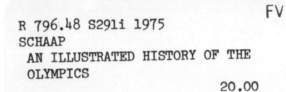

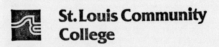

AN ILLUSTRATED HISTORY OF The Olympics

AN ILLUSTRATEI

HISTORY OF **The Olympics**

*Third Edition, Enlarged*

**By DICK SCHAAP**

ALFRED · A · KNOPF    New York    1975

THIS IS A BORZOI BOOK

PUBLISHED BY ALFRED A. KNOPF, INC.

ISBN: 0-394-48757-5

Library of Congress Catalogue Card Number: 75-8243

Manufactured in the United States of America

THIRD EDITION, ENLARGED

# Contents

*COLOR ILLUSTRATIONS WILL BE FOUND*

*FOLLOWING PAGE 274.*

# INTRODUCTION

# The Conquerors and the Conquered

*"Themistocles, being asked whether he would rather be Achilles or Homer, said, 'Which would you rather be—a conqueror in the Olympic Games, or the crier that proclaims who are conquerors?'"*

—PLUTARCH
Apophthegms of Kings and Great Commanders

What do Alexander the Great, Emperor Nero, inventor A. C. Gilbert, General George S. Patton, Jr., Dr. Benjamin Spock, and boxer Ingemar Johansson have in common? In different times and in different sports, all six competed in the Olympic Games. But only three of them won championships. One failed because, in an ancient race, he ran too slow. One failed because, at a decisive moment, he lost his touch with a pistol. And one failed because, under pressure, he discovered the meaning of fear.

The history of the Olympic Games is rich with famous names. It is rich, too, with drama and pageantry, goodwill and controversy, humor and pathos. The Olympics are sports at the summit, and because the stakes are so high and the tension so great, the games seem to bring out and intensify the most basic emotions. Men cry in defeat and sing in victory. Spectators cry too. For the observers and the observed, the Olympic Games are the most compelling spectacle in sports.

Yet the Olympics go beyond sports. They approach art. They offer ritual in the symbolic freeing of the pigeons, the solemn lighting of the Olympic flame, the quiet dignity of the Olympic oath. They offer competition, with the animal excitement of physical combat, strength matched against strength, style against style, stamina against stamina, courage against courage. And, above all, they offer a singular spirit of a camaraderie born of shared victories, an understanding born of shared defeats.

The purpose of this book is to capture the essence of the Olympics, the ritual, competition, and spirit, from the days of Coroebus of Elis, a cook who won the first recorded Olympic event in 776 B.C., to the days of Spitz of California, a swimming genius who won seven gold medals in the 1972 Olympics. The highlights are here—the magnificent Marathon race of 1908, the gripping struggle of a man who pushed his body far beyond its physical limits; the incredible accomplishments of Paavo Nurmi, the Phantom Finn who ran as smoothly and as efficiently as the finest machine; the exquisite beauty of Sonja Henie, the Norwegian girl who brought ballet to the ice; the sheer willpower of runners like Ray Barbuti, John Woodruff, and Emil Zatopek, who made up in heart what they lacked in form; and the brilliance of skiers Jean-Claude Killy and Toni Sailer and boxers Cassius Clay and George Foreman, who through their virtuosity lent new prestige to their sports.

Words tell part of the story. Pictures add a dimension. Few subjects lend themselves so well to illustration as the Olympic Games. Leaf through the pages of this book, and the games come vividly to life. You can watch Jesse Owens leaping to a record in the broad jump, Dorando Pietri weaving and sagging as his strength ebbs, Andrea Mead Lawrence flashing down a treacherous slope, Peggy Fleming invoking the poetry of figure skating. You can see the muscles of the weight lifters, the comic step of the walkers, the fierce determination of female athletes, the grace of the sailors, the fencers, and the gymnasts. You can study skill on the ground, skill in the water, skill on snow, and skill on ice.

Statistics, too, cold and lifeless as they may seem in themselves, reflect the glory of the Olympics. In the back of this book, you will find a listing of all the modern Olympic champions and their performances. Glance down the lists, and you can trace man's increasing ability, his fulfillment of the Olympic motto, *Citius, Altius, Fortius,* "Swifter, Higher, Stronger." Etched indelibly into the background are the improved training facilities, the improved techniques, the improved diet, all the dozens of big and little factors that contribute to the constant evolution of athletic records.

This is not a complete history of the Olympic Games. It could not be. A thick volume could be written on each sport, or on each renewal of the Olympics, or on dozens of the countries or hundreds of the individuals who have earned Olympic honors. I have sought to present the bulk of the track and field history, plus the leading events and the leading stars of the other Olympic sports.

I have singled out one athlete in each of the chapters on the eighteen modern Olympic Games, except for Chapter Seven (1908) and Chapter Seventeen (1960), where I have concentrated upon two. Eleven of the protagonists are Americans; the other nine represent nine different nations. All but five excelled in track and field, all but two are men, and all but two competed in summer sports. This emphasis upon individuals is proper, I believe. The Olympics, ultimately, are a test of individuals, not of nations.

In gathering material for this history, I stumbled upon an enormous amount of confusion. From the first games of the ancient Greeks to the last games of the modern period, the records of the Olympics abound with contradictions and calumnies, fables and fiction.

Consider a matter as simple as a name. In several accounts of the 1896 Olympics, the first of the modern games, there is a French runner named Albin Lermusiaux. In other accounts, his name is Lemursiaux.

Or take physical characteristics. At least one historian claims that Hannes Kolehmainen, a great Finnish runner, was six feet six inches tall. But Dan Ferris, a veteran American athletic official who saw Kolehmainen race sixty years ago and visited him in Finland half a century later, told me that Kolehmainen was no taller than he. And Ferris was decidedly shorter than average height.

Or take age. Another Finn, Albin Stenroos, ran in the Olympics of 1924. He was then thirty-five years old, or thirty-eight, or forty, depending upon your source.

Or take the details of a race. In 1904, Harry Hillman won the 400-meter run, dramatically, by one meter, or easily, by five meters.

If Olympic facts sometimes conflict, Olympic fancy often confounds. Greek historians assert that Milo of Croton, six times a wrestling champion in the ancient Olympic Games, was so steady he could mount an oiled disc and never slip off, no matter how furiously a rival assaulted him. The imagination boggles at the thought.

The Greeks may have been masters of myths, but they held no monopoly. Modern journalists solemnly put forth a conversation between King Gustav V of Sweden and Jim Thorpe, the American Indian, which ran like this:

Gustav: "Sir, you are the greatest athlete in the world."
Thorpe: "Thanks, King."

I have attempted to avoid both the false fact and the false fancy. In cases of conflict, where no authoritative source is available, I have accepted the most common spelling, or the most logical age, or in some instances, admittedly, the most dramatic description. I have debunked some of the myths, but I have unquestionably compounded others. I have repeated the story of Felix Carvajal, the Cuban distance runner, but how much of it is truth and how much fiction, no one seems to know.

Several sources were invaluable. I found particularly fascinating, and helpful, a document called *Official Report, Olympic Games, 776 B.C.—1896 A.D.* Originally published in 1896 by the Greek Olympic Committee, the report includes a history of the ancient games written by S. P. Lambros and

N. G. Polites, both professors at the University of Athens; an account of the birth of the modern games written by Baron Pierre de Coubertin, the individual most responsible for the Olympic revival; a summary of the Greek preparations for the first modern games written by Timoleon Philemon, the secretary-general of the Greek Olympic Committee; and a detailed, event-by-event description of the 1896 Olympics written by C. Anninos, a reporter who had a gift for observation, a gift for language, and an understandable Greek bias. I drew too upon an equally delightful view of the 1896 games, "High Hurdles and White Gloves," an article written by Thomas P. Curtis, a member of the first United States team. The article appeared originally in *The Sportsman* in 1932 and was reprinted by *The Atlantic Monthly* in 1956.

For details of the modern games and modern stars, I am indebted to many sources, but particularly to the autobiography *This Life I've Led* by Babe Didrikson Zaharias as told to Harry Paxton; the biography *Bob Mathias, Champion of Champions* by Jim Scott; and the reference work *The Association of Track and Field Statisticians Olympic Handbook* compiled by D. H. Potts and R. L. Quercetani. I also discovered a wealth of biographical and anecdotal background in articles from *Sport, True, Esquire, Sports Illustrated, Reader's Digest, Time*, and *Newsweek* magazines. For day-by-day coverage, I turned, of course, to the files of newspapers, particularly *The New York Times*.

I am grateful to Henry Robbins and Ash Green, the editors of the book, both patient and encouraging; Arthur Hawkins, who created the imaginative designs; Larry Klein, the former sports editor of *Newsweek*, who buried himself in Olympian piles of research material and emerged only slightly scarred; Tom Murray of *Sport* magazine, who helped research the closing chapters; Jim Kenney, of *Newsweek*, who helped collect the accompanying photographs; Arthur G. Lentz, former assistant executive director of the United States Olympic Association, who provided access to his files; and Dan Ferris, of the Amateur Athletic Union of the United States, who offered his recollections. I must express my appreciation also to the thousands of reporters who have covered the Olympics since 1896 and to the tens of thousands of Olympic competitors, the conquerors and the conquered, whose performances made this book possible.

AN ILLUSTRATED HISTORY OF The Olympics

As the Olympic flame flares, the 1960 winter games open at Squaw Valley.

# The Spirit
# of the Olympics

## CHAPTER ONE

*"If everyone in the world were an athlete,
we would have a much better chance
for peace. We would break records—
not each other's heads."*
—VASILY KUZNETSOV
Honored Master of Sport of the U.S.S.R.

He is a Greek shepherd with a passion for prayer. He is an American Indian with a thirst for firewater. He is a Czech soldier with a tortured look. He is Chinese and Russian, fat and thin, tall and short, handsome and ugly, intellectual and stupid. He is all ages, all nationalities, all races, and all religions. He is an Olympian.

Every four years, in some major city of the world, thousands of Olympians gather for athletic competition. Only a select few emerge as heroes. But almost all emerge with new appreciation and respect for people whose backgrounds contrast drastically with their own.

It has become a cliché to say that the Olympics generate international goodwill. Yet this cliché, like most, has a hard core of truth. There is something about competition on the athletic field, something about physical combat, that inevitably draws the competitors, the combatants, closer together. One athlete may admire another or even worship him, fear him or even hate him, but he cannot simply dismiss him. Empathy is unavoidable, and empathy, in time, leads to understanding.

Understanding has been the keynote to the Olympic spirit ever since the ancient festival was revived in Athens in 1896. "My most lasting memory," Ellery Clark, who represented the United States in the first modern Olympics, recalled several years later, "is the fine spirit which underlay the games, the bringing together of the nations of the world on a common footing—the true ideal, in a realm of sport, of the brotherhood of man."

I

Equally exhausted, winner Murray Halberg of New Zealand (foreground) and loser Friedrich Janke of Germany lie on the turf after the 5,000-meter run in 1960.

Demonstrations of international goodwill are sprinkled throughout Olympic history. In 1896, a gracious Greek lent a discus to Robert Garrett of the American team; Garrett, who had never seen an authentic discus before, promptly beat the Greeks at their own specialty. In 1904, a cheerful little Cuban, Felix Carvajal, charmed so many members of the United States squad with his wit and amiability that the Americans shared their food and quarters with him. In 1912, Hannes Kolehmainen, a Finnish runner, found the American athletes so friendly that he accepted an invitation to compete in the United States and, eventually, married an American girl. In 1936, a German broad jumper named Luz Long offered Jesse Owens the advice that helped the American Negro win the Olympic broad jump championship. And in 1960, young Cassius Clay, a boxer from Kentucky, spent so much time chatting and laughing with athletes from all over the world that he reigned as unofficial mayor of the Olympic Village in Rome.

One of the most stunning cases of mutual understanding sprang from the 1956 Olympic Games in Melbourne. Harold Connolly was a husky, handsome hammer throwing champion from the United States; Olga Fikotova was a sturdy, striking discus throwing champion from Czechoslovakia. They met and, despite the barriers of language and politics, fell in love. Olga spoke some English, and both enjoyed opera; they saw *Il Trovatore* together in Melbourne. She called him "Mickey Mouse"; he called her "Minnie Mouse." In 1957, after the United States State Department helped cut Czechoslovakia's red tape, Olga Fikotova married Harold Connolly in Prague. "The H-bomb overhangs us like a cloud of doom," said *The New York Times* in an editorial. "The subway during rush

Cheers for a conqueror, Sweden's Johan Oxenstierna (above), champion in the 1932 modern pentathlon; despair for a conquered, Belgium's Roger Moens (left), runner-up in the 1960 800-meter run.

hours is almost impossible to endure. But Olga and Harold are in love, and the world does not say no to them." From 1960 through 1968, the Connollys competed as United States teammates.

An equally dramatic example of cooperation—on a vastly different level—occurred during the 1960 winter Olympics in Squaw Valley, California. Nikolai Sologubov, a sharp-featured Muscovite with a lean, muscular body and a shock of blond hair, helped win the Olympic ice hockey championship—for the United States.

The United States had never before won the hockey title, but, following unexpected victories over Canada and the Soviet Union, the Americans had a chance to clinch the championship simply by defeating Czechoslovakia in their final game. After two periods, however, the Czechs led, 4–3. Playing in the thin air high in the Sierra Nevadas, the Americans looked almost lethargic.

Then, during the intermission before the final period, Sologubov, who spoke no English, went to the United States dressing room and, through gestures, suggested that the Americans inhale oxygen. They did—and when they returned to the ice, revived and eager, they routed the Czechs, 9–4, and won the Olympic championship. With his helpful gesture, Nikolai Sologubov, now a captain in the Red Army, personally captured the spirit of the Olympic Games.

The Olympic spirit can take curious forms. In 1956, after an American heavyweight wrestler, Bill Kerslake, offered a pair of sponge kneepads to a Hungarian wrestler, the Hungarian, in turn, gave the American a salami. In 1960, after an American athlete presented a Soviet track star with a Louis Armstrong record, the Russian reciprocated with a

East-West camaraderie flourishes in Rome in 1960: American gymnast Doris Fuchs dances with Russian boxer Boris Nikonorov (left), Russian Tamara Press and American Al Oerter discuss discus technique (below), and four track and field stars—Russian Vladimir Bulatov, American Don Bragg, Russian Igor Ter-Ovanesyan, and American Al Cantello—trade tips and quips (right).

record of Lenin giving a speech in 1919. One of the most popular American athletes in recent years, Earlene Brown, an ebullient Negro shot-putter who competed in Melbourne, Rome, and Tokyo, won hundreds of friends from dozens of nations by giving jitterbug lessons in the Olympic Village. Earlene weighed 225 pounds, and she had a smile to match.

At times, of course, the harmony of the Olympics has been violently broken. The 1908 games in London, which degenerated into a running battle of accusations and counteraccusations, probably strained British-American relations more than any other single event since the War of 1812. The 1936 games in Berlin, with their undertones of anti-Semitism and pro-Aryanism, stirred up great bitterness throughout the world. Ever since the Soviet Union entered the Olympic fold in 1952, charges of state subsidization—and the intense Soviet-American athletic rivalry—have added heat to the cold war. Surely, the 1956 Olympics mirrored the passions of international politics. Against the bloody background of the Hungarian revolution, a Russia-Hungary water polo game resembled war in miniature and did, in fact, draw blood in the water. And, in 1972, came the most terrible assault on the Olympic ideal— the Arab terrorist massacre of eleven Israeli Olympians.

Twice, during World War I and World War II, the modern Olympics were suspended while nations turned their energies to destruction. "The ancient Greeks used to stop fighting to stage the games," Avery Brundage, the American who long presided over the International Olympic Committee, once said unhappily. "Now we stop the games to stage our wars."

Yet Brundage always clung to a belief that the Olympic Games in particular—and amateur sports in general—lead to peace. "People of all nations will turn to the high ideals of

4

amateurism," he commented, after World War II, "away from the tragedies of war."

Brundage's philosophy has had its critics, among them Paul Gallico, the novelist and former sportswriter. "Brundage suffers from the dangerous illusion that public competition on the athletic field engenders good sportsmanship, makes nations love one another, and is good for peace," Gallico once wrote. "It does nothing of the kind. It's the finest stewpot for cooking up international hates between wars, and keeping them alive, next to a round-table gathering of diplomats."

If Brundage tended to be overly optimistic, Gallico veered to the opposite extreme. The truth is that whatever international antagonism arises from the Olympics is the creation of officials and of fans. The spectators, not the athletes, are the chauvinists. Ira Davis, an American hop, step, and jump specialist, aptly expressed the competitors' viewpoint during the 1960 Olympics. "I'm here to win for myself," Davis said. "If the best man in my event is a Russian, then I want to beat the Russian. If he's a Frenchman or a Brazilian, I want to beat him just as much. I'm not interested in any national rivalries. I want to win—and I want my friends to win, whether they're Americans, Russians, or anything."

"For nations to want to collect a lot of gold medals, as proof of national superiority, degrades the whole idea of competitive sports," said Dick McTaggart, a British boxer.

"There shouldn't be any room for quarrels in the Olympics," insisted Tsuyoshi Yamanaka, a Japanese swimmer. "It profanes the gods of Olympia."

Certainly, nationalism is not the only sore spot in the modern Olympics. A good deal of controversy centers around the issue of amateurism. Theoretically, only amateurs may compete in the games, and according to the Olympic definition, "an amateur is one who participates . . . solely for pleasure and for the physical, mental and social benefits he derives therefrom, and to whom participation is nothing more than recreation without material gain of any kind, direct or indirect." Athletes who intend to become professionals are specifically barred from the games.

But after the 1960 Olympics, for example, at least seventeen members of the United States team turned professional, and, obviously, not all of them acted on impulse. They violated the spirit, if not the letter, of the Olympic amateur code.

The Russian system of amateurism, too, stretches the Olympic spirit. There is no such thing as an acknowledged professional athlete in the Soviet Union, but every outstanding athlete unquestionably receives special privileges. For instance, Vasily Kuznetsov, a superb competitor who was the leader of the Soviet team in the 1960 Olympics, taught anatomy and physiology in a Moscow high school. His teaching schedule was deliberately arranged so that he would have every afternoon free to prepare for the Olympics. And when he left his job to compete in international athletics, his family continued

Rivals in politics and performances peacefully coexist: 1936 broad jump foes, Luz Long of Germany and Jesse Owens of the United States, relax in Berlin (left) and three 1960 decathlon men—C. K. Yang of Nationalist China, Rafer Johnson of the United States, and Vasily Kuznetsov of the Soviet Union—join hands in Rome.

to receive his regular income. This is hardly amateurism at its purest.

"Olympic athletes may have been gentlemen amateurs in the period before World War I, today they clearly are not," Chris Chataway, a 1952 and 1956 British Olympian who became a Member of Parliament, wrote in his book *The Road to Rome.* "It may have been reasonable, then, to keep the professionals out; to pretend to do so today is hypocrisy." The problems of the Olympics will persist, but they are far less significant than the benefits of the Olympics.

On a July day in 1976, the president of the International Olympic Committee will turn to the Prime Minister and announce, "I have the honor to invite the Prime Minister of Canada to proclaim open the Games of the XXI Olympiad of the Modern Era, initiated by the Baron Pierre de Coubertin in 1896."

Then the Prime Minister will rise and say, "I declare open the Olympic Games of Montreal, celebrating the XXI Olympiad of the Modern Era."

Bands will play, and the traditional parade of the athletes will begin. The Olympic Flag—five interlaced rings of blue, yellow, black, green and red set against a white background—will lead the parade. The Greeks, the founders of the games, will march first, as always. Then all the other nations will follow in alphabetical order, except the hosts, the Canadians, who will march last.

Hundreds of pigeons will be released, to symbolize the spirit of peace, and cannons will roar, to punctuate the pageantry. Finally, a Canadian runner, bearing a torch that was originally lit by the rays of the sun in Olympia, will trot into the stadium, circle the track, and ignite the Olympic flame.

The games will begin. Friendship will thrive. An Englishman may befriend a Bulgarian. A Russian may help a Canadian. An American may teach Africans new dance steps in the Olympic Village. A romance may sprout between representatives of different nations. Men will acquire new understanding and new respect.

And, of course, amid the tension of the most brilliant sports spectacle in the world, there will be friction, too. As the athletes strain for the medals—gold medals to all who finish first, silver medals to all who finish second, bronze medals to all who finish third—there will be conflicts and arguments and even fights. The atmosphere cannot be perfect. After all, the Olympic Games are a gift to modern civilization, a gift from the Greeks, and that is fair warning.

Outside Berlin's crowded Olympic Stadium in 1936, German gymnasts stage a mass exhibition.

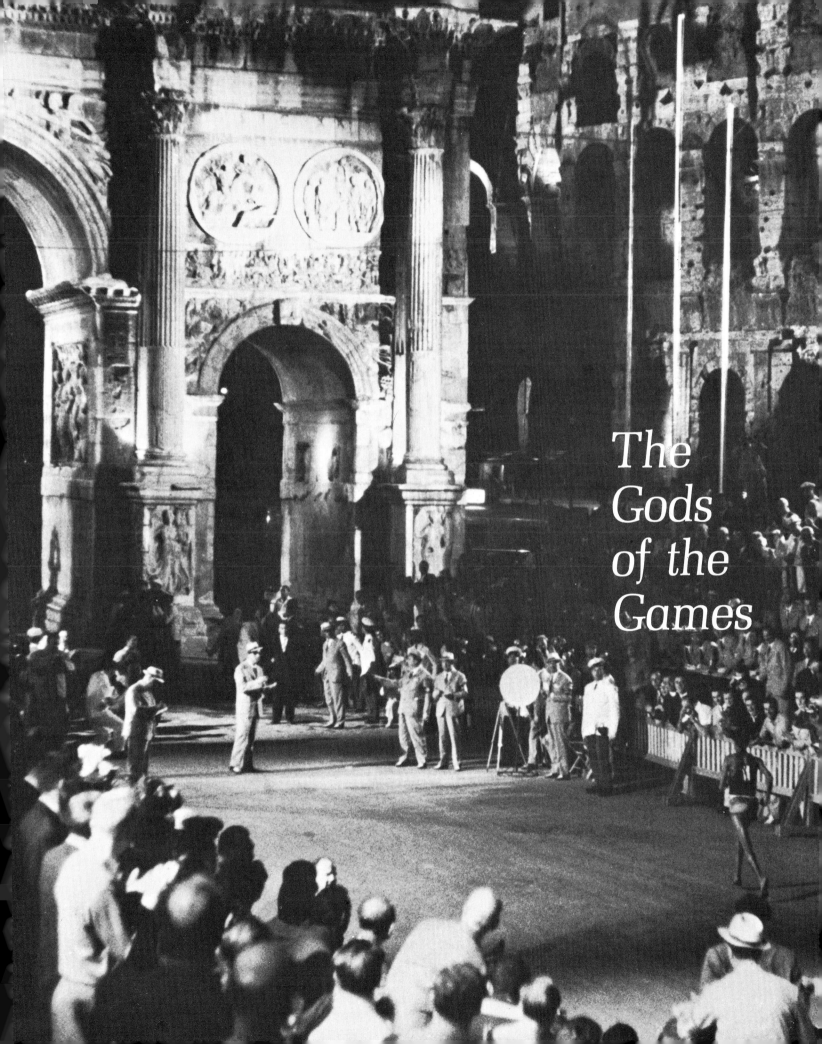

The
Gods
of the
Games

JIM THORPE, UNITED STATES, 1912

3

4

1  Passing the torch, Australia, 1956
2  End of the Marathon, Rome, 1960

5   6

PAAVO NURMI, FINLAND, 1920—1928

7        8

JESSE OWENS, UNITED STATES, 1936

10

11

14

12

13

14

15

EMIL ZATOPEK, CZECHOSLOVAKIA, 1948—1956

17

16

18

19    20                                    21

BOB MATHIAS, UNITED STATES, 1948—1952

22

23

24

25

26

FANNY BLANKERS-KOEN, NETHERLANDS, 1936—1952

27

28

RAFER JOHNSON, UNITED STATES, 1956—1960

29    30

31  32

33

23

The ruins at Olympia.

# The Ancient Games

CHAPTER TWO : 776 B.C. – 394 A.D.

*"There is no greater glory for a man as long as he lives than that which he wins by his own hands and feet."*
—HOMER
*The Odyssey*

If the myths of the Greeks can be trusted, if the ancient fables ring true, then the first contest in Olympic history was fixed. The fixer's name was Pelops, and through his deception, he won a beautiful girl, Hippodamia, the daughter of Oenomaus, the King of Pisa in the ninth century B.C. So far as anyone knows, a woman was never again awarded as an Olympic prize. The custom is not likely to be revived.

Oenomaus had offered his daughter in marriage to any suitable suitor—with one catch. To claim Hippodamia, the suitor first had to steal the girl away from her home in a chariot, then had to withstand the spirited, and deadly, pursuit of her protective father. Thirteen young men bid for Hippodamia, thirteen young men whisked her away, and thirteen young men lost the chase to King Oenomaus. The King, apparently, was not one for frivolity. Each time he caught a suitor, he killed him.

Pelops was the fourteenth candidate. He was young and strong, and most important of all, he was shrewd. He bribed Myrtilos, the King's charioteer, to weaken an axle on the King's chariot. After Myrtilos sabotaged the chariot, Pelops raced off with Hippodamia. The King followed, bold as Ben Hur, sure as Spartacus, and, inexorably, he began to cut down the margin between his chariot and the eloping lovers. The King knew that his horses were the fleetest in the world. He knew that his spear was the sharpest. He knew a great deal, but he did not know that his axle had been damaged.

25

Myron's discus thrower demonstrates classic form.

As King Oenomaus closed in on his fourteenth victim, his chariot suddenly sagged, lurched, and toppled. The King crashed against the turf and died. Pelops had lost a father-in-law, but he had gained a bride.

Pelops had promised Myrtilos half the kingdom of Pisa, but the ambitious young man disposed of the obligation by tossing his coconspirator off a handy cliff. Then in celebration of his triumphs, the legend runs, Pelops instituted the Olympic Games. He chose what the poets called "the most lovely site in Hellas," the valley of Olympia, a few miles west of Pisa on the southwestern coast of the Greek peninsula. The Alpheus River, now called the Rouphia, flowed through Olympia on its way to the Ionian Sea. The Kladeos River ran nearby. Mount Kronius looked down upon the valley, and rich foliage brightened the area.

No one knows for certain whether Pelops actually set up athletic competitions in the valley of Olympia. No one even knows whether the legend of Pelops and Hippodamia is close to truth. One theory proposes that prayers and human sacrifices were offered in Olympia for hundreds of years before Pelops, and that in time, as the Greeks grew more civilized, sports were substituted for sacrifices.

It is known, definitely, that in 776 B.C., a young cook, Coroebus of Elis, won a one-stade race (approximately 200 yards) in Olympia. The ancient Greeks, in fact, dated their calendar from 776 B.C. Formal records of the Olympic Games go back to that date—and no further.

Archeologists today are convinced that Olympia was a religious center before 776 B.C. Ruins seem to prove that the Temple of Hera in Olympia dates back to at least 1000 B.C. In all likelihood, several other shrines rimming the Altis, the sacred grove of Zeus that stood in the heart of Olympia, also predate the victory of Coroebus.

At the beginning of the recorded Olympics, the festival was largely local in nature. The Pisates competed, and so did the Eleians, for they came from the villages closest to the sacred site. The Eleians, who lived at the mouth of the Alpheus River, presided over the early games, but for one competition, in 748 B.C., the Pisates, aided by an alliance with King Pheidon of Argos, took command. Sparta, which lay to the southeast of Olympia, quickly helped Elis regain control.

During the *Hieromenia*, the month of the Olympic Games, all wars among the Greeks were voluntarily halted, a tradition that has not survived to the modern games. No one bore arms within the sacred limits of Olympia; anyone carrying arms deposited them in Elis before advancing. This honorable truce was violated only once, in 364 B.C., when the Pisates once more reigned over the Olympics. The Eleians, certain that their cause justified drastic methods, swept down upon Olympia during the festival and routed the Pisates.

Eventually, the games expanded to Panhellenic proportions, and when the Greek city-state system crumbled and gave way to great empires, the Olympics drew athletes first from the wide Macedonian world and later from the entire Roman Empire. After the Romans conquered Greece in the second century A.D., the decline and fall of the Olympic Games began.

But when the games were the glory of all Greece, symbolizing the combination of strength and beauty that the Greeks revered, brilliant men walked in the vale of Olympia. In the fifth century B.C. alone, Herodotus, the historian, roamed among the spectators; Socrates spread his wisdom at the festivals; Pindar, the poet, composed odes to athletic greatness; and Phidias, who kept his own workshop on the Olympic grounds, was one of many sculptors who honored the heroes

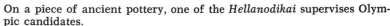
On a piece of ancient pottery, one of the *Hellanodikai* supervises Olympic candidates.

27

A Greek javelin thrower rears back.

of the games. The Temple of Zeus at Olympia housed an awesome statue of Zeus, forty feet high, bearing the inscription, "Phidias the Athenian, the son of Charmides, made me." Sculptors carved statues commemorating almost every champion, but only after a man won three championships did he have a statue built exactly in his own likeness.

A man did not have to be rich to compete in the ancient Olympics, but wealth certainly helped. Each athlete had to devote himself exclusively to training for eleven full months before the games. After ten months practicing at home, he reported in Elis to the *Hellanodikai,* the Olympic judges, usually ten in number. Each candidate—at least for the first several centuries of the games—had to swear that he was a freeborn, native Greek. He had to make pledges to the Greek gods, too, for the Olympic ceremony, basically, was a religious ceremony. The games and the rituals were designed to please the gods.

For nearly a month, under the stern supervision of the judges, who whacked the athletes with rods to emphasize their instructions, the candidates trained in Elis. To keep their muscles supple, they anointed themselves in oil. In the early years of the games, the athletes ate only fresh cheese and drank only water; later, the diet also included meats and wines. Shortly before the games began, the judges selected the best athletes and took them to Olympia. "If you have exercised yourself in a manner worthy of the Olympic Games," the judges announced, "if you have been guilty of no slothful or ignoble act, go on with courage. You who have not so practiced, go wither you will."

Women were allowed neither to compete in the Olympic Games nor, with the exception of one special priestess, to observe. The women had their own festival, the Heraea, which was held once every five years and featured a 100-foot race for young girls. Any woman discovered at the Olympic Games was to be punished by death; she was to be thrown from a nearby cliff.

Apparently, this edict was disobeyed only once, when Pherenice of Rhodes accompanied her son, Pisidores, to the games. She disguised herself as an athlete, but when her son won the boxing competition, she rushed to him and embraced him so eagerly that her robe slipped, betraying her sex. But because her father, Diagoras, and her brothers had been Olympic champions and because her husband had died while their son was in training, Pherenice was spared. From then on, to avoid deception, all athletes in all events had to compete naked.

Many thousands of Greeks descended upon Olympia once every four years to watch the athletes and to join in the religious ceremonies. People planned the trips month in advance, for attendance at the Olympic Games was a status symbol, somewhat the way attendance at the World Series is in the United States today. Kings and merchants jammed Olympia. There was a carnival air, with booths and tents everywhere, and acrobats and magicians performing.

The stadium at Olympia was roughly 215 yards long and 35 yards wide, surrounded on four sides by grassy slopes capable of seating comfortably more than 40,000 spectators. When Coroebus became the first known Olympic champion in 776 B.C., the only event was the one-stade race, a sprint nearly the length of the stadium. In 724 B.C., a double-stade race was added and then, four years later, a distance race of approximately three miles.

During the next century, the schedule broadened considerably. Wrestling, boxing, chariot races, races in armor, the grueling pentathlon, and the crippling *pankration* became Olympic events.

An ancient painter captures the style of the short-distance runners.

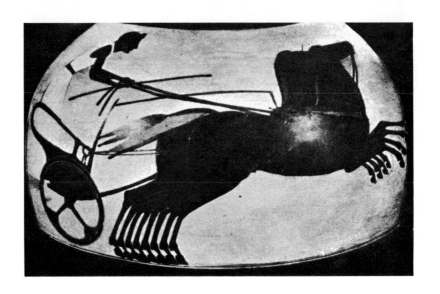

The rules of the ancient wrestling matches were simple. The athlete who knocked his opponent to the ground three times was the winner; there was no wrestling on the ground. The boxers wore leather straps around their fists, and their battles, continuing until one man surrendered, were brutal. Greek boxers suffered cauliflower ears and pug noses—and worse. The boxers absorbed so much punishment that one ancient sportswriter reported: "After twenty years, Ulysses returned home and was recognized from his appearance by his dog Argus. But thou, Stratophon, after boxing for four hours, hast been so altered that neither dogs nor any person in the town could possibly recognize thee."

In the pentathlon, competitors broad jumped (carrying weights in their hands to improve their distance), threw the javelin and the discus (to the accompaniment of flutes to improve their rhythm), ran one stade, and wrestled. The exact order of events is uncertain, but one suggested possibility is that all the entrants broad jumped, and everyone who leaped a specified distance qualified for the javelin throw. The four leaders in the javelin advanced to the sprint, and then the three swiftest hurled the discus. Finally, the two best men in the discus wrestled for the championship.

The pankration combined boxing and wrestling, with no holds barred. In this pleasant sport, the battle continued on the ground until one man raised his hand and conceded defeat. The viciousness of the contest can best be indicated by one incident. Arrachion, who had previously won a boxing championship, grappled with a rugged opponent on the ground and began twisting his rival's foot. The opponent, in turn, put a stranglehold on Arrachion's neck. Arrachion choked to death, but as he was dying, he twisted his opponent's foot so violently that the man raised one hand in surrender. Arrachion, dead, was judged the winner, so the story runs.

As new sports and variations of old sports won places on the Olympic calendar, the games grew, in the fifth century B.C., from a one-day to a five-day festival. The first day was devoted to religious rituals and the second to events for boys. One curious practice was the method of separating the men from the boys. Age made no difference. The division was based solely on physical development, as determined by the judges.

Incredible heroes, whose accomplishments were perhaps half fact and at least half fancy, sprang from the Olympic Games. Poulydamas of Thessaly and Theagenes of Thasos excelled in the pankration. Poulydamas, supposedly, once killed a lion on Mount Olympus with his bare hands, once grabbed a bull by a hind foot and held it fast, and once stopped a chariot at full speed by seizing the back of it. Theagenes, not to be outdone, first demonstrated his enormous strength when he was nine years old. He carried a large bronze statue a long way to his home and, when he was told that he could not keep it, carried it back again. In his career in boxing, sprinting, and the pankration, he won a total of 1,400 different championships, probably an all-time amateur record.

But Poulydamas and Theagenes were weaklings compared to a wrestler named Milo of Croton. Milo had a hearty appetite. His typical meal included seven pounds of meat, seven pounds of bread, and four or five quarts of wine. He lived in the sixth century B.C., and one day at Olympia, he ate an entire bull. History records that the bull was four years old at the time; no one knows how old Milo was.

Milo won the Olympic wrestling championship six times, but he earned more fame for his tricks than his victories. For instance, he carried his own life-size statue to its proper place in Olympia. He had the knack of holding a pomegranate in his fist so tightly that no one could open his hand, yet so gently that not a single drop of juice dripped out. He could stand on an oiled disc and brush away attackers without ever losing his footing. He could wrap a piece of cord around his forehead and, by swelling his veins, slice the cord in half. He had a trick for every occasion, and a trick finally did him in. Wandering through a forest, he came upon a tree that had been cut with an ax. Wedges had been placed in the cuts. Milo boldly tried to widen the cuts with his bare hands, but he made one wrong move. The wedges slipped out, and his hands slipped in, trapped by the trunk of the tree. Milo was stuck, and a group of wolves, who did not realize he was an Olympic champion, came along and ate him. No one knows how old the wolves were.

The chariot races were wild affairs, so hazardous that once, in a forty-chariot match, only one man, Arcesilaus of Cyrene, completed the full nine-mile course. In the early part of the first century A.D., Tiberius of Rome, before he became Emperor Tiberius Claudius Nero, won an Olympic chariot championship.

Another regal Olympian was Alexander the Great, who, as a youth, entered one of the sprints—and lost the race.

Even women, although they were barred from the games, won Olympic championships. This paradox unravels easily.

A relay runner passes along an early version of the Olympic flame.

31

In the chariot races, the owners of the horses, not the drivers, won the prizes. Cyniska, the sister of Agesilaus, the King of Sparta, was the first woman to earn a chariot championship. In later years, Belestiche of Macedonia, the mistress of Ptolemy Philadelphus, entered her favorite chariots and dominated the Olympics.

For a victory in the Olympic Games, each champion received an olive wreath, but that was only the start of his rewards. He became an idol in his home city, and his fellow citizens showered him with gifts. Often he returned home through a gap especially cut in the city's protective wall. He generally received a free home, free meals for a lifetime, and large sums of money. A street in his city sometimes was renamed after him. He had achieved the ultimate in success. When Diagoras, the father of Pherenice, won his Olympic championship, a friend told him, "Die, Diagoras, for thou hast nothing short of divinity to desire."

Receptions grew so lavish that the champions, inevitably, became spoiled. In the early history of the games, one champion, Oebotas of Achaia, decided that his city had not rewarded him sufficiently for his feat. In retaliation, he placed a curse upon the city, and for the following three hundred years, not one Achaian won an Olympic event. Then, upon the advice of the Oracle of Delphi, the city built a statue to the memory of Oebotas. In the next Olympics, in the sprint for boys, the champion was Sostratas of Achaia.

Losers, naturally, earned only scorn. "By back ways," wrote Pindar, "they slink away, sore smitten by misfortune, nor does any sweet smile grace their return."

Cheating was even worse than losing. Athletes who violated the Olympic code had to erect statues, called Zanes, at the foot of Mount Kronius. The Zanes bore the name of the guilty and his offense. Surprisingly, in more than eleven centuries of ancient competition, only thirteen Zanes sprouted in Olym-

pia. The crime of at least one man, Sarapion of Alexandria, was understandable. He had entered the pankration and, the night before the event, had changed his mind and fled.

With the emergence of the Romans and the subjugation of the Greeks, the Olympic Games withered. They reached their nadir in 66 A.D., when Emperor Nero, accompanied by five thousand bodyguards, turned the competition into a farce. The tyrant entered several events, including some that he had invented on the spot, and, not surprisingly, he won every event that he entered. In the chariot race, he tumbled from his mount, and all his rivals, who knew what was good for them, politely waited until the Emperor was reseated. He won going away. He was the best singer, the best musician, the best herald.

Although the Olympics outlived Nero, they had lost both their purity and their strength. Occasionally, a Greek managed to win a championship, but contestants poured in from all corners of the Roman Empire, skilled and eager to conquer, but oblivious of the traditions. Prince Varastades, who later became King of Armenia, was the last recorded Olympic champion. Around 388 A.D., in the 291st Olympic Games, Varastades won the boxing competition.

Five years later, a marauding band of Goths ravaged the sacred shrine of Olympia. And in 394 A.D., Emperor Theodosius of Rome, a Christian opposed to pagan spectacles, formally abolished the Olympic Games.

The valley itself began to decay. In 395 A.D., the statue of Zeus, the masterpiece of Phidias, was hauled away. In 426 A.D., Emperor Theodosius II ordered all the remaining temples to be destroyed. Fire failed to topple the Temple of Zeus, but a century later, violent earthquakes shook the area and reduced the temple to ruins. The Kladeos changed its course and swept through the Altis. No one lived in the valley any more. No one prayed there. No one cared. The Olympic Games were dead.

Spiridon Loues (in white) poses with American athletes—the three in front on the right are James B. Connolly, Ellery Clark, and Robert Garrett—and with Greek princes (in uniform).

# A Shepherd
# Named Spiridon

## CHAPTER THREE : 1896 – ATHENS

It is solemnly recorded in the history of the modern Olympic Games that at 2 p.m. on Sunday, April 10, 1896, a Greek army colonel named Papadiamantopolous fired a revolver signaling the start of a foot race from Marathon to Athens. Twenty-five young men promptly trotted off toward Athens, nearly twenty-five miles away, followed at a discreet distance by carts bearing doctors and medical supplies.

Colonel Papadiamantopolous, the starter, had a special interest in the race. One of the competitors, a shepherd named Spiridon Loues, had served under the colonel in the Greek First Infantry Regiment and had demonstrated great stamina during endurance marches. When Athens had been named as the site of the first modern Olympic Games, Colonel Papadiamantopolous, a member of the organizing committee, had persuaded Loues to enter the long-distance race.

The race from Marathon to Athens fell on the fifth day of the 1896 Olympic Games, and during the four preceding days not a single Greek had won a track and field event. By winning his race, Spiridon Loues, twenty-five years old, with bright gray eyes, handsome mustache, and dark hair, could give this modern Greek drama a happy ending.

In Athens, within the handsome reconstructed Panathenaic Stadium where the race would end, a capacity crowd, perhaps 70,000 people, including King George and Crown Prince Constantine, awaited the runners from Marathon. On the hills overlooking the stadium, another 70,000 spectators strained for a view. Tens of thousands of Greeks lined the road from Marathon to Athens, eager to press food, drink, and encouragement upon the runners, particularly upon Spiridon Loues, the short, slender shepherd from the hills of Maroussi.

Thirty minutes after the start, Albin Lermusiaux of France, running at a recklessly fast pace, galloped through the village of Pikarni in first place, leading Australian Edwin Flack by more than a mile. Then came an American, Arthur Blake, and a Hungarian, Gyula Kellner. Several minutes later, Spiridon Loues reached Pikarni. Informed by anxious villagers that he was far behind, Loues shrugged. "Never mind," he said. "I will overtake them and beat them all." Then Spiridon the shepherd stepped up his pace, spurred by the hopes of modern Greece and the feats of ancient Greece.

Nearly twenty-four centuries earlier, another young Greek, Pheidippides, had run the same route from Marathon to Athens. In 490 B.C., on the plains of Marathon, Pheidippides fought for Miltiades, the brilliant Athenian general, against the invading Persians. Although far outnumbered, the Athenians forced back the mighty invaders, and as the Persians retreated to their ships, leaving twenty thousand of their dead behind them, Miltiades called upon Pheidippides, a champion Olympic runner, to carry the news of the stunning victory to Athens. Weary after a full day of battle, Pheidippides shed his armor and set off from Marathon. Hours later, his feet bloody, his lungs aching, Pheidippides staggered into the market place in Athens. "Rejoice—we conquer!" he cried—and died.

The idea of commemorating Pheidippides' heroism with a "Marathon" race in the 1896 Olympic Games came from Michel Bréal, a French writer and a student of Greek mythology. Bréal's interest in the games stemmed from his friendship with Baron Pierre de Coubertin, the man who fathered the modern Olympic Games. Beyond reasonable doubt, without Baron de Coubertin, the Olympic Games would still be as dead as Pheidippides.

A short man, barely five feet three inches tall, Baron de Coubertin attended St. Cyr, the famous French military academy, and early decided that military life was not for him. He resigned before he graduated, turned to the study of political science, and eventually devoted his life and his wealth to the field of public education. He published hundreds of books and pamphlets on educational theory, wrote a history of the world in four volumes, and developed a plan, "The Fundamental Charter of New Teaching," to modernize French schools.

Baron de Coubertin believed that mental development and physical development were inseparable, a belief that put him at odds with French educational tradition. In French schools, de Coubertin complained, "physical inertion was considered an indispensable assistant to the perfecting of intellectual powers."

In 1888, when he was only twenty-six, Baron de Coubertin helped create *l'Union des Sports Athlétiques*, an organization

Forty years after the first modern Olympics, Loues attends the games in Berlin.

Baron Pierre de Coubertin sees his dream fulfilled—the revival of the ancient Greek games (commemorated in stamps, left).

which stimulated physical education programs in schools and colleges throughout France. In 1889, he started a monthly paper, *La Revue Athlétique*, to stir up national interest in sports. Representing the French ministry of public instruction, Baron de Coubertin toured Europe and North America studying physical education systems in many countries. During his travels, he visited the ruins at Olympia, which had been excavated between 1875 and 1881 by a German archeological team.

The baron was disturbed by an international trend toward commercialism in sports, and he gradually began to dream of a cure—a revival of the ancient Greek Olympic Games. His plan was simple: Amateur athletes from all nations would gather every four years and compete in various sports. Everywhere he went, Baron de Coubertin outlined his idea, and almost everywhere he went, people dismissed him as a misguided idealist.

Twice in the nineteenth century, the Greeks themselves had tried to revive the ancient games. Financed by a bequest from Evangelios Zappas, a wealthy Greek who had lived in Rumania, Olympic Games were held in Athens in 1859 and 1870. But both times the competition was small, mismanaged, confused, and totally unsuccessful. If the modern Greeks couldn't sustain the Olympics on a national scale, it seemed unlikely that Baron de Coubertin could succeed on an international scale. Yet he persisted. "I was the sole author of the whole project," de Coubertin later explained, immodestly but accurately.

In 1893, the baron invited sportsmen from all over the world to join l'Union des Sports Athlétiques in an international athletic congress at the Sorbonne. Deliberately, Baron de Coubertin implied that the congress would discuss only general topics of international athletics; the subject of the Olympic Games was nowhere on the agenda. "I carefully refrained from mentioning such an ambitious project," he said, "afraid it might raise such a storm of contempt and scorn as to discourage beforehand those who favored it."

Few countries responded favorably at first to Baron de Coubertin's invitation, and he feared the international congress might be a fiasco. But he kept prodding and pleading, and when the congress opened on June 16, 1894, delegates were present from the United States, England, Sweden, Spain, Italy, Belgium, Russia, Greece, and, of course, France. Then Baron de Coubertin sprang his Olympic plan. Stressing the development of youth fitness and the development of international understanding, the baron convinced even the most skeptical delegates. Unanimously, the international congress voted to revive the Olympic Games. Baron de Coubertin's original proposal was to stage the first modern Olympic Games in Paris in 1900, as part of the Paris International Exposition. But swayed by history and the arguments of the Greek delegation, the congress—with the baron's approval—chose Athens in 1896. It was, as matters turned out, a most fortunate switch.

When the Greek citizens heard that the Olympic Games were going to be revived in Athens, they rejoiced. Then a sobering note set in. To stage the games, the Greeks needed money, and money was one thing the Greek government could not spare. The government, to be blunt, was bankrupt. Only national pride dissuaded the Greeks from sending the gift horse promptly back to Paris.

Crown Prince Constantine became honorary president of the Greek Olympic Committee and immediately went to work raising money. A public appeal netted approximately $65,000 in gifts. The government decided to issue eight commemorative stamps and pledged the revenue, a minimum of $100,000, toward the games. The government also promised to waive the tax on admission charges to the games. Still one enormous problem remained. There was no adequate stadium in Athens, and none in sight until Crown Prince Constantine suggested that the committee appeal to George Averoff, a Greek philanthropist living in Alexandria, who had donated hundreds of thousands of dollars to Greek educational institutions. Averoff liked the Olympic idea and agreed to pay for the restoration of the Panathenaic Stadium, the stadium of Herodis, originally constructed in 330 B.C. Nothing remained of the ancient stadium but rubble, and the restoration, in marble, with a capacity close to 70,000, cost Averoff $386,000. Finally, the stadium was ready, the games approached, and in the hills of Maroussi, Spiridon the shepherd trained and ran and prayed.

Other countries did not share the full fervor of the Greeks. Slowly, quietly, handicapped by a lack of national enthusiasm, England, France, Switzerland, Denmark, Germany, and Hungary assembled teams for the games.

There was no official Olympic organization in the United States, and the New York Athletic Club, which included a large percentage of the national track and field champions, ignored the games entirely. The most influential American advocate of the Olympics was William Milligan Sloane, a Princeton history professor who had met de Coubertin on one of the baron's North American tours. Professor Sloane won one convert in Robert Garrett, a wealthy young man who was captain of the Princeton track and field team. Garrett had prepared for college with a private tutor at home and had never competed in athletics. But when he entered Princeton, he tried out for the weight-throwing and jumping events and quickly developed into an outstanding shot-putter. In 1896, Garrett, six feet one inch tall and 176 pounds, decided to enter the Olympic Games. According to persistent stories, which Garrett refused to confirm, he paid the traveling expenses to Athens for three of his Princeton teammates—sprinter Francis Lane, pole vaulter Albert Tyler, and quarter miler Herbert Jamison.

The Boston Athletic Association, also lured by the luster of the Olympics, sent to Athens five of its track and field men—sprinter Tom Burke, hurdler Thomas Curtis, jumper Ellery Clark, pole vaulter Welles Hoyt and distance runner Arthur Blake. Another Bostonian, James B. Connolly, a Harvard undergraduate and a fine jumper, was so determined to make the Olympic pilgrimage that he applied for a leave of absence from his college. When Harvard turned down his bid, he quit school and paid his own way to Athens. Connolly never returned to Harvard. He later became an author of sea sagas and a newspaperman for the Boston *Globe* and Boston *Post*.

The totally unofficial thirteen-man American team—ten track and field athletes, swimmer Gardner Williams, and brothers John and Sumner Paine, both Army captains and revolver experts—sailed from New York on March 20, 1896, aboard the *Fulda,* a tramp steamer. "We sailed by the southern route to Naples, passing the Azores," hurdler Thomas Curtis wrote years later, "and we kept in condition as well as we could by exercising on the afterdeck. At Gibraltar the British officers invited us to use their field for practice, and we managed to get rid of our sea legs to a certain extent. But when we arrived at Athens on the day preceding the opening of the games—after crossing Italy by train, spending twenty-four hours on the boat from Brindisi to Patras, and then crossing Greece by train—we were not exactly in the pink.

Beyond the reconstructed Panathenaic Stadium stretches the city of Athens and the Acropolis.

"Nor did our reception at Athens, kind and hospitable as it was, help. We were met with a procession, with bands blaring before and behind, and were marched on foot for what seemed miles to the Hôtel de Ville. Here speech after speech was made in Greek, presumably very flattering to us, but of course entirely unintelligible. We were given large bumpers of the white-resin wine of Greece and told by our advisors that it would be a gross breach of etiquette if we did not drain these off in response to the various toasts. As soon as this ceremony was over, we were again placed at the head of a procession and marched to our hotel. I could not help feeling that so much marching, combined with several noggins of resinous wine, would tell on us in the contests the following day."

When Curtis reached his hotel, the proprietor politely asked him what his specialty was. Curtis said he was a hurdler, and the hotel owner burst into laughter. "It was some time before he could speak," Curtis recalled, "but when he had calmed down enough, he apologized and explained that it had seemed to him inexpressibly droll that a man should travel 5,000 miles to take part in an event which he had no possible chance to win. Only that afternoon, the Greek hurdler in practice had hung up an absolutely unbeatable record."

After the wine and the marching, this news heightened Curtis's fears. Reluctantly, the American asked the proprietor what the Greek's record was. "He glanced around guiltily," Curtis said, "led me to a corner of the room, and whispering in my ear like a stage conspirator, said that the record was not supposed to be made public but that he had it on unimpeachable authority that the Greek hero had run the hurdles in the amazing time of nineteen and four-fifths seconds. Again he was overcome with mirth but recovered to say that I should not be too discouraged, perhaps I might win second place." Curtis was not too discouraged, perhaps because he regularly ran the 110-meter high hurdles in eighteen seconds flat.

On April 6, 1896, the seventy-fifth anniversary of Greek independence from Turkey, the modern Olympics began. It was a cloudy day, but starting early in the morning, huge crowds jammed the roads to the Panathenaic Stadium. By 2 p.m., the seats were filled. Nearly three hundred competitors drawn from thirteen countries were assembled on the playing field. At 3 p.m., King George and Queen Olga arrived, surrounded by Crown Prince Constantine, Prince George, Prince Nicholas, Baron de Coubertin, assorted noblemen, and sundry diplomats. At the official request of the Crown Prince, King George rose and announced: "I hereby proclaim the opening of the First International Olympic Games in Athens." Fifteen hundred and two years after the Roman Emperor Theodosius had killed the ancient games, the French Baron de Coubertin had brought them back to life.

The modern Olympic Games began with three heats of the 100-meter dash, approximately half the distance Coroebus of Elis had run in 776 B.C. The American squad certainly was not an overwhelming one—only Tom Burke, in the quarter mile, held a United States championship—but it was far stronger than any other in Athens. Americans won all three 100-meter heats, first Lane, then Curtis, and finally Burke.

Before his heat, Curtis noticed that one of his rivals, a short, stocky Frenchman, was wearing white kid gloves. "Why the gloves?" Curtis asked.

"A-ha," said the Frenchman, "zat is because I run before ze Keeng!"

After the Frenchman failed to place before the King, Curtis asked him what events he had entered. "Ze *cent* meter and ze Marathon," said the Frenchman.

The combination struck Curtis as a curious one. "How do you train for such different events?" the American said.

The Frenchman smiled. "One day I run a leetle way, vairy quick," he explained. "Ze next day, I run a long way, vairy slow."

The first final of the 1896 games was the hop, step, and jump, and the first champion in modern Olympic history was the Harvard renegade, James B. Connolly. Although Connolly won by a comfortable margin, the official Greek historian of the games, a confirmed chauvinist, noted that the third-place finisher, Joannis Persakis of Greece, "was considered by everybody the most graceful jumper."

"Why it was a moment to inspire!" Connolly later wrote of his own victory. "The young fellow was seeing things through a purple haze by then, and the haze deepened and glowed when over in a corner a group of countrymen, officers and sailors of a warship in port and the not-to-be-mistaken tourists, suddenly flashed into view a lot of American flags and split classic airs with an assortment of American yells. But, eyes for flag aloft and ears to strain below, he stood to attention, and not until shouts had died away did he regain his balance. He made his way across the field and through the tunnel to the dressing room, and there graciously posed for four artists and any number of photographers."

For the Greeks, the highlight on opening day was the discus throw, an event in which Panagiotis Paraskevopolous, the local champion, was heavily favored. Princeton's Robert Garrett, who had never seen a real discus before he reached Athens, also entered the event. At Princeton, Garrett had heard about the discus and had asked a friend to make him a steel model which vaguely resembled the real thing. At Athens, before the competition began, he had borrowed a discus from a friendly Greek and had found, to his great satisfaction, that the platter was much easier to handle than his rough imitation.

Still, Paraskevopolous and a fellow Greek, Sotirios Versis, had the advantage of experience. Versis, whose best throw traveled ninety-four feet five inches, "showed a harmony and dignity in his attitudes which would not have disgraced an ancient discus thrower," the partisan historian reported. "He himself is beautiful of form like an ancient statue." With the form of the *Discobolus*, Paraskevopolous, on his final throw, spun the discus ninety-five feet, well in front of Garrett's best effort. The Princetonian still had one chance remaining.

In action in Athens: Robert Garrett of the United States prepares to put the shot (left), Thomas Curtis of the United States and Grantley Goulding of Britain clear the hurdles (below, top) and Thomas Burke of the United States shows the sprinters the four-point stance (below, bottom).

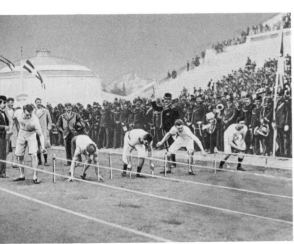

With a comfortable but far from classic form, Garrett's last throw surpassed the Greek champion's by seven inches. "Most of the spectators were rather disappointed by this result," the Greek historian noted, with restraint.

There were more disappointments for the Greeks on the second day of the games. France won a fencing championship, Denmark and England divided the two weight-lifting titles, and the United States continued to dominate track and field. Curtis of the Boston A.A. won one heat of the 110-meter high hurdles, a brash Britisher named Grantley Goulding won the other, and the Greek who couldn't lose failed to place in either heat.

The Boston A.A. provided two champions. Ellery Clark won the broad jump, pressed by Ivy Leaguers Garrett and Connolly, and Burke scored easily in the 400-meter run. To celebrate each victory, the other Bostonians shouted: "B! A! A! Rah! Rah! Rah!" The noisy outburst delighted the Greeks, especially the royal party. The King himself asked the Bostonians to repeat the cheer.

In the shot-put, Garrett earned his second championship, but as the ubiquitous historian saw it, the spectators "did not forget to cheer most heartily the Greek champion who had maintained the honor of his nation with as much valor, but alas with less success than his antagonist." Miltiades Gouskos, the Greek champion, lost by less than three inches.

The American monopoly on track and field championships ended in the 1,500-meter run. Albin Lermusiaux, a Frenchman with strong legs and a weak sense of pace, sprinted to an early lead, then faded in the stretch. Both Edwin Flack of Australia, running for the London Athletic Club, and Arthur Blake of Boston passed Lermusiaux, and with a final spurt, the Australian won by a stride.

On the third day, only one final was held, a cycling race won by a Frenchman. But the following day, finally, the hosts had native champions to cheer. Greeks won individual titles in rifle shooting, fencing, and gymnastics. The Germans enjoyed themselves too, with three gymnastics victories. In the only track and field event, Flack, the Australian, won his second championship, the 800-meter run.

Soon after his victory, Flack departed for Marathon, where the long-distance runners were going to spend the night. Spiridon Loues, the little Greek shepherd, fasted the entire day preceding his race. A devout man, he spent most of the evening in prayer.

On Sunday, April 10, the final day of track and field competition, spectators filled the Panathenaic Stadium by 10 a.m. Excitement among the Greeks reached a peak. " 'If only the Cup of Marathon would be gained by a child of the soil!' was the ardent wish of every Greek," the historian wrote. "All kinds of rewards were promised to the victorious champion, should he be a Greek. Some hotelkeepers had pledged themselves to give him board and lodging free of expense—some for a fixed term of years, some for his whole lifetime. Tailors, barbers, hatters offered their services for nothing."

In Athens, during the morning, a Greek and a German won gymnastics events, and Captain John Paine won the revolver match at 25 meters, with his brother, Sumner, placing second. In Marathon, at the same time, Spiridon Loues received Holy Communion. He prayed, and he thought of Pheidippides, and he thought of the long road to Athens.

Precisely at 2 p.m., Colonel Papadiamantopolous's shot sent the twenty-five distance runners scurrying off the Bridge of Marathon. They fell easily into line, a full forty kilometers (approximately twenty-four miles and 1,500 yards) in front of them. At Pikarni, where France's Lermusiaux held a large lead, a few starters collapsed; the doctors following the field began a long afternoon of treatments.

Halfway through the race, Blake, the American, was holding up surprisingly well, running third behind Lermusiaux and Flack, the Australian double champion. But Blake was a miler by habit, not a long-distance runner, and after twenty-three kilometers, exhaustion forced him to quit.

At the village of Karvati, Lermusiaux's lead seemed so commanding that the townspeople, who had built an arch of triumph, prematurely placed a champion's garland upon the Frenchman's head. But after Karvati, the course swept uphill, and Lermusiaux's overambitious pace began to wear him down. He slowed to a walk, and Flack trotted past him into the lead. Soon Lermusiaux surrendered second place. Who passed him? The slender shepherd, Spiridon Loues.

After thirty-two kilometers, Lermusiaux dropped out, his energy totally spent. One kilometer later, running comfortably and smoothly, Spiridon Loues took the lead. For three kilometers, Flack stayed within twenty meters of the shepherd, but then, perhaps feeling the effect of his 800-meter run the previous day, Flack fell back. Then Flack fell down. Doctors came to his aid, but he was out of the race. Loues sprinted briefly, and his lead grew to two kilometers. With less than four kilometers to run, merely two miles, Loues looked like a certain winner. Only collapse could stop the Greek hero.

At the stadium in Athens, the spectators received periodic reports of the long-distance race, and the mood of the crowd mirrored the progress of the runners. The Greeks were sad as Lermusiaux built his early lead, hopeful as the Frenchman faltered, exultant as Loues moved in front. Within the stadium, two Bostonians earned their second championships. Tom Burke won the 100-meter final, and Ellery Clark won the high jump, trailed by Connolly and the versatile Garrett. "One can imagine the joy of the Americans," the historian said, "which expressed itself in their absurd shouts."

In the hurdles final, Boston's Tom Curtis met Britain's Grantley Goulding, who had been waging psychological warfare against his American rival. "He had quite a number of medals hung on his waistcoat," Curtis reported, "and these he insisted on showing me. 'You see this medal,' he would say. 'That was for the time I won the championship of South Africa. This one here was from the All-England games'—and so on. I never met a more confident athlete."

A packed and partisan crowd awaits the arrival of the Marathon runners.

43

Goulding's skill almost matched his confidence. The Englishman led Curtis over the eight obstacles, but in the flat run to the finish, the American pulled even, then won moving away. Goulding promptly gathered his old medals, left the stadium, and took the first train out of Athens.

In the pole vault, Welles Hoyt, later a star for Harvard, defeated Princeton's Albert Tyler. Except for the race from Marathon, the track and field competition was over. The makeshift American team had won nine championships, Australia's Flack the other two.

During the pole vault competition, word reached the stadium that Spiridon Loues, the shepherd from Maroussi, was in Athens and, leading by a wide margin, was jogging toward the finish. At last, a Greek, a child of the soil, was going to win a track and field championship. Closer and closer Loues came, and the murmur of the crowd swelled to a roar. Prince George, six feet five inches tall, and Crown Prince Constantine left the royal party and hurried to the entrance of the stadium. Loues entered, obviously weary but still trotting, and the two Princes ran along at his side on his final lap. Happily, easily, seven minutes in front of his nearest competitor, Spiridon Loues, the ex-infantryman, completed the course. He had conquered. All Greece rejoiced. Loues advanced before his King, the King congratulated the shepherd, and several members of the Greek Olympic Committee embraced the young hero. Doves were released in the stadium. Hats were waved. Thousands cheered, and to make joy complete, five of the first six finishers in the race were Greek. Spiridon Loues, weighed down with gifts, had saved the reputation of Greece.

"The impression produced by the Greeks' performances in the earlier events of the competition," *The New York Times* editorialized, "was that the course of physical development had taken its way westward and that, if the school of sculpture were to be renewed, it would do better to seek its models in Chicago than in Olympia. . . . The long-distance race has changed all that. This was precisely the contest that proved most as to high physical powers and high physical training."

After the Marathon race, the rest of the 1896 Olympics seemed anticlimactic. Captain Sumner Paine won the revolver match at 30 meters for the eleventh American victory; Greece had the second highest number of victories, eight. An English tourist named I. P. Boland entered the tennis tournament on a whim and won, Emile Masson of France won three cycling championships, and a Hungarian, Alfred Hajos, scored twice in swimming events. The American swimmer, Gardner Williams, entered the 100-meter race, which was held in the Bay of Zea, just off the Mediterranean Sea. When the starter fired his revolver—one American team member later reported—Williams, accustomed to the warm waters of indoor pools, dove head first into the icy bay, bobbed to the surface, shouted, "I'm freezing," and promptly climbed out of the water.

On the seventh day, King George gave a breakfast party for all the Olympic participants, and in the middle of breakfast, at the King's request, the Americans gave the B.A.A. cheer once more. "The whole Grecian royal family are regular bricks," said Arthur Blake, when he returned from Athens. "We played leap frog with the King and the Crown Prince, had a game of baseball with them, too, and they jumped and romped about with great glee." In the baseball game, after the rules and objectives had been hastily explained to the hosts, Prince George served as pitcher and Crown Prince Constantine as catcher. The bat was a stick, the ball an orange, and on the first pitch, Thomas Curtis, as he said, "struck not wisely, but too well." The orange split, and both halves splattered the chest of the regal court uniform of the Crown Prince.

In formal ceremony, on the tenth and final day of the 1896 Olympic Games, the King of Greece presented each champion with a gold medal and an olive branch. Then the medal winners marched slowly around the stadium, and in the front row, most proudly of all, marched Spiridon Loues. He carried his gold medal and his olive branch, a silver cup and an ancient vase, and in one hand he clutched a small Greek flag. He waved the flag at the cheering crowd, and he smiled and he bowed. Then, as the little shepherd from the hills stood smartly at attention, King George rose and said: "I announce hereby the close of the First Olympiad."

King George of Greece presents an olive branch to Spiridon Loues.

The
Muscle
Men

4

1 Stockholm, 1912: American shot-putters
2 Los Angeles, 1932: International weight lifters
3 Wrestling in the Basilica of Maxentius, Rome, 1960
4 Free Style: Ivanov (left), Bulgaria, vs. Geldenhuys, South Africa, 1960
5 Free Style: Hasan Gungor (right), Turkey, middleweight champion, 1960
6 Greco-Roman Style: Hovars (top), United States, vs. Albrecht, Germany, 1960
7 Free Style: Shelby Wilson (right), United States, lightweight champion, 1960
8 Free Style: Wilfried Dietrich (right), Germany, heavyweight champion, 1960

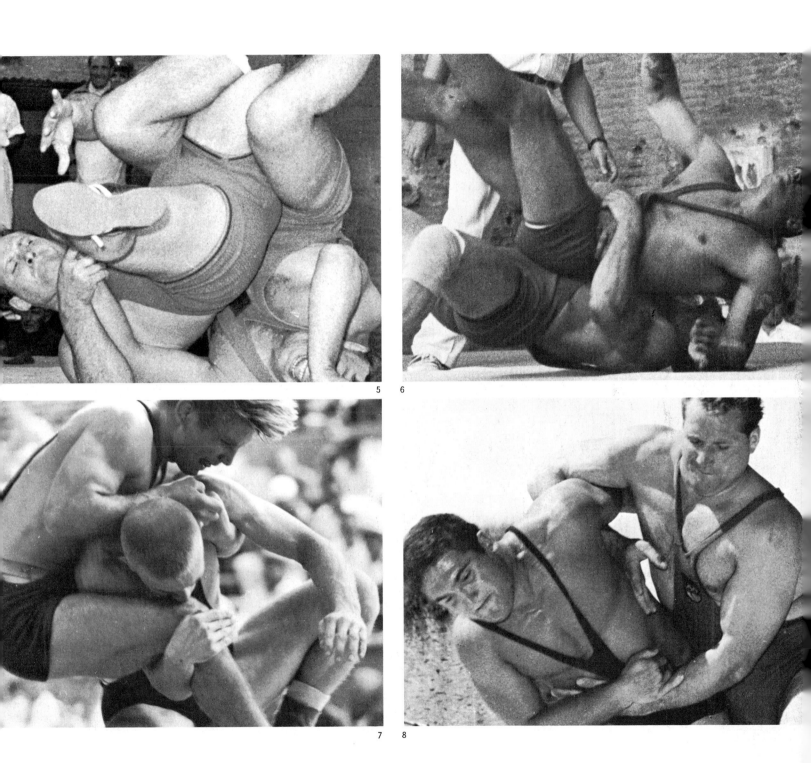

5  6

7  8

9  10

11  12

13

9 Free Style: Gamarnik (left), U.S.S.R., vs. Horvat, Yugoslavia, 1960
10 Free Style: Nasuch Akar (top), Turkey, bantamweight champion, 1948
11 Free Style: Safepour (right), Iran, vs. Aliev, U.S.S.R., 1960
12 Free Style: Evans (standing), United States, vs. Bard, Great Britain, 1952
13 Free Style: Emmali Habibi (top), Iran, lightweight champion, 1956

14    15

16

17

18

**14** Evgeni Minaev. U.S.S.R., featherweight champion, 1960
**15** John Davis, United States, heavyweight champion, 1948 and 1952
**16** Weight lifter at work, 1960
**17** Esmail Elm-Khah, Iran, bantamweight, third place, 1960
**18** Arkady Vorobiev, U.S.S.R., middle-heavyweight champion, 1956 and 1960

19 Terence Spinks (left), Great Britain, flyweight champion, 1956
20 Pete Rademacher (left), United States, heavyweight champion, 1956
21 Cassius Clay (right), United States, light-heavyweight champion, 1960
22 Francesco De Piccoli (right), Italy, heavyweight champion, 1960

19

20

21

22

24

23  Jack Torrance, United States, shot-put, fifth place, 1936
24  Giuseppe Tosi, Italy, discus throw, second place, 1948

Ray Ewry displays the form that made him the greatest standing jumper in the world.

# Nobody Jumped
# Like Ewry

## CHAPTER FOUR : 1900 – PARIS

When Ray Ewry was a child, growing up in Lafayette, Indiana, he was so frail that his family feared he might not live. After he survived a polio attack, doctors suggested that he try to build up his muscles by exercising. Ewry obediently took up calisthenics and, as he gained strength, added jumping to his daily regimen. Gradually, he grew tall and slender. His once weak legs became incredibly powerful. By the time he reached maturity, he was, in all likelihood, the greatest jumper who ever lived.

Ewry's specialties were the standing jumps—the high jump, broad jump, and hop, step, and jump, all without a running start. At his peak, between the ages of twenty-six and thirty-four, no one could beat him in any of the jumps. And at his peak, from 1900 through 1908, he established an Olympic record that should last forever. In four Olympics, including the semiofficial games of 1906, Ewry entered ten events and collected ten gold medals. He won all three standing jumps in 1900 and 1904, and then, after the standing hop, step, and jump was dropped from the Olympic schedule, he won the standing high jump and broad jump in 1906 and 1908. No other man in Olympic history has won more than seven track and field events.

"Deac" Ewry, six feet three inches tall, attended Purdue University from 1890 through 1897, earning both an undergraduate and a graduate degree in mechanical engineering. He captained the Purdue track team and played one season of football. If a shoulder injury had not forced him off the football field, some observers said, he might have become one of Purdue's greatest ends. For a year after he left Purdue, Ewry competed for the Chicago Athletic Association. Then he moved to New York, to work for the city as a hydraulics engineer, and from 1898 on, he represented the New York Athletic Club. He was still a member of the New York A.C. in 1912 when, as he trained for the Olympics in Stockholm, he realized that his skills had faded.

"Ray, you're getting to be an old man," said Martin Sheridan, a shot-putter and discus thrower who had been Ewry's teammate in the 1904, 1906, and 1908 Olympics. "You ought to quit."

At the age of thirty-eight, Ray Ewry quit.

He left a glittering record, and no facet was more brilliant than his performance on Monday, July 16, 1900. On that one day in Paris, Ray Ewry won three Olympic gold medals. His marks in the standing broad jump and the standing hop, step, and jump were admirable, but his leap in the standing high jump was almost unbelievable. From a stationary start, Ewry cleared the cross bar at five feet five inches. No other contestant came within four inches of this height. To appreciate the full magnitude of Ewry's feat, consider this: In the first four Olympic Games, only one man was able to jump higher than six feet with a *running* start. Ewry was a phenomenon, an athlete far ahead of his time, yet, paradoxically, he was an athlete perfectly suited to his time. Had Ewry been born later, he might never have had a chance to demonstrate his talents. For after 1912, the standing jumps were eliminated from the Olympic program.

"Ewry's performance is marvelous," Malcolm Ford, a former trackman, wrote in the New York *Mail and Express* the day after the triple victories. "A man who can stand still before a bar five feet five inches high and lift himself over it not only must have wonderful spring, but also the ability to handle his legs very rapidly. The standing high jump is made by the athlete standing sideways to the bar. When the spring is made, the leg nearest the stick is put over first, and it begins descending on the other side again before the trailing leg is well up. The dropping of the forward leg over the bar after clearing it counterbalances the raising of the trailing leg. It is essentially a motion which only can be acquired with much practice and differs very much from the standing broad jump, the movements of which are so simple that anyone can go through them. Ewry's new record is apt to stand a long time." Ewry's Olympic record, of course, still stands unbroken.

The 1900 Olympic Games, which marked the start of the Ewry era, were notable for a less pleasant reason. They were the most ill-planned of all modern Olympic Games. They were so disorganized that many of the 1,000 competitors from twenty countries, as strange as it may seem, did not even realize they were taking part in Olympic Games.

The problem with the 1900 Olympic Games was that they

A group of American competitors gather for a team picture in Paris. The wearers of the "P" are J. Walter Tewksbury and Irving Baxter.

were run as a sideshow, almost as an afterthought. After the highly successful 1896 games in Athens, considerable sentiment existed for holding the competitions permanently in Greece. The athletes at Athens, in fact, circulated a petition to this effect. But Baron de Coubertin, the founder of the modern games, insisted that the Olympics, in order to be truly international, had to be rotated among the leading nations of the world. Besides, he was a Frenchman, and he had committed himself to holding the Olympic Games in conjunction with the 1900 International Exposition in Paris.

The French government, which was supervising the exposition, took over supervision of the games, too, and quickly demonstrated that French officials knew no more about sports than the 1896 French runner Lermusiaux knew about pace. The government felt that the games were strictly a secondary attraction, not nearly so significant as the massive industrial exhibits of the exposition. To keep sports in the background, the authorities decided not to use the designation of Olympic Games. The events were called simply international championships, and nowhere on the official program did the word "Olympics" appear.

Baron de Coubertin himself was stuck in an obscure committee post, and the government deliberately forgot him and his Olympic ideas. Unfortunately, the government also forgot to prepare for the athletic competitions, and as the opening of the events drew close, no facilities were ready. The government hastily remembered the baron, placed him in charge of the sports committee, and told him he could call the games Olympic.

The baron tried his best to salvage the games, but it was too late for him to undo all the confusion. The track and field events were scheduled to be held on the grounds of the Racing Club of France, in the Bois de Boulogne. The site was lovely—for picnicking, not racing. There was, for one thing, no track. The idea of installing a cinder track and disturbing the splendor of the grass appalled French authorities; Baron de Coubertin had to settle for a 500-meter oval laid out on grass that was not even level. The jumpers had no proper pits. The broad jump take-off was on a slight incline. The vaulters, instead of thrusting their poles into dirt, had to use a wooden platform. The hurdles, one meter high, were as solid as telephone poles, perhaps because some *were* telephone poles, bent and broken. Bushes grew under the hurdles.

Despite the French mismanagement and apathy, interest in the United States was considerably greater than in 1896. Among American colleges, Yale, Princeton, Chicago, Georgetown, Michigan, Penn, and Syracuse all agreed to send representatives to the games. The New York A.C., which had spurned the first modern games, sent a sizable squad, including Ray Ewry; several individuals, including 1896 veterans Robert Garrett and James B. Connolly, went to Paris at their own expense. A total of thirty-five Americans, among them most of the national champions, competed in the 1900 track and field events.

The American delegation precipitated the first major international incident of the modern Olympic Games. When the French scheduled the games to begin on July 15, a Sunday, the Americans insisted that Sunday competition was sacrilegious. Start on Saturday, July 14, the Americans demanded. The French politely pointed out that July 14 was Bastille Day, a national holiday marked by parades and military demonstrations certain to lure Frenchmen away from the track and field contests. But the Americans complained so long and so loud that the French shrugged and, apparently, gave in. As the Americans departed for France, their understanding was that the games would begin on Saturday, then recess until Monday.

On the way to Paris, many of the American athletes paused in England and won most of the British track and field championships. Then they moved on to France and settled into their temporary quarters. Most of the Americans stayed in Paris, the Princeton team in Neuilly and the Penn team in Versailles. They soon learned that the French had compromised the original agreement. The events were going to begin on Saturday—but they were going to continue on Sunday. The Americans howled.

"The programme of events sent out by the French managers states that the preliminary heats will take place Saturday and the final heats Sunday," the famous Amos Alonzo Stagg—who lived long enough to celebrate his 100th birthday in 1962—complained in a letter to the New York *Herald*. Stagg, then thirty-eight and manager of the University of Chicago team, had borrowed $2,500 on his own to take his athletes to Paris. "Everybody here feels that it is a most contemptible trick. Not a single American university would have sent a team had it not been definitely announced that the games would not be held on a Sunday. Even at this late date, it is likely that the American teams will unitedly refuse to compete if the French officials persist in carrying out what seems to us a very nasty piece of business—to use no stronger term."

Alvin Kraenzlein clears the hurdles with one leg extended, a revolution in form.

But the French persisted in carrying out their plans, and the American teams were not at all united in their reactions. Princeton, Syracuse, and Penn were the most outspoken critics of Sunday sports, but when the time came for a showdown, Penn backed down and permitted its athletes to compete at their own discretion. Georgetown and the New York A.C. made the same choice. Bitterly, Yale, Princeton, Syracuse, Chicago, and Michigan decided to keep their athletes out of the Sunday events; their decision, prompted by admirable motives, unquestionably weakened the American team in Paris.

The weakening, however, was so slight as to be almost imperceptible. The United States could have dominated the track and field competition simply by sending to Paris four men—Ray Ewry and three University of Pennsylvania students, Alvin Kraenzlein, Irving Baxter, and J. Walter Tewksbury. The three Penn men, coached by Mike Murphy, were close friends; during the school year, they shared an apartment in Philadelphia. After their performances in Paris, they could have decorated every wall with Olympic medals and still have had a few left over.

In a total of twenty-three Olympic track and field events, Ewry, Kraenzlein, Baxter, and Tewksbury collected eleven gold medals, five silver medals, and one bronze medal. Ewry, of course, scored three firsts; Baxter two firsts and three seconds; Tewksbury two firsts, two seconds, and a third; and Kraenzlein became the first—and only—man in Olympic track and field history to win four individual championships in one year.

Kraenzlein, twenty-three years old, had competed for the University of Wisconsin, the Chicago A.A., and the New York A.C. before representing Penn in Paris. He gained his first victory in the 110-meter high hurdles, one of the two finals staged on Saturday. John McLean of Michigan took an early lead, but on the next-to-last hurdle, Kraenzlein moved in front and won by less than a meter. Kraenzlein, a master stylist, revolutionized hurdling. Until he came along, runners skimmed over hurdles with both their legs tucked up under them. He was the first outstanding hurdler who cleared the barriers with one leg extended.

Arthur Duffy of Georgetown was the favorite in the 100-meter dash, but halfway through the race, as he was holding first place, he suddenly collapsed, crippled by a pulled tendon. Frank Jarvis of Princeton sprinted home first, trailed by Tewksbury.

The uniforms of the Americans made almost as deep an impression as their performances. "The natty college costumes of the Americans," one reporter wrote, "were a decided contrast to the homemade attire of some of the best European athletes who, instead of donning a sweater or bathrobe after the trials, walked about in straw hats and light overcoats."

The crowd was shocked by the college cheers of the Americans—"What a band of savages!" one spectator said—and the

Irving Baxter sets sail toward the pole vaulting championship.

Americans, in turn, were shocked by the small size of the crowd. Barely a thousand people watched the Saturday competition, and a sizable percentage of the gathering were Americans. On Bastille Day, Parisians, obviously, preferred to watch the President's review of the troops at Longchamps.

On Sunday, too, the Parisians apparently had better things to watch than young men flexing muscles. Again the crowd was small, probably under a thousand.

Even though more than half the best American athletes skipped the Sunday competition—some of them still mistakenly assuming that no finals would be decided—the United States won eight of the ten events contested. Only Hungary's Rudolph Bauer, in the discus, and Great Britain's Charles Bennett, in the 1,500-meter run, spoiled the Americans' sabbath festival.

With his toughest American rivals withdrawn from the high jump and the pole vault, Irving Baxter won both events. George Orton of Penn won the 2,500-meter steeplechase, Maxey Long of the New York A.C. won the 400-meter run, Richard Sheldon of the New York A.C. won the shot-put and, most disheartening from the French point of view, Tewksbury won the 400-meter hurdles. This event was a European specialty, not introduced in American championships until 1914, and Henri Tauzin of France had never been defeated. But Tewksbury jumped in front at the start and held the lead all the way.

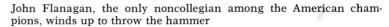

John Flanagan, the only noncollegian among the American champions, winds up to throw the hammer

Rudolph Bauer of Hungary (center) wins the discus championship.

Kraenzlein added two more titles, the first in the 60-meter dash and the second, somewhat tainted, in the broad jump. Myer Prinstein of Syracuse, the holder of the world broad jump record, had been the leading qualifier in the Saturday trials, but his school refused to give him permission to compete on Sunday. With six extra jumps on Sunday, Kraenzlein surpassed Prinstein's best qualifying jump by one centimeter, less than half an inch. Prinstein challenged Kraenzlein to a jump-off on Monday, but the Penn star, whose Sunday participation had already stirred up considerable bitterness in the American camp, refused the bid.

Monday was Ewry day. Baxter placed second in all three of the standing jumps. Prinstein earned a measure of consolation by winning the hop, step, and jump and setting an Olympic record that survived for twelve years. The 1896 champion, James B. Connolly, finished second in the triple jump. The only noncollegian among the American champions, John Flanagan, an Irish-born policeman representing the New York A.C., won the hammer throw. To break the monotonous string of United States triumphs, Englishmen won the 800-meter run and the 4,000-meter steeplechase.

65

Besides diving and swimming, Olympians went still-fishing in the Seine.

Kraenzlein picked up his fourth championship in the 200-meter hurdles, winning easily, with roommate Tewksbury in third place. "That was my last race," Kraenzlein announced after his victory. "I am through with athletics and shall devote myself to something more serious." Kraenzlein promptly retired and devoted himself to something more serious—coaching athletics. Shortly before World War I, the Germans brought him to Berlin to train their national track and field team for the ill-fated 1916 Olympics.

After Monday, the track and field competition sputtered on till the end of the week, and sports events, of one type or another, were held until October 28. Tewksbury won the 200-meter sprint, defeating, among other rivals, a young man who was the champion of South Africa. "Ten thousand people had gone to the boat to see him off," Tewksbury once recalled. "He had let them down and after the race he was crying. I went over and told him I was sorry. I never felt so bad about winning a race in my life."

The Marathon race, as usual, stimulated strong feelings. Originally, the race was scheduled to be run on a forty-kilometer course from Paris to Versailles. But at the last moment, after the American, British, Swedish, and South African runners had carefully studied the Versailles route, the French switched to a different course—four times around the track at the racing club, then a circular route around Paris and back to the racing club. Michel Teato, a French bakery boy, won the race, followed by two of his countrymen and a Swede named Ernest Fast. "It may be that the chief reason for the Frenchmen's success in this event," one tactful American reporter wrote, "is that they were familiar with the course."

Other American observers were less charitable. The story spread—and grew stronger with each passing year—that Arthur Newton of the New York A.C., who finished fifth officially, overtook the French contingent early in the race, took

66

the lead at the halfway mark, and was never passed the rest of the way. Yet when Newton reached the finish, the three fast Frenchmen and Fast the Swede were waiting for him. Cynics suggested that the French knew the course—and its detours—exceedingly well. "There wasn't a drop of mud on the three Frenchmen," Walter Tewksbury later said. "Everyone else in the race was drenched with the stuff." Nobody ever did explain satisfactorily how Fast found his way.

While the Marathon provided the only French victory in track and field, the hosts scored heavily in other sports, particularly shooting, yachting, and croquet, and finished the 1900 Olympics with a total of twenty-eight gold medals. (Croquet was far from the strangest sport on the calendar; competition was held for still-fishing in the Seine, but no champion was crowned.) The United States had seventeen gold medals in track and field and five in other events, including one in the tug of war. Only two teams—one from France and one from the united country of Sweden and Norway—had originally entered the tug of war, but the Scandinavian group, after defeating the French, graciously agreed to risk its title against a pick-up American squad. The Americans—including shot-put champion Sheldon, hammer champion Flanagan, and the 1896 veteran, Bob Garrett, who took third places in the 1900 shot-put and standing hop, step, and jump—beat the Scandinavians and, according to official Olympic records, won the championship.

The United States secured its final gold medal late in August, more than a month after the track and field competition ended. In rowing, an Olympic event for the first time, the Vespers Boat Club of Philadelphia won the eight-oared championship.

When the games finally dragged to a close, only one thing seemed reasonably certain. If Baron de Coubertin had held to his original plan, if the modern Olympics had begun with the Paris competition of 1900, the heady French blend of confusion and controversy could have killed the games in their infancy. But fortunately for the baron, the splendid competition at Athens had already demonstrated that Olympic Games could be successful.

The Scandinavians (left) win the tug of war from the French, before losing the championship to the United States.

With long-sleeved shirt, clipped trousers, and low-cut street shoes, Felix Carvajal (No. 3) lines up for the start of the Marathon.

# Our Man from Havana

## CHAPTER FIVE : 1904 – ST. LOUIS

*"All I knew was that you had to run, run, run without knowing why . . . through fields you didn't understand . . . into woods that made you afraid . . . over hills without knowing you'd been up and down."*
—ALAN SILLITOE
*The Loneliness of the Long-Distance Runner*

Nobody heard of Felix Carvajal before 1904, and nobody heard of Felix Carvajal after 1904. The suspicion persists that Felix Carvajal did not exist, which is an exaggeration, because he was very short, but not that short.

Carvajal was a mailman in Havana, and neither snow, nor rain, nor heat, nor gloom of night could stay him from the swift completion of his appointed rounds. Felix was proud of his endurance. When the news filtered through to Cuba that the 1904 Olympic Games were going to be held in St. Louis, he decided that he would enter the Marathon race.

But before Carvajal could compete in the Marathon, he had to solve one slight problem. He had to get to St. Louis. In 1904, Cuba had no official Olympic team, Felix had no money, and great as his endurance was, he could not run to the United States. Felix found a novel solution. He went to the public square in Havana and began running around in circles, and eventually a crowd gathered about him. Then he climbed on top of a wooden box, announced that he was going to St. Louis to win the Olympic Marathon championship, and asked for contributions. Strangely enough, he got them.

Felix promptly sailed to the United States, and on the way to St. Louis, he passed through New Orleans, a city known for fine food and fine gamblers. Felix never did get a chance to try the food. He soon found himself in a dice game and soon afterward found himself out of funds. Working and begging, eating meager meals, he somehow managed to continue on to St. Louis.

Once Carvajal reached the Olympic site, he became a mascot of the weight throwers on the United States team. The American giants shared their food and lodgings with the tiny Cuban and tried to teach him some of the finer points of running. Felix, unfortunately, was not an apt student. To him, running was running, and all the talk about pace and strategy was simply Yankee propaganda. He ate the Americans' food, slept in their quarters, listened eagerly to their jokes, told tales of his native Havana in broken English—and ran the same undisciplined way he always had.

On August 30, the second day of the 1904 Olympic Games, with the temperature in the nineties and the humidity no lower, Felix showed up for the start of the Marathon wearing a faded long-sleeved shirt, a pair of long trousers, and a pair of low-cut street shoes with heavy heels. Perhaps as a concession to the heat, the little Cuban allowed Martin Sheridan, a New York policeman and a discus thrower, to take a pair of scissors and clip his trousers at the knee.

The start of the St. Louis Marathon was sheer chaos. Men on horseback rode off in front of the runners to clear the course. Trainers on bicycles rode off next to the runners to give advice and encouragement. Doctors in automobiles rode off behind the runners to salvage the victims. "The roads were so lined with vehicles," one witness reported, "that the runners had to constantly dodge the horses and wagons. So dense were the dust clouds on the road that frequently the runners could not be seen by the automobiles following them."

But in dust or heat or heavy shoes the mailman must go through. Felix trotted off as casually as if he were making his daily rounds in Havana. He had no trainer to advise or encourage him, so as he jogged along, he chatted with spectators, trading jokes and idle comments. Once he asked a picnicking bystander for some peaches, and when he was refused, he grabbed two and ran off eating them. Later he detoured temporarily, climbed into an apple orchard, and ate some green apples.

Felix was not the only blithe spirit in the 1904 Marathon race. Fred Lorz was another. A New Yorker representing the Mohawk Athletic Club, Lorz led the early part of the race. At the halfway mark, his fast pace, combined with the killing heat, forced him to retire. Exhausted, suffering painful cramps, Lorz dragged himself to the side of the course, and, his chances gone, waved to the other runners as they passed him.

After a comforting rest, Lorz accepted a ride in one of the automobiles cruising along the Marathon course. The car soon began overtaking the competitors, and Lorz, a good-natured fellow, smiled and shouted at his rivals as he went by. He was out of the running, but he was in good spirits. Eventually, Lorz on wheels passed all the Marathon men on foot. Then, roughly five miles from the finish, the car suddenly broke down. Refreshed by his ride, Lorz hopped out of the car and, to keep his muscles from tightening, jogged to the finish line. Naturally, he arrived far ahead of the other contestants and, naturally, the crowd hailed him as the winner Lorz knew he was ineligible and knew the victory reception was ridiculous, but he found the whole scene amusing. He decided to play along with the gag. When Alice Roosevelt, the daughter of President Theodore Roosevelt, was about to present him with the championship cup, Lorz realized that his joke had gone far enough and confessed that he had not run the entire distance. It was all very funny—but not to the Amateur Athletic Union of the United States. The A.A.U. suspended Lorz for life. Thanks largely to testimony from Lorz's rivals, all of whom felt that the hoax was merely a prank, the A.A.U. ultimately rescinded the suspension. Without benefit of an automobile, Lorz won the Boston Marathon in 1905.

While Lorz was motoring playfully toward the finish of the St. Louis Marathon, an excellent race developed on the course. With Lorz eliminated, two other New Yorkers jockeyed for the lead. Sam Mellor maintained a slight advantage over Arthur Newton, the man many people thought had won the

Thomas Hicks, the Marathon champion, sits dazed after the race.

1900 Olympic Marathon. Thomas Hicks, an English-born Bostonian, was running third. The terrible heat polished off Mellor—seventeen of thirty-one starters failed to finish—and with nine miles remaining, Newton slowed to a walk, giving Hicks the lead. While the United States runners fought for first place, Felix Carvajal happily stayed back in the pack, a towel wrapped around his waist, still grinning and talking with spectators.

Hicks proved to be a reluctant leader. Seven miles from the finish, he was ready to give up the race. He felt too tired to continue. But two of his handlers, who had been trailing him in an automobile, ran up to him, fed him the white of an egg, and gave him small doses of strychnine. The drug—later barred by Olympic rules—dulled Hicks' pain and his reactions. He plodded on, refreshed periodically with water splashed on him by his handlers. "I want something to eat as soon as I get there," Hicks yelled to his aides. "I'm nearly starved."

Two miles from the finish, as he approached the last of seven steep hills on the brutal course, Hicks stopped running and started walking. Still leading by more. than a mile, he walked to the peak of the hill. Then, when a group of spectators cheered his approach, he began running once more. Barely conscious of what he was doing, he trotted the rest of the way to the finish. Hicks arrived in a daze—just as the furor over the Lorz hoax was subsiding—and had to be carried to a dressing room. Four doctors worked to revive him. When Hicks was finally strong enough to leave the stadium, he took a trolley back to his quarters at the Missouri Athletic Club and slept all the way. Albert Corey of Chicago placed second, six minutes behind Hicks and thirteen minutes in front of Arthur Newton.

And where was Felix? The green apples he had plucked from the friendly orchard had turned upon him. He had developed cramps in the latter part of the race and had been forced to rest for a considerable time. Still the tiny Cuban managed to finish fourth. Then he disappeared completely from athletic competition. No one seemed to know where he went or what he did, but for years afterward, many witnesses insisted that if Felix Carvajal had curbed his taste for green apples, he would have won the 1904 Olympic Marathon. Even without victory, little Felix clearly was the hit of the St. Louis games.

The 1904 Olympic Games almost weren't held in St. Louis. They had been scheduled originally for Chicago, but after an official United States Olympic Committee was formed for the first time and Theodore Roosevelt agreed to be honorary president of the group, the President suggested that the games be shifted to St. Louis. The Louisiana Purchase Exposition was being held in St. Louis during 1904, and Roosevelt felt that it was foolish to conduct two major international events at the same time in two different American cities. Each would detract from the other, the President believed. Roosevelt's intentions were good, but the effect was that the Olympics again

Sprinter Archie Hahn, a master of the start, sets himself for the gun.

Harry Hillman (left) and Jim Lightbody each earned three gold medals

became a secondary attraction, as they had been in Paris. The St. Louis crowds, although much larger than the ones in Paris, didn't come close to matching the Athens turnouts. Attendance averaged about 10,000 and went as high as 20,000 only on the last of the five track and field days.

Because of the great expense and time involved in sending teams to the United States, European representation in St. Louis was minimal. An overwhelming majority of the 500 competitors, representing eleven countries, were Americans. England, then the second strongest track and field nation in the world, did not send a squad. Nor did France. Germany and Hungary sent a few athletes, but they were mostly swimmers. The imbalance of national representation showed up vividly in the results. In twenty-three official track and field events, the United States scored twenty-two firsts, twenty-two seconds, and twenty thirds.

The Americans' domination was not merely impressive; it was ridiculous. Never before or since has any one nation demonstrated such superiority in the Olympic Games—and, amazingly, several of the best American athletes did not even compete in 1904. None of the large Eastern universities bothered to send teams to St. Louis. The United States was represented almost entirely by a dozen athletic clubs. The strongest was the New York Athletic Club. Competing for a team trophy donated by the sporting goods manufacturer, A. G. Spalding, the New York A.C. defeated the Chicago Athletic Association by a single point after a heated debate over the eligibility of one New York competitor.

During the St. Louis games, one complaint, which has since become almost standard for track and field competitions, cropped up in print for the first time. "Unquestionably the greatest array of athletic officials ever seen at one meet swarmed the arena and made life miserable for the athletes," the New York *Sun* noted in its coverage of the first day's events. "When they were tired of ordering the contestants around, they exercised their official authority on each other."

Four Americans each won three track and field events. Ray Ewry, naturally, captured the three standing jumps. Stocky Archie Hahn, a master starter who had just graduated from the University of Michigan, won the 60-meter, 100-meter, and 200-meter dashes. Harry Hillman, who later became track coach at Dartmouth, scored in the 200-meter hurdles, the 400-meter hurdles, and the 400-meter run. Silent Jim Lightbody, representing the Chicago A.A., demonstrated both versatility and endurance and won the 800-meter run, the 1,500-meter run, and the 2,500-meter steeplechase.

Probably the finest races of the 1904 Olympics were the 400-meter and 800-meter runs. In the shorter event, four Americans each had a strong shot at victory. H. C. Groman led for more than half the distance, but as he entered the stretch, Hillman, Frank Waller, and George Poage, the first Negro to represent the United States in the Olympics, pulled even with him. Poage seemed to have the best position, but he suddenly stumbled and fell. Groman, tiring, faded to third place, and with a brilliant finish, Hillman defeated Waller by a stride.

In the 800-meter run, Lightbody was content to lay back and let his American rivals set the early pace. Harvey Cohn wore himself out in the first 400 meters. Then Emil Breitkreutz took the lead and held it until the final 100 meters. "I don't remember anything after that point," Breitkreutz said

Myer Prinstein (left) wins the hop, step, and jump, and weight-thrower Etienne Desmarteau of Canada makes the only dent in the American track and field monopoly.

Charles Dvorak clinches the pole vaulting championship.

later. He finished the race on pure instinct. Howard Valentine, the national half-mile champion, passed Breitkreutz, and in the stretch, Lightbody made his bid. Running on the outside, he sprinted past opponent after opponent. With thirty meters to go, Lightbody flashed in front of Valentine and won pulling away. Breitkreutz finished third, then fell and passed out.

The fifth-place finisher, Johannes Runge of Germany, might have threatened Lightbody had he not been the victim of a curious mix-up. There were dozens of junior, novice, and handicap competitions conducted during the St. Louis Olympics, and a few minutes before the 800-meter championship race, Runge by mistake entered an 800-meter handicap race. He won the handicap event, then discovered his error, and with hardly a chance to catch his breath, ran another 800 meters against Lightbody.

If Runge was the most disappointed athlete in the games, the most satisfied were two Americans—Myer Prinstein and Charles Dvorak. In the Paris Olympics, Prinstein had been favored in the broad jump and Dvorak in the pole vault, but both had been frustrated when their schools refused to allow them to compete on a Sunday. After four years of waiting, Prinstein and Dvorak each won his specialty in St. Louis. Prinstein also retained his hop, step, and jump championship.

Ralph Rose, Martin Sheridan, and John Flanagan, three of the American weight throwers who had befriended Felix Carvajal, enjoyed greater success than their Cuban mascot. Rose won the shot-put and finished second in the discus; Sheridan won the discus and finished fourth in the shot-put; and Flanagan won the hammer throw for the second straight Olympics, finished second in the 56-pound weight throw, and finished fourth in the discus. Flanagan, the world-record holder, had been favored in the weight throw, but he was upset by a fellow policeman, Etienne Desmarteau of the Montreal police force. Desmarteau was the only man to disturb the United States monopoly in track and field.

Besides track and field, competitions were held in nearly twenty other sports, including such temporary Olympic events as roque (a form of croquet) and archery. But as in track and field, the vast majority of contestants were Americans. In recognized Olympic events, the United States collected a total of seventy-seven gold medals, precisely seventy more than the next country, Cuba. Despite the failure of Felix, Cuba won seven gold medals, all in fencing. Boxing and catch-as-catch-can (free style) wrestling, later permanent fixtures, appeared on the Olympic schedule for the first time, and Americans won all seven weight classifications in both sports. The United States also swept the rowing events, with the Vespers Boat Club of Philadelphia retaining its eight-oar title.

United States superiority disappeared in a series of sub-Olympic events staged on August 12 and 13. These two days were called Anthropology Days and featured competition among Pygmies and Kaffirs from Africa, Ainus from Japan, Patagonians, and Moros and Igorots from the Philippines. A Patagonian won the shot-put, an Igorot won the pole climb, and the Pygmies convinced everyone that they were the best in the mud fight. The host nation did contribute one champion; a Sioux Indian managed to win the 100-yard dash.

"In no place but America would one have dared to place such events on a program," Baron Pierre de Coubertin said later, "but to Americans everything is permissible, their youthful exuberance calling certainly for the indulgence of the ancient Greek ancestors."

An American triumphs in roque (above), and a giant Patagonian tries the high jump (left).

By the time the St. Louis festival ended, Baron de Coubertin's faith in the Olympic idea must have been wavering. The 1900 Olympic Games in Paris had attracted an international field but had been terribly organized and dreadfully attended. The 1904 Olympic Games in St. Louis had been decently organized and reasonably attended but had failed to draw an international field.

Half in desperation, the baron reconsidered the Greeks' standing offer to be permanent hosts for the Olympic Games. Baron de Coubertin arranged a compromise: Starting in 1906, and every four years thereafter, mid-Olympic competitions would be held in Athens. These would not be official Olympic Games, but they would serve to fan the Olympic flame. The first mid-Olympics was held in 1906, but when internal difficulties forced the Greeks to cancel the 1910 competition, the idea quietly died. Yet the 1906 competition in Athens served a significant purpose. The Greeks once more provided efficient organization, splendid attendance, and handsome pageantry; England, France, and other European nations returned to the Olympic fold. Considering the mismanagement of 1900, the disinterest of 1904, and the bitterness that was to come in 1908, it is not at all unreasonable to conclude that the Greeks of 1906 saved the Olympic Games.

"To Americans, everything is permissible, their youthful exuberance calling certainly for the indulgence of the ancient Greek ancestors."

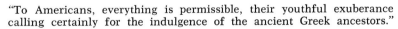

1

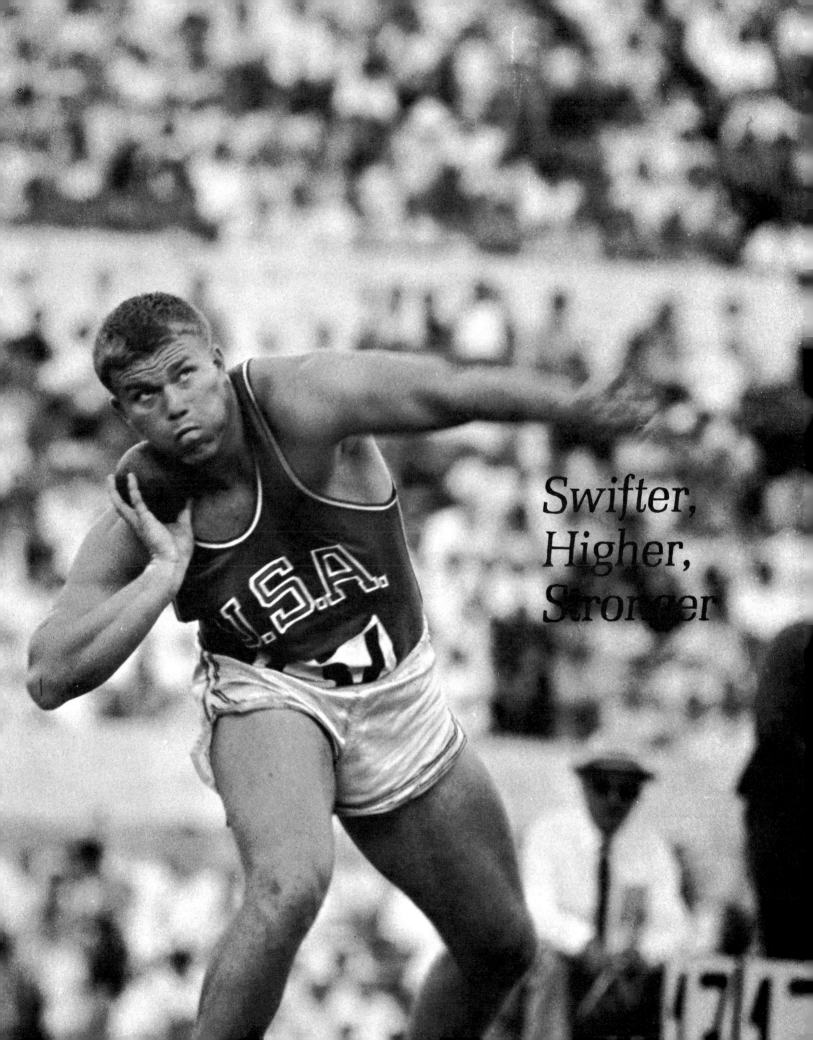

Swifter,
Higher,
Stronger

3

1 Start of the 10,000-meter run, 1960
2 Dallas Long, United States, shot-put, third place, 1960
3 Start of the decathlon sprint, 1936
4 At 20 meters, the 100-meter dash final, 1952
5 At 40 meters
6 At 60 meters
7 At 80 meters
8 After the tape, the winner, Lindy Remigino (981), United States

4

5

6

7

8

9 Finish of the 110-meter hurdles final, 1960, won by Lee Calhoun (left), United States
10 Heat of the 1,600-meter relay, 1960
11 Finish of the 100-meter dash final, 1960, won by Armin Hary (bottom), Germany
12 Herb Elliott, Australia, 1,500-meter champion, 1960
13 Chris Brasher, Great Britain, 3,000-meter steeplechase champion, 1956
14 Peter Snell, New Zealand, 800-meter champion, 1960: 800- and 1,500-meter champion, 1964

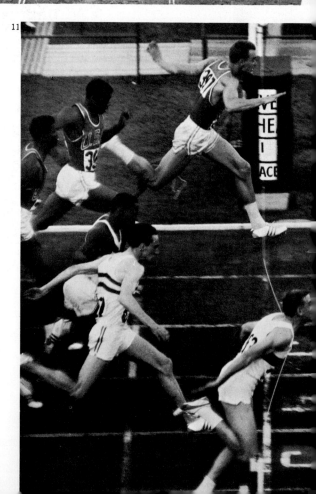

12

13

14

15

15 Finals of the 110-meter hurdles, 1952, won by Harrison
   Dillard (center, leading), United States
16 Glenn Morris, United States, decathlon champion, 1936
17 Heat of the 110-meter hurdles, 1960
18 Glenn Davis (foreground), United States, 400-meter
   hurdles champion, 1956 and 1960

16

17

18

19

20

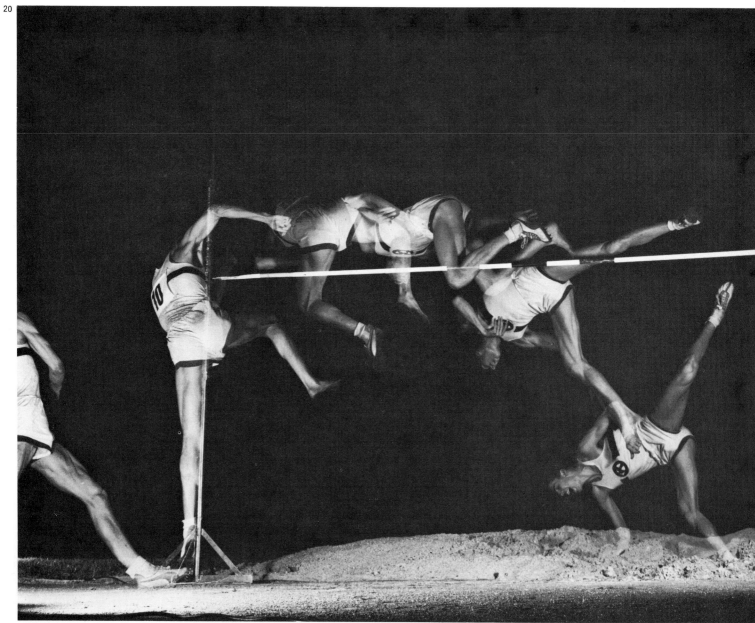

86

21
22

19  Charles Dumas, United States, high jump champion, 1956
20  Stig Pettersson, Sweden, high jump, fifth place, 1960
21  Cornelius Johnson, United States, high jump champion, 1936
22  Robert Shavlakadze, U.S.S.R., high jump champion, 1960

23

24    25

26

27

**23** Ralph Boston, United States, broad jump champion, 1960
**24** Greg Bell, United States, broad jump champion, 1956
**25** Vasily Kuznetsov, U.S.S.R., decathlon, third place, 1960
**26** Bob Richards, United States, pole vault champion, 1952 and 1956
**27** Don Bragg, United States, pole vault champion, 1960

28  Zora Singh, India, and Ron Zinn, United States, 20,000-meter walk, 1960
29  Don Thompson, Great Britain, 50,000-meter walk champion, 1960
30  Bob McMillan, United States, during the 3,000-meter steeplechase, 1948
31  Walking race, 1920
32  3,000-meter steeplechase, 1956

31

32

Paul Pilgrim, holding second place on the outside, challenges the leader, Jim Lightbody, in the 800-meter run.

# Pilgrim's Progress

## CHAPTER SIX : 1906 – ATHENS

From an American point of view, the Olympic Games of 1906 served an invaluable purpose. Certain technical procedures, which later became standard, were introduced for these off-year Olympics. For the first time, American athletes wore an official uniform. For the first time, the United States Olympic Committee selected an official team. And for the first time, the selection committee made a terrible mistake. The committee ignored Paul Pilgrim.

No competitive tryouts were conducted for the 1906 team, and the committee based its choices entirely on the athletes' reputations. Paul Pilgrim was a twenty-year-old member of the New York Athletic Club who had no reputation at all. He was an obscure candidate for the Olympic squad in the 400-meter and 800-meter runs. He had accomplished nothing in national events, and the committee felt he was not needed in Athens.

The committee's feeling certainly appeared justified. After all, the United States had the defending champion in each event, Harry Hillman at 400 meters and Jim Lightbody at 800 meters. Hillman was backed up by Fay Moulton, a fine sprinter, and Charles Bacon, a fine hurdler; Lightbody, who had followed his twin victories in the 1904 Olympics by winning the half-mile and mile races in the 1905 United States championships, didn't seem to need any backing up. There wasn't much point in spending money to take an unknown like Pilgrim to the Olympic Games.

But Pilgrim was a protégé of Matt Halpin, the New York A.C. official who was serving as manager of the American Olympic team in 1906. Shortly before the team was scheduled to leave for Athens, James E. Sullivan of the United States Olympic Committee approached Halpin and told him that the committee's fund-raising campaign had been a resounding success. "Matt," said Sullivan, "we're in such good financial shape that you can add any one man you want to the squad."

With some misgivings, Halpin decided to add Pilgrim. When the young New Yorker won his qualifying heat of the 400-meter run, Halpin's misgivings disappeared. "That's wonderful, Paul," the manager said. "Now no one can criticize us for bringing you."

Pilgrim was strictly a long shot in the 400-meter final. Because Hillman, the defending champion, had bruised his knee during the boat trip to Athens and had failed to regain his top form, Lieutenant Wyndham Halswelle, a swift Englishman, was the prerace favorite. Halswelle's most dangerous rival seemed to be Nigel Barker, an Australian who had scored the fastest time in the preliminary heats.

Hillman got off to a good start, but his leg weakened halfway through the race. Halswelle and Barker pulled away from the hobbled American and swept toward the finish. Victory for the British Empire appeared certain, but suddenly, unexpectedly, Pilgrim put on a furious sprint, flashed past the leaders, and won by more than a meter. Halswelle was second, Barker was third, and Halpin was overjoyed.

Lightbody won the 1,500 meters the same day Pilgrim won the 400, and the next afternoon, the two American gold medalists faced a strong field in the 800-meter final. England's Halswelle, determined to make up for his 400-meter failure, presented the greatest threat to the Americans. Lightbody, who had been content to lay back in St. Louis, took the lead at the start in Athens, and after 700 meters, he and Pilgrim drew away from their rivals. A notoriously fast finisher, Lightbody was in a commanding position, but fifty meters from the tape, again suddenly, again unexpectedly, Pilgrim sprinted, caught up to his famous teammate and, by less than a stride, captured his second gold medal. The obscure New Yorker, who got to Athens only on a fluke, had become the hero of the 1906 Olympic Games. No athlete since Pilgrim has won both the 400-meter and 800-meter runs in the Olympics.

As a competitor, Pilgrim faded from fame as abruptly as he had appeared; in the 1908 Olympic Games, he failed even to qualify for the 400-meter final. But as an administrator, Pilgrim continued to contribute to American success in international sports; from 1914 until 1953, he was athletic director of the New York A.C., and sent dozens of his members into the Olympic Games. He was always quiet, always modest, and right up till the day he died in 1958, he was embarrassed by mention of his two Olympic victories.

In 1906, as in 1896, the Americans' journey to Athens was as tense and tiring as the Olympic competition itself. The first

Paul Pilgrim wears the official American uniform and the New York A. C. sweater.

George Bonhag sets the pace for Jim Lightbody in the 1,500-meter run.

official United States team—thirty-one track and field men, four swimmers and divers, and two wrestlers—sailed from New York on April 3 aboard the S.S. *Barbarossa.* One day out of port, the ship steamed into rough water. A huge wave swept over the bow and cascaded into an unsuspecting group of American athletes, smashing them against the deck and against the rails. Six of the athletes, including Moulton, Hillman, and Martin Sheridan, suffered injuries serious enough to require medical treatment. A 265-pound weight thrower named Jim Mitchell dislocated a shoulder as he saved Harvey Cohn, a veteran distance runner, from being swept overboard. The big weight thrower also saved Pilgrim by advising the young runner to go below deck before the damaging wave struck. Mitchell's heroics probably cost him a gold medal. He had been favored to win the fourteen-pound stone throw, but his shoulder injury kept him out of the competition.

The Americans docked in Naples on April 16 and from there followed the familiar 1896 route—across Italy by train, steamship to Greece, then across Greece to Athens by train. In Italy, the Americans experienced a strange setback. They had brought their own mineral water with them, but Italian officials, through some curious reasoning, decided that the water was contraband gin and seized it. In fair trade, the Italians gave the Americans an equal volume of native wines.

Once more the Panathenaic Stadium was the site of the track and field championships, and once more the Greeks did a splendid job of organizing the games. King George and Queen Olga returned to watch the competition, and Crown Prince Constantine, who became King when his father was assassinated in 1913, still served as president of the Greek Olympic Committee. His brothers, Prince Nicholas and Prince George, again helped supervise the games, aided this time by another brother, Prince Andrew. The stadium and the surrounding hills were filled with the familiar crowds, and for the opening ceremonies, Greek soldiers in gleaming armor stood smartly atop the rear tier of the stadium.

"Short-skirted and neat-legged," by 1906 standards, Danish girls give a demonstration in gymnastics.

Matt Halpin provided a sprightly, if irreverent, description of the opening ceremonies. In a cable to the New York *Evening Mail*, Halpin reported: "Before the King and Queen of Greece, all the other available royalty and more than 60,000 people, the Olympic Games at Athens were formally opened yesterday with ceremonies sufficiently impressive for the coronation of some great monarch.

"We paraded—900 athletes from all over the world—and a grand march it was. I headed our bunch, carrying the American flag, and we got a louder hand all around the track than any other group. When I dipped the Stars and Stripes passing the royal box, the King staked me to a smile that made me feel that I belonged." This was the last time that an American flag was dipped during an Olympic parade.

King Edward VII and Queen Alexandra of England were among Halpin's "other available royalty," and so were the Prince and Princess of Wales. Twenty-one different teams were assembled, including small delegations from Smyrna, Salonika, and Bohemia. The gathering watched a demonstration in gymnastics by Danish girls—"short-skirted and neat-legged," an observant English historian noted—and a demonstration in physical fitness by J. E. Fowler-Dixon, a fifty-six-year-old Englishman. Fowler-Dixon walked 1,500 meters in eight minutes and forty-five seconds, rested twenty minutes, then ran 1,500 meters in five minutes and forty-six seconds.

Once the games began, the American team put on its own demonstration—of track and field superiority. The United States delegation included four triple winners from St. Louis —Ray Ewry, Archie Hahn, Hillman, and Lightbody—but none of the four had a chance to defend all his honors in Athens. The Greeks had eliminated the standing hop, step, and jump, so Ewry settled for two gold medals. The Greeks had eliminated the 60-meter and 200-meter dashes, so Hahn settled for the 100-meter gold medal. The Greeks had eliminated the 200-meter and 400-meter hurdles races and Pilgrim took care of the 400-meter run, so Hillman settled for a free trip to Athens. The Greeks had eliminated the 2,500-meter steeple-chase and Pilgrim took care of the 800-meter run, so Light-body settled for the 1,500-meter gold medal.

Lightbody's victory in the metric mile was a curious one. The cofavorites in the race were two Englishmen, and both knew that in order to win they had to withstand Lightbody's finishing kick. Yet for some reason, the British stars let George Bonhag of the United States, who was primarily a long-distance runner, set a ridiculously slow pace. Lightbody was able to conserve his energy, and when he sprinted the last 200 meters, nobody was fast enough to hold him off. He won moving away. Bonhag, who had played his pace-setting role to perfection, faded far out of contention.

In his specialty, the five-mile run, Bonhag finished fourth. Disappointed because he had failed to earn even a bronze medal, Bonhag decided at the last moment to enter the 1,500-meter walk, the first walking race ever to appear on the Olympic program. Bonhag's decision came as a surprise—both to his teammates and to himself—probably because he had never before competed in a walking race.

Nine walkers started the 1,500-meter event, and one by one, most of the best were disqualified for improper heel-and-toe walking technique. Prince George, judging the race, banished the favorite with a firm command: "Leave! You have finished!" With his competition stripped away, Bonhag strolled to victory. Two of the four judges thought Bonhag, too, had violated the regulations, but Prince George, as president of the jury, ruled that the American's walk was legal. Bonhag happily collected a gold medal.

The most versatile American in the 1906 Olympics was Martin Sheridan, the New York policeman who had won the discus throw in St. Louis. In Athens, Sheridan finished first in the shot-put and the free style discus throw and second in the fourteen-pound stone throw, the standing broad jump, and the standing high jump. He also entered the pentathlon—the first pentathlon of the modern games combined the javelin throw, standing broad jump, Greek-style discus throw, Greco-Roman wrestling, and sprint—but had to quit when his leg, injured in the S.S. *Barbarossa* incident, began to bother him.

Sheridan faced two gifted European weight throwers. One was Nicholas Georgantas of Greece, who won the stone throw and finished second in both the free style and Greek-style discus throws. The other was Werner Jarvinen of Finland.

Jarvinen won the Greek-style discus throw and placed third in the free style, earning the nickname of "The Big Finn," but his importance in Olympic history outweighs his performances. He was the first Finn to compete in the Olympics, and when he went home to his job as a railroad fireman, he was greeted as a national hero. He toured Finland, demonstrating his skills and inspiring other Finnish athletes.

Ray Ewry, as usual, wins the standing high jump championship.

Erik Lemming of Sweden, javelin champion in 1906, 1908, and 1912, gets ready to throw (above), and versatile Martin Sheridan of the United States strains to hurl the discus (below).

Spurred by Jarvinen's example, an athletic tradition sprang up in his native country, and from 1912 through 1936, tiny Finland, with a population of fewer than 4,000,000, never placed worse than second in the track and field phase of the Olympic Games. Great athletes followed Werner Jarvinen out of Finland—Hannes Kolehmainen, Paavo Nurmi, Ville Ritola, Volmari Iso-Hollo, and, finally, three brothers named Akilles, Matti, and Kaarlo Jarvinen. They were the sons of Finland's first Olympic champion. Matti Jarvinen won the javelin throw in the 1932 Olympics and finished fifth in 1936. Akilles Jarvinen placed second in the decathlon in both 1928 and 1932; ironically, under the modern decathlon scoring system adopted in 1952, Akilles would have won the championship both times. Kaarlo Jarvinen, a shot-putter, competed in the 1932 and 1936 games, but failed to place in any finals.

For the host Greeks in 1906, the Marathon race again was a great attraction. Memories of Spiridon Loues' magnificent effort in 1896 were still fresh in everyone's mind. All the stores in Athens closed on Marathon day, and once again patriots promised that if the champion were Greek he would receive such prizes as a huge statue of Hermes, a loaf of bread every day for a year, and a free luncheon for five every Sunday for a year. Of the seventy-three starters, thirty-seven were Greek, but not one of the natives showed the speed and stamina of Spiridon Loues.

William Sherring, a Canadian who was five feet seven inches tall and weighed only 115 pounds, went to Greece two months before the games and ran the Marathon-to-Athens course so many times he learned every incline and every dip. Sherring, representing the Shamrock Athletic Club of Hamilton, Ontario, made practice pay off. Halfway through the race, the twenty-seven-year-old Canadian slipped past Billy Frank of New York and took the lead for good. Frank managed to stay close to Sherring until six miles from the finish. Then the Canadian shouted, "Good-by, Billy," and opened up a comfortable margin. When Sherring entered the Panathenaic Stadium, far in front of his rivals, Prince George, still in athletic trim, trotted the final lap with him. As a foreigner, Sherring was ineligible for the statue of Hermes, the free bread, or the free meals, but he did receive a free goat from the Greeks and a free house when he returned to Canada.

With Myer Prinstein retaining the broad jump title and Robert Leavitt winning the 110-meter high hurdles, the United States earned eleven gold medals in twenty track and field events during the 1906 Olympics. "Hearty congratulations to you and the American contestants," President Theodore Roosevelt cabled James E. Sullivan, the United States Olympic official. "Uncle Sam is all right."

Uncle Sam, however, missed out on the over-all championship. One swimming title gave the United States a total of twelve victories in Athens, second to France's fourteen. Fernand Gouder, in the pole vault, was France's only track and field champion, but the French picked up four gold medals in shooting, three in fencing, and three in tennis.

Marathon champion William Sherring of Canada tours the stadium, with Prince George of Greece at his side.

Great Britain placed second in track and field, but to the chagrin of Londoners, two of the three British victories were recorded by Irishmen. Con Leahy won the high jump, and P. G. O'Connor won the hop, step, and jump. After his triumph, O'Connor proudly produced an Irish flag and requested that it be raised to signify his victory. The Greeks, unmoved by this display of patriotism, stuck to protocol and hoisted the British banner.

One glaring international dispute marred the general harmony of the games. Rumors, later proved false, spread through Athens that Josef Steinbach, a huge Austrian weight lifter, was actually a professional. When Steinbach and a Greek named Tofolas matched muscles for the two-hand weight-lifting championship, the crowd showered upon the Austrian a steady stream of jeers. In protest, Steinbach quit the competition. As the Greek flag was run up in victory, the jeers turned to cheers. Then, as the cheers subsided, Steinbach re-entered the stadium, walked up to the weight which Tofolas had strained to lift, and with exaggerated ease, raised it three times above his head. Disdainfully, the Austrian set down the weight, bowed politely to the silenced crowd, and marched out. The following day, before a subdued audience, Steinbach won the one-hand lifting competition.

Steinbach's unhappy experience with the Greek crowd was only a hint of the struggle between athletes and audience that was to erupt two years later. During the Olympic Games of 1908, held in a section of London called Shepherd's Bush, the British spectators waged relentless warfare against the American participants. The antagonism was so great that even now, almost three-quarters of a century later, the 1908 Olympics are remembered as "The Battle of Shepherd's Bush."

Dazed, Dorando Pietri sprawls on the track.

# Marathon Madness

## CHAPTER SEVEN : 1908 – LONDON

His eyes bulge. His legs move up and down, but he does not advance. He staggers, weaves, even totters backward. His body is spent, and only a strange will power forces him on. Then he falls, scraping against the cinders, his legs still churning convulsively. He is a burnt-out distance runner, and no one who has seen his agonies can ever forget the sight.

In London, during the Olympic Marathon race of 1908, 100,000 spectators saw and studied the agonies of a burnt-out distance runner. "It would be no exaggeration," reported one observer, "to say it was the most thrilling athletic event that has occurred since that Marathon race in ancient Greece, where the victor fell at the goal and, with a wave of triumph, died."

The Marathon course for the 1908 Olympic Games stretched twenty-six miles 385 yards—or 42.195 kilometers—the distance that later became standard for Marathon races. The British chose this distance for a simple reason: The race was going to end at the Olympic Stadium outside London, and by beginning the Marathon twenty-six miles 385 yards away, directly in front of Windsor Castle, the Olympic committee enabled the grandchildren of King Edward VII and Queen Alexandra to watch the start.

Fifty-five competitors assembled for the Marathon, including a handful of Scandinavians, a few Englishmen, and several Americans, most notably Thomas P. Morrissey, the winner of the 1908 Boston Marathon and the Olympic favorite. Dorando

Pietri, a short, twenty-two-year-old Italian candymaker from Capri who had won the 1907 Paris Marathon, rated only a slim chance for victory. Johnny Hayes, a twenty-two-year-old Irish-American who had trailed Morrissey at Boston, was equally an outsider.

Hayes was a little fellow, barely five feet, four inches tall and weighing only 126 pounds. His legs were merely thirty inches long, and he liked to quote Abraham Lincoln's mot about the ideal soldier's legs—"exactly long enough to reach from the hips to the ground." Hayes was full of enthusiasm and popular among his American teammates. "Listen, no fast work," he advised his fellow American runners, as they lined up for the start of the Olympic Marathon. "Don't run yourself blind."

Hayes took his own advice, and as the field moved off briskly, he was content to maintain a leisurely pace. He had trained for twenty-five miles, not twenty-six, and he wanted to be certain that he saved enough energy for the extra mile.

During the first ten miles, three Englishmen took turns in the lead, and each wore himself out. Tom Longboat, a strong, silent Canadian Indian, also overextended himself and had to quit halfway through the race. By then, Charles Hefferon of South Africa was in first place, and Pietri, the Italian, was advancing toward second. Hayes, trailing by more than a mile, began to step up his pace. "You're going too fast, Johnny," suggested Mike Ryan, an American teammate who had been trotting even with Hayes.

"No, we've got to move now," said Hayes. "Stick with me, Mike." But Ryan, who later coached United States Marathon teams, quickly fell back and soon retired from the competition.

With six miles remaining, Hefferon held first place, four minutes ahead of Pietri and approximately six minutes ahead of Hayes, who had moved up to third place. But the South African was tiring rapidly, and Pietri began to cut down the margin. According to James B. Connolly, the 1896 hop, step, and jump champion who attended the 1908 games as a newspaperman, Pietri's handler gave the Italian a shot of strychnine to bolster him for the finish.

Less than two miles from the finish, after a steep climb approaching Wormwood Scrubs prison, Pietri sprinted past the fading Hefferon. At this point, the race was strictly among three men—Pietri, Hefferon, and Hayes—and the Italian, by far, had the most favorable position. As the stadium came into sight, Hayes overtook Hefferon. The thirty-four-year-old South African was the oldest man in the race. Neither he nor the American said a word to each other. "I found out later that Hefferon was of Irish descent," Hayes once recalled. "If I had known, I would have talked to him."

Hayes was in second place, but his chances seemed dim. Pietri had reached the stadium at least a full minute ahead of the American. But once inside the stadium, Pietri's grim personal struggle began. First he turned to his left, instead of to his right. "The man was practically delirious," a reporter

At the start of the Marathon, Pietri is near the rear of the pack (above); as he approaches the finish, he staggers "like a man in a dream," aided illegally by British officials (left and below).

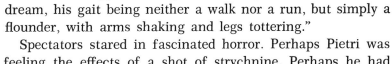

noted. "He staggered along the cinder path like a man in a dream, his gait being neither a walk nor a run, but simply a flounder, with arms shaking and legs tottering."

Spectators stared in fascinated horror. Perhaps Pietri was feeling the effects of a shot of strychnine. Perhaps he had simply run too far too fast. Perhaps the normal heat of a July day had exhausted him. He had only 300 meters to go—and no strength to get him there.

Officials and doctors swarmed around the tiny Italian, pleading with him to turn around and run in the proper direction. Finally, a curious sight in his sweaty and dirty white shirt and red knee pants, Pietri turned, staggered, and collapsed. Illegally, officials pushed him to his feet. "Help him, help him," some spectators cried. The more sensible shouted, "Stop him, don't let him continue," but the British authorities determinedly shoved him toward the finish. Three times more, Pietri lurched and fell. He sprawled on the cinders, dazed, agonized, totally pitiful, and into the stadium trotted Johnny Hayes, still fresh. "Heat never bothered me," Hayes later explained. "My grandfather and father were bakers, and I worked in the bakery as a boy. I was used to heat."

Before Hayes could complete the course, British officials picked up Pietri and literally dragged the game Italian across the finish line. Hayes ended his run thirty-four seconds later, nearly a minute ahead of Hefferon.

Obviously, Pietri had to be disqualified. He had not finished under his own power any more than Fred Lorz, the 1904 automobile rider, had. But British-American relations were so strained during the 1908 games that the hosts raised the Italian flag in victory. "I knew it was going to be all right," Hayes said. "They had to disqualify Dorando."

Several hours later, after an official United States protest, the British reversed themselves and disqualified Pietri. Hayes was awarded first place and Hefferon second. Two Americans, Joseph Forshaw and A. R. Welton, took third and fourth; never since 1908 has the United States scored so heavily in the Marathon.

With Pietri eliminated, it was the Italians' turn to be bitter. They claimed that Pietri would have finished unaided if the British had left him alone. Pietri himself, even though he almost died after the race, felt the same way. "I was all right until I entered the stadium," he said that night, when he finally regained his senses. "When I heard the people cheering and knew I had nearly won, a thrill passed through me and I felt my strength going. I fell down, but tried to struggle to the tape, but fell again. I never lost consciousness of what was going on, and if the doctor had not ordered the attendants to pick me up, I believe I could have finished unaided." Very few non-Italians shared Pietri's belief.

The night of the race, still keyed up, Hayes sat and sipped beers in a London hotel. The first modern Olympic champion, James B. Connolly, and the latest, Johnny Hayes, drank together until two in the morning. Hayes received one congratulatory cable, from friends in Canada who had bet heavily upon him at long odds. They were offering to share their profits with Hayes. As a further bonus, the champion later heard that his New York employers, Bloomingdale's department store, were going to promote him from shipping clerk to head of the sporting goods department. Bloomingdale's plastered photographs of Hayes all over the store and proudly announced that the young clerk had trained for his triumph on the roof of the store.

Ever since 1908, Olympic historians have referred to Hayes as a department store clerk and have pointed to his promotion as a suitable reward. The truth is that Hayes never did get the sporting goods job. As a matter of fact, he never did work in

With Pietri disqualified, Johnny Hayes jogs to the finish (left), then receives the Marathon trophy (below).

Bloomingdale's, much less train on the roof. His so-called job as a shipping clerk had been strictly a convenience, arranged for him by his club, the Irish-American Athletic Club. Hayes drew a steady salary from Bloomingdale's, but instead of working, he spent his time training for the Marathon on a track outside Manhattan. This slight subterfuge merely demonstrates that amateurs have not changed much in half a century.

"It is a question whether public opinion will ever support another Marathon race here," one newspaperman wrote in London. "Dorando's condition when he finished, and the condition of many of the contestants, lead people to think this sport is worse than prize fighting or bullfighting."

The 1908 race did not kill Marathon running, but it did have certain aftereffects. Inspired by the Olympic race, a young American songwriter composed his first hit, a catchy tune called "Dorando." The composer was Irving Berlin. His song helped create the enduring misconception that the Italian's *last* name was Dorando and also helped stimulate Marathon running in the United States. Hayes and Pietri both turned professional, and in a match race at the old Madison Square Garden, the Italian avenged his Olympic defeat by beating Hayes by sixty yards. Hayes toured the United States and Europe, giving Marathon exhibitions, and later became a successful food broker in New York.

Ironically, if it had not been for a volcanic eruption, Pietri would have run the 1908 Olympic Marathon in his native country. The International Olympic Committee originally assigned the 1908 games to Rome, but when Mount Vesuvius erupted in 1906, destroying several villages and placing great financial strain upon the Italian government, the games were shifted to London. Twenty-two nations sent a total of 2,000 athletes to England, and the main sport was bickering. The British—officials and spectators—seemed to take even more delight in the problems of the American athletes than in the triumphs of the native athletes.

The American Olympic Committee in 1908 inaugurated the practice of tryouts for the national team. Two sets of Olympic trials were held—one in Chicago and one in Philadelphia—and a combined team was selected. Once again, the selection committee missed some good men, and at least one of them, Bobby Cloughen, a New York City schoolboy, paid his own way to London and joined the American team. The United States squad was its strongest and largest yet—120 competitors, including seventy-seven track and field men, twenty-one shooters, and scattered candidates in swimming, wrestling, cycling, tennis, archery, and skating. The track and field delegation was fairly evenly divided between athletic clubs and colleges; the Irish-American A.C. contributed the most club members, nineteen, and Cornell the most collegians, seven.

All the Americans were in high spirits—until they reached England. Then everything went wrong. From the start of the Olympics until the end, the Americans and the English feuded.

In 1908, England believed itself the mightiest nation in the world, and even after more than a century of American independence, the British had no great affection for the colonials. To increase friction, a large percentage of the United States team were Irish-Americans. Feelings between the British and the Irish were bitter, as usual, and the British decision to incorporate Irish athletes into a consolidated United Kingdom team—the same policy followed at Athens in 1906—heightened the bitterness. In protest, several of the most talented Irish athletes retired rather than join the British team.

Long before the hectic finish of the Marathon, the athletes of England and the United States stopped speaking to each other. The furor started on opening day. King Edward was present. Queen Alexandra was present. The band of the Grenadier Guards played. Twenty thousand people, adrift in a stadium that seated more than 65,000, looked on. Brilliant flags of the competing nations brightened the stadium. Everything was lovely—except that the British had neglected to display an American flag. The British explained that they hadn't been able to find one. The Americans fumed and, during the opening parade, carried several of their own flags. When the Olympians marched before King Edward, each nation dipped its flag in tribute—but, to the outrage of the crowd, not the Americans. "This flag dips to no earthly king," snapped Martin Sheridan, the weight thrower. The tradition has persisted; the United States still does not dip its flag in Olympic parades.

Other nations had flag trouble too. The Swedish flag, like the American one, was missing from the stadium. The Swedes were equally furious, and when they later disagreed with the

Before J. C. Carpenter of the United States can complete the 400-meter run, British judges slice the tape and disqualify him.

106

Mel Sheppard, champion at 800 and 1,500 meters in London, demonstrates his running style.

British judges in the wrestling events, they quit the competition. The Finns, who were then ruled by Russia, received permission from the Czar to compete as a separate team, but they were refused permission to march under their own flag. Rather than carry the Russian banner, the Finns marched flagless.

From the outset, the Americans were constantly complaining. The British held the drawings for heats in private; the Americans, fearful that their best runners would be placed in the same heats, screamed conspiracy. British officials, waving megaphones, openly coached and cheered British athletes in competition; the Americans screamed knavery. The British permitted Tom Longboat, the Canadian Indian who was considered a professional in the United States, to enter the Marathon; the Americans screamed mockery. Every scheme spawned a scream. "We will knock the spots off the Britishers," predicted Martin Sheridan.

"Probably England was not as charitably inclined toward the American champions as she might have been," said Lawson Robertson, an Olympic athlete in 1908 and later an American Olympic coach, "and it is equally true that the victorious Americans were not as modest as they should have been."

The most stormy controversy of the 1908 games grew out of the 400-meter run. The four finalists were Lieutenant Wyndham Halswelle, the Englishman who had trailed Paul Pilgrim at 400 and 800 meters in 1906, and three Americans, J. C. Carpenter, J. B. Taylor, and W. C. Robbins. British newspaper stories before the final warned that the Americans were likely to gang up on Halswelle, who had set an Olympic record in the semifinals.

In the race, Taylor got off to a poor start and fell far off the pace. Coming into the last 100 yards, Carpenter, Robbins, and Halswelle were closely bunched. Carpenter took the last turn wide, stepped up his pace and pulled in front. At the same time, British officials began yelling, "Foul! Foul!" One of the judges rushed onto the track and stopped Taylor. Another cut the finish tape before Carpenter, Robbins, and Halswelle finished in that order. Then the judges deliberated and declared the race void. They disqualified Carpenter—for interfering with Halswelle—and ruled that the other three men would have to rerun the race.

The Americans were enraged. "As we approached the last bend," said Carpenter, acidly, "Robbins had the pole and was leading by a yard. I made my effort there, and I certainly ran wide, as I have done every time I have been on the track. Halswelle had lots of room to pass me on either side. We just raced him off his feet. He couldn't stand the pace."

"Never in my life," said James E. Sullivan, the distinguished American Olympic official, "and I have been attending athletic meetings for thirty-one years, have I witnessed a scene that struck me as being so unsportsmanlike and unfair. When Carpenter started to leave Halswelle behind, the officials cried,

Three champions at work in 1908: Forrest Smithson captures the 110-meter hurdles, Charles Bacon wins the 400-meter hurdles, and A. C. Gilbert ties for first place in the pole vault.

'Foul!' The announcer also ran around yelling, 'Foul!' The race was as fair as any race ever run."

British newspapers, not surprisingly, did not share Sullivan's view. "It certainly seemed as if the Americans had run the race on a definite and carefully thought-out plan," said *The Times* of London. "It was not as if Carpenter, the one who forced Halswelle to run wide and elbowed him severely as he tried to pass him, had himself taken a wide curve at the bend and then run straight on. He appeared rather to run diagonally, crossing in front of the Englishman so that he was obliged to lose several yards. . . . This is a fair and impartial account of what happened."

Fairly and impartially, *The Sportsman* of London called the 400-meter race "one of the most disgraceful exhibitions of foul play ever witnessed. . . . A slur is cast upon American sportsmanship in the eyes of all Europe which cannot ever be eradicated. . . . There can be no excuse; the thing was open, unabashed and shameless."

To protest the disqualification of Carpenter, the Americans withdrew both Robbins and Taylor from the rerun, leaving Halswelle alone to win the only walkover in Olympic history. This single incident was responsible, largely, for a change in Olympic rules. After the 1908 games, the judging and supervision of events was taken away from the host country and given to international groups.

For the British, the 400-meter victory, tainted as it was, provided some consolation for their surprising setback in the 1,500-meter run. Five of the eight 1,500-meter finalists were British, including the cofavorites, Harold Wilson and Norman

Hallows. The two best Americans at 1,500 meters, J. P. Halsted and Jim Lightbody, had failed to qualify for the final. The faster of the two American qualifiers was Mel Sheppard, a shy New Yorker whose favorite distance was the half mile.

Sheppard ran his best when he was angry, but he did not anger easily or often. Shortly before the start of the 1,500 final, Mike Murphy, the stern and shrewd American coach from the University of Pennsylvania, walked up to Sheppard. "Mel, you might as well stay in the stands," said Murphy. "You don't have a chance." Then Murphy winked at some other American athletes who were standing nearby—and Sheppard marched off steaming. He stayed angry. With a brilliant sprint finish, Sheppard beat Wilson by two yards and set an Olympic record.

"We all went to read the British papers the next day," Johnny Hayes recalled many years later, "and the headline was: 'WHY WILSON DIDN'T WIN.' We had to read almost to the end of the story before we found Mel's name." The following week, Sheppard won his specialty, the 800-meter run, setting both an Olympic and world record. Curiously, Sheppard, who ran for the Irish-American A.C., had been rejected a few months earlier by the New York City police force as physically unfit. Police doctors insisted that he suffered from arteriosclerosis and from chronic endocarditis. He still managed to win the United States half-mile championship five times between 1906 and 1912.

Sheppard, who anchored the winning American 1,600-meter medley relay team, was one of three Americans to win two individual events in London. Martin Sheridan won both discus throws, free style and Greek style; Ray Ewry won both standing jumps, the high jump and the broad jump. Ewry, with his ten gold medals, and Sheridan, with his five, finished their Olympic careers in 1908. So did John Flanagan, who won the hammer throw for the third time in three tries.

To increase the American total of track and field gold medals to fifteen—four more than all other nations combined—Forrest Smithson won the 110-meter hurdles, Charles Bacon won the 400-meter hurdles, Harry Porter won the high jump, Frank Irons won the broad jump, Ralph Rose won the shot-put, and Edward Cook and A. C. Gilbert tied for first in the pole vault. Gilbert was a bright young man who had turned a gift for magic shows into a Yale education and who later turned a gift for Erector sets into a fortune. He was, of course, the founder of the A. C. Gilbert toy company.

The United Kingdom earned seven track and field victories, including two for George E. Larner, a brilliant walker. Larner enjoyed an unfair advantage over his rivals. He was a policeman who patrolled a beat along Brighton Beach, and all year round, as he performed his regular job, he practiced his heel-and-toe technique.

America's monopoly in the sprint events, intact from 1896 through 1906, was shattered by two representatives of the British Empire. Robert Kerr, a Canadian, won the 200-meter dash, and in a tense race, Reginald Walker, a South African schoolboy, scored at 100 meters. Walker, an American reporter wrote, "achieved an ovation seen only once in a lifetime on an athletic field, when 40,000 persons arose with a great cheer and filled the air with hats, while the boy, who this morning was unknown, but whose name is heard all over London tonight, was lifted on the shoulders of enthusiastic friends." The fact that Walker's narrow victory came over an American, Jimmy Rector, unquestionably intensified the enthusiasm.

The British expanded the Olympic schedule to twenty-two separate sports, awarded more than 100 championships, and in the process, generated considerable confusion. "The games were as bewildering to watch as a three-ring circus," one spectator said. "At one time, a dozen bicyclists were wheeling along the outer edge of the oval, while twenty runners were racing on the cinder path just inside of it. Swimmers, with bright-colored caps, were splashing through the long tank, while on the greensward members of the Danish and German gymnastic clubs, arrayed in white uniforms, were performing spectacular feats on the horizontal and parallel bars, and giving exhibitions of calisthenic drills. Judges, scorers, trainers, timers and rubbers of the many nationalities represented swarmed everywhere."

As expected, the United Kingdom, scoring heavily in boxing, cycling, shooting, and tennis, accumulated the most gold medals. As expected, too, the United States finished second.

Henry Taylor, a twenty-three-year-old Englishman, emerged as the first authentic swimming star of the Olympics. Taylor

Ralph Rose wins the shot-put for the second time.

won the 400-meter free style and the 1,500-meter free style and anchored the successful British 800-meter relay team. His most gifted rival was an American, Charles Daniels, who won the 100-meter free style for the second straight time. Daniels had a career total of four Olympic gold medals, including victories at 220 yards and 440 yards in the St. Louis games.

The first winter sport, figure skating, made its appearance on the Olympic calendar, and a Russian named Panin won the men's special figures competition. Panin was Czarist Russia's first Olympic champion—and its last. Not until 1952, long after the revolution, did another Russian earn a gold medal.

The tug-of-war produced a British victory and an international crisis. The rules for the event stated that "no competitor shall wear prepared boots or shoes," only ordinary footwear. But when the American team, again a makeshift group of weight throwers, met the Liverpool police in an elimination match, the British bobbies wore heavy boots rimmed with steel. The Americans protested, but the English officials ruled that the Liverpool police were perfectly free to wear their boots because this was their everyday footwear. The British won the first of the best-two-out-of-three pulls, and the American team immediately quit. The Americans, a British official eagerly announced, "had had enough of it."

The Americans had had more than enough of London. They scurried back across the Atlantic, their admiration for George Washington renewed. Fifty-five years later, Johnny Hayes recalled the 1908 Olympic Games and shuddered. "Oh, the British!" he said. "They were out to get us, you know."

Martin Sheridan wins both the free style and the Greek style discus throws.

While the British and the Americans were feuding, French and Italian Olympians enjoy a tour of London.

1

Rugged
Individualists

3  4

1  Rudolf Karpati (left), Hungary, saber champion, 1956 and 1960
2  Finnish gymnast, 1932
3  Imre Petnehozy, Hungary, modern pentathlon, 1932
4  George Lambert, United States, modern pentathlon, 1960
5  Pat Smythe, Great Britain, show jumping, 1960
6  Thomas Gayford, Canada, endurance, 1960

5   6

8

7   Berndt Rehbinder (left), Sweden, vs. Yves Dreyfus, France, épée, 1960
8   Christian D'Oriola (left), France, foils champion, 1952 and 1956

9    10

9  Gotthard Handrick, Germany, modern pentathlon champion, 1936
10  Igor Novikov, U.S.S.R., modern pentathlon, 1960
11  Winter pentathlon, 1948
12  Pistol shooting, 1936

11

12

13

14

15  16  17

**13** Knud Jensen, Denmark, 1960
**14** Heat of the 1,000-meter cycling sprint, 1952
**15** Vinnie Richards, United States, tennis singles champion, 1924
**16** Helen Wills, United States, tennis singles champion, 1924
**17** Henri Cochet, France, tennis, 1924

18  19                                        20

18  Agnes Keleti, Hungary, gymnastics champion, 1952 and 1956
19  Polina Astakhova, U.S.S.R., gymnastics champion, 1960
20  Muriel Grossfield, United States, gymnastics, 1960
21  German gymnast, 1936

Jim Thorpe sits stiffly in white collar and tie during a victory parade in 1912.

# The World's Greatest Athlete

## CHAPTER EIGHT : 1912 – STOCKHOLM

*"I was not very wise to the ways of the world. I hope I will be partly excused by the fact that I was an Indian school boy and did not know that I was doing wrong."*

—JIM THORPE
United States athlete, 1912

When the United States Olympic team sailed aboard the liner *Finland* to the 1912 games in Stockholm, a cork track rimmed the deck of the ship. Every day, weather permitting, the American athletes trained on the makeshift track. They ran. They jumped. They sweated. All except one man. Jim Thorpe, from the Carlisle Indian School, just sat in a deck chair and dozed.

"What are you doing, Jim?" Francis Albertanti, a reporter for the New York *Evening Mail,* asked Thorpe one day. "Thinking about your uncle, Sitting Bull?"

"No," said Thorpe, opening his eyes. "I'm practicing the broad jump. I've just jumped twenty-three feet eight inches." Then Thorpe closed his eyes, furrowed his brow, and resumed his mental workouts.

Once the team reached Sweden, of course, Jim Thorpe trained differently. After all, he was entered in the decathlon, the pentathlon, the high jump, and the broad jump, and he knew that he had to be in perfect physical condition. In Stockholm, Thorpe didn't sit and doze in a chair. He lay and dozed in a hammock.

Strict Mike Murphy, the veteran American coach, was furious because Thorpe never showed up for practice sessions. One afternoon Murphy wandered through the training quarters and found Thorpe asleep in a hammock. Glenn "Pop" Warner, who coached Thorpe in football and track at the Carlisle School in Pennsylvania, was standing near the hammock.

"Glenn," Murphy snapped, "I've seen some queer birds in my day, but your Indian beats all! I don't see him do anything —except sleep!"

"Don't worry, Mike," said Warner. "All those two-for-a-nickel events you've got lined up for Thorpe won't bother him. He's in shape. What with football, lacrosse, baseball, and track back at school, how could he be out of shape? This sleeping is the best training ever—for Jim."

Jim Thorpe, born in Prague, Oklahoma, on May 28, 1888, a member of the Sac and Fox Indian tribe, six feet tall and 190 pounds in his prime, was the finest athlete the United States has ever produced. In 1950, the Associated Press conducted a poll of American sportswriters to select the greatest male athlete of the half-century 1900–49. Thorpe received 252 first-place votes; all his rivals combined polled only 141.

Thorpe could excel in any sport, but the three he played best were football, baseball, and track and field. In football, he was an All-American halfback for two seasons at little Carlisle. He could punt seventy yards. He could run so hard that sometimes, for fun, he would tell the opposition which way he was going to attack.

In 1911, little Carlisle defeated mighty Harvard, 18–15; Thorpe kicked four field goals, scored a touchdown (which then counted five points), and kicked the extra point. "Watching him turn the ends, slash off tackle, kick and pass and tackle," said Percy Haughton, the famous Harvard coach, "I realized that here was the theoretical superplayer in flesh and blood."

In 1912, little Carlisle defeated mighty Army, 27–6; Thorpe kicked three field goals, scored two touchdowns, passed for one touchdown, and kicked three extra points. Once he returned an Army kick ninety yards for a touchdown. When the run was nullified by a penalty, Army kicked again, and this time Thorpe returned the ball ninety-five yards for a touchdown. In 1912, Thorpe scored twenty-five touchdowns and 198 points; each total has been surpassed only once in major-college football history.

Between 1913 and 1919, Thorpe played no football, but when a professional league sprang up in 1920, Thorpe, at the age of thirty-two, joined the Canton Bulldogs and performed so brilliantly that in 1963 he was voted into the National Football League Hall of Fame. He finished his career with Canton in 1926 at the age of thirty-eight. He insisted, with only slight exaggeration, that he had never been forced out of action by injuries. "How can you get hurt playing football?" he once asked.

In baseball, Thorpe signed with the New York Giants in 1913 and lasted in the major leagues through 1919. He had two glaring weaknesses—the curve ball, which hampered his hitting, and the whiskey bottle, which hampered him in all sports—yet in his final season, playing sixty games for the Boston Braves, he still managed to hit .327.

In track and field, Thorpe's genius is best illustrated by one

Thorpe follows through after throwing the discus.

performance, in a dual meet on May 25, 1912, between Lafayette and Carlisle. Lafayette had forty-eight men on its unbeaten squad, and according to one popular tale, Thorpe showed up for the meet accompanied by only one schoolmate.

"You mean the two of you are the whole team?" said a Lafayette official.

"Nope," said Thorpe. "Just me. The other fellow's the student manager."

According to another version of the same story, Warner and Thorpe and no one else arrived at Lafayette and were greeted by Harold Bruce, the Lafayette coach.

"Where's the team?" asked Bruce.

"Here it is," said Warner, pointing to Thorpe.

Both these versions, like so much athletic lore, are sheer fantasy, no more substantial than Johnny Hayes's job at Bloomingdale's. The truth of the matter is that Thorpe went to Lafayette with six teammates. He didn't need all of them— but they were there.

Against Lafayette, Thorpe won the high jump, broad jump, shot-put, discus, 120-yard high hurdles, and 220-yard low hurdles. He slumped to third in the 100-yard dash. His teammates contributed five other victories, and Carlisle won, 71–41.

Two months later, after his relaxing cruise aboard the *Finland*, Thorpe was in Stockholm, dominating the Olympics. He finished first in the pentathlon, first in the decathlon, fourth in the high jump, and seventh in the broad jump.

In the 1912 version of the pentathlon, a strenuous test of versatility combining five separate events, Thorpe defeated all challengers in the broad jump, discus throw, 200-meter dash, and 1,500-meter run. He proved that he was human by placing only third in the javelin throw. Thorpe won the pentathlon

Finland, ruled by Russia, marches flagless in the opening parade.

gold medal by a mile; another American, Avery Brundage, later the president of the International Olympic Committee, finished sixth.

In the decathlon, a blend of ten events, Thorpe defeated all rivals in the high jump, high hurdles, shot-put, and 1,500-meter run. He accumulated so many points in the other six events that his Olympic decathlon record survived for twelve years. Brundage was in the decathlon too, and although he failed to complete all of the ten events, he wound up fifteenth in the point totals. No one will ever match Thorpe's pentathlon-decathlon double because the pentathlon was abandoned after the 1924 Olympics.

The 1912 Olympic Games provided Jim Thorpe with his greatest glory. They also provided him, as matters developed, with his most bitter setback. In 1913, a year after the games ended, the International Olympic Committee discovered that Thorpe had earlier played baseball for money, declared him a professional, stripped him of his medals, and erased his records from the official Olympic history. The records are gone now, but the memory lingers.

The Olympics of 1912 are still remembered primarily as the Olympics of Jim Thorpe, but their full significance transcends one individual. More important, the Stockholm games guaranteed the permanence of the Olympics; they were strikingly successful in every way. Pageantry was magnificent; in a handsome double-decked stadium, built with funds raised in a national lottery, King Gustav V presided over a colorful opening parade, and a chorus of 4,400 voices sang "A Mighty Fortress is Our God." Attendance was encouraging; daily crowds ranged between 20,000 and 30,000, and perhaps 100,000 people saw at least part of the Marathon race. Participation reached new heights; twenty-eight nations entered, including Chile and Japan for the first time, and 2,500

The Crown Prince, later King Gustav VI of Sweden, greets the Hungarian soccer team.

athletes competed, including fifty-seven women. Performances were excellent; eleven Olympic records were set in track and field. The host team made a strong showing; Swedish authorities convinced Ernie Hjertberg, a native Swede who had become an outstanding coach in the United States, to return home and train his country's athletes. Most amazing of all, international goodwill flourished; when an American relay team was disqualified by the judges, James E. Sullivan, the same official who had condemned so vigorously the 400-meter ruling in London, praised the decision. The Swedish games were such a success that even after the shattering impact of World War I, which wiped out the 1916 competition, the Olympics survived and resumed in 1920.

The United States Olympic Committee, growing steadily stronger, conducted tryouts for the 1912 squad at three separate sites—at Harvard in the East, Chicago in the Midwest, and Stanford in the Far West. Out of all the trials arose the largest American team yet, 176 members, ranging from 111 track and field athletes down to one tennis player. George Bonhag, the veteran distance runner who had competed in the 1904, 1906, and 1908 games and had won the walking race at Athens, carried the American flag in the opening parade.

Yet if there had been no Jim Thorpe, the whole, huge United States team would have been obscured by one slender Scandinavian, a Finn named Hannes Kolehmainen. Without Thorpe, the Olympics of 1912 would be remembered as the Olympics of Hannes Kolehmainen.

Hannes came from a running family. One brother, Willie, was a professional distance runner who toured the United States in 1910, gathered information about pace and strategy, then returned to Finland and shared his knowledge with his family. Another of the Kolehmainen brothers, Tatu, entered the 10,000-meter run and the Marathon in the 1912 Olympic Games.

Hannes Kolehmainen, first of the flying Finns, wins the 5,000-meter run (above) and the 10,000-meter run (right).

Willie and Tatu Kolehmainen were gifted runners, but their younger brother, Hannes, five feet nine inches tall, was far better. He was the first of the world's great distance runners. In the 5,000-meter run at Stockholm, Hannes sprinted brilliantly in the last fifty meters and defeated France's Jean Bouin by a single step. Both men broke the world record by more than twenty seconds, and no other man finished within half a minute of them.

In the 10,000-meter run at Stockholm, Hannes led from beginning to end and defeated the runner-up, Lewis Tewanima of the United States, by more than forty-five seconds. Tewanima, a Carlisle Indian, finished fifteen seconds in front of a young Finn, Albin Stenroos, who was to win the Olympic Marathon fully twelve years later. Tatu Kolehmainen held fifth place halfway through the 10,000-meter race, but worn down by the heat and by the swift pace, he failed to finish.

Hannes gained his third Olympic gold medal in the 8,000-meter cross-country race, winning this event by more than half a minute. The fleet Finn barely missed a fourth gold medal. The 3,000-meter run was staged strictly as a team race; medals were awarded only on the basis of the cumulative performances of each team's three fastest men. Although Hannes turned in the best time of any individual, his teammates lagged, and Finland failed to qualify for the final.

Tatu Kolehmainen tried mightily to add to the family laurels in the Marathon race. It was a terribly hot July day, so draining that a Portuguese runner named Lazaro collapsed after nineteen miles and died the following morning. Tatu stayed in first place for almost ten miles, then slipped back to second, between two South Africans, short, slim Christopher Gitsham and six-foot, sturdy Ken McArthur. Unlike most of the sixty-eight competitors, neither Gitsham nor McArthur wore hats; they were both accustomed to being baked in the sun.

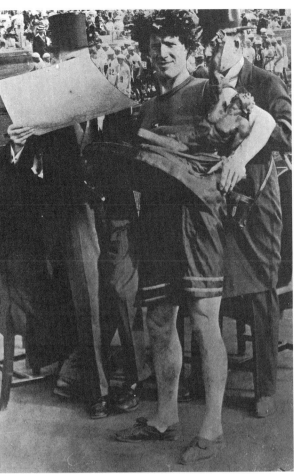
Ken McArthur of South Africa poses with the victor's spoils after the Marathon.

At the halfway mark, Tatu's strength began to disappear, and he soon retired, leaving the two South Africans to fight for the championship. Two miles from the finish, Gitsham, who was leading, stopped for a drink of water, and McArthur sprinted past him. The taller South African won by a minute over his countryman.

Gitsham complained afterward that McArthur had betrayed him. "He said he would wait for me while I took a drink " the trusting Gitsham said. "But he didn't."

McArthur was more practical. "I went out to win or die," he explained.

One American Marathon runner, Gaston Strobino, a young machinist's helper from New Jersey, shared McArthur's Spartan attitude. "I'll finish one, two, three, or break a leg," Strobino told his mother before he went to Stockholm. He finished third.

With neither Finns nor South Africans entered in the final of the 1,500-meter run, the United States was a heavy favorite to win this distance event. Precisely half of the fourteen finalists were Americans, including the defending champion, Mel Sheppard and a trio of great milers, Abel Kiviat, Norman Taber, and John Paul Jones. But the British, who had been stunned by Sheppard's victory in the 1908 1,500-meter run, got their revenge in 1912. Kiviat, Taber, and Jones waged a furious struggle as they stormed down the stretch, but in the final thirty meters, Arnold Jackson of Oxford uncorked a tremendous kick and, with his last ounce of energy, overtook the three Americans. He collapsed at the tape. The British star won by the narrow margin of one tenth of a second over both Kiviat and Taber, with Jones only three tenths of a second farther back. The first five finishers all broke the Olympic record by more than five seconds.

Shut out in the distance races, the United States monopolized the shorter events. Ralph Craig of the University of Michigan stood out among the sprinters. In the final of the 100-meter dash, he watched his rivals make seven false starts. "I decided to win if I could," Craig later explained, "and every time I saw a man go off the mark, I went with him. If we had to stay there for a month, I would have jumped every time I saw another man stir." On one false start, Craig sprinted the entire 100 meters. He still had enough speed left to come from behind on the eighth start and win in the closing strides. Craig also rallied in the late stages of the 200-meter dash and won a second gold medal.

Craig established an Olympic endurance record of sorts when, thirty-six years after his double triumphs, he competed once more for the United States. In 1948, he sailed aboard a boat called *Rhythm* in the Dragon class yachting championships. But *Rhythm* finished eleventh, and Craig missed his chance for a third Olympic gold medal.

In expectation—and in performance—the 800-meter run was the outstanding race of the 1912 Olympics. The brilliant field featured the men who had run one-two-three at London

131

in 1908—Mel Sheppard, Emilio Lunghi of Italy, and Hans Braun of Germany. Sheppard was the favorite. In the trials, the competition was so swift that Lunghi, who held the world record for the half mile, failed to qualify for the final. Six of the eight qualifiers were Americans, and the fastest was a nineteen-year-old student from Mercersburg Academy, James "Ted" Meredith. Despite his fine trial run, the schoolboy seemed to be racing out of his class.

Sheppard broke in front and ran the first 400 meters in 52.4 seconds, an incredibly torrid pace. Meredith, straining to stay close to his teammate, held second place, pressed by Germany's Braun. When the German made his bid in the stretch, the American schoolboy refused to fold under pressure. Instead, he stepped up his own pace, overtook Sheppard in the last ten meters, and won by a step. Sheppard finished second, inches ahead of an American teammate, Ira Davenport, and Braun slipped to fourth, inches ahead of another American, David Caldwell. The first six runners broke the Olympic record; the first three runners broke the world record. In one of the most dramatic finishes in track and field history, only four meters separated Meredith from the fifth-place man.

"A finer lot of men was probably never got together," said *The Times* of London.

"I never expected to win, but I knew I would be close," explained Meredith, who was five feet nine inches tall and weighed 155 pounds. "I felt strong as a lion."

If Ted Meredith was the lion of the 1912 United States team, Pat McDonald was the bull. McDonald, a member of the Irish-American Athletic Club, stood six feet four inches tall and weighed, give or take a few ounces, 350 pounds. A shot-putter by avocation and a policeman by vocation, McDonald was for many years as sturdy and familiar a New York monument as the Statue of Liberty. He directed traffic in Times Square.

McDonald brought a new technique to traffic control. Often he would stop all traffic, walk to the curb, and, arm-in-arm, escort a female pedestrian across the crowded intersection. He seemed to specialize in the least attractive ladies. "Why do you always pick the ugly ones?" Johnny Hayes, the Marathon runner, once asked McDonald.

"For a simple reason," said the policeman. "Most of them have never had a man escort them across a street. You should see the tips I get for my kindness."

At Stockholm, McDonald was decidedly unkind to Ralph Rose, the American who had won the Olympic shot-put championship in 1904 and 1908. Rose led in the shot-put until the final round of throws, and then, with a mighty effort, Pat McDonald captured first place.

In the standing high jump, for years the personal property of Ray Ewry, the competition narrowed down to two Americans—Platt Adams and his brother Ben Adams. When the bar was set at five feet four inches, the brothers shook hands and patted each other on the back. Platt promptly cleared the

Ralph Craig (above) sprints to victory in the 100-meter dash (above, right).

132

height on his first attempt, then turned and whispered some advice to his brother. It must not have been very good advice. Ben jumped three times and failed three times. Then he smiled slightly and once more shook the hand of his brother, the champion.

The 1912 Olympic Games offered championships in thirty separate track and field events, and the United States, including Thorpe's victories, won sixteen, ten more than surprising Finland. The hosts dominated the non-track-and-field activities. The Swedish Olympic Committee set up an "unofficial" over-all scoring system—three points for a first place, two for a second, and one for a third—and under this system, Sweden won the games with 136 points. The United States finished second with 124 points.

In the tug of war, only two teams entered—the Swedish and the British—and the British again wore the heavy police boots that had helped them to victory in 1908. But the Swedes pulled a neat trick on the British bobbies. The tug of war in Stockholm was staged in sand, and the big British boots became a burden instead of a boon. The Swedes won without difficulty.

The 1912 swimming competition was significant on two counts. First, women competed for the first time; Fanny Durack of Australia won the 100-meter free style in exactly the same time that Alfred Hajos of Hungary had won the men's 100-meter free style in 1896. Second, Duke Kahanamoku competed for the first time.

Kahanamoku, a colorful, cheerful Hawaiian who later served as sheriff of Honolulu for a quarter of a century, introduced the flutter kick and the Hawaiian crawl to international swimming. At Stockholm, he won the 100-meter free style so convincingly that, on his last lap, he turned around, saw no one within threatening distance, and coasted home. He also swam on the second-place United States 800-meter relay team.

The Duke became a perennial Olympian. In 1920, he won two gold medals; he retained his 100-meter free style title and swam on the championship American relay team. In 1924, he added a silver medal by placing second in the 100-meter free style. And in 1932, at the age of forty-two, he was an alternate on the United States water polo team.

Kahanamoku remained an international celebrity for half a century, but he never quite matched the fame of one of his 1912 teammates, the only American who competed in the military pentathlon. (Since 1924, when the track and field pentathlon was eliminated, the military pentathlon has been called the modern pentathlon.) This American was a young lieutenant from West Point, and he performed brilliantly in cross-country running, fencing, swimming, and riding, four of the five segments of the military pentathlon. Shooting was the fifth segment, and shooting, supposedly, was the lieutenant's forte. Had he finished first in the shooting, he would have won the military pentathlon. But he slumped to twentieth among forty-two competitors and had to settle for fifth place in the over-all standings.

With a mighty effort, Pat McDonald, the giant policeman, wins the shot-put.

"I don't know whether I lost my nerve or my ammunition was defective," the lieutenant said, after the shooting, "but I did nothing like my best."

The lieutenant never did become an Olympic champion, but he did, in time, become a general. Nicknamed "Blood and Guts," he was General George S. Patton, Jr.

Gustaf Lilliehook of Sweden won the military pentathlon. For years, the event remained a Swedish specialty. Only once, from 1912 through 1956—in 1936—did a non-Swede finish first. Perhaps the greatest pentathlon performer was Lars Hall of Sweden, who earned the championship in 1952 and again in 1956.

When the 1912 Olympics ended, with the decathlon on the final day, King Gustav of Sweden invited Jim Thorpe to visit him at his royal castle. "Immediately following Jim's victory," Dan Ferris, an American official who attended every Olympics for half a century, later recalled, "he and a few of his cronies went on a well-deserved spree. It was a case of too much Swedish punch—at least for Thorpe. Our ship was anchored in Stockholm harbor, and when the tender finally poured Thorpe's party aboard, Jim proceeded to leap about the deck, jumping and kicking in cabin doors. I remember he kept yelling, 'I'm a horse! I'm a horse!' In the midst of all this confusion, a delegate came to our ship to ask Thorpe to visit the King. We had to tell him that Thorpe wasn't aboard."

At the formal closing ceremonies, when Thorpe received his gold medals from the Swedish King, he also received a bronze bust of King Gustav and a jeweled silver model of a Viking ship. "Sir," said King Gustav, solemnly, "you are the greatest athlete in the world."

Years later, when Thorpe killed time between bottles by reminiscing about the Olympics, he told people that he had accepted the regal compliment with two words: "Thanks, King." It is a nice line and a pleasant story, but the odds are infinite that Thorpe never thought of the flip reply until long after 1912.

Platt Adams takes the gold medal in the standing high jump.

After the games ended in Stockholm, Thorpe went back to Carlisle and enjoyed his finest football season. Then in 1913, a New England sportswriter reported that Thorpe, in 1910, had been paid for playing minor league baseball in Rocky Mount, North Carolina. Thorpe candidly confirmed the story; he had played, he had received money, and he had used his own name, James C. Thorpe. The unsophisticated Indian hadn't realized that by playing baseball for money, he had forfeited his amateur standing in other sports.

When the International Olympic Committee ruled that Thorpe was a professional and took away his 1912 medals, first place in the decathlon was awarded to Hugo Weislander of Sweden and first place in the pentathlon to Ferdinand Bie of Norway. Legend has it that both runners-up refused the medals; "Thorpe won—not I," Weislander supposedly insisted.

Legend has it wrong. Both Weislander and Bie did pay tribute to Thorpe's talent, but both did, in 1913, accept the gold medals. Forty years later, Weislander presented his medal to the Swedish sports museum. Bie, a practicing doctor, often indicated that he was willing to return his medal to Thorpe, but he never did.

In 1932, a reporter discovered Thorpe in Los Angeles, too poor to buy a ticket to the Olympic Games. Friends and admirers sent him gifts and cash, and for two decades afterward, reporters periodically campaigned to have the Olympic medals returned to Thorpe. He had paid for his mistake, they pointed out, and he deserved to regain his trophies. But the United States Olympic Committee refused to argue in Thorpe's behalf; ironically, one of the most outspoken opponents of the move to reinstate Thorpe was Avery Brundage, Thorpe's teammate in the 1912 pentathlon and decathlon.

Thorpe died in 1953, poor and lonely. "It'd be great to be a young buck again, just for a season," Thorpe said, shortly before his death. "That was the best time of my life, and I guess I'll never forget it."

In the sand at Stockholm, the British bobbies' boots became a burden.

With a decisive triumph in the 10,000-meter run, Paavo Nurmi begins his Olympic reign.

# The Phantom Finn

## CHAPTER NINE : 1920 – ANTWERP

His heart beat only forty times a minute. His face never betrayed emotion. His legs pumped up and down so smoothly and steadily that his energy seemed endless. One observer called him "a mechanical Frankenstein—created to annihilate time." His name was Paavo Nurmi, and he could run and run and run.

Between 1920 and 1930, Peerless Paavo, the Phantom Finn, set world records for races at one mile, two miles, three miles, four miles, five miles, six miles, 1,500 meters, 2,000 meters, 3,000 meters, 5,000 meters, 10,000 meters, and 20,000 meters. He also ran farther in one hour than any man had before— eleven miles 1,648 yards, an average of one mile, give or take a few inches, every five minutes.

Nurmi was half machine and half myth. He once revealed that he had developed his strength by chasing a morning mail train in Turku, Finland. "This was not a very hot specimen, as mail trains go," commented John Lardner, the humorist. "It went along at a careful eight to ten miles per hour. Still it had good breeding and plenty of stamina, and nobody else in Turku thought of running races with it." Nurmi often outran the train, then paused, gathering his energy until his iron rival caught up with him.

Even after he became the greatest distance runner in history, Nurmi did not run against mere men. He ran against time. He wore a stop watch on his wrist, and as he glided along, barrel-chested, head erect, he constantly checked his

Nurmi: "A mechanical Frankenstein—
created to annihilate time."

times. If he maintained the schedule he had set for himself, he didn't care who was in front of him. He knew that his opponent was running too fast and would eventually tire.

Nurmi's secret power, some people said, came from a daily diet of black bread and dried fish, but one day a reporter followed the Finn and noticed that his taste leaned toward rolls and meats. "No black bread and fish today?" said the disappointed reporter.

"No black bread and fish *any* day," snapped Nurmi. "Why should I eat things like that?" Nurmi's favorite dish, actually, was oatmeal.

He took running so seriously that a training point helped ruin his marriage. When his son, Matti, was an infant, Paavo decided that the child's feet were going to be too small for distance running. He told his wife to put Matti on a special diet designed to stretch his feet. Mrs. Nurmi refused, and a short time later, the runner and his wife separated. "If there is one thing women do not understand," John Lardner noted, "it's feet."

Paavo Nurmi competed in three Olympic Games—1920, 1924, and 1928—and entered a total of ten races. He finished first seven times and second three times; his seven victories were consecutive, following an inaugural defeat. Nurmi might have added to his medals in the 1932 Olympics, but a few days before the games began, the International Olympic Committee declared him ineligible for demanding—and receiving—excessive expense money during a tour of Germany. The Finn had a world-wide reputation for juggling expense money. "Nurmi," said one track official, "had the lowest heart beat and the highest asking price of any athlete in the world."

Nurmi was twenty-three years old when he pranced onto the Olympic scene in 1920. He wore white trunks and a blue shirt bearing the Finnish flag, and from the moment he stepped onto the track for the 5,000-meter run in Antwerp, he set out to demonstrate that he was the successor to Hannes Kolehmainen, the first of the flying Finns.

King Albert of Belgium had flown from Brussels to Antwerp to watch the 5,000-meter race because the popular favorite was Jacques Guillemot, a spirited French soldier who had been badly gassed by the Germans during World War I. Despite the damage to his lungs, Guillemot had quickly established himself after the war as an outstanding distance runner.

Nurmi took the lead early in the race, and Guillemot followed him. By the end of 4,000 meters, the two had drawn away from the field, with Nurmi still holding first place. On the final turn, to the intense pleasure of the crowd and King Albert, Guillemot picked up his pace, sprinted past Nurmi, and won by ten meters.

Three days later, in the final of the 10,000-meter run, Nurmi and Guillemot met again. This time the roles were reversed. Nurmi let the gallant Frenchman set the early pace, then overtook his rival on the final lap and won pulling away. The reign of Nurmi had begun.

Eight years after his triple triumphs in Stockholm, Hannes Kolehmainen wins the Marathon in Antwerp.

In the 10,000-meter cross-country run, the two distance stars faced each other once more. Guillemot, unfortunately, stumbled over an obstacle midway through the race, injured his foot, and had to retire. Nurmi trotted home with his second victory. Because Nurmi's teammates finished third and sixth, Finland won a team gold medal, too, in the cross-country run.

The crowds that witnessed Nurmi's heroics in Antwerp were frustratingly small. The 1920 Olympic Games, of necessity, had been hastily organized. They had been awarded to Belgium only one year earlier, and the Belgian people, still recovering from the war, demonstrated scant interest in international athletics. Although the Belgian government constructed a new stadium, seating 30,000 people, and general admission cost only thirty cents, attendance rose above 10,000 only late in the games when schoolchildren were admitted free.

Despite short notice, the Antwerp games attracted more than 2,600 athletes, representing twenty-nine nations. When the competitors assembled for the opening ceremonies, they witnessed the unfurling, for the first time, of the official

Charlie Paddock, "The World's Fastest Human," leaps toward the tape and wins the 100-meter dash.

Olympic flag. (The flag, symbolizing the spirit of international cooperation, shows five interlocking circles of blue, yellow, black, green, and red. At least one of these colors appears in every national flag of the world. The five circles represent the five major land masses—Europe, Asia, Africa, Australia, and the Americas.)

At Antwerp, too, where each country was restricted to a maximum of four contestants in any one event, the Olympic oath was introduced. Victor Boin, a Belgian fencer, took the oath on behalf of all the international athletes: "In the name of all competitors, I swear that we will take part in these Olympic Games, respecting and abiding by the rules which govern them, in the true spirit of sportsmanship, for the glory of sport and the honor of our country."

The country that gathered the greatest honor at Antwerp was Finland. In the 1920 Olympic Games, the Finns and the Americans each won nine gold medals in men's track and field. By tying the United States, little Finland achieved an amazing feat; in every other Olympics from 1896 through 1968, Americans won more gold medals in men's track and field than any rival nation. In 1972, Russia tied the U.S.

Nurmi, of course, was the ace of the Finnish squad, but he had considerable support. Finland's weight throwers, in particular, were an imposing group; three of the finest Finns— Elmer Niklander, Armas Taipale, and Jonni Myyra—were veterans of the 1912 Olympics. In Stockholm, Niklander had won a silver and a bronze medal, Taipale had won two gold medals, and Myyra had finished seventh in the javelin throw. In Antwerp, Niklander won the discus throw and finished second in the shot-put, Taipale finished second in the discus, and Myyra led Finland to a one-two-three-four sweep in the

140

javelin. Ville Porhola, who had missed the games in 1912 (he was then only thirteen years old), won the shot-put for Finland in 1920. All four of these men returned to Olympic competition in 1924, but only Myyra, who retained his javelin championship, enjoyed success. Myyra's mastery of his specialty was so complete that the only way to excel in this event, decided Pat McDonald of the United States, was to call the spear a "yavelin."

Vilho Tuulus, in the hop, step, and jump, and E. R. Lehtonen, in the pentathlon, contributed Finland's seventh and eighth gold medals at Antwerp. The ninth was won in the Marathon race, and the winner, after leading most of the way, was the hero of 1912, the veteran Hannes Kolehmainen. By that time, Hannes was practically a Yankee; he had married an American girl and had competed in United States championships as a member of—strangely—the Irish-American A.C. When Hannes ran, suggested one American Olympian, "he looked like Ben Turpin." And, of course, when Hannes ran, he made all the Americans look like Charlie Chaplin.

Even with their magnificent performances, the Finns caused only a small share of the Americans' headaches in 1920. The difficulties began on July 26, the day the United States team, 351 athletes strong, sailed from Hoboken to Europe.

The trip was a disaster. Because the United States Olympic Committee did not have time to conduct an extensive fund-raising campaign, Congress—for the first and last time—lent a helping financial hand and authorized the use of a military transport ship for the American Olympians. At first the Olympic team was assigned the *Great Northern*, the fastest and finest of the troop ships, but when she broke down shortly before sailing time, the team had to settle for the *Princess Matoika*. There was nothing regal about the *Princess*. She was old and she was small, and because she had been used as a funeral ship, she reeked of formaldehyde. The women on the American team had cabins on the top deck, but 108 male athletes had to sleep on hammocks deep within the ship. The mess hall was so undersized that the team had to be fed in three sittings, and the temperature of the food varied from group to group. For nearly two weeks, often in rough seas, the Americans suffered aboard the *Princess Matoika*. There was almost mutiny aboard. Norman Ross, a swimmer, played Mr. Christian to the Captain Bligh of Gustavus Kirby, the president of the Olympic Committee. But nothing could be done in the middle of the Atlantic.

The only cheerful note was provided by Duke Kahanamoku and his fellow Hawaiian swimmers, who spent most of each day sitting on the deck strumming ukeleles. The music was conducive to romance, and a romance sprang up between Dick Landon, a studious high jumper from Yale, and Alice Lord, an attractive young diver from New York. They were married not long after the games ended.

If American morale was low on the high seas, it dipped

Dick Landon soars higher than King Albert's head and wins the high jump.

even lower once the team reached Antwerp. The athletes had expected to live in comfortable hotels; but for the men, the only available accommodations were cots in an old schoolhouse. The cots were so small that three huge American weight throwers—Matt McGrath, Pat McDonald, and Pat Ryan—received permission to stay in an Antwerp inn. McGrath and McDonald shared one room; Ryan took a single. Dan Ahearn, a veteran hop, step, and jumper who found he could not sleep in the crowded schoolhouse, also requested separate quarters, but he was refused. Curfew was set in the schoolhouse at 10 p.m., and on the first night, Ahearn missed the deadline. He had found his cot unbearable and had moved into Pat Ryan's hotel room. The United States Olympic Committee promptly suspended Ahearn from the team.

At this move, the other American athletes rebelled. Disgusted by the miserable trip and the miserable accommodations, some two hundred men signed a petition demanding that Ahearn be reinstated. If Ahearn did not compete, the petitioners insisted, they would not compete.

"You can't do that," Judge Bartow Weeks of the United States Olympic Committee told a meeting of the rebels. "You can't betray the people who sent you over here. You must carry on. The committee must carry on. What would you do if the committee quit?"

With American help, Earl "Tommy" Thomson (far left) captures the high hurdles for Canada.

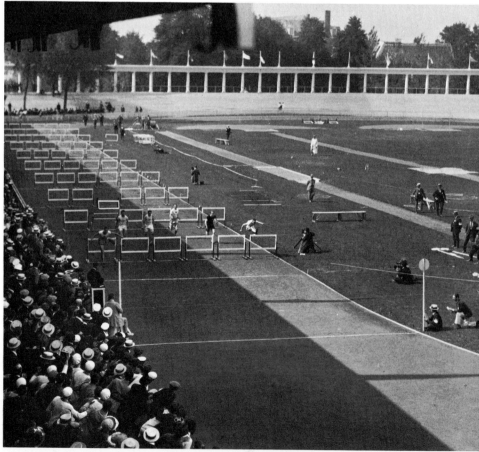

One of the American whales, Pat Ryan, gets set to win the hammer throw.

"Get a better one!" one of the rebels yelled.

Ahearn was reinstated the next morning, and the rebellion subsided. But the bitterness persisted.

Considering the conditions, the Americans did well to survive in Antwerp. Charley Paddock, the first man to be called "The World's Fastest Human," made the first of his three Olympic appearances in the sprint events. He won the 100-meter dash, then made the mistake of celebrating a 200-meter victory the night *before* the event. The following day, he ran out of energy twenty meters from the finish, and Allen Woodring, a hard-working alternate who had been added to the American team at the last minute, captured the gold medal.

Al Wesson, a Navy commander who attended high school and college with Paddock in California, later offered an intimate description of the sprinter's style. "When Charley's foot hit the ground," Wesson wrote, "it immediately bounded up with his knee high in the air ready for another powerful stride. There wasn't the slightest trace of a back kick. The result was that from the side Charley looked as though he were running in a sitting down position; his knees and feet were always out in front. From a head-on or rear view, it looked as though he were flying along about two feet off the ground

In formal team uniforms, Duke Kahanamoku collects his gold medal from King Albert (left), and thirteen-year-old Aileen Riggin, the spring-board diving champion, poses with three of her American teammates.

and never touching it. His feet rebounded with such speed that you couldn't see them hit the track.

"Charley had no great early speed and won nearly all of his races by his explosive finish. His flying leap at the tape was of no value in gaining speed in the air, as he well knew, but it gave him a goal at which to aim. His famous flying leap was twelve feet at the longest, not the fifteen or twenty that is often said. He aimed at a takeoff spot about six feet from the finish and figured on hitting the tape about in the middle of the final drive."

Paddock was probably the most spectacular United States performer in Antwerp, but others were equally effective. Frank Foss, in the pole vault, and Frank Loomis, in the 400-meter hurdles, both broke world records, and Foss, despite a water-logged runway, beat his closest competitor by fully thirteen inches. Perhaps helped by their comfortable beds, Pat Mc-Donald won the fifty-six-pound weight throw, and Pat Ryan won the hammer throw. Triumphs in the 400-meter relay and the 3,000-meter team race swelled the United States victory total.

Dick Landon of Yale clinched the ninth American gold medal by high jumping six feet four and one fifth inches, an Olympic record. After his victory, on the same day as the

5,000-meter race between Nurmi and Guillemot, Landon was brought before King Albert of Belgium. The King, six feet four inches tall, congratulated the American and said, with awe, "You jumped higher than my head!"

A few minutes later, Tom Campbell of Yale, a finalist in the 800-meter run, walked up to schoolmate Landon. "You've shown me how," Campbell said. "I'll lead the pack or they'll pick me up on the track." They picked him up on the track.

Campbell collapsed twenty-five meters from the finish in a sensational race won by Albert G. Hill of Great Britain. Earl Eby of the United States placed second, and Bevil Rudd of South Africa, the 400-meter champion, placed third. Hill won by barely a step over both Eby and Rudd. The exhausted South African fell at the finish. "My legs ached like a toothache," said Eby. "I was absolutely blind coming up the stretch and could not see Hill. I could only feel him when our elbows touched. I must take my hat off to Hill, who is one of the most wonderful half-milers I ever saw or heard of."

Hill, amazingly, was thirty-six years old in 1920. Yet two days after his dramatic 800-meter victory, he won the 1,500-meter race, matching the 800–1,500 double achieved by Flack in 1896, Lightbody in 1904, and Sheppard in 1908.

Joining Hill and Nurmi as a double winner in the 1920 Olympics was a third European, Ugo Frigerio of Italy. Little Ugo, a cheerful fellow who enjoyed trading comments with the crowd, won the walking events at 3,000 and 10,000 meters. Four years later, in Paris, he retained the 10,000-meter championship.

Another noteworthy champion, particularly from the American point of view, was Earl "Tommy" Thomson, a Canadian hurdler. Although he represented his native country, Canada, Thomson had lived most of his life in the United States and had been educated at Dartmouth. When he came in second behind an American in a trial heat of the 110-meter high hurdles, one Canadian official suggested that Thomson had deliberately lost. The truth was that Thomson had strained a muscle in his right leg. Before the final in the high hurdles, Thomson received treatment from Billy Morris, the trainer of the American team. Then he stepped out and won the event in world record time.

Even though Finland managed to tie the United States in gold medals in men's track and field, the American team, clearly, was the strongest overall at Antwerp. The United States accumulated a total of forty-one gold medals—including thirteen in shooting and eleven in swimming—more than twice as many as any other country.

In swimming, Kahanamoku set an Olympic record at 100 meters free style, and Norman Ross, the leader of the rebellion, won both the 400-meter and 1,500-meter free style events. Kahanamoku and Ross each picked up an extra gold medal as members of the 800-meter relay team. Ross had remarkable endurance in the water. There is a story, probably apocryphal, that once, while swimming in Lake Superior, he stopped and shouted to some nearby bathers, "What town's this?"

"Marquette," someone yelled back.

"Damn it," said Ross, "I wanted Duluth." Then he swam away.

Among the female American swimmers, Ethelda Bleibtrey scored a double, winning the 100-meter and 300-meter free styles, and Aileen Riggin won the springboard diving competition. Miss Riggin was exactly thirteen years old at the time.

The crew from the United States Naval Academy captured its specialty, setting up an American eight-oared dynasty that lasted, without defeat, until 1960. But the American rowing star at Antwerp was a young bricklayer from Philadelphia named John B. Kelly. Jack Kelly won the single sculls championship and teamed with his cousin, Paul Costello, to win the double sculls. Kelly was probably the greatest individual oarsman in history; in 1919 and 1920, he won 126 consecutive races. Naturally, Kelly developed a great deal of faith in his own ability. He also developed a reputation for gamesmanship.

Once, before a regatta on the Schuylkill River in Philadelphia, Elliott Saltonstall, who had been assigned to referee the single sculls race, was warned, "Watch that fellow Kelly. He's a tricky fellow at the start and has been known to beat the gun."

As the six starters lined up for the race, Saltonstall cautiously positioned his boat right next to Kelly's shell. "Mr. Kelly," said Saltonstall, "I understand you have a reputation for being somewhat shifty at the start. Well, you'll not get away with it in this race. Remember that!"

Five of the six shells hugged the starting line. Kelly casu-

The Navy crew wins the eight-oared championship.

146

ally lay back about two feet. The tactic looked suspicious to referee Saltonstall. Finally, after studying Kelly carefully, Saltonstall fired the gun. Five shells darted away from the start. Kelly wasn't even rowing. The referee was stunned.

"Is it all right to go now, Mr. Saltonstall?" Kelly asked, politely.

"Of course, you darned fool," Saltonstall shouted.

Kelly took off—and, of course, won the race.

The one race Kelly never won was the classic Diamond Sculls at England's Henley Regatta. The story has been told hundreds of times how Kelly was barred from the gentlemanly competition because he worked with his hands for his living. The story has been told just as often how John B. Kelly, Jr., satisfied his father's pride by winning the Diamond Sculls in 1947 and in 1949. But if millions of people know the story of Kelly *père* and Kelly *fils*, even more know the story of Jack Kelly's daughter, Grace, who gave up a movie career to marry Prince Rainier of Monaco.

A veteran Frenchman and a lovely young French girl dominated the tennis program at Antwerp. The incomparable Suzanne Lenglen won the women's singles championship, then teamed up with her countryman, Max Decugis, to win the mixed doubles title. Fourteen years earlier in Athens, Decugis had won the men's singles and had joined with his wife to win the mixed doubles.

Ice hockey was introduced to the Olympics in 1920, and Canada started a habit by earning the championship. The United States, to the surprise of itself and its rivals, finished first in the rugby football competition.

When the games ended late in August, the American team scored its most satisfying victory: None of the athletes went home on the *Princess Matoika*. Many of them toured Europe, then returned to the United States on commercial liners. Nobody missed the *Princess* at all.

The first ice hockey champions in the Olympics, the Canadians, pose for a team picture (above); the single sculls champion, Jack Kelly, poses for an individual picture (right).

1

The
Team
Effort

3

4

5

6

1 Water polo, 1960
2 Basketball, 1960
3 Great Britain vs. Italy, 1960
4 Soccer, 1960
5 Soccer, 1960
6 Eigil Nielsen, Denmark, goalie, 1948

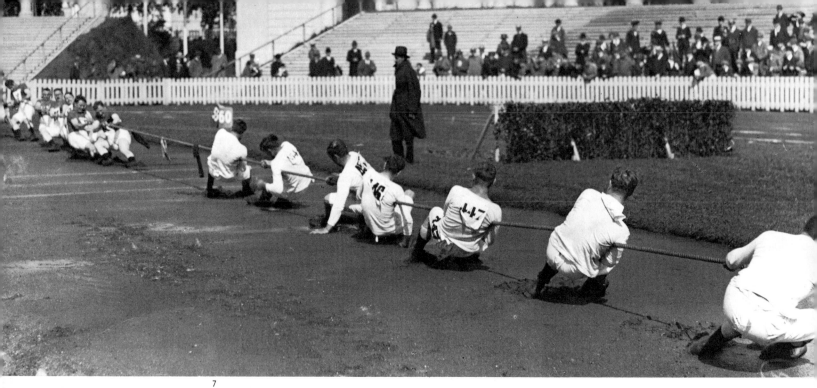

7

8

**7** Belgium vs. Holland, 1920
**8** Polo, 1936
**9** Tandem cycling, 1960

10

11

12    13

10  Bill Russell, United States, scores in 1956
11  Oscar Robertson, United States, scores in 1960
12  Jerry Lucas and Jerry West, United States, rebound in 1960
13  Massoni Domingos, Brazil, scores in 1960

15

16

17

**14** Field hockey, 1960
**15** Field hockey, 1948
**16** Field hockey, 1960
**17** Field hockey, 1932

Johnny Weissmuller splashes to an Olympic championship.

# King of the Water

## CHAPTER TEN : 1924 – PARIS AND CHAMONIX

*"I've seen the most durable of athletes, from Nurmi in track to Cobb in baseball, but I'd have to say Weissmuller had the most fantastic endurance of any champion."*

—ROBERT KIPHUTH
United States swimming coach,
1928 through 1948

The cast of characters assembled in Paris for the 1924 Olympic Games included three men who would, in time, become three of the most famous men in the world. One was a British spectator, the Prince of Wales, and he became first King Edward VIII and then the Duke of Windsor. The second was an American rower, a Yale student named Benjamin Spock, and he became Dr. Spock, seer and savant to millions of mothers. The third was an American swimmer, a nineteen-year-old boy named Johnny Weissmuller, and he became Tarzan the Ape Man.

What Paavo Nurmi was to the track, Johnny Weissmuller was to the tank—and more. Nurmi was strictly a distance runner, but Weissmuller was a distance swimmer and a sprint swimmer. He set world records in sixty-seven different events, ranging from fifty yards (roughly the equivalent of a 200-yard sprint) up to 880 yards (roughly the equivalent of a two-mile run). "Johnny didn't give a damn what the event was," said his coach, William Bachrach, "just as long as they had a tank, timers, and a finish line."

Bill Bachrach, a preposterously fat man with a face always decorated with a mustache and a cigar, coached the swimming team at the Illinois Athletic Club in Chicago. Weissmuller went to him in 1920, a gangly, uncoordinated fifteen-year-old, and said he wanted to be a swimmer. "Swear to me that you'll work a year with me, without questions," said Bachrach, "and I'll take you on. You won't swim against anybody. You'll just

Finland's talented twosome dominates the distance events: Ville Ritola wins the 3,000-meter steeplechase (left), Paavo Nurmi wins the 1,500-meter run (center), and Nurmi leads Ritola home in the 5,000-meter run (right).

Weissmuller poses on the brink of the pool.

be a slave and you'll hate my guts. But in the end you might break every record there is." Six feet three inches tall and 190 pounds at his peak, Weissmuller was the perfect Trilby to Bachrach's Svengali. Whatever the round, red-faced coach said, the trim swimmer did.

Half the secret of Weissmuller's success was skill and dedication, and the other half was relaxation. "Even as a kid," he once said, "I didn't tense up. Not even the Olympics bothered me."

Weissmuller's first Olympic test came in the 100-meter race at Paris. His rugged rivals included Duke Kahanamoku, the defending two-time champion; Sam Kahanamoku, the Duke's speedy brother; and Arne Borg, the "Swedish sturgeon" who had never lost a race.

As the start of the 100-meter free style drew near, the two Kahanamokus and Borg set themselves somberly at the edge of the pool. Each seemed intent, each slightly nervous. A few yards away, Weissmuller stood with a group of female friends, chatting and laughing.

"Come on, Weissmuller," the starter said. "Only five seconds to the start."

"I'll be there on time," Johnny said. "Don't worry."

Weissmuller was there. For seventy-five meters, Duke Kahanamoku clung to a slim lead. Then, using the American crawl stroke that he made famous, Weissmuller splashed past his veteran teammate and won the race in fifty-nine seconds flat, an Olympic record. Duke Kahanamoku placed second, Sam Kahanamoku third, and Borg fourth.

In the 400-meter free style, Borg's specialty, Weissmuller won again, this time shaving fully twenty seconds off the Olympic record. He earned a third gold medal by anchoring the victorious United States 800-meter relay team. For an extra touch, Weissmuller, an All-American water polo player,

picked up a bronze medal as a member of the third-place United States water polo team.

Weissmuller returned to the Olympics in 1928, limited himself to the 100-meter free style and the 800-meter relay and collected two more gold medals. Then, with no more waves to conquer, he retired from competitive swimming and turned to movie acting. In two decades as Tarzan the Ape Man, uttering such deathless lines as "Me Tarzan—you Jane," Weissmuller earned nearly $2,000,000 plus a world-wide fame probably unequaled by any other Olympic champion in history. Swinging from vines, swimming across jungle rivers, and thumping his hairy chest, Johnny Weissmuller became a familiar figure in every country where motion pictures were shown. His fame as Tarzan eventually obscured his fame as a swimmer, and in 1950, when sportswriters voted him the greatest swimmer of the preceding half century, millions of young people were amazed to learn that Johnny Weissmuller's swimming foes had once been men, not crocodiles.

Thanks largely to Weissmuller, swimming emerged from the shadows of the Olympics and became, to Americans at least, a significant segment of the games, second in appeal only to track and field. After Weissmuller and Duke Kahanamoku and Norman Ross, Olympic swimming competition turned out such enduring heroes as Clarence "Buster" Crabbe, who followed Weissmuller to Hollywood and became "Flash Gordon," an even more improbable character than Tarzan; Adolph Kiefer, the brilliant 1936 backstroke champion; Dr. Sammy Lee, the gifted little diver from Hawaii; and Murray Rose, the great Australian who won the 400-meter and 1,500-meter free styles in 1956 and the 400-meter free style in 1960.

Weissmuller was the star of the American delegation in the 1924 Olympics, but the most impressive nation, as in 1920, was tiny Finland. The Finns did not match the United States in men's track and field gold medals, but the margin was so slender—twelve to ten—that the Scandinavians could claim, at worst, a moral victory.

Paavo Nurmi appeared on the track scene once more, which meant, almost automatically, that Nurmi dominated the track scene once more. But this time he had one teammate so talented, so durable that even Peerless Paavo could not completely obscure him. The teammate's name was Ville "Willie" Ritola, and although he had polished his skills competing in the United States, he ran, unquestionably, like a Finn.

Ritola worked for exactly one week in Paris, July 6 through July 12, and this is what he did:

July 6—Ran 10,000-meter final.
July 7—Ran 3,000-meter steeplechase heat.
July 8—Ran 5,000-meter heat.
July 9—Ran 3,000-meter steeplechase final.
July 10—Ran 5,000-meter final.
July 11—Ran 3,000-meter team race.
July 12—Ran 10,000-meter cross-country final.

And on the eighth day he rested. Ritola had run a total of 39,000 meters in seven days, and he had finished first in the 10,000-meter run, first in the 3,000-meter steeplechase, second in the 5,000-meter run, second in the 10,000-meter cross-country race, and second in the 3,000-meter team race. In the 10,000-meter run, racing on a muddy track in extreme heat, he broke the world record. In the 3,000-meter steeplechase, he broke the Olympic record.

Incredibly, Nurmi did even better. Compared to Ritola, Nurmi was on a holiday—he worked only five consecutive days, entered only four separate events, and, including heats, ran only 26,000 meters—but he managed to finish first in the 1,500-meter run, first in the 5,000-meter run, first in the 10,000-meter cross-country race, and first in the 3,000-meter team race. In three different races, Nurmi and Ritola met face to face, and in three different races, Nurmi came in first, Ritola second.

The most spectacular day of Nurmi's spectacular career was Thursday, July 10, 1924. He started off in the 1,500-meter final, a distance shorter than he was accustomed to running, and after 100 meters, he bolted into the lead. Nobody caught up with him. After each lap, Nurmi glanced at his stopwatch, satisfied himself that his pace was proper and jogged on. He jogged home an easy winner, setting an Olympic record. Henry Stallard of Great Britain, who finished third, collapsed at the tape, so exhausted that doctors needed thirty minutes to revive him. Nurmi was not even breathing hard.

After he crossed the finish line in the 1,500-meter race, Nurmi continued running, disappeared into the locker room, and emerged an hour later, fresh and phlegmatic as ever, ready to start the final at 5,000 meters. He and Ritola and Edvin Wide of Sweden shared first place for half the race. Then Nurmi took one last look at his watch, decided that he needed it no longer, heaved it away, and stepped up his stride. He won without difficulty, establishing another Olym-

Double champions for the United States: Clarence Houser (below) adds the shot-put title to his first place in the discus, and Harold Osborn (right) becomes the only man in Olympic history to win the decathlon and an individual event, the high jump.

162

pic record. Without breaking stride, he picked up his sweat-shirt and ran once more to the locker room. "The superman has arrived at last," wrote Grantland Rice after Nurmi's double victories. "Forty-four competing nations must pay tribute to the greatest track phenomenon that any age in sport has ever known."

In the 3,000-meter team race, which did not count for individual honors, Nurmi's dignity—not his supremacy—was threatened. Joie Ray, who represented the United States in three Olympic Games, amused the spectators by mimicking Nurmi. Ray kept a solemn face, thrust out his chest, and studied his watch every few strides. Ray finished eighteenth, and Nurmi, leading Finland to the team championship, had the last laugh.

In the 10,000-meter cross-country race, which included a team title as well as an individual championship, Nurmi scored his most decisive triumph, defeating Ritola by 500 meters, nearly a minute and a half. Nurmi did not even linger on the field long enough to see Ritola come in second and clinch the team victory for Finland.

Between them, Nurmi and Ritola gave the Finns seven gold medals—five individual awards and two team awards. Jonni Myyra retained the javelin championship, E. R. Lehtonen retained the pentathlon championship, and for the second straight time, a Finn won the Olympic Marathon. The successor to Hannes Kolehmainen was Albin Stenroos, forty years old, the same man who had placed third in the 10,000-meter run at Stockholm twelve years earlier. Stenroos had retired from athletic competition before World War I, after breaking a leg in a cross-country race, and few people had expected him even to complete the Marathon course in Paris.

Jonni Myyra of Finland successfully defends his javelin championship.

The stars of the sprints: Jackson Scholz of the United States wins the 200-meter dash (top), and Harold Abrahams of Great Britain wins the 100-meter dash (bottom).

A reporter for the New York *World*, Leonard Cline, offered a unique explanation for the Finnish athletic splurge. "Every single person in that country," Cline wrote, "goes through, day after day, the ordeal of talking in Finnish. After that, why should one be surprised at anything the Finns accomplish?"

Against the glittering array of Finns, the United States sent out its largest team yet, 417 men and women, including 116 track and field athletes. This time, for a change, no one found fault with the trip or the accommodations. Most of the team sailed to France aboard a comfortable chartered liner, the S.S. *America*, and the entire squad stayed at scenic Rocquencourt on the Seine, at the estate once owned by Prince Joachim Murat, who served under Napoleon. The Americans' only complaints concerned the food. "Our first breakfast," Dr. Spock later recalled, "was a little wizened orange, one croissant and one curl of butter. The meals improved."

Pat McDonald, the giant weight thrower who had competed in 1912 and 1920, went along as an honorary member of the team. His specialty—the 56-pound weight throw—had been dropped from the Olympic program, but he was still called "The Prince of Whales." The oldest member of the American team was another whale, Matt McGrath, forty-five, the durable hammer thrower who had placed second in 1908, first in 1912, and fifth in 1920. At Paris, where he added a silver medal to his collection, McGrath carried the American flag in the opening parade.

Originally, the games were scheduled for Amsterdam, but they were switched to Paris at the request of Baron de Coubertin, who was planning to step down as president of the International Olympic Committee in 1925. Baron de Coubertin attended the opening ceremonies; his distinguished companions included the Prince of Wales, the Crown Prince of Sweden, the Crown Prince of Rumania, the Regent of Abyssinia, and the President of France. The chaos of 1900 was replaced by thorough planning. Crowds ranged up to 60,000 daily, and 40,000 Frenchmen viewed the opening parade. Forty-four nations dispatched 3,000 athletes to Paris, setting a record for participation. The Americans had the largest team; Lithuania, China, and the Philippines each sent two men.

Harold Osborn of Illinois and Clarence "Bud" Houser of California were the individual track and field stars for the United States, probably because neither had to compete against Nurmi or Ritola. Osborn won the high jump at six feet six inches, a record that lasted for twelve years, and then became the only man in Olympic history to win both an individual event and the demanding decathlon. Houser also earned a pair of gold medals, capturing the shot-put and the discus.

Other American champions included Fred Tootell of Bowdoin College in the hammer throw, Dan Kinsey in the 110-meter high hurdles, Morgan Taylor in the 400-meter hurdles, William DeHart Hubbard in the broad jump, and both the 400-meter and 1,600-meter relay teams. A seventeen-year-old California schoolboy, Lee Barnes, won the pole vault championship in a jump-off with teammate Glenn Graham, and in the 200-meter dash, Jackson Scholz defeated Charley Paddock.

Paddock, who had lost the 200-meter race in 1920 because he had stayed up too late, lost the 200-meter race in 1924 because he looked back too soon. Ten meters from the tape, Paddock, holding first place, glanced back over his shoulder—and Scholz spurted past him on his blind side.

Two nonwinners on the American squad turned in striking performances. Bob LeGendre, while competing in the pentathlon, broad jumped twenty-five feet six inches, a new world record and a full foot beyond Hubbard's championship leap in the broad jump. LeGendre received nothing more than a bronze medal for placing third in the pentathlon. Clarence DeMar, thirty-six years old, also won a bronze medal. He finished third in the Marathon, and not until 1972 did an American again run so well in the long-distance race. DeMar, a preacher and a printer in New England, ran the Marathon in the Olympics for the first time in 1912 and for the last time in 1928; for several years afterward, in his forties and fifties, he competed in the annual Boston Marathon. When he died in 1958, at the age of seventy, doctors performed an autopsy and found, contrary to the common theory about enlarged "athletes' heart," that DeMar's heart actually was slightly smaller than most. But the arteries leading away from his

Morgan Taylor of the United States breaks the tape in the 400-meter hurdles.

165

heart were two to three times thicker in diameter than average.

For the second straight Olympic Games, no other nation mounted a serious threat to the Finnish-American dynasty in track and field. But Great Britain did show off two outstanding runners—Harold Abrahams, a tall, carefree Cambridge student who drank ale and smoked cigars, and Eric Liddell, a short, serious divinity student. Abrahams upset Paddock and Scholz in the 100-meter dash, and Liddell sprinted away from his rivals in the 400-meter run. Both Britons set Olympic records.

The United States again won the unofficial over-all Olympic championship, concentrating its points in swimming, tennis, and catch-as-catch-can wrestling. Weissmuller, of course, spurred the men's swimming team; the women's team, although boasting no individual star, did include Gertrude Ederle, who two years later became the first woman to swim across the English Channel. Miss Ederle earned a gold medal as a member of the championship United States 400-meter relay team and two bronze medals for her third places in the 100-meter and 400-meter free style races.

In rowing, Jack Kelly and Paul Costello successfully defended their double sculls title—Kelly did not compete in the single sculls, won by Great Britain's durable Jack Beresford—and the slick Yale crew, undefeated for two straight seasons, swept to a decisive eight-oared victory. Rowing number seven for Yale, weighing 175 pounds and standing six feet tall, was the future baby doctor, Ben Spock.

Tennis, which had been a regular Olympic event since the first modern games in 1896, made its final Olympic appearance in 1924. The trouble was that the Olympic Games—the most prestigious international showcase for track and field, swimming, and several other sports—never did provide a true tennis test. To amateur tennis players, victory in the British championships at Wimbledon or in the American championships at Forest Hills meant much more than victory in the Olympics. For instance, Bill Tilden, the greatest amateur tennis star of the 1920's, never did compete in the Olympics. Ironically, the last Olympic tennis competition attracted two of the world's finest amateurs—Helen Wills and Vincent Richards. Led by Miss Wills and Richards, the United States swept all five tennis titles in Paris.

While tennis was fading from the games in 1924, boxing was establishing itself as a permanent—and significant—event. The sport had been staged in only three different Olympics before 1924, and an English-speaking boxer—from the United States, Great Britain, or Canada—had won every championship except one. But in 1924, finally, the boxing championships took on an international flavor. The eight titles were divided among six nations; Denmark, Norway, and Belgium each contributed its first champion. Probably the most gifted of the 1924 Olympic fighters was an American, Fidel LaBarba. He won the flyweight division, then turned professional and soon became flyweight champion of the world.

During the pentathlon competition, Bob LeGendre breaks the world record in the broad jump.

Lee Barnes, a seventeen-year-old California schoolboy, finishes first in the pole vault.

Early in 1924, several months before the summer competition, a separate set of winter games were held for the first time in Olympic history. At Chamonix, France, sixteen nations entered a total of 300 athletes. Norway won the team championship, helped greatly by Thorlief Haug's three gold medals in Nordic skiing events (cross-country and jumping). Clas Thunberg of Finland stood out among the speed skaters, Gillis Grafstrom of Sweden won the second of his three consecutive figure skating titles (before 1924, figure skating had been held with the summer sports), and Switzerland's four-man team captured the only bobsled race.

The most efficient organization in the inaugural winter games, judging from its record, was Canada's ice hockey team. The Canadians defeated Czechoslovakia, 30–0; Sweden, 22–0; Switzerland, 33–0; and England, 19–2. In the final, Canada met the United States, which had turned back Belgium, 19–0; France, 22–0; England, 11–0; and Sweden, 20–0.

"We ought to beat the United States by ten or twelve to nothing," predicted Harry Watson, the star of the Canadian team.

"We'll fight for the match until we drop," predicted William Haddock, the manager of the American team. But, with Watson scoring three goals, Canada beat the United States, 6–1.

The idea of separate winter games was a pleasant one, endorsed by Baron de Coubertin and the International Olympic Committee and incorporated permanently into the Olympic program. The winter games offered the smaller Nordic and Alpine nations an extra incentive to produce Olympic athletes, offered bobsledders and speed skaters a splendid opportunity to test their skills against international opposition, and offered spectators, at the figure skating competitions, some of the most lovely athletes ever seen.

167

At the age of fifteen, Sonja Henie wins her first Olympic gold medal.

# The
# Norwegian Doll

## CHAPTER ELEVEN : 1928 – AMSTERDAM AND ST. MORITZ

When Sonja Henie was the brightest figure skating star on ice, the little Norwegian girl suffered no lack of confidence. "Most always, I win," she said. Most always, she was right. From 1927 through 1936, Miss Henie won ten consecutive world championships and three consecutive Olympic championships.

Sonja Henie was among those rare individuals who competed in four different Olympic Games. Another four-time Olympian, for example, was Matt McGrath, the American hammer thrower, and in 1924, when he made his fourth and final appearance, he was forty-five years old. In 1936, when Miss Henie made her fourth and final appearance, she was, incredibly, only twenty-three years old.

Coached by her father, Wilhelm, an Oslo shopkeeper and a European cycling star, Miss Henie made her Olympic debut at the age of eleven, during the inaugural winter games of 1924. She already had won the championship of Norway, but she finished dead last at Chamonix. Stung by the defeat, little Sonja promptly went home, started studying ballet, and began practicing her skating seven hours a day. Her dedication paid off handsomely. In 1927, at the age of fourteen, she won her first world title. The following year, at St. Moritz in Switzerland, she won her first Olympic title.

Sonja Henie was a genius on skates. Although she was a master of the school figures, the compulsory, classic maneuvers which make up the first half of each figure skating competition, she specialized in the second half, the free skating. Petite and attractive—five feet two inches tall and 109 pounds as an Olympic champion, with stunning blond hair and twinkling brown eyes—Sonja was one of the first figure skaters to transform the sport into an art. She adapted the "Dying Swan" sequence from "Swan Lake," patterned her performance after the great ballerina, Anna Pavlova, and fashioned an icy masterpiece. She developed nineteen separate types of spins, and on some of them, she whirled around eighty times, achieving such speeds that the slightest slip could have caused serious injury. "Music and her skating are inseparable," a reporter once wrote. "With a quick movement, she glides down the ice, gradually gaining speed. Before the onlookers realize it, Sonja is moving in her natural pace, spiraling around the ice on one skate with her arms extended to each side, her head thrown back and a confident smile on her face."

She became an international favorite. King Haakon of Norway sent her a telegram before each of her public appearances. Crown Prince Friedrich Wilhelm of Germany once gave her a diamond stickpin emblazoned with the Hohenzollern crest. She skated before the rulers of England, Sweden, and Belgium and captivated them all. Queen Mary of England once told Miss Henie that she would like to learn to ice skate. "I would suggest, your Majesty, that you try roller skating first," Sonja said. "It's safer."

After her triumph in the 1936 Olympic Games, Miss Henie turned professional and toured the United States with her own ice show. The show, a great success, served two purposes. It made ice skating popular in the United States, and it made Miss Henie the richest athlete in the world. Her gate appeal was so great that she won a Hollywood contract, and although her acting was on a par with Charles Laughton's figure skating, she was, again, an instant sensation. Her movies were largely witless and plotless, transparent devices to put the Norwegian doll on ice, but by 1939, she was, statistically, the number three box office attraction in the United States. Only Shirley Temple and Clark Gable pulled more customers into the movie theaters. By the age of twenty-six, Miss Henie was earning approximately $1,000,000 a year.

At St. Moritz in 1928, with twenty-five countries contributing a total of five hundred competitors, Sonja Henie helped Norway to its second straight winter Olympic championship. She was not the only hero at the plush Swiss resort. Her countryman Johan Grottumsbraaten won two Nordic skiing events, and Clas Thunberg of Finland, the speed skating star of 1924, collected two more gold medals.

Pierre Brunet of France teamed with a lovely young lady named Andrée Joly, won the pairs figure skating championship, and then married his partner. As husband and wife, they retained their title in 1932. Brunet later became a brilliant, if stern, teacher of figure skaters, and in 1960, his outstanding American pupil, Carol Heiss, perhaps as beautiful and skilled as Sonja Henie, won the Olympic championship.

Andrée Joly and Pierre Brunet earn the pairs figure skating championship at St. Moritz.

The United States finished a surprising second in the 1928 winter games, thanks largely to its bobsledders. John Heaton won the skeleton (one-man) race, and a sled captained by William Fiske won the four-man championship.

Five months after the winter games ended in Switzerland, the summer games began in Holland. Forty-six nations enrolled 3,000 athletes, and a capacity crowd of 40,000—minus Baron de Coubertin, who was recuperating from a recent illness—watched Prince Hendrik of Holland preside over the opening ceremonies. In the parade at Amsterdam, as has become traditional, the founders of the Olympics, the Greeks, marched first, and the host team, the Dutch, marched last. Germany, back in the Olympic fold after being excluded from the 1920 and 1924 games, paraded 300 men. Haiti, Panama. and Cuba each paraded one. The single Haitian, Sylvio Cator, won a silver medal by finishing second in the broad jump. Cator, who later in 1928 became the world's first twenty-six-foot broad jumper, remains today the only Haitian ever to earn a medal in the Olympic Games.

The French did not march at all in Amsterdam, and they did not smile, either. Their unhappiness stemmed from an incident the day before the games began. The French athletes went to the stadium to test the running track, but a Dutch gatekeeper, who had already allowed the German team to enter, refused to admit the French. The gatekeeper's remarks indicated clearly that he preferred Germans to Frenchmen, and patriotic punches were exchanged. The French demanded an immediate apology from the Dutch Olympic Committee and the immediate dismissal of the pro-German gatekeeper. The Dutch honored the first request and promised to honor the second. But when the French Olympians showed up for the opening ceremonies, the same gatekeeper was on duty, still quick with nasty remarks. The French fumed, turned around, and hurried back to their hotels. After further Dutch apologies, the French did compete in the games.

To everyone except, perhaps, Haitians and Frenchmen, the most intriguing aspect of the 1928 summer Olympics was the abrupt and unexpected decline of the United States track and field team, particularly in the running events. In seven separate flat races—the 100-meter and 200-meter dashes, plus the 800-meter, 1,500-meter, 5,000-meter, 10,000-meter, and Marathon runs—a total of twenty-one medals, from gold to bronze, were awarded, and not a single one was awarded to an American. A South African won the 110-meter high hurdles, and an Englishman won the 400-meter low hurdles; before 1928, the United States had never lost the low hurdles and had lost the high hurdles only once, in 1920, to Earl Thomson, the American-trained Canadian. In the hammer throw, won exclusively by Americans in earlier games, an Irishman finished first at Amsterdam, and a Swede finished second.

What made these reversals doubly disappointing was that before the games began, Major General Douglas MacArthur, the new president of the United States Olympic Committee, had been bursting with optimism. "Without exception," General MacArthur said, "our athletes have come through the long grind of training into superb condition. They are prepared both mentally and physically for the great test. Americans can rest serene and assured."

What happened? Most observers agreed that the Americans sagged because of four excesses: They were overcoached, overtrained, overfed, and overconfident.

The American track and field squad alone had a manager and three assistant managers, a head coach and ten assistant coaches, a trainer and five assistant trainers. "The boys themselves say they get orders from so many sources that they don't know which to take," reported Wythe Williams, a correspondent for *The New York Times*. "As Father Murray, New York's sporting priest who came over with the boys, said, 'Too much management spells mismanagement.'"

Critics argued, too, that the United States Olympic trials, which had been staged at Harvard only three weeks before the games began, should have been held a month earlier. The extra month, theoretically, would have allowed the competitors time for a natural slump after the high tension of the tryouts.

Nobody could dispute the allegation that the American athletes ate exceedingly well. Sailing on the S.S. *President Roosevelt,* which doubled as the team's headquarters in Amsterdam, the United States squad—300 men and women, including eighty-four track and field performers—once consumed 580 steaks at a single meal. "When the ship left New York," Alexander Weyand, a member of the 1920 team, wrote in his book *The Olympic Pageant*, "a quantity of ice cream was taken aboard that was deemed sufficient for the entire round trip. Before the games began, the supply was exhausted." Frank Wykoff, a schoolboy sprinter from California who was favored in the 100-meter dash, reportedly gained ten pounds between the trials and the games. He finished fourth in his specialty.

Correspondent Wythe Williams also addressed himself to the matter of overconfidence. "Many explanations and suggestions were offered," Williams said, "but the one heard most frequently was that the team, puffed up with conceit, hadn't trained seriously since its arrival in Amsterdam. It might be well for the American committee to return to rough-house methods as in the days of Mike Murphy when an athlete who broke rules was immediately dismissed from the team."

Confused, stale, plump, and cocky, American athletes did not score a single point in individual flat races until the last one was run. Then, in the 400-meter run, there was a little salve for the United States wounds.

The cofavorites in the 400-meter race were James Ball of Canada and Joachim Buchner of Germany, the winners of the two semifinals. The American contenders in the six-man final were Ray Barbuti, a rugged Syracuse football player, and Herman Phillips. Both Americans, on the advice of trainers, sipped sherry and eggnog before the final.

Phillips and Barbuti both broke well, but Phillips, setting a blistering pace, wore himself down in the first 200 meters. As the tight field swept into the final 100 meters, Phillips faded—and Barbuti spurted. In the next fifty meters, the Syracuse football star opened up a five-meter lead over Canada's Ball.

But Barbuti was in difficulty. His sprint at the head of the stretch had cost him most of his strength, and Ball was pounding toward him, cutting into the American's lead with every stride. Closer and closer Ball came, and closer and closer came the tape. Desperately, less than ten meters from the finish, Barbuti flung himself forward, dove toward the tape, cut it, and slammed painfully into the cinders. He had won, by inches. Ball finished second and Buchner third, and everyone in the stadium realized that if the race had lasted another five meters, the Canadian would have won.

Sports ballet in Amsterdam: A Dutch field hockey player leaps through the air against India (left), and soccer players from Chile and Portugal try a *pas de deux*.

"I was going to send the Stars and Stripes up the victory pole," Barbuti said, "if I had to pull it up myself. I never noticed the other runners after the start. I heard them, but all I kept thinking was, 'Run, kid, run.' I don't remember anything of the last 100 meters except a mad desire to get to that tape. It seemed a mile off."

Barbuti earned a second gold medal by anchoring the victorious American 1,600-meter relay team. The United States also won the 400-meter relay and picked up five first places in the field events. Robert King of Stanford led the high jumpers, with defending champion Harold Osborn placing fifth, and Edward Hamm of Georgia Tech led the broad jumpers, with Haiti's Cator second and defending champion William DeHart Hubbard eleventh. Sabin Carr won the pole

Ray Barbuti, Emerson Spencer, George Baird, and Fred Alderman make up the victorious American 1,600-meter relay team.

vault, displacing another defending champion, Lee Barnes, who slumped to fifth.

The only American to retain a championship in the 1928 field events was Dr. Clarence Houser, who had won both the shot-put and the discus in Paris. The California dentist didn't defend his shot-put title, and he almost failed to qualify for the discus final. He fouled twice, then qualified on his last chance. He won the final by three and a half inches. In the shot, John Kuck, another Californian, set a world record and defeated two talented rivals, Herman Brix of the United States and Emil Hirschfeld of Germany.

With a total of eight gold medals in men's track and field, the United States delegation made its worst Olympic showing till 1972. In all other games, from Athens in 1896 through Mexico City in 1968, the United States men scored at least nine victories in track and field.

Still the American performance in 1928 could hardly be considered a complete disaster. No other nation matched the United States. Finland finished second once more, this time with five gold medals.

For the third consecutive Olympics, Paavo Nurmi was the

star for the Finns. Although he won only one race and placed second in two others, the suspicion persists that Nurmi would have won all three events if he had chosen to. Many observers at Amsterdam felt strongly that in the distance races, especially the 5,000-meter run, the sequence of Finnish finishers had been predetermined.

In the first distance race of the 1928 games, the 10,000-meter run, Nurmi and Willie Ritola matched each other, stride for stride, until the final lap. "It's worth crossing the ocean just to see this," said General MacArthur, who left his box seat and moved to the finish line to watch the Finns duel. Nurmi, with a sudden sprint, won the duel by six tenths of a second, setting an Olympic record. "After his victory," a reporter noted, "Nurmi demonstrated that he's the same aloof figure by refusing to shake Ritola's hand and unceremoniously waving aside cameramen as he trotted off the field."

Whatever rift existed between Nurmi and Ritola apparently healed before they met again a few days later in the 5,000-meter run. The two Finns quickly moved out in front, and, once more, they ran together into the last lap. Then, without great difficulty, Ritola pulled away from Nurmi and, for the first time in five Olympic efforts, defeated his famous teammate. "It seemed that Nurmi deliberately handed the victory to his compatriot," one sportswriter suggested, "when he halted, stepped aside and let Ritola pass. Afterward, Nurmi made no effort to take the lead, and at the finish he was looking back as though to make sure he wouldn't be passed by Edvin Wide of Sweden, who ran third."

Wide, by that time, must have developed a passionate distaste for Finns. In 1924, he ran third behind Nurmi and Ritola at 5,000 meters and second behind Ritola at 10,000 meters. In 1928, he ran third behind Nurmi and Ritola at both 5,000 and 10,000 meters.

The day after the 5,000-meter final, Nurmi faced Ritola in the 3,000-meter steeplechase. Nurmi was not exceptionally graceful on the obstacle course. In his qualifying heat, he had tumbled over the water jump on the first lap and, after being helped out of the water by a Frenchman named Lucien Duquesne, had moved from last place to first place, always navigating the water jump slowly and carefully.

In the final, Ritola, the defending champion, also had trouble at the water jump and was forced to quit the race. Finland still placed one-two-three, but the winner was not Nurmi. He took second, trailing Toivo Loukola, a chauffeur from Helsinki.

Nurmi did not bother to defend his 1,500-meter title, but Harri Larva kept the championship in Finland and broke Nurmi's Olympic record. Four different Finns had captured gold medals in four separate distance races. Paavo Yrjola, outstanding in no event but skilled in all, set a world record in the decathlon, and his Finnish teammate, Akilles Jarvinen, placed second. Jarvinen, whose father Werner Jarvinen had earned Finland's first Olympic victory in 1906, also competed in the hop, step, and jump and came in sixth.

El Ouafi of Algeria, the ex-French soldier, approaches the finish of the Marathon.

Another Finn, Martti Marttelin, was favored to win the Marathon run, and for most of the race, he battled for the lead with Kanematsu Yamada and Seiichiro Tsuda, two Japanese stars, and Joie Ray, the American veteran who had mimicked Nurmi in 1924.

A few miles from the finish, El Abdel Baghinel Ouafi, a twenty-nine-year-old French Algerian, suddenly began to close in on the leaders. El Ouafi, an Arab who worked in a Paris automobile factory, turned on a sprint, rushed into the lead and won by 150 yards. Miguel Plaza, a Chilean newspaper vendor who had finished sixth in the 1924 Marathon, had been following El Ouafi all the way and captured second place. Marttelin was a distant third, Yamada fourth, and Ray, slowed by a painful cramp, fifth.

As Ouafi finished, a French official grabbed him and embraced him. As Plaza finished, a woman wrapped a Chilean flag around him, and he ran an extra lap carrying the flag. As Ray finished, he cracked, "I lost because I ran too slow."

El Ouafi, a tiny vegetarian who drank nothing but milk and water, had once been a dispatch bearer in the French Moroccan army. "I had been told to watch the Finns," he explained, "so I kept my eye on Marttelin. When I saw him running slower, I just kept on a little faster."

Next to the American slump, the most striking feature of the 1928 track and field competition was the well-balanced showing of the other English-speaking nations. Great Britain and Canada each won two gold medals, Ireland and South Africa one apiece. These four countries excelled in events previously dominated by Americans.

The victory for Ireland was not particularly surprising. Dr. Patrick O'Callaghan of the Irish Free State went into the hammer throwing competition with the best of training; he had studied under John Flanagan, the three-time Olympic champion who had retired from the New York police force and had returned to his native country. Flanagan's teaching paid off handsomely; Dr. O'Callaghan won the hammer throw in 1928—and again in 1932.

The Canadian triumphs were startling. Percy Williams, a curly-haired, twenty-year-old Canadian schoolboy, had worked his way from his home in Vancouver to his country's Olympic trials in Toronto. He had made the long cross-country train trip by serving as a waiter in a dining car.

In Amsterdam, Williams, the ex-waiter, won both the 100-meter and 200-meter sprints. "That boy doesn't run—he flies," insisted Charley Paddock, the American veteran who was eliminated in the semifinals of the 200-meter dash. "He's a thoroughbred and a great competitor. I didn't have a thing left. I lost eight yards overnight. It must be age. My old kick isn't there."

In the 400-meter low hurdles, Morgan Taylor of the United States, the defending champion, and Thomas Livingstone-Learmonth, who could run faster than he could give his name, won the semifinals and were expected to duel for the title.

En route to championships, Dr. Patrick O'Callaghan of Ireland gets set to throw the hammer (above), and Helena Konopacka of Poland prepares to hurl the discus.

But Taylor, who held the world record, was off form in the final, and Livingston-Learmonth faded in the last 100 meters. Another Englishman, Lord David George Brownlow Cecil Burghley—commonly called "Davy"—raced off with the championship.

"Seldom in the Olympic arena has a more popular hero been acclaimed," one reporter noted. "Even the American contingent, shocked though it was by the failure of Taylor, rose to cheer the smiling young Briton as he was carried off the field by teammates."

Davy is still a popular Olympic figure. He is one of the two vice-presidents of the International Olympic Committee. His impressive address is: The Marquess of Exeter, Burghley House, Stamford (Lincs), England.

In the final of the 800-meter run, five men—Lloyd Hahn of the United States, Erik Byhlen of Sweden, and Earl Fuller of the United States, the winners of the three semifinals; Sera Martin of France, the holder of the world record; and Phil Edwards of Canada, making the first of his three appearances in the Olympic 800-meter run—were given a chance for the championship. None of them won. With a brilliant stretch drive, Douglas Lowe of Great Britain retained his Olympic championship and broke the record set by Ted Meredith sixteen years earlier. Byhlen finished second, nearly

177

ten yards behind. "I reckoned I'd come out all right," Lowe said, "but I was surprised at the effect my spurt had on the rest. I didn't figure on so big a margin. I was jolly glad, though, when I hit the tape."

Female track and field competitors reared their sometimes pretty heads for the first time in modern Olympic history, and Canada ran off with most of the honors. Canada contributed the most victories (two in five events), the prettiest athlete (high jump champion Ethel Catherwood, who was awarded the beauty prize by correspondent Williams of *The New York Times*), and the most heartbroken athlete.

In the 100-meter final, won by Elizabeth Robinson of the United States, Myrtle Cook of Canada, wearing red shorts and a white silk blouse, jumped the gun twice and was disqualified. She promptly sat down next to the starting line and began crying. The starter finally convinced her that she should move to a pile of cushions on the nearby grass. She sat on the cushions and sobbed loudly for fully half an hour.

A German girl was also disqualified for two false starts, but she was tougher than the Canadian. Instead of crying, she shook her fist at the starter and swore revenge.

Female swimmers, too, suffered their share of upsetting incidents. When Hilde Schrader of Germany won the 200-meter breast stroke and set a world record, the German lass swam so furiously that on the last lap the straps of her bathing suit broke. After completing the course, the buxom blonde, modest by nature, stayed in the water until her suit was fixed. "I would have gone even faster," she said, "if I had not been so embarrassed."

The American swimmers had little to be embarrassed about. The girls won five of seven events, and the men won five of eight events. Martha Norelius, in the 400-meter free style and the relay; Albina Osipowich, in the 100-meter free style and the relay; Johnny Weissmuller, in the 100-meter free style and the relay; George Kojac, in the 100-meter backstroke and the relay; and Peter Desjardins, in the springboard and high dives, each earned two gold medals.

In rowing, Paul Costello won a gold medal in the double sculls for the third straight Olympics, with Charles McIlwaine

Despite bathing suit embarrassment, Hilde Schrader of Germany wins the 200-meter breast stroke.

replacing Jack Kelly as his partner, and the California crew, using handsome blue-tipped oars, maintained American supremacy in eight-oared competition. Wythe Williams of the *Times* gave a large part of the credit for the California victory to Don Blessing, the coxswain. "Blessing's lungs are magnificent," Williams wrote, "and for the entire 2,000 meters, he gave what by unanimous accord was one of the greatest performances of demoniacal howling ever heard on a terrestrial planet. Never for a second did he cease. Bobbing up and down in his seat, sometimes raising clear up on the thwarts until it seemed he would slip into the water, he gave the impression of a terrier suddenly gone mad. But such language and what a vocabulary! What magnificent flights of rhetorical vituperation! One closed his eyes and waited for the crack of a cruel whip across the backs of the galley slaves."

The United States again won the most gold medals overall —twenty-four to nine and a half each for runners-up Finland and Germany—but twenty-eight nations, the most till then in Olympic history, scored at least one victory. Uruguay won its second consecutive soccer championship, India its first of five straight field hockey titles. The Swiss collected five gold medals in gymnastics, Lucien Gaudin of France won both the foils and *épée* fencing championships, and Crown Prince Olaf of Norway skippered the winning six-meter yacht and set a regal precedent. Thirty-two years later, Crown Prince Constantine of Greece won the Dragon class.

"Nothing is more synonymous of our national success than is our national success in athletics," said General MacArthur in his official report after the 1928 Olympics. "The team proved itself a worthy successor of its brilliant predecessors." Technically, the general was correct; the United States had outscored all other countries in the Olympic Games. But, considering what was expected and what was accomplished, his words had a hollow ring.

rd David Burghley of Great Britain dashes to the 0-meter hurdles championship.

Urged on by coxswain Don Blessing, the California crew beats England by half a length.

On
Snow
and
Ice

1  Speed skaters, 1956
2  Squaw Valley scene, 1960
3  Aulis Kallakorpi, Finland, 1956
4  Antti Hyvarinen, Finland, ski jump champion, 1956
5  Willis Olson, United States, 1956
6  Helmut Recknagel, Germany, ski jump champion, 1960

5

6

7    8

7  Toni Sailer, Austria, downhill, slalom, and giant slalom champion, 1956
8  Roger Staub, Switzerland, giant slalom champion, 1960
9  Andrea Mead Lawrence, United States, slalom and giant slalom champion, 1952
10  Jean Vuarnet, France, downhill champion, 1960

9

10

11

**11** Tenley Albright, United States, figure skating champion, 1956
**12** Barbara Ann Scott, Canada, figure skating champion, 1948
**13** Carol Heiss, United States, figure skating champion, 1960
**14** Maxie Herber and Ernst Baier, Germany, pairs champions, 1936

15    16

15  Evgeni Grishin, U.S.S.R., speed skating champion, 1956 and 1960
16  Dick Button, United States, figure skating champion, 1948 and 1952
17  Ronnie Robertson, United States, figure skating, second place, 1956

17

18 Canada vs. United States, 1960
19 Canada vs. Germany, 1956
20 United States vs. U.S.S.R., 1956

20

22    23

21  Four-man bobsled, 1936
22  Four-man bobsled champions, Switzerland, 1956
23  Two-man bobsled, 1936

In the heat of the 80-meter hurdles, Babe Didrikson (right) streaks to a world record.

# The Lady
# Wore Spikes

## CHAPTER TWELVE : 1932 – LOS ANGELES AND LAKE PLACID

*"Before I was even into my teens, I knew*
*exactly what I wanted to be when I grew*
*up. My goal was to be the greatest athlete*
*that ever lived."*
—BABE DIDRIKSON ZAHARIAS
*This Life I've Led*

In July of 1932, at the Northwestern University field, the team from the Employers Casualty Company of Dallas, Texas, won the United States women's track and field championship. The team from Texas took first places in the shot-put, javelin throw, broad jump, baseball throw, and 80-meter hurdles, tied for first place in the high jump, scored a fourth in the discus throw, and failed to place in the 100-meter sprint. The team from Texas consisted, in its entirety, of "Babe" Didrikson.

All by herself, the wiry little Texan, barely eighteen years old, the sixth child of an immigrant Norwegian cabinetmaker, won the national team championship. The Illinois Women's Athletic Club, represented by twenty-two girls, finished a distant second.

This sounds suspiciously like pure myth, straight out of Milo of Croton by way of Thorpe of Carlisle, but the feats of the Babe of Texas were unquestionably fact. Roughly five feet four inches tall and 110 pounds, with green eyes and short, sandy hair, Mildred Didrikson put on a performance that has never been matched in American championships, and probably never will be.

Two weeks after her triumphs at Northwestern, Babe Didrikson competed in the 1932 Olympic Games at Los Angeles In the opening parade, she wore a pair of stockings for the first time in her life. The next day, she was comfortable again, in sweat socks and spiked shoes.

Under a special Olympic rule for women, Babe was permitted to enter only three events. She chose the javelin, the hurdles, and the high jump. "Ah'm gonna whup you," she told her rivals, with conviction, not with boastfulness.

On the first day of competition, she won the javelin throw and broke the world record. On the fifth day of competition, she won the hurdles race and broke the world record. She seemed sad because she had only one more event in which to break a record. "I'd break 'em all if they'd let me," said the Babe.

She might have, too. In the high jump, naturally, she broke another world record, but this time she didn't win the gold medal. Miss Didrikson and a teammate, Jean Shiley, tied at a height of five feet five and one-quarter inches. In the jump-off, at the same height, both girls cleared the barrier, but the Babe was disqualified for "diving." In those days, regulations specified that a high jumper's feet had to go over the bar first; the rule has since been rescinded. "My feet went over first," Miss Didrikson insisted. "I'd been jumping the same way all afternoon." She settled for a silver medal.

A rumor spread among the Olympic press corps that the Babe, besides mastering every phase of track and field, also swam, shot, rode, rowed, tumbled, boxed, and wrestled and played tennis, golf, soccer, field hockey, basketball, football, baseball, polo, and billiards. Paul Gallico, then a reporter for the New York *Daily News*, asked Miss Didrikson, "Is there anything at all you don't play?"

"Yeah," she said. "Dolls."

Actually, the rumors were exaggerated—but only slightly. Miss Didrikson did make the All-American women's basketball team three times. She once pitched for the Philadelphia Athletics in an exhibition game, once tackled a Southern Methodist University football player as a movie stunt, once squared off against a boxer named Baby Stribling (Young Stribling's younger brother) as a publicity gag, and once defeated Pauline Betz in a tennis doubles match. But her best game, after she turned professional and abandoned track and field, was golf. In the late 1940's, she won seventeen consecutive golf tournaments, an all-time record.

In 1932, for her Olympic accomplishments, and again in 1945, 1946, 1947, and 1950, for her golf victories, the Associated Press poll of sportswriters voted her the best woman athlete of the year. In 1950, joining Jim Thorpe, the greatest male athlete of the half century, the Babe was elected the finest female athlete of 1900–49.

Babe Didrikson married a huge, friendly wrestler named George Zaharias in 1938 and lived a happy life until in 1956, at the age of forty-two, after a courageous battle, she lost her fight against cancer. She left a brilliant legacy, in golf and in the Olympics.

In the 1932 Olympic Games, a total of six women's track and field events were held, and world records fell in all six. Miss Didrikson personally took care of half of them, Lillian Copeland of the United States won the discus, and the Ameri-

Stanislawa Walasiewicz of Poland, known as Stella Walsh in the United States, wins the 100-meter dash.

can team won the 400-meter relay. The other record-setter was also an incredible athlete, Stanislawa Walasiewicz of Poland. Although she represented her native country, she lived in the United States, where she was known as Stella Walsh, and during her career, she won thirty-five American national championships. Her titles spanned the years 1930 through 1951, and her events spanned the sprints and the broad jump through the discus and basketball throws. In the Los Angeles Olympics, Stella Walsh broke the world record for the 100-meter dash.

New records struck the keynote in the 1932 games. In men's track and field, excluding the 50,000-meter walk, which was being held for the first time, the athletes competed in twenty-two separate events and set nineteen Olympic records. The other three records escaped by a total of twelve inches—eight in the hammer throw, three and a half in the broad jump and one half in the high jump. World records were shattered in seven events.

Had a new breed of supermen—and superwomen—suddenly sprung up? Certainly, athletes seemed stronger and swifter than ever before, but the real secret of the record explosion in Los Angeles was the track. It was made of crushed peat, and it was ideal for running. "This track is the fastest in the world," Paul Gallico reported. "All of the athletes say that they have never encountered one like it. It is like running on a springboard."

The springboard track was only one of the conveniences offered the Olympians of 1932. From an organizational standpoint, too, the Los Angeles games set Olympic records. The United States Olympic Committee, with Avery Brundage succeeding General MacArthur to the presidency, provided magnificent facilities. The Los Angeles Coliseum, later infamous as the baseball home of the Los Angeles Dodgers, was expanded to seat 105,000 spectators and became the main Olympic stadium. Some events were staged in the Rose Bowl in nearby Pasadena, others at the Los Angeles County Museum and the lavish Riviera Country Club. More than one million people witnessed the games, including a record crowd of roughly 100,000 on one day of track and field competition; daily attendance in the Coliseum averaged 60,000.

In Baldwin Hills, twelve miles southwest of Los Angeles, the United States set up the first Olympic Village, a self-sufficient athletic city sprawling over 321 acres and housing 550 bungalows, forty kitchens (with chefs equipped to suit all national tastes), a hospital, a library, and a post office. All 1,300 male athletes, representing thirty-seven countries, lived within the Olympic Village, and the 127 female athletes stayed in Los Angeles hotels. Participation slumped from previous games partly because each country, for the first time, was limited to three entries in each event, and mostly because the Asian and European nations could not meet the expense of sending large squads to the United States. Brazil tackled its cost problem by dispatching its athletes on a ship and giving them coffee beans to sell along the way.

197

President Herbert Hoover was busy campaigning for re-election (which turned out to be a waste of energy), so Vice-President Charles Curtis presided over the opening ceremonies. In the parade, Chung Cheng-liu alone represented 400,000,000 Chinese, Sylvio Cator again marched by himself for Haiti, and 361 Americans brought up the rear. Although he was technically excused from the opening parade because his event was to be held the next day, Morgan Taylor, the veteran hurdler, carried the American flag. When Lord Burghley, the popular British hurdler, learned that his rival, Taylor, was marching, he too, in a sporting gesture, joined the parade. Bands played, trumpets blared, cannons roared, choirs sang, pigeons flew, and Charles Curtis announced: "In the name of the President of the United States, I proclaim open the Olympic Games of Los Angeles."

Once the competition began, the sixty-eight-man United States track and field team set out with a vengeance to make up for its disappointing 1928 showing. Americans captured eleven of the twenty-three events, established ten Olympic records, and broke five world records. No other nation won more than three championships.

Eddie Tolan, a squat sprinter from Michigan, finished first in both sprints, setting a world mark at 100 meters and an Olympic mark at 200. Chewing gum all the way, Tolan wore horn-rimmed glasses held in place by adhesive tape and wrapped a white bandage around his left knee to keep it warm. Ralph Metcalfe of Marquette, who had won the American trials in both events, placed second at 100 meters, third at 200.

The 400-meter run presented a striking American duel, East against West, short, black-haired Bill Carr of Pennsylvania against tall, blond-haired Ben Eastman of Stanford. Twice before, in the intercollegiate championships and in the Olympic tryouts, the two had met, and twice before, even though Eastman held the world record for the quarter mile, Carr had won.

At Los Angeles, Eastman burst out of the starting blocks, grabbed the lead, and ran the first 200 meters in the amazing time of twenty-one and seven tenths seconds, a pace fast enough to have won all but two of the previous Olympic 200-meter dashes. Carr was only four tenths of a second slower. Then he began slicing into Eastman's lead. With eighty meters to go, Carr drew even. Stride for stride, the two Americans pounded down the stretch together until, finally, Carr slipped in front and won by a long stride. Both men broke the world record.

Eight months later, tragically, Bill Carr broke both his legs in an automobile accident. He never raced again. Two other members of the 1932 American Olympic team also met misfortune soon after the games. Only a month after Carr's accident, George Saling, who won the 110-meter high hurdles and set an Olympic mark, died in an auto crash. Lieutenant George C. Calnan—who competed as a fencer in four Olympic Games, won a bronze medal in 1928, and recited the

Little Eddie Tolan captures the 200-meter sprint by an impressive margin.

Olympic oath for all the athletes in 1932—lived less than a year after the Los Angeles Olympics. As a crew member on the *Akron*, he died when the ill-fated Navy dirigible crashed into the Atlantic Ocean off the New Jersey coast.

At Los Angeles, Finland once again placed second in track and field competition. But the Finns were weaker than they had been during the 1920's; despite the efforts of the three Jarvinen brothers (Matti won the javelin, Akilles placed second behind American Jim Bausch in the decathlon, and Kaarlo failed to score in the shot-put) and a remarkable veteran, Ville Porhola (the 1920 shot-put champion came in second in the 1932 hammer throw), Finland collected only three gold medals at Los Angeles.

The Finns obviously missed Paavo Nurmi, who had been declared a professional, and Willie Ritola, who had declared himself a professional, but they did unveil a new long-distance sensation, Volmari Iso-Hollo, a twenty-five-year-old typesetter from Kerava. Iso-Hollo set an Olympic record in a heat of the 3,000-meter steeplechase, then won the final easily, even

Volmari Iso-Hollo of Finland (117) takes an early lead in the 3,000-meter steeplechase.

though an official's error forced him and his rivals to run an extra lap. Iso-Hollo took second in the 10,000-meter run, pressing a surprising Pole named Janusz Kusocinski to an Olympic record. Four years later, in Berlin, Iso-Hollo retained his steeplechase championship and placed third at 10,000 meters.

The American-Finnish rivalry was usually conducted on separate planes—short distances for the United States, long distances for Finland—but in 1932, representatives of the two nations met head on in a magnificent struggle, the 5,000-meter run.

Lauri Lehtinen of Finland, who held the world record, and his teammate, Lauri Virtanen, took the lead early and shared it for half the race. Then an American, Ralph Hill of Oregon, moved up to challenge. Americans, generally, were no more formidable in the long-distance races then than Finns in sprints, and Hill's threat was startling. Soon Virtanen dropped back, and at the start of the last lap, Lehtinen was still leading, but Hill was on his heels. Turning into the homestretch, Hill, a stride behind, swung to the outside, trying to pass the Finn. Lehtinen moved out too, blocking the American. Hill cut back to the inside and, simultaneously, Lehtinen swerved in, again closing the gap. To avoid a collision, Hill had to break stride. He made one more desperate effort and barely missed catching Lehtinen at the tape. The margin was less than a meter. Both men were timed in fourteen minutes and thirty seconds, an Olympic record.

Bob Tisdall of Ireland (left) barely beats Glenn Hardin of the United States to the tape in the 400-meter hurdles.

The huge Coliseum crowd hooted and howled, convinced that Lehtinen had blocked Hill illegally. The American spectators shouted demands that the Finn be disqualified. Bill Henry, the announcer, finally quieted the crowd. "Remember, please," Henry said, "these people are our guests."

After a full hour of deliberation, Arthur Holz of Germany, the chief judge in the 5,000-meter run, announced, "I am of the opinion that No. 125 did not wilfully interfere with No. 433 in the finish." Lehtinen, officially, won the championship.

"I never took Hill for that good a runner," Lehtinen explained afterward. "I swung wide on the last turn, then saw the American trying to get around and went the other way to let him pass. But at the same time he changed his mind. I am very sorry. It was unfortunate."

At the medal-awarding ceremony, which was delayed until the following day, Lehtinen, standing on the top rung of the victory pedestal, reached down and tried to pull Hill up with him. Hill politely declined. After the medals were presented, Lehtinen turned and pinned a small enameled Finnish flag to Hill's sweater. The crowd cheered loudly. Until 1964 Hill's second-place finish was never equaled or surpassed by an American in the Olympic 5,000-meter run.

The 400-meter low hurdles race rivaled the 5,000-meter run for both drama and efficiency. The final attracted a glittering field—Morgan Taylor of the United States, the 1924 champion and third-place finisher in 1928; Lord Burghley of Great Britain, the 1928 champion and fifth-place finisher in

On his way to the decathlon championship, American Jim Bausch clears the high jump.

Canada's Duncan McNaughton, American-trained, soars to a gold medal in the high jump.

the 1932 high hurdles; Glenn Hardin of the United States, the winner of one semifinal; Robert Tisdall of Ireland, the winner of the other semifinal; Luigi Facelli of Italy, the sixth-place finisher in 1928, who was making the third of his four Olympic appearances; and Kjell Areskoug of Sweden, who was happy to be in such distinguished company.

Areskoug, the upstart, broke in front, but the whole field quickly flashed past him, Tisdall setting the pace, Hardin running second. The Irishman opened up a five-meter lead and seemed an easy winner until he smacked over the last hurdle. He staggered, then regained his stride and still managed to beat Hardin to the tape by less than a step. Taylor finished third, Lord Burghley fourth, and Facelli fifth. All five bettered the existing Olympic record, and the first two men broke the world record. Under the rules then in effect, Tisdall was ineligible for either record because he had knocked down a hurdle. Hardin, from Louisiana State University, got credit for both records, but Tisdall got the gold medal. The Irishman demonstrated his versatility by finishing eighth in the decathlon.

The walking event, a 50,000-meter grind, seemed, as usual, more comic than dramatic. Walkers work hard and must be in top condition, but even at their smoothest and swiftest, they look strangely awkward. Fittingly, in a walking contest, the two stars were relatively old men. Tom Green, a thirty-nine-year-old British railroad worker, won by a comfortable margin. The sentimental favorite, Italy's smiling, hand-waving Ugo Frigerio, the 1920 and 1924 champion who had been shut out of the 1928 games by the temporary elimination of walking races, finished third in the five-hour event and then collapsed.

Frigerio must have felt frustrated, but he was no more frustrated than Phil Edwards, a Canadian who had attended New York University. In 1932, Edwards finished third in the 800-meter run (behind Tom Hampson of Great Britain), third in the 1,500-meter run (behind Luigi Beccali of Italy), and third in the 1,600-meter relay (behind the United States). With a third-place showing in the 1,600-meter relay in 1928 and a third-place showing in the 800-meter run in 1936, Edwards finished his Olympic career with the world's finest collection of bronze medals.

One Canadian did manage to win a gold medal in Los Angeles, but he had to sweat for it. After gaining a four-way tie with two Americans and a Filipino in the high jump, Canada's Duncan McNaughton, a student at the University of Southern California, won the jump-off. He was the first non-American to capture the event since Ireland's Con Leahy in 1906.

Juan Carlos Zabala of Argentina approaches the tape at the end of the Marathon.

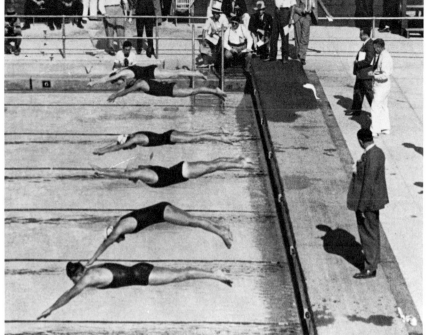

Clarence "Buster" Crabbe (bottom) gets a quick start in the 400-meter free style final.

Crossing the finish line at Santa Monica, California, Attilo Pavesi of Italy wins the 100-kilometer cycling race.

The Marathon, by tradition, concluded the track and field program. Juan Carlos Zabala of Argentina, a brash twenty-year-old schoolboy, predicted that he would win the event—and he did. Breaking Hannes Kolehmainen's Olympic record, Zabala led almost all the way and defeated the runner-up, Sam Ferris of Great Britain, by twenty seconds. Ferris, evidently a glutton for punishment, had finished first in the Olympic Marathon at Paris and eighth at Amsterdam.

Overall, the United States thoroughly dominated the 1932 summer games. The Americans gathered forty-one gold medals, including nine in swimming and five in gymnastics. Italy had twelve, with four in gymnastics; France, ten, with three in weight-lifting; Sweden, nine, with four in Greco-Roman wrestling; and Japan, seven, with five in swimming.

The Japanese men suddenly emerged as the best swimmers in the world. Four different Japanese won individual events, and three of them broke Olympic records; their 800-meter relay quartet cracked the Olympic mark by an amazing thirty-eight seconds. Even more amazing was the youthfulness of the flying fish from Japan: Kusuo Kitamura, who won the strenuous 1,500-meter free style, was only fourteen; Masaji Kiyokawa, the 100-meter backstroke champion, was sixteen; and Yasuji Miyazaki, the 100-meter free style champion, was seventeen.

Only Clarence "Buster" Crabbe of the United States, the future movie actor, cracked the Japanese monopoly in swimming events. Crabbe broke the Olympic record in the 400-meter free style. Two other Americans, Michael Galitzen and Harold Smith, captured the diving championships.

The diving competition attracted an extra, surprise starter. Without submitting an official entry, a fully-dressed man executed a perfect belly flop from the side of the pool. He was a German sportswriter, and he won a hundred-dollar bet for taking his dive.

In women's swimming, Americans swept six of the seven events. Helene Madison led the surge, winning the 100-meter free style and the 400-meter free style and anchoring the championship relay team. An attractive young lady named Eleanor Holm, who had placed fifth at Amsterdam, won the 100-meter backstroke.

The most controversial incident of the Los Angeles games took place in the water polo competition. After Germany defeated Brazil, 7–3, the coffee sellers politely joined hands and gave a cheer for the winning team. Then, impolitely, they turned and attacked the referee, a Hungarian named Bela Komjadi, whose decisions had irritated the Brazilians all day. The Brazilian goalkeeper kicked the referee, which is against water polo rules, and policemen and spectators promptly poured into the free-for-all.

Later, before a judicial board that barred Brazil from the remainder of the games, referee Komjadi stated his case. "The Brazilians have no idea how to play water polo," he insisted. "They have no idea of the international regulations. It stands to reason that if I were to be unfair, I, as a Hungarian, would be prejudiced against the Germans, our big rivals, and not against the Brazilians, whom we do not have to fear." Komjadi's appraisal turned out to be accurate. Hungary won the water polo championship, and Germany finished second.

Two durable Scandinavians were the stars of the wrestling matches. Ivar Johansson, a Swedish policeman, won the catch-as-catch-can middleweight championship, then swore off the *smörgåsbord,* sweated off eleven pounds in less than a week, and won the Greco-Roman welterweight title. Four years later, back up to his normal weight, he added the Greco-Roman middleweight crown to his collection. Johansson's countryman, Carl Westergren, a bus driver by profession, earned a gold medal in the Greco-Roman heavyweight division. Westergren, obviously a growing boy, had won the Greco-Roman middleweight class in 1920 and the light-heavyweight class in 1924. What had happened in 1928? An injury had forced him out of competition.

Argentina won the light-heavyweight and heavyweight boxing championships, which may explain why, on the trip home, the Argentine athletes fought so furiously among themselves that the ship's captain had to lock them up. Upon his return to Buenos Aires, Santiago Lovell, the talented Olympic heavyweight champion, was rewarded with a free room and free meals—in jail.

Gold medals traveled from Los Angeles to all parts of the world. India won the field hockey tournament, an Italian won the 100-kilometer cycling race, and an Australian won the single sculls. India had little competition in field hockey; in the final, Roop Singh, the Babe Ruth of his sport, scored twelve goals, his teammates scored twelve more, and the Indians crushed the United States, 24–1. The Italian cyclist,

Attilo Pavesi, had a remarkable appetite—or one reporter had a remarkable imagination. Although Pavesi's 100-kilometer race lasted only two and a half hours, he carried—according to the observant reporter—a bowl of soup and a bucket of water on his handle bars, and a dozen bananas, cinnamon buns, cheese sandwiches, and cold spaghetti in a bib draped around his shoulders. For an extra touch, he had two spare tires wrapped around his neck. The Australian sculler, Bobby Pearce, won the single sculls for the second straight Olympics, an unprecedented feat.

The other rowing feature, the eight-oared race, matched the University of California crew against a spirited Italian shell. "In all the history of American rowing," wrote Allison Danzig, the rowing authority of *The New York Times*, "there has never been a more thrilling or more magnificently fought boat race. In a Herculean driving finish, that brought a deafening roar from the throats of 80,000 frenzied spectators, the Golden Bears of California cut down Italy's three-foot lead in the last twenty-five yards of the 2,000-meter course to slam over the finish line the victor by the exceedingly close margin of a foot and win the Olympic championship for the United States for the fourth successive time."

In the winter games at Lake Placid, New York, the United States, for the first and probably last time in Olympic history, won the most gold medals. Americans won four victories in speed skating—two each for Jack Shea and Irving Jaffee—and two in the treacherous sport of bobsledding. One reporter, W. O. McGeehan of the New York *Herald Tribune*, suggested that bobsledding was a modern version of an ancient form of suicide. But McGeehan absolved the Greeks of all blame. "When an ancient Greek wanted to end it all," he wrote, "he took hemlock or drank some of the native Greek wine with rosin in it. This left the body intact for funeral purposes." The American four-man sled in 1932, captained by Billy Fiske, a veteran of the 1928 games, included Eddie Eagan, who had won the Olympic light-heavyweight boxing championship in 1920. "It is a shame," McGeehan lamented, "that

India's brilliant field hockey team outclasses the United States.

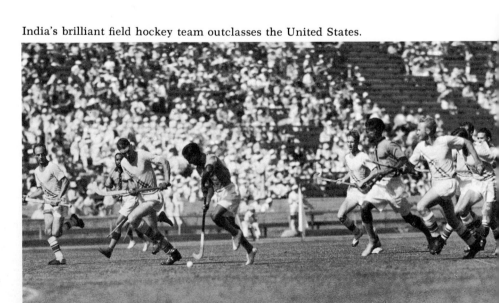

Mr. Eagan, educated at Yale and Oxford and with a fine bringing up in every way, should turn out to be only a bob-sledder." Eagan had never been on a bobsled before he went to Lake Placid in 1932, but he signed a waiver absolving anyone else of blame for a possible injury, hopped aboard a sled, and started down into the frightening eighty-degree banks.

"The first ride will always be vivid in my memory," Eagan later recalled. "In a car, in the cab of a railroad engine or in a plane, speed has never frightened me. But it did on that bobsled. It took only about two minutes to make that run, but to me it seemed like an eon. I remember the snow-covered ground flashing by like a motion picture out of focus. Speeding only a few inches from the ground without any sense of security, I hung on to the straps. My hands seemed to be slipping, but still I clung. We hit a turn. My head snapped backward. We went through Zigzag. I was dizzy as my head snapped first to the right, then to the left. Finally, the sled neared the bottom." A few weeks later, his bobsledding tech-nique polished by continuous practice, Eddie Eagan, shaken but safe, accepted his second Olympic gold medal in twelve years. No one yet has matched his summer-winter double.

At the Lake Placid Olympics, which touched off a ski boom among Americans, the United States had a clear advantage in numbers. Of the 300 winter athletes from seventeen na-tions, fully one fifth were Americans.

Norway, the 1924 and 1928 leader, finished second in gold medals with three. Birger Ruud won the first of his two jumping championships, Johan Grottumsbraaten retained the Nordic combined title, and Sonja Henie, of course, won the women's figure skating crown.

From every standpoint—facilities, performances, attend-ance, sportsmanship—the 1932 Olympic Games had been a thorough success. The Olympic spirit had flourished in a free nation. But four years later, in Hitler's Germany, the Olympic Games, for the first time since the days of the Romans, felt the cold weight of a dictatorship.

In a magnificent finish, California's crew turns back a strong Italian bid.

In Hitler's Germany, Jesse Owens leaps to a world record.

# Owens
# Über Alles

## CHAPTER THIRTEEN : 1936 – BERLIN AND GARMISCH-PARTENKIRCHEN

*"Jesse was always a face boy. When a problem came up, he always faced it."*
—MRS. HENRY OWENS
Describing her son

Brown shirts were in fashion, and the goose step was the vogue. Germans sang the Horst Wessel song ("Storm troopers march with steady, quiet tread . . ."), and Adolf Hitler spread his big lies. The Aryans were supermen; they were the master race. But in the Olympic Games of 1936, the myth of Aryan superiority took a beating. On the sacred soil of the Fatherland, the master race met its master: A slender, twenty-two-year-old American named James Cleveland Owens. Among sixty-six men on the United States track and field team, "Jesse" Owens was one of ten Negroes.

"The Black Auxiliaries!" cried *Der Angriff*, the Nazi newspaper.

"America will have an all-Negro team by 1940," one German reporter predicted.

To the psychotic Nazi mind, white meant might, black meant weakness, and the mere presence of Negroes on the American team meant that the United States was a decaying nation. With his performances in the Berlin Olympics, Jesse Owens ripped this theory to shreds.

Born in Alabama, the seventh child of an impoverished cotton picker, the grandson of slaves, Jesse Owens grew up in Cleveland, attended Ohio State University, and became a national hero on May 25, 1935. Competing as a sophomore in the annual Western Conference track and field championships, Owens, within two hours, won the 100-yard dash, the 220-yard dash, the 220-yard low hurdles, and the broad jump

—and set world records in three of the four events. He slumped in the 100-yard sprint; he only tied the world record. His broad jump—twenty-six feet eight and one quarter inches—was not surpassed for a quarter of a century.

Like many brilliant athletes, Owens had what his Ohio State coach, Larry Snyder, called "a high tension nervous system." Before competing, he worked up such extraordinary tension that his adrenal glands flooded his bloodstream with adrenalin, which stimulated the heart. As a result, Owens had great strength under pressure.

He also had grace under pressure. Even though he churned within, he remained outwardly calm. "Owens is a form runner," Jesse Abramson, the New York *Herald Tribune*'s track and field expert, wrote in 1935. "He is the picture of relaxed ease as he sprints. He never shows any apparent effort. He always appears able to do better."

Owens once revealed a secret to his style. "In the sprints," he said, "I stick with the field, breathing naturally, until thirty yards from the finish. Then I take one big breath, hold it, tense all my abdominal muscles and set sail. I do the same thing in the broad jump. About thirteen yards from the take-off, I get that big breath and then I don't let it out until I'm safely in the pit."

If Owens had a weakness, it was his start. Instead of concentrating on the gun, he watched his rivals out of the corners of his eyes, and when they started, he started. He often was late off the mark, but his relatively short, powerful, seven-foot stride quickly carried him past his opponents.

Larry Snyder groomed Owens carefully for the Olympics of 1936. To prevent his star from burning himself out before the games, the coach deliberately curtailed Owens's activities during the preceding winter. Then, as the Olympics drew closer, Owens grew sharper, and in the final American tryouts, he won the 100-meter and 200-meter dashes and the broad jump. "Without being overconfident," said Owens, confidently, "I think I'll be a triple winner in the Olympics." Owens, as it turned out, was underestimating himself.

On August 3, 1936, the second day of the Olympic track and field program, Owens bid for his first gold medal. In a field of three Americans, one German, one Dutchman, and one Swede, he was favored to win the 100-meter sprint.

Owens had reason to be even more tense than usual. The previous day, *der Führer*, Adolf Hitler, had made a great show of congratulating the first 1936 Olympic champion, who happened to be a German. But later the same day, when an American Negro won a gold medal, Hitler offered the non-Aryan no congratulations. In fact, as the American triumphed, *der Führer* hurried out of the stadium, supposedly to escape a light drizzle. The contrast was so blatant that dozens of reporters charged Hitler with snubbing the Negro out of prejudice. Surely, the Nazi dictator was prejudiced, but the truth is that he snubbed the Negro because he was told to. Under the international Olympic rules, Hitler was informed, the

In the 400-meter relay, Owens turns over the baton to teammate Ralph Metcalfe.

210

leader of the host nation may preside over the opening ceremonies, the closing ceremonies—and nothing more. He could not publicly congratulate any champions, Aryans or non-Aryans.

When Owens stepped to the starting line in the 100-meter final, Hitler was in the stands. So were Hermann Goering and Joseph Goebbels and Heinrich Himmler. "As my eyes wandered across the field," Owens later recalled, "I noticed the green grass, the red track with the white lines. And as my eyes wandered into the stands, I noticed the 120,000 people sitting and standing within that great arena. And as my eyes wandered upward, I noticed the flags of every nation that was represented there, underneath that German blue sky. My attention was diverted from that beautiful picture because the whistle had been blown and we were to receive our final instructions. The starter stepped back about ten paces and he hollered in a loud German voice, 'Aufdieplatz,' and when he hollered, 'Aufdieplatz,' every man went to his mark. And when the starter suddenly said in a soft voice, 'Fertig,' every man came to a set position. Every muscle in his body was strained. The gun went off."

Owens, for once, broke with the gun. He shot into the lead, and although one teammate, Ralph Metcalfe of Marquette University, who had started poorly, made a tremendous bid in the last fifty meters, no one caught up to Owens. He won by a meter. Hitler watched, unhappily.

The following day, Owens competed in the broad jump. Trials were held in the morning, and each contestant was allotted three jumps. In order to qualify for the final, he had to leap at least twenty-three feet five and one half inches.

For Owens, this seemed a simple task. But on his first try, he fouled. On his second try, he fouled. He had only one chance left, and because heats of the 200-meter dash had just been run off, he was obviously tired.

"I kicked disgustedly at the dirt," Owens recalled afterward. " 'Did I come 3,000 miles for this?' I thought bitterly. 'To foul out of the trials and make a fool of myself?' Suddenly, I felt a hand on my shoulder. I turned to look into the friendly blue eyes of a tall German broad jumper. He offered me a firm handshake. 'I'm Luz Long, I don't think we've met,' he said.

" 'Glad to meet you,' I said.

" 'You should be able to qualify with your eyes closed,' he said. 'Why don't you draw a line a few inches in back of the board and aim at making your takeoff from there? You'll be sure not to foul, and you certainly ought to jump far enough to qualify.'

"The truth of what he said hit me. I drew a line a full foot in back of the board and proceeded to jump from there. I qualified with almost a foot to spare."

In the finals, held the same afternoon, Luz Long, the friendly German, provided the sternest opposition to Owens. After Owens set an Olympic record on his second jump, Luz

Glenn Cunningham of the United States clings to the lead late in the 1,500-meter run.

tied it on his fifth—of six—jumps. But Owens was just warming up. On both his fifth and sixth tries, he lengthened the Olympic record. "At the instant I landed from my final jump —the one which set the Olympic record of twenty-six feet, five and one quarter inches—Luz Long was at my side, congratulating me," Owens said. "It wasn't a fake smile, either."

A sincere friendship sprang up between the blond Aryan and the Negro American, but the two never saw each other after the 1936 Olympics. Long, fighting in the German army, died in Sicily during World War II. After the war, Owens revisited Germany and met Long's widow and son. "He was a wonderful guy," Owens said. "It took a lot of courage for him to befriend me in front of Hitler."

The day after the broad jump, Owens easily captured the 200-meter dash, establishing another Olympic mark. Then, a few days later, he ran the first leg on the championship United States 400-meter relay team. He collected four gold medals, but not a single word of praise from Adolf Hitler. "It was all right," Owens later explained. "I didn't go over to shake hands with Hitler, anyway."

In 1950, when the Associated Press polled sportswriters to select the greatest track and field athlete of the half century, Owens finished first, Jim Thorpe second, and Paavo Nurmi third. The slim Negro star drew twice as many votes as the Indian and the Finn combined.

Led by Owens, America's "black auxiliaries"—ten talented men—outscored every national team, including their fifty-six Caucasian teammates, in the 1936 Olympic track and field events. Among them, the ten Negroes earned eight gold medals, three silver medals, and two bronze medals. They won every flat race from 100 meters through 800 meters. All except one of them took home at least one medal. It was enough to make Hitler's pure-blood theory run thin.

The oldest of the Negroes, Ralph Metcalfe, the veteran of the 1932 games, won a silver medal in the 100-meter dash and a gold medal in the 400-meter relay. The youngest of the Negroes, John Woodruff, a University of Pittsburgh freshman who had absolutely no notion of running style, stormed from last place and became the first American in twenty-four years to win the 800-meter run. Fritz Pollard, Jr., of the University of North Dakota, whose father had been an All-American football player at Brown, led for almost half the race in the 110-meter high hurdles, then slipped to third. And David Albritton, Owens's teammate at Ohio State, collected a silver medal in the high jump. Four of the Negroes were Californians—Archie Williams and James LuValle, who came in first and third in the 400-meter run, Mack Robinson, and Cornelius Johnson.

Mack Robinson, who placed second to Owens in the 200-meter dash, was known at the time primarily as a twenty-five-foot broad jumper. He was later known primarily as the older brother of Jackie Robinson, the first Negro to play in baseball's major leagues. Jackie, incidentally, was also a twenty-five-foot

With a furious finish, John Woodruff of the United States wins the 800-meter run.

212

Champion Cornelius Johnson slides over the bar in the high jump.

In hot water, Eleanor Holm Jarrett never got into the swim in Berlin.

broad jumper and a strong candidate for the canceled 1940 Olympics.

"Corny" Johnson was tall and skinny, "a funny-looking kid with a boyishly grave face," according to his Los Angeles High classmate, the novelist Budd Schulberg. The first day Johnson tried out for his high school track team, as a fifteen-year-old freshman in 1930, he leaped six feet two inches. In 1932, at seventeen, he tied for first place in the Olympic high jump, then fell to fourth in the jump-off. In 1936, he was a strong favorite to win the Olympic title. He almost failed to make the American team.

Dick Landon, the 1920 Olympic champion, was one of the judges at the American trials, and when the high jump try-outs began, he noticed that Johnson was nowhere in sight. Landon delayed the event as much as he could, then started without Johnson. When the bar was up to six feet six inches, Johnson, who had been stuck in a traffic jam, reached the stadium. Without warming up, he promptly cleared six feet six inches and went on to qualify.

In Berlin, Johnson soared to victory at six feet seven and seven eighths inches, a new Olympic record, without a single miss. He won on opening day and became the first Negro champion of the 1936 games. It was he who, on accepting his medal, looked up and saw Hitler scurrying out of the stadium. He flashed a broad smile.

The American Negroes almost didn't get an opportunity to show up the master race in Berlin. When Hitler and the Nazis came to power, between the time the games had been awarded to Germany and the time they were to be held, many Americans insisted that the United States should not compete in Nazi Germany. They argued that participation would indicate tacit approval of Hitler's tyranny and his flagrant anti-Semitism. But Avery Brundage, the president of the United States Olympic Committee, argued that the games were international in character, not national, and that they concerned only sports, not politics. He fought steadily for American participation. Brundage is an honorable man, sincerely devoted to amateur athletics, but he has never been a master of tact.

Asked in 1933 about anti-Semitism in Germany, Brundage replied, "Frankly, I don't think we have any business to meddle in this question. We are a sports group, organized and pledged to promote clean competition and sportsmanship. When we let politics, racial questions, religious or social disputes creep into our actions, we're in for trouble."

*The New York Times*, in an editorial, took the opposite tack. When the Nazis "deliberately and arrogantly offend against our common humanity," the *Times* said, "sport does not 'transcend all political and racial considerations.'"

Brundage would not be budged. "Certain Jews must now understand that they cannot use these games as a weapon in their boycott against the Nazis," he wrote in a pre-Olympic pamphlet.

"Among inferior races, Jews have done nothing in the athletic sphere," the Nazis themselves wrote in a pre-Olympic pamphlet. "They are surpassed even by the lowest Negro tribes."

Brundage won a promise from the Germans that they would not discriminate against Jewish athletes or spectators, and he also won his battle to keep the United States in the Olympics. To prove their good intentions, the Germans put one Jew on their winter team—hockey player Rudi Ball—and one Jew on their summer team—fencer Helene Mayer. The fact that Rudi Ball was, by a wide margin, the best hockey player in Germany and Helene Mayer was a former Olympic champion may have influenced the Germans' gesture.

As another concession, the Nazis temporarily took down the anti-Semitic signs dotting Berlin. Hitler ordered everyone whose home faced the athletic fields to paint or clean his house and to decorate his windows with flowers. All the streets sparkled with bright banners, and Germans turned out by the hundreds of thousands to welcome the visiting teams. Brundage was impressed. "No nation since ancient Greece," Brundage said, "has captured the true Olympic spirit as has Germany."

The Germans spent the equivalent of $30,000,000 to turn the 1936 Olympics into a gigantic showcase for Nazism. On the outskirts of Berlin, fifteen minutes by car from the center of the city, they built a 325-acre *Reichssportfeld* housing the Olympic Stadium (seating 100,000), a swimming stadium (18,000), dozens of smaller stadiums, six gymnasiums, practice fields, tennis courts, parking areas, and a railroad station. Closed-circuit television was set up on the grounds for people who could not get inside the stadiums.

Nine miles away, 3,741 male athletes, representing a record total of forty-nine nations, lived in a 136-acre Olympic Village. They were housed in handsome brick-and-stucco cottages, with twin rooms painted in green and cream. Each cottage was named after a German city; the Australians, when they learned they were being quartered in Worms House, had a few anxious moments. The cottages made the Los Angeles

The two discus champions, Ken Carpenter of the United States (left) and Gisela Mauermaver of Germany, demonstrate their muscular styles.

bungalows look like shacks, and just in case anyone didn't remember, the Germans brought over a Los Angeles bungalow and installed it in the village as a monument—and as a propaganda weapon.

The village, as in Los Angeles, was completely self-sufficient, with every convenience for each national peculiarity. The Japanese had special steam baths, and the Finns had sauna baths. The French team, naturally, received wine with all meals. The food was varied and plentiful. An Egyptian weight lifter one morning ate twenty-four fried eggs for breakfast. The hosts provided two hundred buses to transport athletes back and forth between the village and the stadiums. The 328 female Olympians had their own quarters on the grounds of the Reichssportfeld.

To add glamor to the games, the Germans instituted the practice of having a torch lit by Greek maidens, at the reconstructed shrine of Zeus in Olympia, and then having runners carry it to the host country. A relay of three thousand men brought the Olympic flame across seven countries to Berlin, where it burned continuously from the opening to the closing ceremonies.

In the opening parade, the Austrians gave the Nazi salute to Hitler and received loud applause, the Bulgarians goose-stepped and drew long cheers, and the Americans neither saluted nor dipped their flag and attracted several jeers. After the parade, the last of the relay runners ignited the Olympic flame, the crowd sang "Deutschland Uber Alles," and a distinguished guest, Spiridon Loues, the winner of the 1896 Marathon, presented Hitler with an olive branch from Olympia.

Conspicuously missing from the American delegation was Mrs. Arthur Jarrett, who, as Eleanor Holm, had won the 100-meter backstroke in 1932. The lovely young swimmer had been dismissed from the United States squad for drinking during the boat trip from New York to Germany. Mrs. Jarrett, who had once been offered a job in the Ziegfeld Follies and had worked briefly as an actress, protested the decision. "I've never made any secret of the fact that I like a good time and that I am particularly fond of champagne," she said. "But I'll train and not touch another drop if I'm given another chance."

Despite her plea and considerable support—"What sort of Sunday school outing is this . . . dirtying up the name of a decent young married woman with a public order of dismissal for drinking?" demanded columnist Westbrook Pegler—Mrs. Jarrett was not reinstated. "It would wreck the American Olympic team," argued Avery Brundage. "I wasn't the only athlete to break training," the swimmer countered. "There were at least a hundred offenders. Why condemn me because I was unwilling to make a secret of the fact that I like champagne?"

Mrs. Jarrett had company in her banishment. Two boxers were also dropped from the American team, ostensibly because they were "homesick." One of the boxers later admitted that he had demonstrated his homesickness by lifting a camera from a German store.

In the track and field competition, the United States, thanks largely to its black auxiliaries, captured twelve of the twenty-three events. But the hosts had one consolation: Germans dominated the weight-throwing categories.

In the shot-put, the opening event, Hans Woellke, a sergeant in the Nazi police, scored Germany's first victory in Olympic track and field history. Hermann Goering promptly promoted him to lieutenant. To add to the honor of the Fatherland, Karl Hein, a carpenter, won the hammer throw, and Gerhard Stoeck, a school teacher, won the javelin throw. Goering promoted neither.

Willie Schroeder, who held the world record in the discus throw, was expected to give the Germans a clean sweep of the weight-throwing events. As he competed, the spectators chanted: "Take the discus in your hand and throw it for the Fatherland." For the Fatherland, Schroeder finished a disappointing fifth. For the United States, Ken Carpenter finished first.

Germany's total of three gold medals was matched by the Finns, who scored, almost by force of habit, in the 5,000-meter run, 10,000-meter run, and 3,000-meter steeplechase. Japan collected two victories and became the sixth different nation in seven games to contribute a Marathon champion.

Juan Carlos Zabala, Argentina's cocky newsboy, was so determined to retain his 1932 Marathon title that he showed up in Germany fully six months before the games and practiced almost daily. He may have left his strength on the practice track, because after setting a brisk pace and holding first place for more than half the race, he collapsed and had to retire. Kitei Son, a Korean-born Japanese student, thought of passing Zabala early in the race, but Britain's Ernest Harper advised him to save his energy. When Zabala began to slow down, Harper, running side by side with Son, told his Japanese rival to move ahead. Son accepted the suggestion and ran the rest of the way in front, beating Harper by two minutes.

No race drew a more glittering field than the 1,500-meter run. The first five finishers from the 1932 race—Luigi Beccali of Italy, John Cornes of Great Britain, Phil Edwards of Canada, Glenn Cunningham of the United States, and Eric Ny of Sweden—were all back and were all in top form. The United States also was represented by a brilliant young Kansan, Archie San Romani, and New Zealand was represented by Jack Lovelock, a slender redhead who was studying to be a doctor in London.

The veterans dominated the early part of the race. Cornes took the lead at the start, Cunningham led at 400 meters, and Ny moved in front at 800 meters. Then Cunningham, holder of the world record for the mile, regained first place. At 1,100 meters, Lovelock, the studious New Zealander, made his bid. He dashed past Cunningham, sprinted the final 400

After a tip from Britain's Ernest Harper (left), Kitei Son of Japan lopes to the Marathon championship.

Karl Schwarzmann of Germany, winner of three gold medals, displays top gymnastics form.

Volmari Iso-Hollo of Finland retains his title in the 3,000-meter steeplechase.

meters in an amazing fifty-seven and eight tenths seconds, and broke the world record for 1,500 meters by a full second. Cunningham, the runner-up, also bettered the world record. The next three finishers—Beccali, San Romani, and Edwards—all shattered the Olympic mark Beccali had set in 1932.

World and Olympic records also fell in the decathlon, won by handsome Glenn Morris of the United States, and in the 400-meter relay, won by the United States. The relay stirred up a controversy within the American squad. Originally, Frank Wykoff, Foy Draper, Marty Glickman, and Sam Stoller were going to represent the United States. But when Italy and Germany showed unexpected speed in the event, Lawson Robertson, the American head coach, dropped Glickman and Stoller and replaced them with Owens and Metcalfe. The American quartet beat Italy in the final by more than ten meters. Unquestionably, the switch had strengthened the United States team, but because Glickman and Stoller were the only Jews on the American track and field squad, some people charged Robertson with appeasing German anti-Semitism. To this day, Glickman, now a prominent sportscaster, insists that Dean Cromwell, an assistant coach under Robertson, instigated the change because of prejudice. "Sure, Owens and Metcalfe were faster than Sam and I," Glickman says, "but we would have won the championship anyway."

The host country, not surprisingly, won the over-all summer championship, with thirty-six gold medals to the United States' twenty-five. The heaviest scorers among the Germans were two splendidly coordinated gymnasts, Karl Schwarzmann and Konrad Frey, who earned three gold medals apiece. But for sheer crowd appeal, the German gymnasts could not match three gifted young ladies.

Marjorie Gestring was a blonde, tanned Californian filled with all the enthusiasm natural to a thirteen-year-old girl. She thoroughly enjoyed the boat trip across the Atlantic, but one day she entered the ship's sick bay and asked the presiding doctor: "Have you anything for seasickness?"

The doctor took out a pill, dropped it in a glass of water, stirred the blend, and handed the glass to Marjorie. "Drink this," he suggested.

The little girl seemed slightly surprised, but she obediently swallowed the mixture.

"Now you'll be all right," said the doctor.

Marjorie gulped. "But I'm not seasick," she finally said. "It's my mother."

Miss Gestring survived the medication and won the Olympic springboard diving championship.

Yet the star of the women's swimming competition was a Dutch girl, Hendrika Mastenbroek. Hendrika was seventeen years old and a pudgy 150 pounds, but her extra weight didn't seem to slow her in the water. She won the 100-meter free style and the 400-meter free style, placed second in the 100-meter backstroke, and led the Dutch 400-meter relay team to a convincing victory. She gathered three gold medals and a

Profiles in courage: Jack Lovelock of New Zealand (top), 1,500-meter champion, and Glenn Morris of the United States, decathlon champion.

silver medal, and her times in the 100-meter and 400-meter free styles were faster than those recorded by any man in the Olympic Games only thirty years earlier. Her 400-meter clocking, in fact, would have brought her home ahead of Norman Ross, the tireless 1920 Olympic champion.

Helen Stephens, a willowy farmer's daughter from Missouri, showed everyone that she, too, was not only a great female athlete, but simply a great athlete. She won the 100-meter dash in eleven and five tenths seconds, precisely half a second faster than the time recorded by champion Tom Burke in 1896. Miss Stephens earned another gold medal when she led the United States relay foursome to the 400-meter championship.

Germany matched the United States' two gold medals in women's track and field. Tilly Fleischer won the javelin throw, and Gisela Mauermayer took her discus in her hand and won a title for the Fatherland. The Germans, obviously, developed muscles in both sexes.

In the winter games, staged at the twin towns of Garmisch-Partenkirchen, a young lady pleased the fancy of the spectators and *der Führer*. The young lady, of course, was Sonja Henie, who won her third figure skating crown, and Hitler spent most of his time staring at her.

For a large percentage of the crowd, the ice hockey games were even more compelling than Miss Henie. Canada, naturally, was favored, but the United States had a strong team, Germany did too, and Great Britain put forth a squad consisting of two Englishmen and all the rest English-born Canadians. One of the British-Canadians was Jimmy Foster, the most talented amateur goalie in the world, and the Canadians energetically protested his eligibility. Foster was under suspension in Canada because he had defected to Great Britain without permission; Canadian officials demanded that the suspension be honored in the Olympics. Fortunately for the British, the demand was rejected.

When the hockey competition drew to a close, the Canadian team, powerful as always, had scored a total of fifty-four goals and had allowed only seven goals in eight games. No other team in the tournament had scored even twenty goals.

Yet, incredibly, the Canadians did not win the title. Great Britain won, sparked by the miraculous play of Jimmy Foster. In seven games, Foster allowed only three goals to slip past him. He shut out Sweden, Japan, and Czechoslovakia; kept the United States scoreless in a 0–0 tie; held Germany to a 1–1 draw; and sparked victories over Canada, 2–1, and Hungary, 5–1.

Canada finished second with seven victories and one defeat, and the United States placed third with five victories, two defeats, and the tie with England. The American defense was almost as stingy as the British; the United States gave up only four goals, but three of them came at the wrong time. Canada stopped the Americans, 1–0, and Italy scored a 2–1 upset.

The winter team title, after its temporary trip to the United

With Hermann Goering and Joseph Goebbels looking on, Adolf Hitler pays his compliments to Sonja Henie.

States in 1932, returned to Norway. In addition to Miss Henie, the Norwegians provided two male stars—Ivar Ballangrud and Birger Ruud.

Ballangrud, blond, thirty-three years old, was the Jesse Owens of the ice. He entered four speed skating events, and finished first at 500 meters, first at 5,000 meters, first at 10,000 meters, and, inexplicably, second at 1,500 meters. He had won his first Olympic gold medal eight years earlier.

After the 1936 games, Ballangrud was asked if he was going to retire. His reply was perfectly logical. All he said was "Why?"

For the second straight Olympics, Ruud won the ski jumping championship. Then, to demonstrate his versatility, he finished first in the downhill race and fourth in the Alpine Combined championship (downhill and slalom). Ruud came from a jumping family. His brother Sigmund won the United States ski jumping championship in 1937, and his brother Asbjorn won the world ski jumping championship in 1938. A few years later, all three Ruud brothers were guests of the Germans—in a Nazi concentration camp; they had refused to turn Quisling.

World War II blotted out any pleasant memories of the 1936 games. Germany ravaged Europe, and the festivities of the Olympics became only a grim recollection. The 1940 Olympic Games, ironically, had been awarded to Tokyo, but by 1940, the Japanese were preoccupied with plotting their attack on Pearl Harbor.

Twelve years passed between the 1936 games and the next Olympics. Shortly before the war began, Baron Pierre de Coubertin died at the age of 78, not knowing the troubles awaiting his dream and the world. Nations fell, and millions died. Great athletes, men who might have been Olympic champions, lost their lives in battle. The ancient Greeks had stopped their wars for the Olympics, but World War II stopped only when Hitler's hordes lost their might. And then, in 1948, the Olympics began again, larger and more spectacular than ever before.

1

Women
at
Work

3

4

5

1  Russian gymnasts, 1952
2  Inga Britt Loretson, Sweden, high jump, 1960
3  Jaroslaw Jazwiakowska, Poland, high jump, second place, 19
4  Thelma Hopkins, Great Britain, high jump, second place, 195
5  Iolanda Balas, Rumania, high jump champion, 1960
6  Ingrid Kramer, Germany, diving champion, 1960
7  Marjorie Gestring, United States, diving champion, 1936
8  Pat McCormick, United States, diving champion, 1952 and 1

7

6　8

223

9  Tamara Tishkyevich, U.S.S.R., shot-put champion, 1956
10  Earlene Brown, United States, discus, 1956
11  Jaroslava Kritkova, Czechoslovakia, shot-put, 1952
12  Tamara Press, U.S.S.R., shot-put champion, 1960
13  Nina Ponomareva, U.S.S.R., discus champion, 1960
14  Olga Connolly, United States, discus, 1960
15  Elene Gorchakova, U.S.S.R., javelin, 1952

16    17

226

18

16 Betty Cuthbert, Australia, sprint champion, 1956
17 Irina Press, U.S.S.R., hurdles champion, 1960
18 Wilma Rudolph, United States, sprint champion, 1960

**19** Mary Bignall, Great Britain, broad jump, 1960
**20** Norma Fleming, Australia, broad jump, 1960
**21** Elizbieta Krzeskinska, Poland, broad jump, 1960
**22** Vera Krepkina, U.S.S.R., broad jump champion, 1960

23   24

25    26

**23**  Agnes Keleti, Hungary, gymnastics champion, 1952 and 1956
**24**  Larisa Latynina, U.S.S.R., gymnastics champion, 1956 and 1960
**25**  Ernestine Jean Russell, Canada, 1956
**26**  Ikeda Keiko, Japan, 1960

231

Bob Mathias skims over the hurdles during the battle for the decathlon championship.

# The
# All-American Boy

## CHAPTER FOURTEEN : 1948 – LONDON AND ST. MORITZ

Once upon a time, in a little California town called Tulare, not far from where Disneyland stands today, there lived a sickly little boy who suffered from anemia. He was short and thin and weak, but he was an obedient little boy. He listened to his mother and his father, and he ate all the right foods, and he slept at least twelve hours every day. And when he grew up, tall and husky and strong, he was the best athlete in the whole world, and he married a beautiful girl and became a rich, handsome movie actor. Ridiculous, isn't it?

And it all happens to be true.

The story of Robert Bruce Mathias, the boy who grew up in Tulare, sounds like a fairy tale. In March, 1948, Bob Mathias was completely unknown outside California's San Joaquin Valley. Five months later, when he represented the United States in the Olympic decathlon championship, Bob Mathias became known everywhere in the world.

After the first three events of the decathlon, Enrique Kistenmacher, a sturdy Army officer from Argentina, held first place. A Frenchman, Ignace Heinrich, was second, a few points ahead of Mathias. The fourth event was the high jump.

To stay in contention for the championship, Mathias knew he had to high jump at least six feet. But when the bar was set at merely five feet nine inches, he failed to clear it on his first try. On his second attempt, he crashed into the crossbar once more. He had only one chance left.

The air was heavy and the ground damp at Wembley Stadium in London, and Mathias wrapped himself in a blanket to keep warm. As he waited before his final jump at five feet nine inches, he worried and thought and, finally, came to a decision. "Forget about form," he told himself. "Just get over that bar."

Then, instead of approaching the bar from the side, as he normally did, he lined up almost directly in front of it, took a deep breath, sprinted, and jumped. He was awkward. He was off balance. But he was effective. He cleared the crossbar, then went on to leap six feet one and one quarter inches.

One of the spectators at Wembley Stadium, Brutus Hamilton, the track coach at the University of California and a former Olympic decathlon man, nodded knowingly. "The kid's going to win it," Hamilton told a companion.

The kid won it.

Defying all logic, Bob Mathias won the 1948 Olympic decathlon championship. Since the days of Jim Thorpe, the decathlon has been the supreme test of track and field ability and versatility. By common consent, the man who wins the decathlon is accepted as the greatest athlete in the world. But the man who won the decathlon in 1948 was just a boy. He was only seventeen years old.

Mathias was not only young. He was incredibly inexperienced. Four months before the Olympics, he had never held a javelin in his hand, had never pole-vaulted, had never run 1,500 meters in competition, and had rarely run 400 meters or the sprints or broad jumped. He was simply a talented schoolboy athlete—with a knack for the hurdles, high jump, and discus throw—until the day late in April, 1948, when his Tulare High coach, Virgil Jackson, suggested he take up the decathlon. "You'll be a cinch to make the Olympic team in 1952," Jackson predicted.

Mathias progressed far more rapidly than he or his coach or anyone else could have dreamed possible. Barely a month after he started training for the ten-event competition—at the beginning, he couldn't vault even eight feet—Mathias entered a decathlon meet for the first time. Competing against several college stars, he won first place. Two weeks later, he won the United States decathlon championship. Six weeks later, he was in the Olympics.

The Olympic decathlon was a murderous test, split over two days as always, five events to a day. Even with his fine showing in the high jump, Mathias finished the first day in third place, still trailing Kistenmacher and Heinrich. The muscular young American, six feet two inches tall and 190 pounds, arose at 7 a.m. the following morning, ate a steak for breakfast at 8 a.m., and at 10:30 a.m., competed in the 110-meter high hurdles, the first of the day's events.

Before the race, Kistenmacher approached Mathias and tried to apply gamesmanship. "Mathematically," said the Argentinean, "I have it figured out you can't beat me."

Mathematically, the Argentinean was wrong.

After the completion of the hurdles and the discus, Mathias

swept into first place. In a steady rain, he added to his lead in the pole vault and in the javelin. A little more than an hour before midnight, after twelve full hours of intense pressure and competition, with the track softened to mud, with floodlights spraying weird shadows, with only a handful of the original 70,000 spectators remaining in Wembley Stadium, Bob Mathias completed the 1,500-meter run and became the youngest decathlon champion in Olympic history.

"What are you going to do to celebrate?" someone asked.

"Start shaving, I guess," said Mathias.

Then the young star turned serious. "I never worked so long and so hard for anything in my life," he said. "I wouldn't do this again for a million dollars."

But Mathias did do it again, and again, and again. He won the United States decathlon championship in 1949 and in 1950, then skipped the 1951 competition. In the fall of 1951, he put his strength and skill to work on the football field for Stanford University. Although he had played no football during his first two years in college—at Tulare High, he had excelled in both football and basketball—he quickly became Stanford's most dangerous runner. Playing fullback, he averaged better than four yards per carry, ran ninety-six yards for a touchdown in the decisive game against Southern California, and led Stanford to the Rose Bowl. (In the Rose Bowl, with Mathias hobbled by an ankle injury, Illinois crushed Stanford, 40–7.)

In 1952, Mathias returned to the decathlon and regained his United States championship. Then, in July, in the Olympic Games in Helsinki, he broke the world record in his specialty and won the championship by more than nine hundred points, the widest margin in Olympic history. Event for event, Mathias surpassed Jim Thorpe's 1912 performances in everything except the 1,500-meter run. Man for man, he would have defeated Thorpe by 1,600 points.

At the end of 1952, largely for his decathlon record and partly for his football play, Mathias won the Associated Press poll as the outstanding athlete of the year. By then, of course, he was accustomed to honors. In 1948, he had earned the James E. Sullivan Award, presented annually to the "amateur athlete who, by performance, example and good influence, did most to advance the cause of good sportsmanship during the year."

Mathias retired from athletic competition after 1952. He acted for a while, then was elected to Congress. His imprint on sports was indelible. He had never in his life been defeated in a decathlon competition.

The amazing rush job that Mathias had performed in preparing for the 1948 decathlon was matched only by the British rush job in preparing for the 1948 Olympics. Lord Burghley, the prewar hurdles champion, was chairman of the British Olympic Committee, and considering that England still bore the scars of World War II, his organization did a magnificent job. For the most part, the British utilized existing facilities.

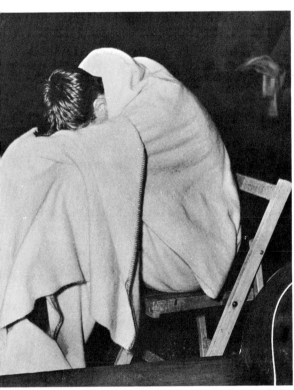
Before the 1,500-meter run, the final phase of the long decathlon grind, Mathias tries to rest.

Mel Patton (71) beats Barney Ewell (70) to the tape in the 200-meter dash.

The country could spare neither the money nor the materials necessary to construct an Olympic Village. Instead, the men stayed at an Army camp in Uxbridge and the women in dormitories at Southlands College.

After a lapse of twelve years, the lure of the Olympics proved stronger than ever. A record total of fifty-nine countries entered 4,030 men and 438 women in the 1948 summer games. King George VI presided over the opening ceremonies, and as 83,000 spectators filled Wembley Stadium to its capacity, the pigeons of peace flew once more, the Olympic flag waved again, and the Olympic torch glowed bright as ever. Notably absent from the games were the Germans and the Japanese, the instigators of World War II.

In men's track and field, still the core of the games, the traditional assault upon the Olympic records was remarkable for its mildness. In the twenty-two standard events (excluding the two walking races, which have been held at various distances at various times), only seven Olympic records fell, an historical low. Had athletes suddenly stopped progressing? Not at all. One logical explanation was that international athletic contests, of course, had been suspended during World War II, and without the incentive of topflight competition, the best athletes had suffered in their development. A second, and equally logical, explanation was that the conditions in London were abominable. It rained almost every day during the competitions, and on the rare occasions when the sky was clear, the track remained soggy. It was a meet for mudders.

The United States demonstrated convincingly that, wet or dry, it still had the most powerful track and field team in the world. But, significantly, more countries than ever before produced individual stars; ten different nations, an Olympic high, contributed track and field champions. The United States won eleven events, Sweden won five (including the two walks) for its finest showing since the 1912 games in Stockholm, and eight other countries won one apiece. Jamaica, Belgium, and Czechoslovakia each boasted its first Olympic track and field champion. Belgium's Gaston Reiff, at 5,000 meters, and Czechoslovakia's Emil Zatopek, at 10,000 meters, ended the long Finnish reign in the distance races. The Finns, in fact, were totally shut out in running events for the first time since 1908; they did maintain their mastery in one field event. Tapio Rautavaara gave Finland its fourth javelin championship in six Olympics.

For the first time in Olympic history, no man won more than one individual track and field event. But there were dramatic contests and dramatic heroes.

Mel Patton, a tall, slender Californian, was the chief United States hope in the 100-meter dash. On May 15, 1948, he had run 100 yards in nine and three tenths seconds, a world record that remained unmatched for six years. Patton was an incredibly tense competitor. "Before a race," he once said, "I feel weak, weak as a kitten. I feel too tired to warm up, and I don't warm up much." In a race, with his high knee action and his short back kick, all Patton's tension turned to speed. Afterward, usually, he disappeared under the stands and got sick. "It's gotten to be a damn bad habit," he said.

Patton knew that his opposition in the Olympic 100-meter sprint was formidable. Lloyd La Beach, a Panamanian, and Barney Ewell, an American, posed the most serious threats. La Beach had shared the world record for 100 yards until

Harrison Dillard (far left) gets a quick start in the 100-meter dash.

Patton shattered it in May. Ewell, although he was thirty-one years old, had beaten Patton and had won the 100-meter dash in the United States Olympic trials in ten and two tenths seconds, faster than the Olympic record.

Two Englishmen, Alistair McCorquodale and Emmanuel McDonald-Bailey, and another American, Harrison "Bones" Dillard, also qualified for the final, but none of the three figured to press Patton, La Beach, and Ewell. Dillard, unfortunately, seemed to be in the wrong event. A Negro from Cleveland, a childhood worshiper of Jesse Owens, an ex-soldier whom General George S. Patton, Jr., once called "the best goddam athlete I've ever seen," Dillard was unquestionably the finest high hurdler in the world. In one stretch spanning 1947 and 1948, he won eighty-two consecutive races, some of them sprints, most of them over the hurdles. But in the Olympic trials for the 110-meter high hurdles, Dillard, an overwhelming favorite, hit one hurdle so hard that he slipped, fell, and didn't even bother to finish the race. He barely salvaged an Olympic trip by placing a distant third behind Ewell and Patton in the 100-meter trials.

In the 100-meter final at London, Patton, Ewell, and La Beach, the leading contenders, drew lanes one, two, and three. Then came the two Englishmen and, in the outside lane, Dillard. Ewell broke well at the start and pounded down the track, watching his two rivals out of the corners of his eyes. Patton faded early, the victim of a poor start, and as Ewell lunged toward the tape, he knew he had beaten La Beach by inches. When he passed the finish line, Ewell leaped into the air and danced a victory dance. "Well, I guess I took that one," said Ewell, happily, to Dillard.

"I'm not so sure," said Dillard. "Let's wait and see."

Ewell soon saw his error. While he had been studying Patton and La Beach, Dillard had stormed out of the blocks on the outside, built up tremendous speed during the middle of the race, and held on to win. Bones Dillard, the retread hurdler, mounted the victory pedestal.

"When I stood there listening to the Star-Spangled Banner and seeing the American flag fluttering and watching my name hoisted on that huge scoreboard," said Dillard later, "I felt that this was the end—the absolute climax to everything for me. On my neck, the hair was standing out and I tingled all over with the greatest moment I'll ever experience."

Four years later, in the 1952 Olympic Games, Dillard experienced another great moment. In Helsinki, he won his specialty, the 110-meter high hurdles, and added another gold medal to his collection.

Patton finished a dreadful fifth in the 100-meter dash. But he had one chance left to redeem himself. Three days later, he reached the final of the 200-meter dash. Once more, he had to face Ewell and La Beach. Dillard was not entered, but Herb McKenley of Jamaica presented a definite challenge.

Shortly before the start of the race, Marshall Smith, the

Mudders in action: Enrique Kistenmacher of Argentina (432) leads Irv Mondschein of the United States (616) in the decathlon 1,500-meter run (above), and Henry Eriksson of Sweden (194) beats his favored countryman, Lennart Strand (195), in the 1,500-meter final (right).

sports editor of *Life* magazine, visited Patton in the locker room. The two had become friendly before the games.

"Hello, Mel," Smith said.

Patton said nothing.

"What's the matter?" Smith said.

Patton stared at the ceiling.

"What happened in the hundred?"

Patton finally looked at Smith. "I guess I tied up, that's all," he whispered.

Smith realized that Patton was still tied up, and that, unless he relaxed soon, he was going to lose the 200-meter dash, too.

"Are you all through over here after this race?" Smith asked.

"Got the relay tomorrow," said Patton.

"That's great!" Smith said. "I'm going over to Paris the day after tomorrow, and you're going with me."

"Can't," said Patton. "No money."

"Forget it," Smith said. "I'm loaded. I'll wangle it on the expense account. The plane fare doesn't amount to anything and we can share a hotel room. We'll have the wildest weekend on record. You ought to be about ready to break training."

For the first time since his defeat, Patton brightened. "This is going to be great," he said.

A few minutes later, in the final of the 200-meter dash, Patton exploded from the start and—although Barney Ewell made a brilliant bid in the last twenty meters—never surrendered the lead. Ewell finished second, La Beach third, and McKenley fourth.

McKenley was not particularly disturbed by his failure to win a medal in the 200-meter dash. He knew, and everyone else knew, that his specialty was the 400-meter run. McKenley, by a wide margin, was the finest 400-meter runner in the world. He held the world record for 400 meters and for 440 yards. Jesse Abramson of the New York *Herald Tribune* called McKenley "the strongest kind of favorite, the surest sure thing of these games."

"Once I go around that last turn into the homestretch in the lead," McKenley once said, "nobody is going to beat me."

In the Olympic 400-meter final, McKenley went around the last turn into the homestretch four meters in the lead. It appeared that nobody was going to beat him. Then, with enormous nine-foot strides, another Jamaican, Arthur Wint, six feet four inches tall, began cutting into McKenley's lead.

McKenley and Wint were old friends and old rivals. They had been schoolmates at Calabar High School in Jamaica. But for the five years preceding the 1948 Olympics, McKenley had been living in the United States, attending Boston College and the University of Illinois, and he hadn't seen much of Wint. Now, in London, he was suddenly seeing too much of Wint.

With twenty meters to go, Wint drew even with McKenley. Then, inexorably, Wint pulled in front and won by one of his huge strides.

For days before the event, McKenley had been telling sports-

Mal Whitfield (136) takes over the lead during the 800-meter final.

writers that he was not a cinch to win, that Wint could beat him. "Now," said McKenley, after the race, "will you believe all that I told you about Wint?"

In Helsinki four years later, Wint and McKenley dueled again in the 400-meter final. Wint couldn't catch McKenley in 1952, but McKenley couldn't catch a third Jamaican, George Rhoden, and Rhoden captured the race. McKenley finally got his gold metal, however, in Helsinki. He, Wint, Rhoden, and Leslie Laing won the 1,600-meter relay championship.

Next to McKenley at 400 meters, the surest bet in the 1948 games was Sweden's Lennart Strand at 1,500 meters. Strand had run the distance in three minutes and forty-three seconds, and no one ever ran faster until 1954. But, like McKenley, Strand failed in London. In rain and mud, another Swede, Henry Eriksson, a twenty-nine-year-old fireman who had made a career of trailing Strand, won the Olympic 1,500 meters. Ironically, three heavy favorites—Patton at 100 meters, McKenley at 400, and Strand at 1,500—had each been beaten by a countryman.

There were other male stars in track and field—Mal Whitfield, a United States Army Air Force sergeant, broke the Olympic record in the 800-meter run, and Adolfo Consolini, a thirty-one-year-old Italian giant, broke the Olympic record in the discus throw—but none of them could match the spectacular performance of a thirty-year-old Dutch housewife, a lean, likable blonde named Fanny Blankers-Koen.

When she was seventeen years old, in 1935, Fanny had set her sights on becoming an Olympic champion. "I've made up my mind to go in for sports," she explained to a Dutch swimming coach, "but I don't know which to pick—swimming or track and field."

In a semi-final of the 80-meter hurdles, Fanny Blankers-Koen of the Netherlands demonstrates her championship style.

The coach recommended track and field. "We have plenty of good swimmers already," he said.

At the Berlin Olympics, Fanny tied for sixth place in the high jump. Then she went home to wait twelve long years for another chance in the Olympics. She did not waste her time; she acquired a husband and two children.

In 1948, at Wembley Stadium, Fanny Blankers-Koen compiled the finest record of any woman in Olympic history. Surpassing the 1932 accomplishments of Babe Didrikson, the quiet housewife won the 100-meter dash, the 200-meter dash, and the 80-meter hurdles, then anchored the Netherlands 400-meter relay team to another championship. Because, like Didrikson sixteen years earlier, she was limited to three individual events, Fanny did not enter the broad jump or the high jump—even though she held the women's world record in both events.

When she returned to the Netherlands, with her four gold medals, thousands of Dutchmen staged a reception for her in Amsterdam. She rode, with her husband and her two children, from the railroad station to the town hall in an open coach drawn by four white horses. "All I've done is run fast," she said. "I don't quite see why people should make so much fuss about that."

Aside from the men's track and field performers—and, perhaps, including the men's track and field performers—Fanny Blankers-Koen, who made a final, unsuccessful Olympic appearance in 1952, was clearly the outstanding competitor in London. But others, too, in sports that are rarely publicized, stirred up a fuss. Denmark introduced a brilliant twenty-year-old sailor named Paul Elvstrom. In 1948, Elvstrom, a husky 200-pounder, won the Firefly class in yachting competition. When the Firefly class was dropped after the London games,

Elvstrom switched to the Finn Monotype and earned Olympic championships in 1952, 1956, and 1960. He is known today throughout the small-boat sailing world as "The Master."

The modern master of canoeing also made his first Olympic appearance in 1948. Gert Fredriksson of Sweden paddled his way to two victories in 1948, one in 1952, two in 1956, and one in 1960, matching Elvstrom's feat of winning gold medals in four consecutive Olympics.

Fredriksson helped Sweden to second place in the over-all standings in the London games. The Swedes collected seventeen gold medals; the United States collected thirty-eight. For the Americans, three men of widely varying sizes made significant contributions. One was broad (five feet nine inches tall and 220 pounds), one was towering (seven feet tall), and one was tiny (five feet one and one quarter inches tall).

The tiny American was Dr. Sammy Lee, a Korean-American who served as an eye, ear, and nose specialist in the Army Medical Corps. He was also a specialist in high diving. He won the Olympic championship in 1948 and then, after a temporary retirement, came back in 1952, at the age of thirty-one, and successfully defended his title.

The towering American was Bob "Foothills" Kurland, a graduate of Oklahoma A.&M. who, naturally, played center on the United States Olympic basketball team. With Kurland and such future professional stars as Alex Groza, Ralph Beard, and Vince Boryla, the Americans had no trouble winning the 1948 basketball championship. The United States, in fact, never had trouble winning the Olympic basketball title—till 1972. Through 1968, Americans won every game they played in the Olympics.

The broad American was John Henry Davis, a Brooklyn garage mechanic who reigned, by acclamation, as the strongest man in the world. Davis won the heavyweight weight-lifting championship in the 1948 Olympics and again in 1952. Olympic weight-lifting competition combines three different lifts—the military press, the snatch, and the clean and jerk; the man who lifts the most total pounds in the three categories earns the championship.

"In the press," Davis once explained, "you pull the barbell to your chest. Then you push it to locked arms overhead, maintaining an erect position and using only the strength of the arms and shoulders.

"To perform the snatch, you must pull the barbell from the floor to fully locked arms overhead without a pause. You are permitted to lunge or split under the barbell by springing your legs front and back—or you can squat under it as it goes up.

"The clean and jerk is done by pulling the barbell to your chest in one movement, splitting or squatting under it when you can't pull it all the way up. Then you have to drive it overhead by a combined leg and arm thrust, again splitting under the weight as it goes up."

It sounds complicated, but Davis always made it look easy. He lifted 997 pounds in 1948, then went up to 1,013 pounds in 1952.

American Bob Kurland, seven feet tall, towers over Egypt and over his teammates.

The strong man's real ambition was to sing at the Met. He once gave four concerts in Sweden and made a record, "The Blind Ploughman," for a Swedish recording company. "I was supposed to collect royalties after 3,000 records had been sold," he said a few years later. "At the last count, the total was seventy-one, so you can see there's plenty of room for improvement."

Davis had no monopoly on muscles in the 1948 Olympics. Two tough boxers had muscle and skill to match. And both had their share of headaches.

Pascual Perez, a flyweight from Argentina, had to keep his weight at the prescribed limit of 112 pounds or lower. When he weighed in before his quarter-final match, he was slightly over the limit. His teammates promptly began to trim his black hair. Then they rubbed him down with towels, scraped dirt off the soles of his feet, and dusted off the scales with a paint brush. Perez stepped back on the scales. Still too heavy.

Overweight meant automatic disqualification, and Perez grew furious. He began to cry and tore the remaining hairs out of his head. He yelled and shouted and protested.

And then someone examined the scales. They were out of order. Perez had been under the weight limit all along. He went on to win the Olympic championship, later won the professional flyweight championship of the world, and established himself as one of the greatest flyweights in history. His hair, eventually, grew back.

Laszlo Papp of Hungary almost lost his hair in the Olympics too. But for Papp, the cause would have been old age, not fury. In 1948, he won the middleweight championship. In 1952, he won the light middleweight championship. In 1956, he retained the light middleweight title. He was the first boxer in Olympic history to earn three gold medals, but he was not happy. All his best early opponents had turned professional, and Laszlo wanted to turn professional too. There was only one problem. Communist Hungary, like Communist Russia, did not recognize professional athletes. For Papp, the Hungarians made an exception. In 1957, at the age of thirty-one, he began his professional boxing career. By the fall of 1963, at the age of thirty-seven, he was still undefeated in some twenty-five pro fights. And he was the professional middleweight champion of Europe.

In 1948, by tradition, separate winter Olympics were conducted several months before the summer games. When President Enrico Celio of Switzerland proclaimed the opening of the winter games at St. Moritz, he called them a "symbol of a new world of peace and good will."

On the same day, American bobsledders found that two of their sleds had been sabotaged, a hockey game between Canada and Sweden ended with fists flying on both sides, speed skaters from eleven nations threatened to strike over the racing rules, and two separate hockey teams showed up to represent the United States. The new world of peace had a familiar touch of chaos.

Dr. Sammy Lee of the United States Army slices the water after a perfect back dive.

Eventually, of course, most of the problems were ironed out. But the problem of the two American hockey teams was never solved. One had been sent by the Amateur Hockey Association, one by the United States Olympic Committee. The Amateur Hockey Association was the proper organization to deal with international events, but the Olympic Committee, of course, was the proper organization to deal with Olympic events. What could be done? The authorities took direct action. They made both American teams ineligible for the Olympic championship. It didn't make much difference. Canada, as expected, won the ice hockey title, anyway.

Two of the most glamorous stars to emerge from the winter games were the two figure skating champions, Barbara Ann Scott of Canada and Dick Button of the United States.

Miss Scott, the heir to Sonja Henie, had achieved notoriety a year before the Olympics, when her native city, Ottawa, in celebration of her skill, presented her with a canary yellow convertible automobile. Avery Brundage—then simply a member, not president, of the International Olympic Committee—took offense. He notified Miss Scott that if she accepted the car, she would be dangerously suspect of professionalism. All patriotic Canadians promptly declared war upon Brundage; he was vilified from Quebec to Vancouver.

Miss Scott, a sparkling, blue-eyed, brown-haired twenty-year-old beauty, cried as she gave up the car in order to maintain her amateur standing. Then, in January, 1948, she went to St. Moritz, captured the Olympic championship and, a short time later, bid farewell to amateurism. In May, 1948, she allowed Ottawa to give her the car again, repainted this time a handsome powder blue.

No one offered to give Dick Button a car before the 1948 games. It was just as well. He was only eighteen years old, and he had no time to polish his driving technique. At St. Moritz, in the weeks leading up to the figure skating competition, he followed a Spartan schedule. Each day, he began skating at 9 a.m. and practiced compulsory figures until 11. Then he worked on his free skating for an hour and a half, sneaked in a quick lunch, and returned to the ice for two more hours of figures and an extra half hour of free skating. "I'm all set to be carried to bed at about 8:30," Button confessed.

When he was younger, his mother had wanted him to be a pianist. As a reward for practicing the piano faithfully, he received his first pair of ice skates, a $13 pair. "This is so that you'll practice the piano more often," his mother said.

"Now," said Button, in St. Moritz, "my father buys me $100 skates and my mother never even mentions the piano."

Button won the Olympic figure skating title in 1948 and again in 1952. Then, generally considered the finest figure skater in history, he decided to turn professional. Button, a student at Harvard Law School, did not receive a car. He received a contract guaranteeing him $150,000 for one year of appearances with "The Ice Capades."

Gretchen Fraser hurtles through the gates of the slalom course.

Figure skating champion Dick Button glides across the ice at St. Moritz.

Dick Button was the first American ever to win a figure skating championship in the Olympics. The United States made another breakthrough at St. Moritz in 1948. An attractive twenty-eight-year-old housewife who wore her hair in pigtails, Gretchen Fraser of Vancouver, Washington, upset the highly favored European girls and won the women's downhill skiing title. "I'm surprised," Mrs. Fraser admitted after her victory. "Surprised and very happy."

Sweden and Norway each collected four gold medals to lead all nations in the snow sports. The Swedes won three Nordic skiing championships and one speed skating championship; the Norwegians reversed the scheme and won three speed skating titles and one Nordic skiing title. By the end of the winter games, which attracted a record total of 878 competitors from twenty-eight countries, peace and goodwill were in evidence once more.

Yet a shadow hung over the 1948 Olympic Games, over the winter sports and the summer sports. It was the shadow of the Russian bear. In 1947, the Soviet Union had been admitted to the International Olympic Committee. The Russians could have competed in the 1948 Olympics, but they chose not to. They simply sent observers to study the stars and styles of other countries. Behind the Iron Curtain, the Russians were gathering their strength. They didn't want to make a weak start. They were aiming at the 1952 Olympics, and they were aiming to be best.

245

Emil Zatopek of Czechoslovakia grunts, groans, and runs all
rivals into the ground.

# Emil The Terrible

## CHAPTER FIFTEEN : 1952 – HELSINKI AND OSLO

*"Bobbing, weaving, staggering, gyrating, clutching his torso, flinging supplicating glances toward the heavens, he ran like a man with a noose about his neck."*

—RED SMITH
Describing Emil Zatopek

To watch Emil Zatopek run a race was to watch torture endured. He suffered with every stride. He trembled with every turn. He died with every lap. "He runs," an admirer once said, "like a man who has just been stabbed in the heart."

Born in Koprinivince, Czechoslovakia, the short, wiry son of a poor carpenter, Emil Zatopek made agony his trademark. As he ran—5,000 meters or 10,000 meters or longer—his face burned red, his tongue jutted out, his hands tightened into fists, and his whole expression shouted pain.

But the strangest part of Zatopek's strange contortions was that, in fact, he felt no pain at all. His legs betrayed him. Flicking across the ground in short, smooth strides that almost never varied, never faltered, never even hinted of fatigue, they revealed his secret: His tortured looks were only for effect, like the grunts of a boxer delivering a hard punch or the moans of an actor playing a death scene.

Zatopek could be Lear one moment and Falstaff the next. He loved a broad joke. Once, in a trial heat of an Olympic race, while all his rivals strained for speed, Zatopek playfully accelerated and decelerated, changing gears until he dropped back next to a lagging American runner and said, "Hurry up—or you'll miss the bus." Then Zatopek dashed away, in high gear once more.

If Zatopek seemed part actor and part artist, he was all perfectionist. Britain's Roger Bannister, the first man to run a mile in less than four minutes, called Zatopek "without doubt the greatest athlete of the postwar world." His greatness sprang from dedication. A career military man—he achieved the rank of colonel in the Czech Army—Zatopek arose at six each morning during his competitive years, exercised every day, and ran at least ten miles each day. Sometimes he ran twenty miles, sometimes twenty-five, alternating between sprinting and jogging. Often he trained in heavy army boots. "Hundreds of lesser athletes have only given themselves blisters trying to follow his example," Bannister said.

In 1948, in London, Zatopek, then twenty-five years old, his blond hair already thinning, entered the Olympics, won the 10,000-meter race and placed second in the 5,000-meter race. "Witnesses who have long since forgotten the other events," columnist Red Smith later wrote, "still wake up screaming in the dark when Emil the Terrible goes writhing through their dreams, gasping, groaning, clawing at his abdomen in horrible extremities of pain."

In 1952, in Helsinki, before Finns conditioned to long-distance excellence, before an audience that included Paavo Nurmi and Hannes Kolehmainen, Zatopek staged the most impressive demonstration of long-distance running in Olympic history.

He competed first in the 10,000-meter run. For more than a quarter of the race, he stayed back in the pack. After 3,000 meters, his face twisted in anguish, Zatopek moved into the lead. From then on, no one could catch him. Occasionally, he would appear to be on the brink of collapse, and suddenly he would sprint to discourage his pursuers. He won the event in twenty-nine minutes seventeen seconds, forty-two seconds faster than his own Olympic record.

"I am disappointed," Zatopek complained afterward. "I was not fast. I was bad, very bad. I will try to do better in the 5,000-meter run."

Not since 1912, when Kolehmainen won the 5,000-meter and 10,000-meter races in Stockholm, had any man captured both Olympic championships. To match Kolehmainen, Zatopek had to overcome an imposing field, led by Herbert Schade of Germany, who had set an Olympic record of fourteen minutes fifteen and four tenths seconds in his qualifying heat.

For 4,000 meters in the 5,000-meter final, Schade clung to the lead. Then Zatopek briefly took command. Eight hundred meters from the finish, Schade and Britain's Chris Chataway slipped past him; 400 meters later, Zatopek surged back in front. But as he entered the backstretch on the final lap, he fell behind Schade, Chataway, and Alain Mimoun, a French Algerian. On the last turn, as a three-man traffic jam on the inside caused Chataway to tumble to the track, Zatopek stormed past his opponents on the outside, and cutting nine seconds off Schade's Olympic mark, won the 5,000-meter championship. Mimoun came in second, a fate he knew well. The Algerian had finished second to Zatopek at 10,000 meters in 1948 and in 1952.

A few minutes after the 5,000-meter run, the Zatopek family

collected another gold medal. Emil's wife, Dana, was an athlete too. She won the women's javelin competition and, naturally, set an Olympic record.

To celebrate his victories at 5,000 and 10,000 meters, Zatopek announced that three days later he would compete in the Marathon. Few people expected him to win, mainly because he had never run a Marathon before. But Zatopek had no doubts. "If I didn't think I could win," he said, "I wouldn't have entered."

Fifteen miles after the start of the twenty-six-mile endurance test, Zatopek, Gustav Jansson of Sweden, and Jim Peters of Great Britain were well in front of the field, trotting along at a brisk pace. Zatopek, who spoke five languages, slowed down and allowed Peters, the prerace favorite, to draw even with him. "Excuse me," said the Czech, in fluent English. "I haven't run a Marathon before, but don't you think we ought to go a bit faster?"

Zatopek may have been seeking advice—or he may have been practicing gamesmanship. A few miles later, Peters, unable to keep pace with the Czech, developed cramps and quit the race. Calmly, smoothly, foregoing his usual groans and grimaces, Zatopek breezed to victory, breaking the Olympic record by more than six minutes and defeating the runner-up by more than two and a half minutes, the most decisive Marathon margin since the 1924 games. "The Marathon," Zatopek told reporters, "is a very boring race."

From the Finnish spectators' point of view, it was appropriate that a long-distance runner emerged as the hero of the Helsinki games. From a historical point of view, it was appropriate that the hero came from a country behind the Iron Curtain. For in 1952, for the first time, the Soviet Union entered the Olympics.

The Russians could have competed in 1948; their entry had been cleared by the International Olympic Committee in 1947. But the Soviets realized that their athletes were not yet gifted enough to dominate the games and, rather than risk embarrassing defeats by capitalist countries, sent only coaches and trainers to London. The Russian delegates analyzed American and Western European athletes, took copious notes, and snapped thousands of photographs. Then, filled with new knowledge of techniques and training methods, they returned home, eager to prepare for 1952.

Between 1948 and 1952, the Soviet government lavished millions of dollars on a national sports program designed to develop international champions. The Russians admitted that they intended to use the Olympic Games for propaganda purposes. "Sports," said Pjotr Sobolev, secretary-general of the Russian Olympic Committee, "will be a weapon in the fight for peace and for the promotion of friendship among all peoples."

In 1952, with the Korean War still raging, peace and friendship were taking a beating. The Russians began the sports year by spurning the winter Olympics in Oslo. Then

Even in Helsinki, Stalin dominates the Russian training camp.

they refused to allow the Olympic torch to be carried across Soviet territory, a decision that added thousands of miles to the trip from Greece to Finland. Finally, although the Soviets did enter the summer games, they announced that their athletes would not live within the Olympic Village in Helsinki, but would fly in daily from Leningrad.

Eventually, the Russians abandoned their scheme for an airlift each day and, instead, set up a separate Iron Curtain Olympic Village in Otaniemi, near the Soviet-owned Porkkala Naval Base in Finland. Surrounded by barbed wire, the Communist village housed the Russian squad and the teams of the satellite nations. The Russians decorated their quarters with a huge banner bearing a portrait of Stalin; the Hungarians, not to be outdone, put up an even larger portrait of Stalin. The Soviets seemed chillingly aloof; at first, they allowed no visitors within the Iron Curtain village.

But once the Russians settled down and started sharing Finnish practice facilities with athletes from the West, their attitude began to soften. Gradually, the Communist camp opened up, and East and West mingled.

The Reverend Robert Richards of the United States, the finest pole vaulter in the world, carried on limited conversations with his three Soviet rivals. "The three Russians knew one word of English—beautiful," Richards said later. "I knew one Russian word—*khorosho*—good. So when I finished a jump, they all cheered, 'Beautiful,' and when they finished, I said, '*Khorosho.*'"

When a Soviet rower pinned a hammer and sickle emblem on rower Dick Murphy of the United States Naval Academy, the Russian joked, "If you should wear this in the United States, they would put you in the electric chair."

But when a Russian official pinned a dove of peace emblem on diver Sammy Lee of the United States Army, the American did not find it funny at all. "I can't wear that Red propaganda," said Major Lee.

Helsinki, of course, could not escape reflections of the cold war. East Germany applied for Olympic recognition and was rejected; West Germany cheerfully competed. Red China applied for Olympic recognition and was accepted; Nationalist China immediately withdrew. (Red China's team never showed up in Helsinki.)

During the opening ceremonies, as sixty-nine countries paraded almost 5,000 athletes around a muddy track, the Russians marched in handsome white flannels, the Americans in smart blue blazers. But for the 70,000 Finnish spectators, a special treat obscured the East-West fashion show. When the last relay runner trotted into the stadium, holding high the Olympic torch, his stride was unmistakable. Fifty-five years old and balding, but still trim and graceful, Paavo Nurmi jogged once around the track and, amid booming applause, ignited the Olympic flame. Then, to heap climax upon climax, Nurmi turned and handed the torch to Hannes Kolehmainen, the hero of 1912. Kolehmainen ran easily up the

Horace Ashenfelter splashes through the water jump in the 3,000-meter steeplechase.

250

steps to the top row of the modernistic stadium and lit a second Olympic flame. Then the 1952 Olympic Games began.

From the outset, the theme of the Helsinki games was clear: East versus West, Communism versus capitalism, Russia versus the United States. Only once before—in Berlin in 1936—had the Olympics been the scene of such sharp political contrast. National prestige was at stake. Which country would win the most gold medals? Which country would score the most unofficial points? Who would dominate, the Russians or the Americans?

The Soviets harbored no false hopes in men's track and field. They knew they could not possibly match the speed and the varied skills of the American squad. But the Russians did expect to win one, two, or at best three gold medals in men's track and field. No Olympian seemed a safer bet than Vladimir Kazantsev of Kiev, who had set the world record of eight minutes and forty-eight seconds for the 3,000-meter steeplechase.

Horace Ashenfelter of the United States, a twenty-nine-year-old FBI agent who had run only eight steeplechase races before the 1952 Olympics, did not appear capable of pressing Kazantsev. Neither Ashenfelter nor any other American had ever run the 3,000-meter obstacle course in less than nine minutes. But, suddenly, in his preliminary heat, Ashenfelter showed that he might be a threat. The skinny Penn State graduate qualified in eight minutes fifty-one seconds, fifteen seconds faster than he had ever run before.

After three of the seven laps in the final, Ashenfelter trotted into the lead, Kazantsev only a stride behind him. The FBI man and the Russian maintained this pattern until the last lap. Then, leaving the backstretch, Kazantsev, as expected, dashed past the American; Ashenfelter's bold bid seemed doomed. But on the water jump, Kazantsev slipped and lost his stride. Ashenfelter cleared the hurdle, landed on his left foot, stepped off quickly on his right, overtook Kazantsev, and began pulling away. The unheralded American rushed home in front, setting an Olympic and world record of eight minutes forty-five and four tenths seconds. After the finish, Kazantsev, who barely outlasted Britain's John Disley for second place, warmly embraced Ashenfelter. The atmosphere was charged with good sportsmanship and goodwill until a Soviet official arrived and, unsmilingly, led the defeated favorite away.

"I sped up going to the last water jump," said Ashenfelter, who received the Sullivan Award in 1952, largely as a result of his Olympic performance, "and when Kazantsev stumbled coming out of it, I really laid it on. I hit the last hurdle with my leg. It threw me off balance, but I was going so fast, I knew I was all right."

After Kazantsev, the Russians' leading candidate for a track and field victory was Yuri Lituyev, who recorded the best time in the semifinals of the 400-meter hurdles. But in the final, an American once again scuttled the Soviet hopes. Cornell's Charles Moore, whose father had been a reserve

Repeating his 1948 triumph, Mal Whitfield holds first place in the 800-meter run.

on the 1924 United States team, led almost all the way. When Lituyev drew close on the last hurdle, Moore sprinted and beat the Russian decisively.

The athletes of the Soviet Union wound up without a single gold medal in men's track and field, the most prestigious phase of the Olympics. The Russians did salvage four silver medals—for Lituyev, Kazantsev, Leonid Shcherbakov in the hop, step, and jump, and the 400-meter relay team. Shcherbakov leaped within an inch of the world record, but he had the misfortune of competing against an incredibly talented Brazilian, Adhemar Ferreira da Silva, who broke the world record four times in his six jumps. The slender, amiable Brazilian, fluent in seven languages, retained his Olympic championship in 1956.

Man for man, the Russian 400-meter relay runners were not nearly so swift as their American opponents. But the Soviet quartet had mastered the art of the baton pass and, thanks to precision teamwork, lost the final to the United States by only two tenths of a second.

If the pressure of their first Olympic test seemed to hamper the Russians in men's track and field, the Soviet debut unquestionably inspired the Americans. Performances generally were brilliant in Helsinki—in the twenty-two standard events, excluding the two walks, seventeen Olympic records were broken and two were tied—but American performances, in particular, far exceeded all expectations. Faced with the strongest field ever, the United States team won fourteen gold medals, its greatest total since World War I.

Three Americans who had earned championships in 1948 picked up fresh gold medals in Helsinki. Bob Mathias, of course, repeated his decathlon victory; although he insisted, "I've never been so tired in my life," after the first day's five events, he set a world record on the second day. Mal Whitfield, who had flown twenty-seven bomber missions in Korea since leaving London, once again led the 800-meter field, tying his own Olympic mark; he failed once again in his bid for a 400–800 double, finishing sixth to Jamaica's George Rhoden in the shorter race. Harrison Dillard, the surprise winner of the 100-meter dash in 1948, won his favorite event, the 110-meter high hurdles, in 1952; "Good things come to those who wait," said Dillard happily.

Two of the most consistently successful Americans in Olympic history earned their first gold medals in Helsinki. Pole vaulter Bob Richards, who had placed third in 1948, finished first in 1952 and again in 1956. Shot-putter Parry O'Brien, only twenty years old during the Helsinki games, placed first in 1952, first in 1956, and second in 1960. For their Olympic feats, both Richards, who worked as a preacher, and O'Brien, who worked in a bank, became immensely popular among the anticlerical, anticapitalist Russians. "In Moscow," said one Soviet sportsman, "every school child knows who Bob Richards and Parry O'Brien are."

The triumphs by Richards and O'Brien were hardly sur-

On the brink of a gold medal, Sim Iness strains before releasing the discus.

Bob Richards, the premier pole vaulter of the 1950's, clears the crossbar.

prising; some of the other American victories were downright startling. Cy Young, a six-foot five-inch, 220-pound giant, celebrated his twenty-fourth birthday by becoming the first American to win an Olympic javelin championship. Even more embarrassing to the host Finns, whose representatives had brought home the javelin title four times in the six previous Olympics, another American, Bill Miller, placed second. The best of the Finns, Toivo Hyytianen, came in third. For the first time since 1912, Finland did not win a single gold medal in men's track and field.

In the discus, Italy's Adolfo Consolini, the defending champion, and Fortune Gordien of the United States were favored. Both were masters of their craft. Consolini, an outstanding discus thrower even before World War II, competed in four Olympics after the war; Gordien competed in three. But in 1952, Consolini had to settle for second place, Gordien for fourth. The winner, Sim Iness, a sturdy Californian who had attended Tulare High School with Bob Mathias, broke the Olympic record on each of his six throws, then cabled his wife in Los Angeles: "We did it. I love you 1,000 times. Distance 180 feet, 6.58 inches."

For sheer closeness of competition, no event matched the final of the 100-meter dash. There was no clear favorite, mainly because the three best 100-meter men in the world—all Americans—were not competing. Andy Stanfield had passed up the 100 to concentrate on the 200 (which he won),

Jim Golliday had injured himself before the Olympic trials, and Art Bragg had pulled a muscle during the preliminary rounds. Among the six starters, only Britain's Emmanuel McDonald-Bailey, sixth in London, had Olympic experience at 100 meters. Herb McKenley of Jamaica, Dean Smith of the United States, and Vladimir Sukharyev of the Soviet Union had all run the distance in ten and three tenths seconds, only a tenth of a second off the world record. The other two finalists were John Treloar of Australia and Lindy Remigino of the United States. Remigino, twenty-one years old, had almost quit the Manhattan College team three months earlier because he felt he was "a drag on the team." After his coach convinced him to keep running, he barely qualified for the United States Olympic squad.

But Remigino burst out of the starting blocks with stunning speed and, halfway through the race, held a sizable lead over Smith and McDonald-Bailey. In the last ten meters, Smith and McDonald-Bailey tightened the gap, and McKenley caught up with the front threesome. All four crashed over the finish line almost simultaneously. All four, in fact, were timed in ten and four tenths seconds. The winner? Either Remigino or McKenley. Remigino congratulated McKenley. Sukharyev congratulated Remigino. The official photograph confirmed the Russian's choice. Remigino was one inch in front of McKenley, who was three inches in front of McDonald-Bailey, who was one inch in front of Smith.

"I thought Herb won," Remigino told reporters. "Another yard and he would have licked me." (McKenley's disappointment was compounded four days later; he lost the 400-meter final to Rhoden by twelve inches.)

Remigino, a New Yorker who had been named after Charles Lindbergh, was a modest, frank young man. "Do you think you could have beaten Stanfield and Golliday?" someone asked him.

"Are you kidding?" Remigino replied. "If they were in the race, I wouldn't be here."

Another American, Bob McMillan of Occidental College, almost pulled as shocking an upset as Remigino's. McMillan, who had run the steeplechase race in London and had fallen flat on his face on a water jump, was given no chance to win the 1,500 meters in Helsinki. But with a brilliant sprint finish, he came within an inch of tying the champion, a man almost as lightly regarded as the American, Joseph Barthel of tiny Luxembourg. England's Roger Bannister, who was to break the four-minute barrier in the mile two years later, placed fourth. With Barthel's victory—Luxembourg's first and only in Olympic history—the little European nation could claim that in 1952 it had earned one gold medal per 300,000 inhabitants, a distinction no other country could match.

As the 1952 Olympic Games progressed, interest focused increasingly upon the duel between the world's two major powers, the United States and the Soviet Union. In men's track and field, with unofficial points awarded on a basis of ten-five-

Titles run in the family, and Emil Zatopek's wife, Dana, celebrates her javelin victory by turning a cartwheel.

Joseph Barthel (406) turns back Bob McMillan (992) in the 1,500-
meter final and collects a gold medal for tiny Luxembourg.

four-three-two-one for the first six places, the Americans
crushed their Russian rivals, 215 to 49. But once competition
began in other sports, the Soviet Union flexed its athletic
muscles.

In women's track and field, while the United States could
muster only a relay victory, two muscular Russian girls—
discus thrower Nina Romaschkova and shot-putter Galina
Zybina—gained gold medals. In gymnastics, with Viktor
Tchoukarine winning three gold medals (he won two more
in 1956), the Soviet Union outpointed the United States, 188 to
0. In Greco-Roman wrestling, Russians took four gold medals,
Americans none. The huge lead the United States had built
up in men's track and field quickly vanished. Soon the Russians held a commanding advantage, first 323½ points to 221,
later 496½ points to 376.

Only occasionally did athletes from other countries share
the spotlight with the American-Russian rivalry. Marjorie
Jackson of Australia won both women's dashes, Henri St. Cyr
of Sweden was the star of the equestrian events, and a Frenchman, Jean Boiteux, scored his country's first Olympic victory

in men's swimming. When young Boiteux won the 400-meter free style, his excited father—wearing coat, vest, pants, and beret—leaped into the pool and kissed him on both cheeks.

Boiteux was one of two non-Americans to win a final in men's swimming; John Davies of Australia won the 200-meter breast stroke. The Japanese had been expected to set a swift pace in the water, but they failed miserably; their greatest star, Hironshin Furuhashi, the Flying Fish of Fujiyama, finished last in the 400-meter free style. The United States gathered six gold medals, led by Sammy Lee, who retained his high diving title, and little Ford Konno of Honolulu, who captured the 1,500-meter free style crown and cut forty-two seconds off the twenty-year-old Olympic record.

Slowly, the United States began reducing the Soviet point lead. In weight-lifting, while the favored Russians settled for three gold medals, the surprising Americans won four, only one less than they had earned in all previous Olympics combined. John Henry Davis, the 1948 heavyweight champion, was the only American athlete in Helsinki who did not have to abide by any training rules. "He can eat, drink and stay out as late as he pleases," said his coach, Bob Hoffman. "He's been world champion since 1938. We can't tell him how he should act." Davis successfully defended his title, but he had to divide American honors with a scholarly-looking, bespectacled twenty-two-year-old named Tommy Kono.

A Japanese-American who had been born in California and had spent part of World War II in a United States relocation camp, Kono was a remarkable athlete. Five feet six inches tall, he could vary in weight from 148 to 184 pounds without ever losing his strength. He won the Olympic lightweight championship in 1952 by lifting 798 pounds and the Olympic light-heavyweight championship in 1956 by lifting 986 pounds. In 1960, because he knew that the Russians had a rugged middleweight named Alexander Kurynov, Kono slimmed down to the middleweight division. Kurynov proved too rugged; Kono lifted 942 pounds, but ended up in second place. At various times, Kono set world records in the lightweight, middleweight, light-heavyweight, and middle-heavyweight divisions. "Successful weightlifting is not in the body," he once said. "It's in the mind. You can lift as much as you believe you can."

In women's swimming, while the Russians drew a blank, Patricia Keller McCormick, like Vicki Draves in 1948, won both diving events for the United States. Four years later, at Melbourne, Mrs. McCormick retained both titles. No one else has ever won two diving championships in two Olympics.

In basketball, with three men roughly seven feet tall—Clyde Lovellette, Marcus Freiberger, and 1948 veteran Bob Kurland—towering over all opponents, the United States maintained its undefeated Olympic record. The Americans beat the Russians twice—86–58 in a preliminary match and 36–25 in the final.

Despite the heavy American scoring in weight-lifting and swimming, the Russians, on the morning of the last full day of Olympic competition, still led the unofficial standings, 533½ to 499. On the final day, five American boxers competed in championship matches—and five American boxers emerged with gold medals. The best of the United States fighters was a seventeen-year-old Negro from Brooklyn, a growing middle-weight named Floyd Patterson. His main problem in Helsinki was the language barrier. "Every time I get my suit pressed," he told coach Pete Mello, "it costs me 300 kilocycles." For Patterson, life in the ring was much less confusing; he won one decision, then knocked out his last three opponents. In the final, he took only twenty seconds to dispose of Rumania's Vasile Tita. "I think he could take Ray Robinson right now," said Eddie Eagan, the 1920 Olympic light-heavyweight champion.

"Patterson has faster paws than a subway pickpocket and they cause more suffering," wrote Red Smith. "He confuses opponents with his impetuous style, lunging forward to throw his first blow, sometimes missing with that opening punch. He doesn't mind if he does miss because he has six or seven other hands to follow up."

Next to Patterson, the most promising prospect among the American boxers was heavyweight Ed Sanders of California. "Sanders scored four straight knockouts, in effect," reported Jesse Abramson of the New York *Herald Tribune*, "though his final opponent, a Swede, was disqualified for running for his life." Seven years later, the frightened Swede won the professional heavyweight championship of the world. His name was Ingemar Johansson, and the man he won the title from—and later lost it back to—was Floyd Patterson. By then, Ed Sanders, who might have been a champion, was dead, the victim of a brain injury suffered in a professional fight.

Led by its boxers, the United States went on a scoring rampage during the last day of competition. When the Helsinki games drew to an end, the Russians had an unofficial total of 553½ points, the Americans 614. The United States was still the strongest sports country in the world. But the margin was slim, and the Soviet Union had demonstrated that it was as powerful a threat in sports as it was in politics.

The emphasis on the American-Russian rivalry, which had nearly obscured the rest of the games, distressed many people, particularly Avery Brundage, the newly elected president of the International Olympic Committee. "If this becomes a giant contest between two great nations rich in talent and resources," Brundage warned, "the spirit of the Olympics will be destroyed."

During the winter Olympics preceding the Helsinki games, smaller nations had a chance to shine. Norway, which played host to thirty teams and some seven hundred athletes at Oslo, outscored its guests in the snow and ice sports. The Norwegian ace was a twenty-eight-year-old truck driver named Hjalmar

With style and grace, Pat McCormick adds the high diving title to her springboard championship.

Anderson, who set a pattern for Zatopek to follow a few months later. In speed skating competition, Anderson won three distance events—1,500 meters, 5,000 meters, and 10,000 meters. To make his accomplishment even more impressive, Anderson scored his three victories on three consecutive days. By adding three gold medals in Nordic skiing events, Norway clinched the over-all team title.

In its most impressive winter showing since 1932, the United States earned four gold medals and finished second in the unofficial team standings. The brightest star of the American squad was a hardy veteran of the 1948 games, a New Englander who had been skiing for sixteen years. She was Andrea Mead Lawrence of Vermont, and she was only nineteen years old.

Andy Mead had, at the age of fifteen, finished thirty-fifth in the downhill and eighth in the slalom at St. Moritz. During the years between Olympics, she had acquired polish, confidence, and a husband—Dave Lawrence, a member of the United States men's skiing team. "I race for fun," she insisted. "It's not worthwhile unless you enjoy it. I'm hardly ever nervous before a race. And I absolutely do not feel bad when I lose."

In Oslo, Mrs. Lawrence, a tall, graceful brunette, felt good. First she won the women's giant slalom, twisting through the fifty-nine gates of the long course in two minutes six and eight tenths seconds, more than two seconds faster than runner-up Dagmar Rom, a lovely Austrian movie actress.

Then, in the forty-nine gate, two-heat regular slalom, Andy Lawrence staged a remarkable recovery. During the first heat, she snagged a ski in a flagpole near the top of the course, tumbled to the snow, got up, and, although her fall cost her at least four seconds, completed the run in one minute seven and two tenths seconds, only one and two tenths seconds behind the leader, Ossi Reichert of Germany. In the second heat, after discussing strategy with her husband, studying the gates, and waxing her skis, Mrs. Lawrence charged down the slope so boldly and so brilliantly that she made the run in one minute three and four tenths seconds—swift enough to overtake Ossi Reichert and earn a second gold medal. "I knew what I had to do," Mrs. Lawrence explained, "so I just cut loose."

Dick Button, the United States figure skating genius, also cut loose in Oslo. The 1948 champion not only retained his title, but for the first time in any competition, executed an incredible triple-loop jump—taking off on one skate going backward, spinning around three times, and landing on the same skate going backward. "I can't copy anybody else," said Button, candidly, "because nobody else has anything new."

Canada won the ice hockey championship for the sixth time in seven Olympics; the American team was widely criticized for its rough style of play. Germany won both bobsled titles; Andreas Ostler, a cheerful, thirty-two-year-old innkeeper, captained both the two-man and the four-man sleds.

Eddie Sanders of the United States bears in on his target, the future heavyweight champion of the world, Ingemar Johansson.

And in the Alpine skiing events, a young Austrian chemistry student, Othmar Schneider, captured the slalom and finished second in the downhill; another Austrian, Christian Pravda, placed second in the giant slalom and third in the downhill. Austria had never before won an Olympic championship in men's Alpine skiing, but the performances of Schneider and Pravda hinted at their country's emerging strength. Back in the skiing villages of Kitzbühel and Innsbruck, Austria was assembling the most gifted collection of Alpine skiers the world had ever seen. The Austrians were aiming squarely at the winter Olympic Games of 1956, and their aim, as events were to prove, was stunningly accurate.

Ducking under a right, Floyd Patterson advances toward the Olympic middleweight title and, eventually, the world heavyweight title.

259

1

The
Wet
Set

3

4

1  Flying Dutchman yachting, 1960
2  Diving in Rome, 1960
3  Ingrid Kramer, Germany, diving champion, 1960
4  Ingrid Kramer
5  Gary Tobian, United States, diving champion, 1960
6  Gary Tobian

5                    6

263

7

8

9

10

11

12

7  William Mulliken, United States, 200-meter breast stroke champion, 1960
8  Heat of women's 200-meter breast stroke, 1960
9  Hendrika Mastenbroek, Netherlands, free style champion, 1936
10  Men's 200-meter butterfly stroke, 1952
11  Underwater view, 1936
12  Start of men's 100-meter back stroke, 1936

13    14    15

266

16

13 Dragon Class, 1960
14 Dragon Class, 1956
15 Dragon Class, 1956
16 Six-meter class, 1948

18

19

20

**17** Yale crew, eight-oared champions, 1956
**18** Two-man kayaks, 1960
**19** Two-woman kayaks, 1960
**20** One-man kayaks, 1960

Besieged by admirers, Toni Sailer enjoys a hero's reception at Cortina.

# The Blitz
# from Kitz

## CHAPTER SIXTEEN : 1956 – MELBOURNE AND CORTINA D'AMPEZZO

*"Toni Sailer is the most perfect skier I ever saw. He is the perfect athlete in perfect condition with perfect technique. He never makes a mistake."*
—FRED ROSSNER
Austrian skiing coach

For twenty-four days in a row during the month preceding the 1956 winter Olympic Games in Cortina d'Ampezzo, not a single flake of snow fell upon the picturesque Italian resort. Just as the Italian government nervously began lugging in snow from the Alps, a sudden storm blew up, and fourteen inches of snow blanketed the area. Then a thaw set in, then a freeze. By the time the Olympics began, the slopes at Cortina, slick with ice, were terribly swift, terribly treacherous. The conditions were frightening for most skiers. The conditions were ideal for Anton Sailer.

"Toni" Sailer was a sturdy, handsome, brown-haired, twenty-year-old Austrian, born and raised in the Tyrolean village of Kitzbühel, where everyone skis and some are great and some are only good. Sailer, whose father was a glazier, started skiing at the age of two—and he was one of the great ones. He had a magic touch, a gift of sensitivity on the slopes.

"He is gentle with the snow," explained Zeno Colo, an Italian who had won the Olympic downhill race in 1952. "He is never rough to his skis. His every movement is controlled, not by reason, but by lightning subconscious reflex. The language that the skis talk through the feet, to the legs and body, is a language unknown to most men and women, but it is the whisper Sailer understands best."

As a teen-ager, Sailer idolized Kitzbühel's Christian Pravda, and when Pravda won two medals in the 1952 winter games at Oslo, Sailer set his own sights on the 1956 Olympics. He

Sailer streaks to victory in the giant slalom, the first of his three triumphs.

trained hard. Whenever there was snow on the mountains around Kitzbühel, Sailer slipped away from his father's glass shop and practiced for four hours a day. By 1956, he was six feet tall and weighed 174 pounds, and for extra strength, he drank a mixture of milk, honey, and sugar every morning. For relaxation, he drank wine with two meals each day.

"He trains just like the other boys," said Fred Rossner, the coach of the Austrian Olympic team. "We let them work as they like. We don't want a unified style. We want each to develop his individual ability."

Sailer's individual ability flourished. Crouching, bending, twisting, he roared down slopes with unmatched calm—and unmatched speed. He could not explain his success. "I put myself on skis," he said, "and just let go."

At Cortina, Sailer's first event was the giant slalom, a race one and two thirds miles long, with a 2,000-foot vertical drop and seventy-one gates to be navigated. Anderl Molterer, "The White Blitz from Kitz," and Sailer, the younger "Blitz from Kitz," were the cofavorites.

Molterer started sixth in a field of nearly one hundred, and he sped down the rocky, hazardous course in three minutes six and three tenths seconds, a fantastically fast time. Thousands of the 30,000 spectators who had descended upon Cortina cheered loudly for Molterer, positive that he had clinched a victory. Molterer himself was less certain. "Toni hasn't come yet," he said.

Sailer, starting eighteenth, came down the course like a bullet, so poised and controlled that he was actually grinning. Unlike most of his rivals, he kept his skis firmly on the slick snow, riding with the bumps rather than soaring over them. He finished his dazzling run in three minutes one tenth of a second, more than six seconds better than Molterer's time. No one else could approach the two boys from Kitzbühel. Sailer won the gold medal, Molterer the silver, and a third Austrian, Walter Schuster, the bronze.

After the giant slalom, the next contest in Alpine skiing was the special slalom—two runs, both over hard, narrow courses, the first with seventy-nine gates, the second with ninety-two. Experts agreed it was the toughest slalom setup they had ever seen. But Sailer was the man to match the mountain. He made the fastest runs over both courses, and with a combined time of three minutes fourteen and seven-tenths seconds, defeated runner-up Chiharu Igaya, a Dartmouth College student from Japan, by exactly four seconds.

To complete an unprecedented Alpine Grand Slam, Sailer still had to win the downhill race. He was confident that he would. "I like downhill racing the best," he said the day before the event. "In slalom, you have to brake all the time. I like to run free into the wind."

But even Sailer conceded the difficulty of the Olympic downhill course. More than two miles long, with roughly 3,000 feet of vertical drop, the course was sheer ice, dotted with bumps so dangerous that of seventy-five starters fifty-eight

Beautiful and gifted, Carol Heiss sparkles on the ice.

A Canadian lands aboard a Russian hockey player, but the Soviets won the game and the title.

fell at least once and twenty-eight fell so violently that they had to quit. All through the competition, skiers were hitting bumps and soaring through the air, sometimes landing upright, more often tumbling to the ground.

Sailer, a yellow silk scarf wrapped around his neck, bounced into the air only once. He hit the first bump and sailed more than thirty feet, skis apart, control seemingly lost. But he recovered beautifully and, from then on, he dominated the course. He completed the run in two minutes fifty-two and two tenths seconds, beating the second-place man, Raymond Fellay of Switzerland, by three and a half seconds. Molterer placed third. "It was a murderous course," said Sailer afterward. "I have never known such hazards. My third medal was the hardest to get."

To celebrate Sailer's triple victories, the Austrian government awarded him its highest medal, the Golden Cross of Merit. He was a hero to all Europe. He received 3,300 fan letters within a month and some two dozen offers to teach at ski clubs. He became a movie actor and played the lead role in a German film, "A Bit of Heaven," portraying a gas station attendant who fell in love with a beautiful countess. He socialized with the Aga Khan and danced with actress Romy Schneider. He recorded a song called "I Know More Than You Think," which sold 100,000 copies. Rich, famous, skilled, he never outgrew his home village.

"Whenever he is through with visiting the world," said one Kitzbühel resident in 1958, "Toni always returns here, where he is comfortable."

Sailer was unquestionably the individual star of the 1956 winter games, but even with his three gold medals, he could not carry Austria to the unofficial team championship. The most powerful team in Cortina—the most powerful group of winter athletes in the world—came from the Soviet Union.

In their first shot at the winter Olympics, the Russians collected six gold medals and 121 points, far outdistancing Austria, which placed second with four gold medals and 78½ points. The pace-setter for the Russians was their only athlete who had previous Olympic experience. Evgeni Grishin, a twenty-four-year-old Moscow engraver, had competed in Helsinki as a cyclist. In Cortina, he switched from bikes to skates, and with a combination of speed and stamina, won both the 500-meter and 1,500-meter speed skating championships. His teammate, Boris Shilkov, a twenty-eight-year-old engineer, won the 5,000-meter race to give Russia three of the four speed skating titles.

The strong Russian showing in speed skating had not been unexpected. What embarrassed and upset the West much more was the Soviet showing in ice hockey. The sport had never been played in Russia before World War II, yet by 1956 the Soviets had the best team in the world. In the six-team final round, the Russians scored five consecutive victories, shutting out the United States, 4–0, and Canada, 2–0. The Canadians, the pretournament favorites and champions

273

in six of the seven preceding Olympics, slipped to third place after losing to the United States, 4–1.

For the first time in the Olympics, Americans won both the men's and women's figure skating championship. In the men's division, with two-time champion Dick Button no longer competing, Hayes Alan Jenkins of Colorado Springs, a master of the school figures, ranked as the favorite. But an eighteen-year-old, red-haired Californian, Ronnie Robertson, who specialized in free skating, presented a strong threat. Jenkins, as expected, built up a sizable lead in the school figures. Then, on the next day, Robertson bid for the title.

"He started smoothly and slowly as a showman should," reported Fred Tupper of *The New York Times*. "Suddenly he spun into a double flip and double Axel and then faster, into a camel with jump sit, all intricate figures that he executed with ease. Then, building speed again, the Californian leaped into the triple loop—a jump only America's Dick Button had done before him and a feat so dangerous that no European skater had ever tried it. The leap didn't quite come off, but Robertson recovered quickly and burst into the triple Salchow as the crowd roared."

Then Hayes Jenkins gave his free-skating exhibition, and while he did not match Robertson's acrobatics or artistry, he skated gracefully and efficiently. For two hours afterward, the judges studied the scores, and the skaters waited. "If they take this one away from you," said David Jenkins to his older brother, "I'll never skate again."

When the judges announced their decision, Hayes Jenkins was champion by a slender margin. Robertson placed second and David Jenkins third.

The drama in the women's division was almost as great. Tenley Albright, an attractive premedical student from Radcliffe, held the world championship and planned to gain the Olympic title without great difficulty. But two weeks before the event, training in Cortina, Miss Albright slipped on the ice and, with her left skate, sliced a deep gash in her right ankle. In the championship, although the wound was still open and painful, Miss Albright put on a magnificent free-skating show to the tune of an Offenbach medley and narrowly defeated a fellow American, Carol Heiss.

The figure skating sweep provided the only American victories at Cortina—and the Russians, not surprisingly, gloated. "We came here expecting triumphs in our strong events and expecting to gain experience in the others," said Nikolai Romanov, the Soviet minister of sports. "We did both—and we're going to win in Melbourne, too."

As the Melbourne games approached—they were scheduled to begin late in November, which was summer in Australia— the world suddenly plunged into turmoil. Israel, aided by Great Britain and France, marched into the Gaza Strip. Russian tanks rolled into Budapest to crush the Hungarian revolution.

Ironically, seventeen members of the Hungarian Olympic

With raised arm, Vladimir Kuts of the Soviet Union breaks the tape in the 10,000-meter run.

274

1

3

4

8

team were already on their way to Australia aboard a Soviet steamship, the *Gruzia*. The rest of the team had assembled in Czechoslovakia, waiting to board a flight to Melbourne. For a while, the Hungarians in Prague considered abandoning the Olympics and returning home to join the fight against the Russians, but they were told that the border between Hungary and Czechoslovakia had been firmly sealed. Reluctantly, fearing for the lives of family and friends, they decided to compete in Melbourne.

Hundreds of Hungarian expatriates, who earlier had moved to Australia to escape the Communist regime, were gathered at Essendon airport when the bulk of the Hungarian Olympians landed. The crowd shouted, "Huj, huj, hajra," the Hungarian equivalent of "Hip, hip, hooray," and sang "Isten Ald Meg a Magyart," the anthem of pre-Communist Hungary. The Hungarian athletes were a somber, saddened group; they did not disguise their hatred for the Russians in Melbourne. They took down the flag over their quarters, ripped off the Communist symbol, and raised the flag of free Hungary. They had several gifted athletes—particularly such distance-running stars as Laszlo Tabori, Sandor Iharos, and Istvan Rozsavolgyi—but, depressed by the bloodshed in Budapest, they did not perform up to their ability in Australia. "I am regaining control of their physical condition," said the brilliant Hungarian coach, Mihaly Igloi, "but their minds are in Hungary." After the games, forty-five of the Hungarians, including coach Igloi, chose to defect and remain in the West.

With open arms, Ron Delany of Ireland breaks the tape in the 1,500-meter run.

To protest the Israeli invasion of Egypt, Lebanon and Iraq withdrew from the Olympics. To protest the Russian rape of Hungary, three nations—Spain, Switzerland, and The Netherlands—also withdrew. To protest the raising, by mistake, of the Nationalist China banner over their camp, the Red Chinese withdrew. Some people suggested that, with the world tangled in conflict, the Olympics should be canceled. Avery Brundage, president of the International Olympic Committee, was determined to hold the games. "The Olympics belong to the people," Brundage argued. "They are contests for individuals and not of nations." There was one encouraging note: East and West Germany competed as a united team.

Little by little, tension subsided—although it never completely disappeared—and the games went on. Russians and Americans fraternized freely in the social centers of the Olympic Village—the Soviet Union this time had no separate village—and the Australians proved gracious, considerate hosts. The Australians provided, among other comforts, 841 neat, handsomely landscaped homes for the Olympic athletes, a total of 770 oversize beds for men more than six feet two inches tall, forty-five superbeds for athletes over six feet six inches tall, and several hundred pounds of turkey for the Americans to eat on Thanksgiving Day. Most important, the Australians provided goodwill and enthusiasm.

When the opening ceremonies were staged at the Melbourne Cricket Ground—with Norman Armitage, a forty-nine-

275

On his way to the high jump championship, Charlie Dumas clears the crossbar.

year-old fencer who had competed in every Olympics since 1932, carrying the United States flag; Australia's John Landy, who held the world record for the mile run, taking the Olympic oath on behalf of the 3,500 assembled athletes; and Russia's Galina Zybina, the 1952 women's shot-putting champion, fainting in the heat—103,000 Australians filled the stadium. For each program of track and field events, a capacity crowd turned out.

Australians may well be the most sports-minded people in the world. With a population of only slightly more than 10,000,000, Australia consistently develops the finest tennis players in the world and a sizable percentage of the best swimmers, best runners, best cricket players, and best sailors. The Australians had ample opportunity to cheer for their countrymen during the 1956 games. Although Landy, hampered by leg injuries, could do no better than a gallant third behind Ireland's Ron Delany in the 1,500-meter run, Australia did produce a triple gold medal winner in women's track and field. Betty Cuthbert won the 100-meter and 200-meter sprints, then paced her team to the 400-meter relay championship.

Australia's most convincing demonstration of strength came in the water. The swimmers from Down Under captured five gold medals in the men's division and three in the women's. Most gifted of the Australians was Murray Rose, a seventeen-year-old prodigy who had been swimming since he was three years old. Rose, a strict vegetarian, ate seaweed jelly for pep, and his strange formula seemed to work. He set Olympic records in both the 400-meter and 1,500-meter free styles—and repeated his 400-meter triumph four years later in Rome.

On the basis of population, the Australians made as impressive a showing as any team in the Olympics. But, naturally, they could not match the over-all strength of the Soviet Union and the United States. A sign on the Olympic scoreboard within the Melbourne Cricket Ground read: "Classification by points on a national basis is not recognized." Nobody paid any attention to the sign. Everybody wanted to know once again how the Americans stacked up against the Russians.

The Russians, obviously progressing in track and field, unveiled their first international running champion, a remarkable, twenty-nine-year-old Soviet navy officer named Vladimir Kuts. A short, muscular Ukrainian with long blond hair, Kuts entered the 5,000-meter and 10,000-meter races.

The longer event was held first, and although Kuts was the favorite, he knew that Britain's Gordon Pirie, a veteran of the 1952 games, would be a dangerous threat. So Kuts devised a bold strategy to kill Pirie's bid. The Russian took the lead from the start and ran the first of twenty-five 400-meter laps in sixty-one and four tenths seconds, practically a sprinting pace. Pirie, afraid to let his rival open up too big a gap, stayed close to Kuts, and the two men moved in front of the field.

Then Kuts ran three brisk, sixty-eight-second laps, drawing Pirie with him farther and farther away from the rest of the runners. Suddenly, just when Pirie was beginning to feel that he—and he alone—could stay with Kuts, the Russian sprinted and opened up a ten-yard gap. For the next 4,000 meters, Kuts followed the same pattern, forcing Pirie to keep up a stern pace and, simultaneously, showing Pirie that he could sprint clear whenever he wanted to. At 5,000 meters, incredibly, Kuts matched Emil Zatopek's Olympic record for the 5,000-meter run. He and Pirie had drawn more than 100 yards ahead of anyone else.

After 6,000 meters, Kuts slowed down several times and waved to Pirie to take the lead. The Englishman refused. Around the 8,000-meter mark, Kuts slowed literally to a walk, and Pirie reluctantly moved in front. That was all the Russian was waiting for. He let Pirie lead for 100 meters, and then he broke into a sprint, whizzed past the Englishman, and opened up a wide margin. Pirie's spirit sagged. He was beaten and knew it. While Kuts went on to win Russia's first track and field championship and set an Olympic record, Pirie faded to eighth place. Jozsef Kovacs of Hungary finished second, then pointedly refused to shake hands with his Russian conqueror.

As soon as he crossed the finish line, Kuts's poker face split in a wide grin, and he jogged an extra lap around the track, waving to the crowd and holding his hands over his head in a victory gesture. "The public were very kind," he said, "and I appreciated the way they applauded me."

The master of the hop, step, and jump, Brazil's Adhemar Ferreira da Silva earns his second straight Olympic title.

Pirie was exhausted, physically and mentally. "It wasn't the fact that he beat me," he said. "It was the way he did it. He murdered me. I hope I never have to compete against a runner like him again."

Unfortunately for Pirie, he had to compete against Kuts again five days later, in the 5,000-meter final. This time Pirie had help from two countrymen, Derek Ibbotson and Chris Chataway, and did not have to press Kuts by himself. But the presence of the three Britons did not seem to disturb Kuts. He ran a straight, solid race, leading almost all the way, and won his second gold medal, again in Olympic record time. Pirie, careful not to burn himself out, sprinted in the stretch and took second place.

With Leonid Spirine winning the 20,000-meter walk, Russia collected three gold medals in men's track and field at Melbourne, a distinct improvement over their shutout in Helsinki. But once more the Soviets could not come close to matching the Americans in men's track and field. The United States squad, again rising to the Russian challenge, won an amazing total of fifteen events.

The Americans' answer to Vladimir Kuts was Bobby Morrow, a tall sprinter with a nine-foot stride. A twenty-one-year-old student at Abilene Christian College in Texas, Morrow dominated the sprints as decisively as Kuts dominated the long-distance events. In the 100-meter dash, Morrow overtook Australia's Hector Hogan after fifty meters and won pulling away. The night before the 200-meter final, the Texan was so nervous he couldn't sleep. The lack of rest didn't bother him in the least. He won the event in Olympic record time, forcing Andy Stanfield, the defending champion, back to second place. Then, in the 400-meter relay, Morrow anchored the United States quartet to a world record of thirty-nine and five tenths seconds and picked up his third gold medal.

In the 400-meter relay, Bobby Morrow takes the baton from teammate Thane Baker.

Morrow was not the only American hero. Four other United States athletes slipped to the brink of defeat—and recovered. Bob Richards almost suffered the most humiliating setback of his career. Beyond question the world's best pole vaulter, he had cleared fifteen feet so many times, with such ease, that any lesser height hardly seemed a challenge. But in the early stages of the Olympic competition, Richards twice tried thirteen feet one and one half inches and twice failed to clear the bar. On his last chance, he succeeded. He then went on to set an Olympic record at fourteen feet eleven and one quarter inches.

High jumper Charles Dumas, like Richards, was considered unbeatable in his specialty. Only a few months before the games, the husky, nineteen-year-old Californian had become the first man to leap seven feet, a full foot above his own head. In Melbourne, when his most dangerous opponent, Sweden's Bengt Nilsson, ruptured a muscle and failed to qualify for the final, Dumas seemed a cinch.

But Charles Porter, a young Australian who had never before gone as high as six feet nine inches, stuck with Dumas

278

right up until the bar reached six feet eleven and one half inches. Then both men missed their first two attempts. Dumas made the height on his last try, and when Porter failed, the American earned the gold medal. Dumas admitted that he had spent the entire night before the event lying awake and thinking about his opponents. "I rested all right," he calmly explained. "I just didn't sleep."

The field for the 800-meter final included four men capable of winning—Tom Courtney and Arnie Sowell of the United States, Audun Boysen of Norway, and Derek Johnson of Great Britain. Courtney burst in front at the start, then fell back into second place behind Sowell. In the last 100 meters, Courtney of Fordham moved to the outside and, straining himself, inched past Sowell of Pittsburgh. The two Americans hurried toward the tape, but fifty yards from the finish, Britain's Johnson, with a tremendous sprint, overtook both leaders and, seemingly, snatched the championship. But Courtney refused to quit. With his last few strides, he summoned superhuman strength, hurled himself past Johnson, hit the tape, and collapsed. "When Johnson got a yard ahead of me—I guess it must have been about fifty yards from the finish— I thought the race was all over," said Courtney, after he regained his senses. "I thought I had lost. I don't even remember what happened after that."

Dan Ferris, the veteran American amateur sports official who had seen every Olympics since 1912, called Courtney's victory one of the two most dramatic events he had ever witnessed in the games. "The only thing that matched it," Ferris said, "was Ted Meredith's victory at 800 meters in 1912."

The hammer throw presented the most direct case of Russian-American competition. Harold Connolly, a New England schoolteacher, and Mikhail Krivonosov, a Minsk schoolteacher, had been taking turns all year breaking the world record. Krivonosov, a slightly more consistent performer, was rated a slim favorite. But Connolly was eager to face the Russian, so eager, in fact, that he kept a picture of Krivonosov on his automobile windshield visor to remind him of his rival.

Krivonosov took the lead in the second of the six rounds and held it until the fifth. Then Connolly got off a throw six inches beyond the Russian's best, broke the Olympic record, and won the championship. "Man, I was nervous," Connolly conceded later. "My hands were sweating so bad I could hardly hang on to the handle."

How had he managed to win?

"Krivonosov," Connolly explained, "was nervous, too."

Connolly took more than a gold medal away from the Iron Curtain countries. During the games in Melbourne, he met a young lady named Olga Fikotova, who happened to throw the discus for Czechoslovakia, happened to win the Olympic championship, and happened to be unusually attractive. Connolly took an immediate liking to the tall, brown-eyed, auburn-haired Czech girl and began escorting her around the Olympic Village. After the games, when Connolly went home

The master of the shot-put, Parry O'Brien, earns his second straight Olympic title.

to Boston and Olga went home to Prague, the romance flourished by mail. The following year, Connolly went to Czechoslovakia on a ten-day visa and asked Antonin Zapotocky, the president of Czechoslovakia, for permission to marry Olga and bring her back to the United States. At first, President Zapotocky turned down the request. From the Czech point of view, the President's reluctance was understandable. After all, Czechoslovakia wasn't gaining a hammer thrower; it was losing a discus thrower.

"No force in the world will be able to separate me forever from the girl I love with all my heart and soul," thundered Connolly. He was right. With an assist from the United States Department of State, Harold Connolly married Olga Fikotova in Prague on March 27, 1957. Emil Zatopek, who placed sixth in the 1956 Marathon race, acted as best man at the wedding. Three years later, both Connollys represented the United States in the Rome Olympics.

During the early stages of the games in Melbourne, when mostly track and field events were being held, the United States built up a comfortable margin over the Soviet Union in the unofficial point totals. But just when the American lead seemed insurmountable—262 to 150 at one point—the Russians began to catch up. Once more the Soviets rolled up a huge score in gymnastics; their star was a lovely young lady

Future pros in action: Laszlo Papp of Hungary (right) scores with a right, and Pete Rademacher of the United States turns away after flooring a Russian opponent.

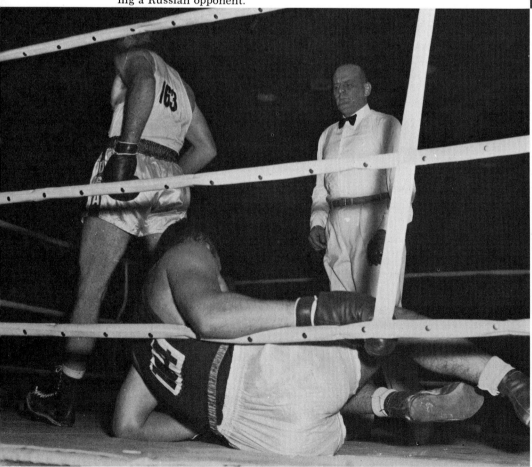

named Larisa Latynina, who won four gold medals. The Russians won five firsts in Greco-Roman wrestling, the Americans none.

The Russian-American rivalry grew keenest in weight-lifting and in boxing. In weight-lifting, for the second straight Olympics, the United States won four gold medals to the Soviet Union's three. Among the Americans, Tommy Kono, the 1952 star, and Paul Anderson, a heavyweight lifter from Georgia, presented a study in contrasts. Kono was eating six meals a day to bring his weight up to 181 pounds for the light-heavyweight division; Anderson was eating only one meal a day to keep his weight down below 310 pounds. Both diets paid dividends. Kono, strong at 181, won the light-heavyweight division. Anderson, in the heavyweight division, lifted exactly the same number of pounds as a giant from the Argentine, Humberto Selvetti. In case of a tie in weight-lifting, the lifter who weighs less than his rival wins the championship. Anderson won. He weighed 304 pounds, Selvetti 316. Who says calories don't count?

But if the United States outmuscled the Soviet Union in weight-lifting, the Russians got even in boxing. Three Russians won championships; only two Americans scored. One of the Americans, Pete Rademacher, won the heavyweight title, promptly turned professional, and in his first pro fight, met the 1952 Olympic middleweight winner, Floyd Patterson, for the world heavyweight championship. Patterson gave Rademacher a rude introduction to the professional sport; he knocked out his fellow Olympian in six rounds.

In basketball, the Russians exhibited a seven-foot three-inch center, Yan Kruminsh, a Latvian woodchopper, but the extra height did the Soviet team no good. The United States had Bill Russell and K. C. Jones, fresh from the University of San Francisco, and the two Californians spurred the Americans to an 89–55 victory over Russia in the finals. Kruminsh, who had been playing basketball only a few years, was awkward and ineffective, often jeered at by the spectators. "I do not mind the people," he said. "If I play good, they like me. If I play bad, they don't." He managed to retain a toothy grin at all times.

"Kruminsh ought to be a Russian poet," one reporter suggested. "His face reflects the sorrow of the soil."

Another Russian newcomer, young Vyacheslav Ivanov, turned back American Jack Kelly, the son of the 1920 champion, in the single sculls. But the star of the crew races in Melbourne was not an individual; it was a full eight-oared crew, with coxswain.

The Yale crew, seeking to score the eighth consecutive victory for the United States in Olympic eight-oared racing, received a severe shock in its opening race. Australia and Canada both finished in front of the Americans. But, under Olympic rowing rules, Yale still had one chance left; it could compete in a repechage race for losers, and if it won, it could enter the semifinals. The youngsters from New Haven won the repechage, then won the semifinal, too. They entered the

A matter of perspective: American Bill Russell looks up at Russia's Yan Kruminsh (left), then jumps far above his Japanese rival.

Yale's comeback crew (top) wins the eight-oared championship by edging Canada.

final against their two first-round conquerors—Canada and Australia—and Sweden.

Canada and Australia shared the lead at the beginning of the 2,000-meter race, but halfway down the course, Yale swept in front. The Elis couldn't relax; Canada and Australia kept up relentless pressure. Yale raised its stroke to 38, and Australia fell back. Then Yale went up to a murderous 40 beats a minute and, with 40,000 spectators looking on, beat back the Canadian bid by barely half a length. Some of the Yale oarsmen collapsed; others got physically sick; a few cried. "We're the toughest crew ever put together," said captain Tom Charlton, "and we beat the finest." No one argued his statement.

The Russians, too, had a rugged experience in the water—and the game was the rugged one of water polo. In the semifinals, Russia met Hungary. It was the battle of Budapest all over again. From the stands, Hungarian expatriates hurled insults at the Russian players, and in the water, the tough Hungarians hurled elbows at their enemies. In a struggle for a loose ball two minutes from the end, with Hungary holding a comfortable 4–0 lead, Russia's Valentin Prokopov butted Hungary's Ervin Zador, drawing blood from above the Hungarian's eye.

"It looked to me like the Russian was justified," Wally Wolf, a veteran American water polo player, said later. "The Hungarians had been pushing him around all game. It really wasn't much of a cut, but with the water dripping down, it looked like he was bleeding to death. After the incident, the Hungarians caucused at one end of the pool, probably trying to decide who they would hit to get even. The Russians, at the other end, decided to leave the pool and forfeit the match. They were lucky to get out of the stadium alive."

One other distressing incident marred the Melbourne games. In the platform diving competition, Gary Tobian of the United States impressed everyone as the best performer—everyone except a Russian and a Hungarian among the judges. Each time Tobian dived, the two Communist judges rated him far more severely than the other five judges did. As a result, Joaquin Capilla of Mexico won a tainted victory by the slimmest of margins. Even Capilla was unhappy with the result; he admitted that Tobian deserved the title.

Slowly but inexorably, as the games progressed, the Russians cut into the American point lead. Finally, on Thursday of the second week of competition, only two days before the closing ceremonies, the Russians broke loose, gained a fistful of championships in gymnastics and Greco-Roman wrestling, and moved ahead of the United States, 690½ to 558½. "The Golden Thursday of Soviet Sport," *Komsomolskaya Pravda*, the Russian youth newspaper, announced. "The American lead has been liquidated," said *Pravda*.

The American lead was indeed finished. By the time the games ended, the Russians had thirty-seven gold medals and 722 unofficial points, the Americans thirty-two gold medals and 593 points. The Soviet Union had become the strongest athletic nation in the world.

In the closing ceremonies, with thoughts of Budapest and the Gaza Strip still lingering, a curious thing happened. For the first time in Olympic history, the athletes did not march by nations. Instead, they marched informally, Russians with Englishmen, Frenchmen with Australians, Americans with Czechs, Africans with Asians, all mixed together, all caught up in the Olympic spirit of friendship. It was a pleasant ending to a tense two weeks, and it was a harbinger of the international goodwill that was to thrive at the 1960 Olympic Games in Rome.

Attacker and attacked: Russia's Valentin Prokopov (top) drew blood when he banged heads with Hungary's Ervin Zador.

283

With quiet grimness, Rafer Johnson dogs the steps of C. K. Yang in the decathlon 1,500-meter run.

# Just Friends and Brave Enemies

## CHAPTER SEVENTEEN : 1960 – ROME AND SQUAW VALLEY

*"Tonight, I'm going to walk for about four hours and look at the moon. I don't know where—just walk, walk, walk. I've got to unwind. I'm through, man, through."*

—RAFER JOHNSON
After the ordeal

It was night, and in the eerie artificial glow that lit Rome's Olympic Stadium, two husky young men, glistening with sweat, awaited the start of the 1,500-meter run, the exhausting climax to every exhausting decathlon competition. Neither spoke. There was nothing to say. The Olympic decathlon championship hinged upon the outcome of the race.

The quiet rivals were, at other times, close friends. They both attended the University of California at Los Angeles, and they both trained under U.C.L.A. Coach Ducky Drake. But in Rome in 1960, Rafer Lewis Johnson, twenty-six, six feet three inches tall and 198 pounds, a graduate student from Kingsburg, California, and Yang Chuan-kwang, twenty-seven, six feet one inch tall and 185 pounds, an undergraduate from the island of Formosa, temporarily set aside their friendship. They were, beyond question, the two most gifted decathlon men in the world, and each wanted the Olympic championship for himself.

For two days, they had been matching speed and strength, skill and stamina. Yang had defeated Johnson in all six of the running and jumping events, but Johnson had scored so heavily in the three weight-throwing events that he carried a slim sixty-seven-point lead into the final test. Johnson's margin was hardly a safe one. If Yang could outrun Johnson by ten seconds or more in the 1,500-meter run, he would capture the Olympic title.

Then the race began, and Yang, the pride of Nationalist

China, his belabored nation's only hope for an Olympic gold medal, moved quickly into the lead. Johnson, the dignified captain and flag-bearer for the mighty American team, slipped in behind Yang. Johnson's strategy was clear. All he had to do was stay close to Yang, stay within ten seconds of Yang, and he would win the championship. Grimly, almost automatically, the pair jogged along, matching stride for stride, the Formosan leading the American, barely a yard separating them. Desperately, Yang stepped up his pace, and Johnson, reacting, accelerated too. Yang's strength was ebbing, but still he struggled to break clear. Johnson stayed with him. "I could see him behind me at the turns," Yang said afterward. "I could see his dark form and I knew he would never let go of me unless he collapsed."

Three hundred meters from the finish, Yang's energy seemed spent. His chin slumped forward on his chest. But, somehow, drawing on his last reservoir of strength, he summoned new speed. Johnson met the challenge. With sheer will power, he clung to Yang, clung to his friend and enemy, almost to the tape. Yang lunged across the finish line in four minutes forty-eight and five tenths seconds; Johnson's time was only one and two tenths seconds slower. By 8,392 points to 8,334—both scores well above the previous Olympic record—Rafer Johnson won the Olympic decathlon championship. Russia's Vasily Kuznetsov, once the holder of the world record, placed a distant third with 7,809 points.

Yang and Johnson staggered off the field together. Then Yang collapsed into the arms of Wei Chen-wu, the head coach of the Formosan track and field team. "I'm sorry," said Yang, fighting tears. "I'm so ashamed. I disappointed you."

Wei shook his head. "You are a hero and a great athlete," he said. "Do not feel badly."

Later, in the dressing room, still wet with sweat, Yang tried to explain his defeat. "I knew I had lost my chance as soon as I found out I was in Rafer's 1,500-meter heat," he said. "If I had run alone, if Rafer had not run in the same heat with me, I would have won the gold medal, not Rafer."

Johnson nodded, sympathetically. "I wanted that one real bad," he said. "But I never want to go through that again—never."

Yang managed to smile. "Nice going, Rafe," he said.

After the 1960 Olympics, the friendly enemies went opposite ways. Back at his studies and his training, Yang began pointing to the 1964 Olympic Games in Tokyo. Johnson quit competition, turned briefly to movie acting, and then went to work for the United States People-to-People Foundation. "Eventually, I'd like to work for the State Department," he said. "I'd travel and meet people and talk with them. I'd really like to help improve international relations."

Johnson, who had competed in Melbourne, was already an old hand at bolstering international relations. Shortly before competition began in Rome, Kuznetsov, the Russian decathlon star, approached Johnson and asked him to pose for a photo-

In eerie spotlights, Johnson hurls the javelin.

graph. "Sure," said Johnson, pleasantly. "You and me and Yang."

Neither Yang nor Kuznetsov, understandably, was anxious to pose with the other. As a Formosan, Yang was naturally anti-Communist; as a Communist, Kuznetsov was naturally anti-Nationalist China. But Johnson persuaded both of them to join him. Kuznetsov grinned. "Okay," he said, turning to Yang, "but, remember, I don't know you."

International goodwill soared to an Olympic peak in Rome. Part of the explanation was that the world, at the time, was reasonably free of violence; neither a Korean War, as in 1952, nor a Hungarian revolution, as in 1956, cast its pall over the games. Equally important, the American and Russian athletes had come to know each other in the years since the Melbourne Olympics. In 1958, the United States national track and field team had competed in Moscow. In 1959, the Soviet Union national track and field team had competed in Philadelphia. The two meets stimulated friendship and understanding.

In Rome, Vladimir Bulatov, a veteran Russian pole vaulter, chatted amiably with his American rival, Don Bragg, who had shared a spaghetti dinner with Bulatov in Philadelphia; Igor Ter-Ovanesyan, a talented Soviet broad jumper, traded jokes and souvenirs with dozens of American friends; and Earlene Brown, an extroverted, 225-pound Los Angeles housewife, showed photographs of her child to her discus throwing and shot-putting rival, Tamara Press of the Soviet Union. New friendships flourished too. Tasia Tchenshik and Vera Ozolina, two Russian girls, talked John Thomas, an American high jumper, into posing for pictures with his arms around them. Ben Northrup, a United States wrestler, danced with Luchilla Klipowa, a Soviet swimmer, and Doris Fuchs, an American gymnast, danced with Boris Nikonorov, a Russian boxer.

Soviet officials, icily aloof in the past, encouraged the East-West fraternization. "Politics is one thing, sports another," said Constantin Andrianov, the chairman of the Russian Olympic Committee. "We are sportsmen."

It was hard for anyone to be bitter in the magnificent setting the Italians had provided for the 1960 Olympic Games. The Italian Olympic Committee spent more than $24,000,000 fusing the futuristic sports palaces designed by architect Pier Luigi Nervi with the ancient wonders of Rome to produce a glittering Olympic network sprawling from one end of the seven hills to the other. Basketball, a modern game, was played in Nervi's modern Palazetto; wrestling, an ancient sport, was staged in the ancient Basilica of Maxentius.

Of course, not everyone among the record total of 5,396 athletes, representing eighty-four nations, was completely satisfied. Some competitors objected to the questionnaire they were asked to fill out. They were supposed to reveal their sexual temperaments, the state of their marriages, their social levels, their eating and drinking habits, and their favorite colors. "The athletes may ignore certain or even all of the questions and still be permitted to compete," said an Italian

Yang picks up points in the broad jump.

287

Olympic spokesman. "It's just that if they do reply, their answers will be of immense scientific value."

Once the games began, the track and field events, as usual, attracted the most attention. The keynote was variety. As Olympic records fell in every event except the 110-meter high hurdles, 5,000-meter run, and 20-kilometer walk, ten different countries won gold medals, and nineteen different countries won medals of gold, silver, or bronze. Several nations that never before had entered the Olympics couldn't resist the temptation of Rome; tiny Surinam, for instance, dispatched one athlete, Wim Essajas, an 800-meter runner. For four years, Essajas had trained diligently. But, in Rome, he didn't win. He didn't even race. The only athlete from Surinam slept through the trials in his event. "What are the folks back home going to say?" he wondered.

The folks back home in Australia, New Zealand, and even Ethiopia had pleasant things to talk about. The 1,500-meter run attracted so brilliant a field of sub-four-minute-milers that Roger Bannister, the original four-minute-miler, predicted "not more than ten meters will separate the first six finishers." But Australia's Herb Elliott made a shambles of both the prediction and the race. Running so swiftly that he pulled the next five finishers past the Olympic record, Elliott won by more than twenty meters and set a world record of three minutes thirty-five and six tenths seconds. Elliott took his victory calmly. "It's an experience I'll never forget," he said, simply.

An unknown New Zealander, twenty-one-year-old Peter Snell, went to Rome looking only for experience and found a gold medal. With a blistering stretch run that cut down famous rivals, Snell set an Olympic record in the 800-meter run. "I never really expected to win," he confessed. "I thought maybe I would have a bronze. I was relaxed, you know. I'm really very pleased."

An Ethiopian as obscure as Snell, Abebe Bikila, a skinny member of Emperor Haile Selassie's palace guards, scored his country's first Olympic victory. Bikila ran the Marathon in his bare feet and covered the twenty-six miles in two hours and fifteen minutes, eight minutes faster than Emil Zatopek's Olympic record. Only a quarter of a century before Bikila's triumph in Rome, Italy had conquered Ethiopia.

The most stunning aspect of the 1960 track and field competition was the unexpected letdown of the American squad. Heralded as the best United States team ever, supposedly a threat to the 1956 team's record of fifteen gold medals, the American delegation lost eight of the first eleven events it entered.

It wasn't only that the Americans lost. It was the way they lost. Seven of the United States athletes entered their events as favorites—and four of the seven were soundly beaten. Not one of the upset American losers finished as high as second.

"This is a lesson in modesty for Americans," crowed *Il Paese,* a left-wing Italian daily.

The lesson was painful. Gloom hung over the American

Australia's Herb Elliott holds the lead in the 1,500-meter run (left); Ray Norton, the goat of the games, takes the baton from teammate Frank Budd (top); and two-time champion Glenn Davis sweeps over the hurdles.

quarters in the Olympic Village. Shock and disbelief, bitterness and sorrow, recriminations and apologies—all set off an explosion of explanations. "The boys have been living it up," charged one American reporter at the scene. "You can't win gold medals when you're not in condition. And you don't get in condition sitting up half the night drinking wine."

The American athletes angrily denied the charges of high living. They blamed their food (dozens of them suffered from diarrhea), their hard beds (many slept on the floor), and their managers (who scheduled three major meets in the month leading up to the games).

But, unquestionably, the athletes were at fault too. Overconfidence hurt them. They had been told repeatedly that they were unbeatable—and they had believed it. No one seemed so unbeatable as John Thomas of Boston University, the greatest high jumper in history.

From the start of the pre-Olympic training sessions in California, Thomas appeared totally relaxed and confident. One morning he went out for an early workout, and when he returned to his dormitory, a coach asked, "Where've you been, John?"

"We decided to work out before it got too hot," Thomas said.

"Who," said the coach, "is we?"

Thomas shrugged. "Me and all the parts of my body," he replied.

In Rome, whenever Russians were watching him practice, Thomas casually set the crossbar at seven feet and cleared it easily. The Russians walked away shaking their heads. "I psyched 'em," said Thomas.

"Thomas is unbeatable," said Harry Korobkov, the Soviet coach.

But in the Olympic competition, the Russians stopped shaking their heads—and started jumping. When Thomas went over the bar at seven feet one quarter inch, all three Russian entrants went over too. Thomas was visibly surprised; he was not accustomed to having so much company above seven feet. When the bar was raised to seven feet one inch, two Russians —Robert Shavlakadze and Valery Brumel—cleared it with the highest jumps of their lives. Thomas missed on his first two tries. On his final attempt, he took short, deliberate steps, leaped—and failed. Shavlakadze won first place on the basis of fewer misses; a graduate student in physical education, he had written his thesis on "Stability in Results in the High Jump."

Brumel finished second, Thomas third. "If Thomas psyched anyone," said a Russian official, "it was himself."

"They beat me fair and square," said Thomas, without bitterness. "I'm not disappointed. I got a bronze medal and that's a lot better than most people in the world can do."

The day the Russians beat Thomas soon became known as "Black Thursday" in the American camp. In the 800-meter run, won by the United States in every Olympics since 1932,

289

not a single American qualified for the final. In the six-man final of the 100-meter dash, won by the United States in every Olympics since 1928, a Californian named Ray Norton was the overwhelming favorite. "I expect to win three gold medals," Norton said before he competed. "The 100-meter dash, 200-meter dash, and 400-meter relay."

But after one false start in the 100-meter final, Armin Hary, a cocky young German, shot out of the starting blocks with incredible speed and held on just long enough to nip Dave Sime of the United States at the tape. Norton finished dead last.

"Rudolph Valentino was called the Thief of Hearts," said Hary. "I am the Thief of Starts." He was, too. The normal human being reacts to sound in twelve hundredths of a second; Hary reacted in four hundredths.

Two days after "Black Thursday" came "Black Saturday" for the United States. Harold Connolly, holder of the world record, defending champion, and strong favorite in the hammer throw, didn't even qualify for the final round. Vasily Rudenkov of the Soviet Union won the championship, followed by a Hungarian and a Pole.

In the 200-meter dash, Norton, once again the favorite, once again finished last. A slender Italian named Livio Berruti, who wore sunglasses as he ran, delighted the home crowd by beating American Les Carney to the finish. The United States, which had won both sprints in the five previous Olympics, now had lost both. "I did awful," said Norton. "I don't know what's wrong."

When someone told him that he had left his spiked shoes on the track, Norton snapped, "I don't want to see them again."

Norton did see his spiked shoes again—when he wore them in the 400-meter relay final—and again he failed. Teamed up with Frank Budd, Stone Johnson, and Sime, Norton ran the second leg in the relay. As he took the baton from lead-off man Budd, Norton stepped out of the passing zone. Because of Norton's misstep, the American quartet, after winning the event in world record time, was disqualified. "I ran too slow in the sprints and too fast in the relay," said Norton, acidly. "I'm through with track. I've had it."

Despite the horrors of its disastrous start, the American team managed to maintain some of its prestige. Three 1956 champions successfully defended their titles: Discus thrower Al Oerter, 110-meter high hurdler Lee Calhoun, and 400-meter hurdler Glenn Davis led the United States to one-two-three sweeps in their events.

To salve American wounds, Don Bragg, whose frustrated ambition was to play Tarzan in the movies, pole-vaulted fifteen feet five and one eighth inches, nearly six inches above the old Olympic record, and celebrated with a chest-thumping jungle yell. Teammate Ralph Boston, tall and loose, won the broad jump with a leap of twenty-six feet seven and three quarters inches, erasing the oldest existing Olympic mark set twenty-four years earlier by Jesse Owens.

After a barely unsuccessful bid to overtake American Otis Davis in the 400-meter final, Germany's Carl Kaufmann sprawls on the track.

Oerter, Calhoun, Glenn Davis, Bragg, and Boston were all favorites, but no one expected a victory from Otis Davis, a twenty-eight-year-old Air Force veteran who had never competed in track and field until he was twenty-five. Then, while attending the University of Oregon on a basketball scholarship, Davis, six feet one inch tall, decided to try out for the track team as a high jumper. He wasn't much good, so he switched to the short sprints. He wasn't much good there, either, so, in 1959, he switched to the quarter mile. "You'll never make a runner out of me," he told Oregon coach Bill Bowerman. But Bowerman kept pushing him, and suddenly Davis was very good, good enough to make the United States Olympic team as the number three 400-meter man, behind Earl Young and Jack Yerman.

In Rome, Davis improved steadily. He won his first heat in forty-six and eight tenths seconds, his second heat in forty-five and nine tenths seconds, and his semifinal heat in forty-five and five tenths seconds. "That's as fast as I can go," he announced after the semifinal. He was wrong.

In the final, Mal Spence of South Africa grabbed the lead immediately and held it for more than 200 meters. Then Davis made his move, swept past Spence, and, at 300 meters, held a sizable lead over Spence and teammate Young. Spence and Young started to fade, but Carl Kaufmann, a New York-born German, started to pick up speed. He rushed past the second and third men and began closing in on Davis. Step by step, Kaufmann gained, and then, just as the tape loomed in front of him, he flung himself forward, crossed the finish, crashed to the ground, and lay stretched out, almost lifeless. He and Davis, who had turned his head to the side to watch Kaufmann's driving finish, had hit the tape almost simultaneously. Both men were timed in forty-four and nine tenths seconds, a world record. For several agonizing minutes, the judges studied the photographs of the finish. Then one judge walked over to Davis and whispered the result to him. Davis leaped in the air, flushed with victory, and clasped his hands over his head. "I owe it all to Bowerman," he said later. "I never dreamed I could ever do all of this."

The four American shot-putters who gathered in Rome could not match Davis's modesty. The headmaster of the quarrelsome quartet was Parry O'Brien, twenty-eight, 1952 and 1956 Olympic champion, self-styled master of psychology. His rivals were Bill Nieder, twenty-six, a disbeliever in psychology; Dallas Long, twenty, an occasional victim of psychology; and Dave Davis, twenty-three, erratic in performance and behavior.

The chief antagonists were O'Brien and Nieder; their feud dated back to 1957, when Nieder, then a Kansas University freshman, upset O'Brien in the Kansas Relays. "It griped O'Brien so much," said Nieder afterward, "that he wouldn't speak to me."

After 1957, the two spoke rarely to each other, often of each other. "Nieder is a cow-pasture performer," O'Brien charged. "He can't win under pressure."

Even a pigeon can't slow up Italy's Livio Berruti (right), the 200-meter champion.

Harold Connolly flexes his muscles, but fails to retain his hammer-throwing championship.

"O'Brien avoids me," Nieder riposted. "He is the Los Angeles dodger."

When Long and Davis joined the club in 1960, both sided with Nieder. "Let's whip O'Brien in Rome," Long ended each letter he wrote to Nieder. "O'Brien bugs me," said Davis, eloquently.

O'Brien scorned all three. "All of them take senior-citizen psych," he said, "and I'm the senior citizen of the shot."

In the United States Olympic trials, Long finished first, O'Brien second, Davis third, and Nieder fourth. "The worst day of my life," said Nieder, unhappily.

"In big meets," O'Brien reiterated, "Nieder chokes up."

Nieder became an alternate on the American squad, but in practice sessions, he consistently outthrew his three rivals. Rumors spread that Larry Snyder, the coach of the United States Olympians, was going to replace Davis, who had a slight wrist sprain, with Nieder. "They should leave Davis on," O'Brien insisted, somewhat nervously. "That injury's nothing."

In the final tune-up meet in the United States, Nieder heaved the shot sixty-five feet ten inches, a world record. The next day, coach Snyder announced that Nieder would compete in Rome and that Davis would make the trip only as an alternate. "I just want to prove," Nieder said, "that I don't choke. I promise I'll come back with a gold medal."

The week before the competition began in Rome, the war of the whales reached a peak. Nieder, Long, and O'Brien trained separately, roomed separately, and ate separately. "When people are fighting to be the best in the world in something," said Nieder, "they can't be friends. There must be tension. There has to be hate." O'Brien confidently prepared to fire his psychological salvos.

"You can't psych anybody," said Nieder, "when you're always two feet behind them."

"O'Brien can't psych anybody because he's gone to his limit," Long added. "And he knows we know it."

Then came the competition. After four of the six throws, it looked as though Nieder and Long had been whistling in the dark. O'Brien's brand of psychology seemed to be holding up. He was first with an Olympic record throw of sixty-two feet eight and three eighths inches, Long second, Nieder third. But on his fifth try, Nieder hurled the sixteen-pound shot sixty-four feet six and three quarters inches, a foot farther than O'Brien had ever thrown in competition. Nieder clinched the championship. "O'Brien might as well shoot himself now," suggested a spectator.

Davis, standing nearby, pulled a toy pistol from his pocket. "I'll give him the gun," he said.

The United States wound up the track and field events with nine gold medals, its lowest total since 1928, and the Soviet Union wound up with five, its highest ever. In addition to the high jump and the hammer throw, Russians won the javelin throw, 10,000-meter run, and 20-kilometer walk.

In the women's events, too, the Soviet Union staged its

Ralph Boston breaks the record set by Jesse Owens in the Olympic broad jump.

most impressive showing. As Olympic records toppled in all ten events, the Russians, led by the Press sisters, captured six gold medals. Tamara Press, the broader and older of the sisters, won the shot-put and placed second in the discus. Irina Press won the 80-meter hurdles race. Discus thrower Nina Ponomareva, who had won her specialty in 1952 under her maiden name of Romaschkova, and javelin thrower Vera Ozolina gave the Soviets a sweep of the weight-throwing events.

The United States would have been shut out in the women's events were it not for a long-legged, attractive, twenty-year-old named Wilma Rudolph. Her friends called her "Skeeter." The French called her "La Gazelle."

Born in Tennessee, the seventeenth child in a family of nineteen children, Wilma suffered double pneumonia and scarlet fever at the age of four and could not walk properly until she was eleven. Then she began exercising to build her strength. Soon after she entered Tennessee State University, she proved she was the fastest female sprinter in the United States. "There's not a nerve in her body," said Ed Temple, the Tennessee State coach. "She's almost lazy. She often goes to sleep between the semifinal and final runs. Then she gets over those starting blocks and—boom—all that harnessed energy explodes into speed."

Wilma exploded in Rome. First she won the 100-meter dash in eleven seconds flat, cutting half a second off the Olympic record. Then, after setting an Olympic record in the trials of the 200-meter dash, she breezed to victory in the final. For an extra touch, she came from behind on the anchor leg of the 400-meter relay team and led the United States to another triumph. She was the first American girl ever to win three gold medals in Olympic track and field competition.

The United States and the Soviet Union, to no one's surprise, far outdistanced all other nations at collecting gold medals in Rome. But the drama generated by the international rivalry, so compelling at Helsinki in 1952 and at Melbourne in 1956, had faded. In Rome, almost everyone expected the Russians to outscore the Americans—and the Russians lived up to expectations.

Perhaps the turning point came in the weight-lifting competition. In both previous Olympics, the underdog American squads had won four gold medals, the favored Russians three in the seven weight-lifting divisions. But in Rome, the Soviets won five championships, the Americans only one. Even Tommy Kono, the remarkable Japanese-American who had earned gold medals in Helsinki and in Melbourne, had to settle for a silver medal in Rome.

The United States picked up some ground in boxing. While the Russians were limited to one champion, the Americans contributed three—three vastly different individuals. Wilbert McClure, a quiet, polite, twenty-one-year-old college student, won the light-middleweight division; Eddie Crook, a rugged, versatile, thirty-one-year-old army sergeant, won the middleweight division; and Cassius Marcellus Clay, a brash, flashy, eighteen-year-old high school graduate, won the light-heavy-weight division.

"That was my 144th and last fight of my life," said McClure, an education major at the University of Toledo, after beating a tough Italian in the final. "I'm sick of sports. I want no part of them from here in." McClure reconsidered after the Olympics, turned professional, and promptly won his first fourteen pro fights.

"I thought I was so far ahead I could coast," said Crook, after winning a disputed decision from a Polish middleweight. "I'll tell you one thing. I'll never turn pro." Then Crook, who had learned to box in the army, went back to Fort Campbell, Kentucky, where he was a football and baseball star and a veteran paratrooper.

Clay started talking before the Olympics began and never shut up. In Rome, he seemed to be running for mayor of the Olympic Village. Of all the 5,000 international athletes, he was, by design, the best known. He roamed from one national area to the next, pausing long enough to exchange greetings and snap pictures with his Brownie camera. He took hundreds of photos of Russians, Americans, Chinese, Italians, Congolese, everyone. Once, when he was talking with an American reporter, a group of Indians walked by. "Excuse me," Clay said. "I gotta get some shots of those cats with the beards."

After he won the Olympic championship, he wore his gold medal around his neck for the next forty-eight hours. "First time in my life I ever slept on my back," Clay said later. "Had to or that medal would have cut my chest."

When he arrived in New York after the games, Clay quickly set off on a tour of the city. Everywhere he went, he wore his blue Olympic blazer, with "USA" embroidered upon it, and his gold medal, with "Pugilato" engraved on it. It was only two days after his final fight, and his face was still fresh in the minds of millions who had viewed the Olympics on television.

As Clay strolled through Times Square, a bypasser did a double-take and asked, "Aren't you Cassius Clay?"

"Yeah, man," Clay said. "That's me. How'd you know who I was?"

"I saw you on TV," said the stranger. "So did lots of people. They all know who you are."

Clay hung his head, feigning modesty. "Really?" he said. "That's wonderful."

Dozens of people stopped him on the street and, for each, Clay had a grin and an air of amazement. "I guess everybody do know who I am," he conceded.

Later in a cab heading toward Greenwich Village, Clay talked about the recognition he had found. "It's great," he said. "Real great. All those people know who I am." He leaned forward and tapped the cab driver on the shoulder. "Why," he said, "I bet even you know that I'm Cassius Clay, the great fighter."

Clay became a professional a few weeks later and rapidly

The two shot-put champions, Bill Nieder of the United States (left) and Tamara Press of the Soviet Union, combine energy and enthusiasm.

grew into the heavyweight division. He recited bad poetry and predicted the rounds in which he would knock out his opponents, and, in time, he became the youngest heavyweight champion in the history of boxing.

In basketball, no other country could even threaten the United States. With the two best college players in the country, Oscar Robertson of Cincinnati and Jerry Lucas of Ohio State, who averaged seventeen points apiece during the Olympic tournament, the American team swept to eight consecutive one-sided victories. The United States averaged 102 points a game, allowed opponents an average of only 60 points a game. In its closest match, the United States crushed the Soviet Union, 81–57; Robertson scored sixteen points, Jerry West of West Virginia scored nineteen, and Lucas helped keep Russia's seven-foot three-inch center, Yan Kruminsh, from scoring a single point.

The American and Russian wrestlers grappled to a standoff in Rome. In the free style category, where the Russians were shut out, three Americans won championships. Curiously, not one of the three United States gold medalists—Terry McCann, Shelby Wilson, and Doug Blubaugh—had won his division in the American Olympic trials; each had earned a late promotion to a first-string job. In the Greco-Roman category, where the Americans were shut out, three Russians won championships. But the Soviet performance was tainted by one unpleasant incident. In the lightweight division, Avtandil Koridze of Russia and Dimitro Stoyanov of Bulgaria wrestled on even terms for eleven minutes. Under the wrestling scoring system, a draw would have eliminated both men and given the gold medal to Branco Martinovic of Yugoslavia. Suddenly, without warning, Koridze threw the Bulgarian and won the match. A Japanese judge accused Stoyanov of deliberately losing to his Russian rival. The International Amateur Wrestling Federation disqualified Stoyanov and barred him from further competition, but although "a suspicion of collusion" existed, Koridze was not disqualified. The Russian then won by decision over Martinovic and earned a gold medal.

Led by Boris Shakhlin, who collected four gold medals, two silver, and one bronze, and Larisa Latynina, who gathered three gold medals, two silver, and one bronze, the Soviet gymnasts won a total of ten championships. In this sport, where medals are shelled out in wholesale lots, the United States, as usual, went home empty-handed.

But the Russian swimmers and divers found out how the American gymnasts felt. The Soviets looked on helplessly as the United States men and women, exceeding expectations, won eleven events. Jeff Farrell, a courageous young man who competed and qualified in the United States Olympic trials only eight days after an emergency appendectomy, and Chris von Saltza, a sixteen-year-old Californian who kept a toy frog at poolside for good luck, picked up most of the hardware for the United States. Farrell earned two gold medals by anchoring both the 800-meter free style relay team and the 400-meter medley relay team to world records. (Even with Murray Rose, the veteran who won the 400-meter free style, and seventeen-year-old John Konrads, the newcomer who won the 1,500-meter free style, the Australian 800-meter relay quartet could finish no better than third.) Miss von Saltza earned two gold medals and one silver. She anchored the American 400-meter free style relay team to victory in world record time and divided the two individual free style races with her arch rival, Australia's Dawn Fraser. Miss Fraser, who had a toy koala bear to match Miss von Saltza's frog, won the 100-meter free style; Miss von Saltza captured the 400-meter race.

Despite their highly successful performances, both the American men and the American women were disturbed by the championships that got away. Paula Myers Pope, competing in her third Olympics, finally was favored—after the retirement of 1952 and 1956 double champion Pat McCormick—to win both the springboard and platform dives. American girls had dominated both events in seven straight Olympics. But a chubby, blonde, blue-eyed, seventeen-year-old high school student, Ingrid Kramer, an East German competing for the combined German Olympic team, spoiled Mrs. Pope's plans. The young lady from Dresden ended an American dynasty and won both diving events. "I had never even heard of Ingrid until two weeks ago," said Mrs. Pope, sadly, as she collected a pair of silver medals.

The American men's unhappiness sprang from the final of the 100-meter free style. With Jeff Farrell, the logical favorite, confined to the relays by his appendectomy, teammate Lance Larson rated a slight edge. Larson's main challenger was John Devitt of Australia.

Devitt held first place with roughly twenty meters to go, but then Larson, a tall blond from California, rallied, caught up, raced stroke for stroke to the finish, and, apparently, touched the wall slightly ahead of Devitt. Larson thought he had won; he broke into a broad grin. Devitt, too, thought Larson had won; "I congratulated Lance, climbed out of the water, and tried not to think about it." But two of the three first-place judges disagreed with both swimmers and gave the championship to Devitt. The ruling seemed absurd; electronic timing devices had caught Larson in fifty-two and one tenth seconds, Devitt in fifty-two and two tenths seconds. Still the Australian, by the judges' majority decision, kept the gold medal.

What bruised American egos more than anything else was that the Soviet Union outscored the United States, two gold medals to one, in rowing, and matched the United States, with one gold medal apiece, in that most capitalistic of all sports, yachting. In rowing, Russia's powerful single sculler, Vyacheslav Ivanov, won his specialty for the second straight Olympics. This was not unexpected. But the unexpected occurred in the eight-oared championship, a United States monopoly since World War I.

The Naval Academy eight-oared shell, representing the

Harold Connolly and his wife, the former Olga Fikotova, relax in Rome.

Oscar Robertson of the United States grabs a rebound against Japan.

Champion in 1952 and 1956, Tommy Kono earns a silver medal in 1960.

United States in Rome, not only failed to win, but finished a dismal fifth. The championship went to coach Karl Adam's German crew, using its revolutionary tulip-shaped blades (shorter and wider than the traditional blades), its revolutionary high stroke (almost always forty or above), and its revolutionary seating positions (with the number four and five oars both rowing on the starboard side).

In the yachting Star class, Timir Pinegin, a Moscow draftsman, guided his boat, *Tornado*, to a decisive victory. To American sailors, the Russian victory, only a few years after Star racing was introduced in the Soviet Union, seemed incredible. But the Americans took some consolation in the discovery that Pinegin had used sails made in the United States and that his boat, in fact, had been built in Old Greenwich, Connecticut. After the event, a generous Russian spokesman jokingly announced that the American sailmakers and boat builders could, if they wished, use Pinegin's photograph in advertisements.

By collecting eight gold medals in canoeing, cycling, riding, and fencing—events in which the United States failed to score a victory—the Soviet Union swept easily to the unofficial over-all championship. The Russians outscored the Americans in gold medals, forty-three to thirty-four, and in unofficial points, 807½ to 564½. The Soviet Union had almost doubled its 1956 victory margin. Twice in a row now, the Russians were masters of the summer games.

Earlier in the year, at Squaw Valley, California, the Soviet Union had won the winter Olympics, too, for the second straight time. The Russian victory formula depended upon two factors: women and speed skaters—and particularly women who speed-skated. Lidija Skoblikova, a blonde, blue-eyed, twenty-one-year-old physiology student from the Urals, best personified the success formula. The Soviet speed skater finished first at 1,500 meters, first at 3,000 meters, and fourth at 1,000 meters, an event won by a Russian teammate. The Soviets added three gold medals in the men's speed skating competition—two for Evgeni Grishin, the converted cyclist who retained his Olympic 500-meter and 1,500-meter titles—and one in women's cross-country skiing.

With seven gold medals (actually six and a half because Grishin was tied at 1,500 meters by Norway's Roald Aas), the Russians accumulated an unofficial total of 165½ points, more than the runner-up, Sweden, and the third-place team, the United States, combined.

Unlike 1956, when Toni Sailer emerged as the star, or 1952, when Andrea Mead Lawrence dominated the slopes, no individual won more than a single Alpine skiing event. Three separate countries—France, Austria, and Switzerland—contributed one champion each in the men's division, and three separate countries—Germany, Canada, and Switzerland—contributed one champion each to the women's division.

The leading American candidate in the Alpine events was Penny Pitou, a frank, ambitious, twenty-one-year-old blonde.

Australia's Dawn Fraser smiles after winning the 100-meter free style for the second time.

"If someone asked me if I wanted a 300 SL Mercedes or a six-year college scholarship," Penny said before the games, "I wouldn't want either. The Olympics are the only thing I want. You talk yourself to the point where a gold medal is the only thing."

Miss Pitou bid boldly for a gold medal in Squaw Valley. She started in the downhill event, and she schussed down the side of KT-22 at breakneck speed, faster and faster until, only fifteen seconds from the end of the course, she hit Airplane Turn, a ninety-degree corner with two small but treacherous humps in the center of it. Penny came into the turn too late, moving too fast for control, staggered, slowed down, and almost fell. By the time she recovered, she had lost several seconds. They proved the difference between a gold medal and a silver medal. Heidi Beibl, a nineteen-year-old German, lost no time at Airplane Turn and beat Penny for first place by exactly one second.

In the giant slalom, Penny again lost by one second, this time to a Swiss girl, Yvonne Ruegg. Then, with her last chance, in the regular slalom, Penny overextended herself on her second run, tumbled to the snow, and finished thirty-third.

If the American spectators were disheartened by the results of the Alpine events, they were cheered by the results in the figure skating competition. Following the example set by Tenley Albright and Hayes Alan Jenkins in 1956, Carol Heiss, the runner-up in Cortina, and David Jenkins, the younger brother of the Cortina champion, brought the United States both individual figure skating titles.

"I love to skate in front of people," said Miss Heiss, after her free-skating performance. "I was tense, almost shaky, when my name was called. But when I got out on the ice and heard all the cheering, I felt everybody was for me. I was happy."

Dave Jenkins felt the same way. "I'm so happy I could cry," he admitted, after his victory. "I think it was the best I've ever done under pressure."

Not long after the games, the men's champion and the women's champion became in-laws. Carol Heiss married Dave's older brother, Hayes Alan.

The unquestioned star of the 1960 winter Olympics was not an individual, but a team, the United States hockey team. Never in Olympic history had the United States won the ice hockey championship, and the 1960 team, at first, seemed no stronger than usual.

In the championship round, the United States started off by beating Sweden and Germany, the two weakest teams in the field, 6–3 and 9–1. Roger Christian of Minnesota scored three goals in the opening victory, assisted on each by his brother William. William Cleary of Massachusetts scored four goals in the second game; his brother Robert scored one.

Canada, the tournament favorite, opened with a 12–0 victory over Germany and followed with a 4–0 victory over strong

Czechoslovakia. Russia also beat Czechoslovakia, 8–5, but was held to a draw by Sweden, 2–2.

In its third game, the United States met Canada. For more than half the opening period, neither team scored. Then Robert Cleary took a pass from John Mayasich and slammed in the first goal. With goalie John McCartan performing brilliantly and stopping thirty-one Canadian shots, the Americans achieved an upset victory, 2–1.

Next the Americans tackled Russia, tied but still unbeaten. Many of the Soviet players, including goalie Nikolai Puchkov and defenseman and captain Nikolai Sologubov, were veterans of the team that had won the championship in Cortina. The United States had never before defeated a Soviet hockey team. William Cleary scored the first goal, but the Russians battled back, tallied twice, and, at the end of the first period, held a 2–1 lead.

Midway through the second period, William Christian, assisted by brother Roger, fired home a goal that brought the Americans even. With superb goal tending by McCartan for the United States and Puchkov for the Soviet Union, the score stayed at 2–2 until less than six minutes remained in the game. Again, William Christian broke loose, again aided by one of his brother's passes, and, suddenly, surprisingly, the United States led, 3–2. The game ended without further scoring. The United States had clinched at least a tie for the Olympic title. By defeating Czechoslovakia on the last day of the games, the Americans would earn the championship.

But the Czechs battled furiously, twice came from behind, and moved in front, 4–3, at the end of the second period. Then, in the most memorable gesture of the 1960 winter Olympics, Nikolai Sologubov, the gregarious captain of the Russian hockey team, visited the United States locker room and indicated with gestures that the Americans should inhale oxygen. Most of the Americans did. Then they returned to the ice, shattered the Czech defense, racked up six goals—all by the Cleary and Christian brothers—and scored a decisive triumph, 9–4. For the first time in Olympic history, the United States won the ice hockey championship.

A few hours later, Avery Brundage, the president of the International Olympic Committee, stood and announced, "I declare the games of the VII winter Olympiad closed." As they listened to the final words, the members of the United States hockey team, still cold and bruised after their battle with Czechoslovakia, knew the feeling of Olympic champions. Some of them shivered. Some of them smiled. But none of them smiled so broadly as Nikolai Sologubov, an officer in the Red Army, a gifted hockey player, and, above all, a true Olympian.

Canadian goalie Don Head slides across the ice as the winning American goal eludes him.

Rounding the last turn in the 1,500-meter run, Peter Snell looks back at his rivals.

# The Kiwi
# Who Could Fly

## CHAPTER EIGHTEEN: 1964—TOKYO AND INNSBRUCK

In Australian slang, the inhabitants of neighboring New Zealand are called, with a mixture of paternalism and mockery, Kiwis, after the strange bird that shares Down Under with the two island nations. The Kiwi, by definition, is a flightless bird.

Peter Snell destroyed the definition.

On a track of cinders or of grass, indoors or outdoors, at distances ranging from 200 yards to more than a mile, Peter Snell, born in the New Zealand coastal town of Opunake and raised in Te Aroha, could fly. His specialties were the half mile and the mile—and their metric equivalents, the 800-meter and 1,500-meter runs. During the first half of the 1960s, carrying his spiked shoes to five different continents, Snell thoroughly rewrote the records in his specialties.

Yet when Peter Snell made his first Olympic appearance, in 1960, he was completely unknown outside his native land. He was so lightly regarded, in fact, that when he showed up for his first heat of the 800-meter trials in Rome—entered against only three other men, the first three finishers to qualify for the semi-finals—a commentator from the British Broadcasting Company announced in the press box: "This is ridiculous. A four-man field and you can write down the first three names before the race starts."

The man from the BBC was right. It was ridiculous. The name he had omitted was Snell.

Peter Snell, then only twenty-one years old, stormed through the trials in Rome and won the 800-meter championship, simultaneously breaking the Olympic record, outracing men with glittering reputations and running far faster than he had ever run before. Then he went home to New Zealand and, following the rigorous training schedule conceived by his coach Arthur Lydiard, added stamina and strength and began pointing toward the 1964 Olympic Games in Tokyo. By 1962, when, in a single week, he reduced the world mile record to 3:54.4 and the world half-mile record to 1:45.1, Snell had established himself as the most strikingly talented figure in international track and field.

Snell cut a striking physical figure, too. Most middle-distance runners are noticeably slender men, some tall, some short, but almost all lean and bony, as though to slice the air cleanly. The curly-haired Snell, in contrast, seemed remarkably husky, with his thick sixteen-and-a-half-inch calves and his bulging thighs. Next to some of his rivals, he looked like a weightlifter, and people who studied him sometimes got carried away by the contrast. One sportswriter likened Snell, in appearance, to a Sherman tank. In his prime, Snell actually was five feet ten and a half inches tall and weighed 171 pounds, with hips so slim his pants had to be specially tailored.

His muscular legs carried Snell to a nine-foot stride, and he possessed another physical gift, the low pulse rate shared by so many masters of endurance. Snell's normal pulse was 42, only two heartbeats a minute faster than Paavo Nurmi's.

Between his unexpected triumph in Rome and the competition in Tokyo, Snell decided that he wanted, in 1964, to win the Olympic 1,500-meter championship, even if he had to surrender his 800-meter title. "There is a possibility that I'll try for the double," Snell said not long before the Games. "I'd like to think I'd run both, and at the moment the opposition in the 800 looks easy. But I would rather win the 1,500, and I don't want to jeopardize my chances. The 1,500 is a glamour event."

Snell's training before the Olympics seemed geared mainly for the 1,500. Stealing time from his sales job with a cigarette company and from his recent marriage, Snell started, in April 1964, running approximately 100 miles each week, stressing development of stamina. In ten weeks, he clocked exactly 1,012 miles. Whenever he could, he adhered to a specific schedule: Running ten miles on Monday, fifteen on Tuesday, twelve on Wednesday, eighteen on Thursday, ten on Friday, fifteen on Saturday, and twenty-two on Sunday, most of them over reasonably flat surfaces. At the end of June, Snell turned to six weeks of running shorter distances, four to eight miles at a time, over hilly terrain, primarily to strengthen his already powerful legs. "At this stage, I was planning everything toward the 1,500 meters," Snell recalled in his autobiography, *No Bugles, No Drums*. "I knew the program [in Tokyo] would suit an attempt on the 800–1,500 double, [but] this was more a dream than a serious consideration. I felt that some of my former sharpness, which was necessary for 800-meter running, had gone."

In the middle of August, two months before the Olympics began, Snell shifted to speed workouts, to sprinting quarter miles and less, often at Lovelock Track, named after New Zealand's 1936 Olympic 1,500-meter champion. One memorable August day, Snell sprinted twenty separate quarter miles, with a quarter-mile jog between each, in an average time of 61.5 seconds. While he was concentrating on speed, he would still trot an extra five or six miles each morning.

Even at his physical best, Snell, a self-questioning type, fluctuated between periods of acute depression and acute elation. Shortly before leaving New Zealand for Japan, he ran a half mile in the plodding time of 2:02, and he felt terrible. When a touch of the flu ruined his first few days in Tokyo, Snell felt even worse. But then, in an 800-meter time trial against his own countryman John Davies and the American Tom O'Hara, Snell suddenly felt right. He covered the distance in 1:47.1, within eight tenths of a second of his Olympic record, handing both of his rivals a physical and psychological setback. Snell decided then that he would attempt the 800-1,500 double.

Snell's boldness even in bidding for the double was impressive. No Olympian had won both the 800-meter and 1,500-meter runs since 1920, when Albert Hill, the thirty-six-year-old Englishman, captured both titles. Earlier, three men—Edwin Flack in 1896, Jim Lightbody in 1904, and Mel Sheppard in 1908—had achieved the middle-distance double. But the competition was not nearly so fierce in those early Olympics, and the races were not nearly so demanding; only Sheppard, with a 1:52.8 clocking in the 800, had turned in a really outstanding performance, for his day.

The physical strain of attempting the double seemed every bit as formidable as the psychological. The first heats of the 800-meter run were scheduled to be held Wednesday, October 14, four days after the Games opened in Tokyo, and the semifinals were to be held the following day. The 800-meter final came on Friday and the first heat of the 1,500-meter run on Saturday, meaning, of course, that Snell had to run four races on four consecutive days against the finest competition in the world.

He did not sleep well the night before his first trial. "All sorts of doubts crowded into my mind," Snell later recalled. "When it really came down to a choice, the 1,500 was the one I wanted most. But obviously, now that I was committed to the 800, I had to ignore the 1,500 to avoid holding any reserves back that might be needed to get me home in the 800. I was in a rather confused state."

There were six heats in the first round of the 800-meter run, and the top four men in each heat were to advance to the semifinals. This did not present any great challenge to Snell, even though his heat, as it developed, was the only one that sent three of its entries all the way to the eight-man final.

Snell's heat was the fourth to be run, and he had watched a young, obscure Kenyan, Wilson Kiprugut, win the first heat in the fine time of 1:47.8. Of all people, Snell did not have to be told how swiftly an unknown runner could develop into an Olympic champion. The third heat gave Snell something else to worry about. Morgan Groth, an American who had run the fastest 800 meters in the world in the first nine months of 1964, finished a fading sixth and did not even qualify for the semifinals.

Without straining, Snell lagged in third place for most of his heat, then, when he felt like it, moved into the lead and, even though he didn't particularly care about finishing first, won the heat in 1:49 flat. "My time was pleasing," he said, "in relation to the effort it took."

The following day, in the semifinal heats, only the first two finishers were guaranteed a place in the final, so Snell wanted to finish first. He held third place going into the final bend, slid to the outside, passed the two leaders and won, by only a tenth of a second, in 1:46.9, the fastest time recorded till then in Tokyo.

Snell saw his mark lowered in the second semifinal. George Kerr of Jamaica, who had placed third behind Snell at Rome, beat Wilson Kiprugut to the tape by inches, and both men were timed in 1:46.1, breaking Snell's Olympic record by two tenths of a second. "I'd been absolutely sure that my Olympic record wouldn't be broken in Tokyo," Snell said afterward, "and logic battled with inner fears as I tried to tell myself that this fantastic semifinal time would spell disaster for these two in the final."

In the 800-meter final, Snell drew the inside lane, which offered him the choice of sprinting for the early lead or conserving his energy and hanging back in the pack. He expected Kiprugut, who had shown himself to be a front-runner, to set the early pace, and he decided he would start strong, then fall in behind the Kenyan. But Kiprugut did not start as swiftly as Snell had anticipated, and although the New Zealander slipped into second, the field remained bunched, with an American, Tom Farrell, boxing Snell in. Snell reached the start of the final lap still trapped, unable to move straight after the leaders.

Deliberately choosing a bold strategy, Snell fell back, out of the box, to the rear of the field, swept out wide and began his bid for the lead. As he entered the final curve, Snell found Kerr and Kiprugut still in front of him and, straining now, using the energy he had developed in his lifetime of athletics, he overtook the leaders, perhaps feeling the effects of their semifinal race, widened his margin in the final straightaway, and broke the tape, still the Olympic 800-meter champion. His time was 1:45.1, clipping a full second off the mark Kiprugut and Kerr had set the previous day.

Bill Crothers of Canada sprinted into second place, Kiprugut brought home a bronze medal for Kenya, its first Olympic prize, and Kerr finished fourth, all of them completing the run in times faster than 1:46.

"This was a much tougher race than the one in Rome," Snell said. "I am really happy about winning, especially the time." He collected his gold medal, spotted his wife Sally standing in front of the grandstand, walked over and handed her the medal. Then he went out to celebrate with a dinner of prime New Zealand lamb chops. The celebration did not last too late, because Snell had to run 1,500 meters the next day.

Snell was hoping his first-round heat at 1,500 meters would be an easy one, a slow one, and it was, the slowest of the day. Snell appreciated the pace.

He knew that the top four men in each heat would move

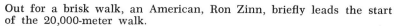
Out for a brisk walk, an American, Ron Zinn, briefly leads the start of the 20,000-meter walk.

on to the semifinals, so he contented himself with securing fourth place, never pressing, spending the last 150 yards looking back over his shoulder to make certain he wasn't being challenged. His time was 3:46.8, the slowest turned in by any man who qualified for the semifinals.

Now, before the semifinals, Snell had a day to rest. "On my off day," he later wrote, "I did an hour's easy jog in the morning and on the day of the semifinals I ran for half an hour before breakfast and felt then that the strength had come back into my legs."

Again, assured that the first four in each of the two semifinals would reach the final, Snell felt no necessity for victory. When Michel Bernard of France set a swift early pace, Snell followed him with the rest of the field. Snell did not, at the time, realize how fast a pace Bernard was setting.

"It was so fast, in fact," Snell said afterward, "that there was no sprint over the last 200 meters and, although I had intended not to win, I found myself going through and passing the finish in the front of the field." Snell defeated Witold Baran of Poland by one tenth of a second in 3:38.8. No one in the other semifinal ran faster than 3:41.5.

After another day off—"I eased out any stiffness with an hour's jogging"—Snell was ready for his sixth major race in eight days, the race he had been pointing for, the 1,500-meter final. "By this time," said Snell, "I was beginning to enjoy racing over the 1,500-meter distance. I hadn't until I reached Tokyo. It involved a curved-line start at the beginning of the back straight, so that by the time the field had settled down there were suddenly only three laps to go. I always found that a pleasant thought."

The Frenchman, Bernard, led the field through the first lap of the 1,500-meter final. Then he gestured for the second-place runner, Dyrol Burleson of the United States, to take the lead. Burleson had no urge to run in front, so, for perhaps 200 meters, the field slowed down. Then Snell's fellow New Zealander, John Davies, who had been beating Snell often a year earlier, moved in front. Snell accelerated into second place.

And then, just as in the 800-meter final, with slightly more than a lap to go, Snell found himself boxed in. He decided he wasn't going to fall back this time. He would try to slide over to the next lane and cut in front of the runner who had boxed him in.

"Fortunately," Snell explained in his book, "it wasn't necessary to use the discourteous elbow-jolt so common in races of this kind. I merely glanced back to see who was behind me as we rounded the bottom bend and then extended my arm, rather like a motorist's hand signal, to show my intentions. I breathed a sigh of relief when the athlete on my shoulder, John Whetton, with the manners of a true Englishman, obligingly moved aside. As simply as that, I was out."

Then he was off. With 200 meters to go, charging into the lead, Snell burst into a furious sprint, opening up a sizable gap, so sizable that, coming around the last turn, he looked back over his shoulder, saw he had the race won and eased home in 3:38.1, fully a second and a half, and more than ten yards, in front of the runner-up, Josef Odlozil of Czechoslovakia. John Davies came in third, earning another medal for New Zealand.

Peter Snell, from tiny New Zealand, from a nation of two and a half million people, had achieved the middle-distance double, the first in forty-four years. After the Games, he went home to New Zealand and, in the space of five days, broke the world records for the mile and for the 1,000-yard run. Then he spent most of the next year touring the world, collecting the cheers and the admiration he had earned in Tokyo. Finally, with his times tapering off and his incentive ebbing, he announced, at the age of twenty-six, his retirement from competitive running.

He left behind him an indelible mark upon the Olympics and the people of New Zealand. He and John Davies and Murray Halberg, who set the world record for three miles, and Bill Baillie, who held the world record for 20,000 meters, had touched off a running revolution in New Zealand, a nation dedicated to tennis, cricket, sailing, and auto racing. One afternoon in 1964, 273 New Zealanders participated in a 37-mile relay race, each man, including Peter Snell, running some five miles. The Kiwis were proving their endurance and speed.

Snell's feats supplied the individual high point of the 1964 Olympic Games, but there were, of course, equally dramatic accomplishments. For sheer surprise impact, nothing matched the outcome of the 10,000-meter run, one of the two championships decided on the first day of track and field competition.

The favorite in the race was Ron Clarke of Australia, who held the world record for both six miles and 10,000 meters. Murray Halberg of New Zealand, the 1960 Olympic champion at 5,000 meters, seemed to pose the greatest threat, and Russia's Petr Bolotnikov, the defending Olympic champion, and Canada's Bruce Kidd figured to challenge the two men from Down Under. Only one American, Gerry Lindgren, a short and slight eighteen-year-old, rated any chance at all, and his chance grew slimmer when, two days before the race, he twisted his ankle in a hole in the ground while running in Meiji Park just outside the Olympic Village. Lindgren's American teammates in the race—Billy Mills, a twenty-six-year-old Marine lieutenant who had never run the distance under 29:10 (the world record was 28:15.6), and Ron Larrieu, who was even slower—appeared to be out of place against international distance runners.

Thirty-eight runners set off in the 10,000-meter race, for twenty-four laps around the track. Billy Mills broke well, clinging surprisingly to the leaders, and after a few laps, as the field began to spread out, he moved into second place, behind Clarke. Four separate times, Clarke opened sizable leads over Mills, and the American, who was seven sixteenths Sioux Indian, seemed ready to fold. But each time Mills revived, and each time he caught up to Clarke and took the lead

Billy Mills keeps his lead in the 10,000-meter run despite an attempt by Tunisia's Mohamed Gammoudi to jostle his way past.

himself. For most of the race, either Clarke or Mills led, although occasionally an Ethiopian, Mamo Wolde, or a Tunisian, Mohamed Gammoudi, slipped in front. With two and a half laps to go, Wolde fell back, and now, with Halberg, Bolotnikov, Kidd, and Lindgren all far behind, it was a three-man race among an Australian, a Tunisian, and, of all things, an American.

"The worst possible outcome I could foresee," said Peter Snell, who watched the race after winning his first 800-meter heat, "was victory for an American. The Americans are traditional masters of the short track events and we other nations are naturally not too keen to see that mastery extended to the longer races."

No American had ever won the 10,000-meter run in the Olympics, or even come close. When the race was introduced to the Olympics in Stockholm in 1912, Lewis Tewanima, a Carlisle schoolmate of Jim Thorpe's, took second place, fully forty-five seconds behind the great Hannes Kolehmainen. Since 1912, no American had finished among the first three in the 10,000-meter run. To cover any distance greater than 1,500-meters, the feeling was, Americans took cars.

Yet, in Tokyo, the unknown Billy Mills matched strides with the finest distance runners in the world, and on the next-to-last lap, the American caught up with Clarke once more and moved into the lead. At the start of the last lap, Clarke decided to launch his sprint, but he found himself boxed in, trapped by Mills and by a straggler who was being lapped.

Clarke slid out and bumped against Mills, and as both men struggled for the lead and for balance, the Tunisian, Gammoudi, opening his stride, made his bid. He put his hands together and aimed them, like a diver, squarely between Clarke and Mills, and then he drove through them, brushing both men off their strides. Mills stumbled to the right, Clarke to the left, and Gammoudi opened up a four-yard lead.

"It was a break for me," said Mills afterward. "Luckily, I was knocked outside where the track was firmer, not so chewed up as on the rail. I found better traction and I was able to pick up immediately."

But now Gammoudi was in front, and Clarke was second, and Mills's chase seemed desperate. With thirty yards to go, he caught Clarke and passed him, and twenty yards from the tape, he went by Gammoudi and then burst across the finish line, three yards and four tenths of a second in front of the Tunisian, his hands clasped over his head in victory. An American had won the 10,000 meters.

"In all the time you've been here," someone asked Mills after the stirring finish, "did a single newspaperman speak to you?"

Nobody, said Mills, had even said hello.

Mills's surge from obscurity was incredible. He won the race in the Olympic record time of 28:24.4, forty-five seconds faster than he had ever run in his life. He had never won a major race before anywhere. An orphan who had attended the Haskell Indian School in Kansas and the University of Kansas, Mills had originally started running so that he could get in shape to be a boxer. He had never distinguished himself in either sport. Nobody knew him when he arrived in Tokyo, and nobody expected to know him afterward.

"I realized nobody else thought so," Mills said, "but I'd been training so well I knew I had a chance, if I could stay with the leaders."

His victory was an early sign of the American superiority in track and field that was going to be so decisive in Tokyo,

Shoulders bent and heads up, the Olympic cyclists begin their grueling road race.

that was going to erase, in large part, the memory of the disappointing Games in Rome.

To compound the felony—the theft of the 10,000-meter gold medal by an American—four days later another American, Bob Schul, ran off with the 5,000-meter championship, another title never won before by an American Olympian. Again, only one American, Ralph Hill in 1932, had ever finished among the top three.

Schul's triumph was not nearly so surprising as Mills's. He had set a world record for two miles less than two months before the Olympics, and he had been running 5,000 meters in less than fourteen minutes. He had twice bettered four minutes in the mile. Yet he was twenty-seven years old and asthmatic, a tall, skinny Ohioan, and he was up against a brilliant and experienced field, including Gammoudi and Clarke, still stung by their experience with Billy Mills.

The 5,000-meter race was run on a rain-splattered track, with mud caking the contestants, and for most of the race, Schul hung back, Clarke again setting the pace, sometimes sprinting, sometimes coasting, hounded by Michel Jazy of France and Harald Norpoth of Germany. Schul's American teammate, Bill Dellinger—they had finished in a dead heat in the United States Olympic trials—lagged near the end of the twelve-man field.

With a lap and a half to go, Dellinger sprinted from the back to the front, and Jazy, Norpoth, Clarke, and Schul chased him. Then Jazy opened up, stormed into the lead, and entered the final turn perhaps ten yards in front of Schul. Jazy looked back at Schul.

"I remember him looking," said Schul later, "and I thought he must be mighty worried."

Schul's big kick cut swiftly into Jazy's lead and, halfway down the stretch, Schul drew even, then pulled away and,

Drenched by rain and mud, Bob Schul of the United States pulls away from France's Michel Jazy in the 5,000-meter run.

The future football star Bob Hayes wins the 100-meter dash for the United States.

smiling, won the championship. Norpoth came in second, Dellinger took a bronze medal for the United States, and Jazy faded to fourth place.

"One of my easy races," said Schul, after he had collected his gold medal.

If the Americans were cheered by their new mastery in the long-distance runs, they were equally heartened by their regained mastery in the short-distance sprints. The loss of both the 100- and 200-meter dashes, for the first time in thirty-two years, had probably been the most stunning reversal of form in Rome. But now, in Tokyo, the United States took back both titles.

First Bob Hayes, from Florida A. & M., captured the 100-meter dash. In the semifinals, he ran the distance in 9.9 seconds, which, if there had not been an excessively strong following wind, would have been a new world and Olympic record. In the final, Hayes slowed down to 10 seconds flat, tying the world record and setting an Olympic record.

Then Henry Carr, from Arizona State, won the 200-meter dash. He ran four 200-meter races in two days, showing perfect progress, accelerating from 21.1 seconds in his first heat to 21 flat in the quarter-finals to 20.6 in the semifinals to 20.3, an Olympic record, in the finals. Livio Berruti, the Italian who had captured the gold medal in Rome, finished fifth.

Hayes and Carr, teammates in Tokyo, later became rivals in professional football. Hayes, playing for the Dallas Cowboys, established himself as the most dangerous long-pass-catching end in the National Football League. Carr, joining the New York Giants, became one of the league's best defensive backs.

No other nation could disturb the American gold-medal monopoly in all races, on flat ground or over hurdles, demanding individual sprinting speed. In the 400-meter dash, Mike Larrabee, a thirty-year-old California schoolteacher, overtook Wendell Mottley, a Yale graduate running for Trinidad-Tobago, won by a tenth of a second, then announced: "No one yet has been able to hang onto me when I really pour it on." Cheerfully, Larrabee revealed his training secret. "I made it fun," he said. "I didn't sacrifice. I only trained about three hours a week."

Both American sprint relay teams shattered world records. In the 400-meter relay, which was lost in Rome for the first time in forty-eight years, Bob Hayes started the last leg in fifth place and flew into first, beating the runner-up, from Poland, by three yards in 39 seconds flat. With the running relay start, Hayes covered his 100 meters in an incredible 8.6 seconds.

In the 1,600-meter relay, with Larrabee running the second and Carr the last leg, the Americans cracked the world and Olympic record by more than a second, sprinting the distance in 3:00.7.

"Hank Carr could run 400 meters in 44 seconds flat," said Larrabee, in awe, after the race. "Trouble is he's lazy."

"Why should I run 400 meters?" Carr replied. "I'm the world's best at 200. I'm not greedy."

Hayes Jones, who had finished third in Rome, won the 110-meter hurdles and Rex Cawley won the 400-meter hurdles to complete the American sweep under 800 meters.

There were three more gold medals for the United States in men's track and field, for a final total of twelve in twenty-four events, supplemented by five silver and three bronze medals. "The Star-Spangled Banner" was played so frequently that the Japanese adopted an abbreviated version, which didn't satisfy one American spectator, an unabashed track and field fanatic named Uan Rasey. Rasey played lead horn in the M-G-M studio orchestra, and at Tokyo's National Stadium, he positioned himself, with his trumpet, just below the Olympic torch. Whenever the abbreviated "Star-Spangled Banner" blared, Rasey finished it off with his horn.

Al Oerter, still only twenty-eight years old, won the gold medal in the discus for the third straight Olympics, matching the mark of Martin Sheridan, who won in 1904, 1906, and 1908. Only five days before the event, Oerter ripped muscles in his rib cage, but, in pain, he still managed to spin the discus to an Olympic record. No man since 1908—Ray Ewry, the genius of the standing jumps, and John Flanagan,

More than a foot above the old Olympic record, Fred Hansen of the United States soars to the pole-vault championship.

the hammer thrower, did it then—had won gold medals in one track and field event in three consecutive quadrennial Olympics.

Fred Hansen of the United States won the pole vault, raising the Olympic record more than a foot, to sixteen feet eight and three quarters inches. The effect of the revolution in vaulting, the new heights made possible by the switch to fiberglass poles, was clear in Tokyo. Nine competitors broke the Olympic record.

To complete the American gold-medal collection, Dallas Long, who finished third as the youngster in the psychological war of the whales in 1960, set an Olympic record in the shotput. Parry O'Brien, the senior whale, winner of gold medals in 1952 and 1956 and a silver medal in 1960, finished fourth, eight inches short of a bronze medal.

Ten different nations gathered gold medals in men's track and field, but no country except the United States took home more than two. Snell, of course, accounted for New Zealand's pair, a total matched by Russia and Great Britain.

For the Soviets, Tokyo was a distinct disappointment, particularly after their trackmen had collected five gold medals in Rome. Only Romuald Klim, in the hammer throw, and Valery Brumel, in the high jump, scored for the Soviet Union. Brumel's victory was a surprisingly close one, over John Thomas, the American who had been so heavily favored in Rome, but whose chances had been almost dismissed in Tokyo. Brumel, holder of the world record, and Thomas each leaped seven feet one and three quarter inches, but Brumel earned the gold medal on the basis of fewer misses. Russia's Robert Shavlakadze, who beat Brumel in Rome on the same technicality, finished fifth in Tokyo.

The broad jump was expected to be a duel between the 1960 champion, Ralph Boston of the United States, and the 1960 bronze medalist, Igor Ter-Ovanesyan of the Soviet Union. Boston won the personal duel, but he lost the gold medal. Lynn Davies of Great Britain outjumped Boston by almost two inches, Ter-Ovanesyan by more than three.

In the tightest decathlon competition in Olympic history, with only 240 points separating first place from sixth, a German named Willi Holdorf ended an American reign that had begun in 1932. Holdorf, so fatigued he fell flat on his face at the finish, outlasted a Russian, Rein Aun, by a mere 45 points, the thinnest margin of victory ever, and no American finished better than fourth.

C. K. Yang, the Formosan who had come so close to Rafer Johnson in 1960, but now weakened by injuries, a lack of competitive preparation, and a change in the scoring system, could place no higher than fifth.

Finally came the Marathon, an event followed so eagerly in Japan that one television station showed the entire two-hour, 26-mile run. Abebe Bikila, the Ethiopian palace guard, came to Tokyo in defense of his 1960 championship, and he had changed in only one respect: He now wore shoes. But he ran as fluidly as ever, and once again loped to victory, cutting almost two minutes off the world record, more than three minutes off his Olympic record, making himself the first Marathon champion ever to repeat in the Olympics. He celebrated by capping his long run with a few calisthenics in the stadium. To sadden the local crowd, an Englishman named Benjamin Heatley overtook the Japanese star, Kokichi Tsubaraya, in the last hundred yards for second place.

For the second straight Olympics, Abebe Bikila of Ethiopia leads the field home in the Marathon.

In women's track and field, no performer quite so brilliant as Wilma Rudolph emerged. Two Americans—Wyomia Tyus at 100 meters and Edith McGuire at 200 meters—split the sprint titles, Rumania's Iolanda Balas retained the high jump championship, and Russia's husky Tamara Press achieved a field-events double, successfully defending her 1960 shot-put title and advancing from second place to first in the discus, breaking the Olympic record in both events. (Tamara's sister, Irina, won the women's pentathlon, a new Olympic event.) The defending discus champion, Vera Ozolina of the Soviet Union, slumped to fifth, which dismayed her so much that, in the great tradition of female Olympians, she rushed to the Olympic Village beauty salon and demanded that all her hair be cut off.

Ann Packer of Great Britain breezes to her second medal, crossing the tape in the 800-meter run.

Betty Cuthbert of Australia, the winner of both sprints in Melbourne eight years earlier, moved up to 400 meters, a new event, in Tokyo and won the gold medal by a stride over an English girl named Ann Packer. Miss Packer, who had won both her heat and her semifinal, raced on six consecutive days in Tokyo. The day after the 400 final, she entered the 800-meter run and barely qualified for the semifinal, finishing fifth in her heat in 2:12.6, the slowest time of any semifinal qualifier.

In the semis, Miss Packer perked up, cut her time to 2:06, and qualified for the final. Six of the finalists had faster times than she, but suddenly Miss Packer found new speed. She ran 800 meters in 2:01.1, a world record for women, and she picked up her gold medal, putting her two medals ahead of her fiancé, Robbie Brightwell, who missed third place by one tenth of a second in the men's 400-meter run.

"I ran well because Robbie had not won a medal," Ann Packer explained. "I was thinking about him and not about myself, and so I wasn't nervous."

"If Ann had not been there when I lost," said Brightwell, after his 400-meter final, "I think I would have leaped off a building."

As brilliant as the Americans were in track and field, they were even more successful in swimming. The American track and field athletes, men and women, won fourteen gold medals in thirty-six events; the American swimmers and divers, men and women, won sixteen gold medals in twenty-two events. The oldest male American swimmer was twenty-three, the

After winning the 400-meter free style, America's Don Schollander pushes himself out of the pool.

oldest female nineteen. And none of them was so spectacularly talented as a blond, eighteen-year-old Californian named Don Schollander.

"First," said Schollander's coach, George Haines, "he is almost flawless mechanically. Second, he has a tremendous desire to win. Finally, he is a thoroughly intelligent competitor with a wonderful tactical sense."

All of Schollander's gifts came into play in Tokyo. In the 100-meter free style, he set an Olympic record of 53.4 seconds. Then, in the 400-meter free style, he set a world record of 4:12.2. And, finally, he anchored both the 400-meter free style relay and the 800-meter free style relay to world-record victories. He gathered four gold medals, a feat never before achieved in Olympic swimming. Schollander's teammates

The only American boxing champion in Tokyo, heavyweight Joe Frazier jabs with his left and readies his right.

broke world records for the 200-meter backstroke (Jed Graef), the 400-meter individual medley (Richard Roth), and the 400-meter medley relay. The American girls were equally devastating; they destroyed world records for the 100-meter backstroke (Cathy Ferguson), the 100-meter butterfly (Sharon Stouder), the 400-meter free style relay, and the 400-meter medley relay. Sharon Stouder competed on both relay teams, giving her, like Schollander, a hand in three world records.

Dawn Fraser, the durable Australian, won the women's 100-meter free style for the third straight Olympics and lowered her Olympic record to 59.5 seconds, fast enough to press Johnny Weissmuller in his prime.

Outside of swimming and track and field, the American showing, as usual, was not impressive. The United States was shut out completely in wrestling and in weightlifting, and was reduced to a single gold medal in boxing, the heavyweight title, won by Joe Frazier, who promptly turned professional and set out in pursuit of Cassius Clay's world championship. These three muscular sports had yielded seven gold medals to Americans in 1960, seven in 1956, and ten in 1952.

In rowing, an American trio won the pairs with coxswain, and a surprising American crew bid for the eight-oared cham-

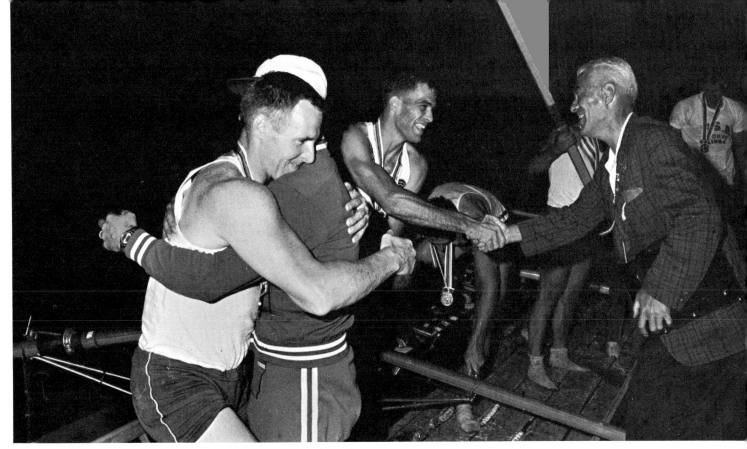

Members of the Vespers Boat Club eight-oared crew happily accept congratulations after their victory.

pionship. The United States had won the eight-oared event in every Olympics from 1920 until 1960—when the Germans shocked the Americans—and in every Olympics since 1904, the United States had been represented by a collegiate eight-oared crew. Earlier, in 1904 and 1900, the United States Olympic crew came from the Vesper Boat Club of Philadelphia.

Now, in 1964, a club crew once again represented the United States and, once again, after a sixty-year lapse, the representative was the Vesper Boat Club of Philadelphia. Vesper had earned its place in the Games by turning back the two finest college crews, Harvard and California, both previously undefeated, in the Olympic trials.

The Vesper lineup included a forty-six-year-old Hungarian refugee, Robert Zimonyi, who had served as coxswain for three previous Hungarian Olympic crews; a thirty-five-year-old father of six, Bill Knecht; and a stroke, Bill Stowe, two years out of Cornell. It did not seem to be the strongest crew ever to represent the United States.

In its first heat, Vesper drew the defending champions, the Germans, who won by a slender margin, forcing the Americans back into the repechages, the second-chance races for first-round losers. Vesper made the most of its second chance. The American rowers won their heat, then, in the final, in a stiff breeze, swept to a stunning victory over Germany by more than a full length.

For the fourth straight Olympics, the basketball competition came down to a battle between the United States and the

Soviet Union. The American team, captained by Princeton's brilliant Bill Bradley, was led in scoring by Jerry Shipp and in playmaking by Walt Hazzard. The Soviet Union still had its seven-foot-three-inch Latvian woodchopper, Yan Kruminsh, who had gained a little polish. Both teams reached the final without being seriously pressed.

"There will be a surprise for everyone," warned the Soviet coach, Alexander Gomelski. "We are fed up with second."

Tickets for the final, staged in a handsome new gym seating merely 4,000, were scarce, and Paul Drayton, an American sprinter, got in only by using Walt Hazzard's competitor's pass. "No sweat," said Drayton. "The Japanese think all us Negroes look alike."

If there was any surprise in the final, it was the ease of the American victory. With Bradley directing play and Lucious Jackson scoring seventeen points, the United States spotted the Russians a 4-0 lead, then quickly caught up, pulled away, and won without difficulty, 73-59. In the locker room afterward, Larry Brown, an American backcourt man, studied his gold medal with appreciation. "It's worth $12, that's all," he said. "And you couldn't buy it away from me if you had a million."

The captain of the American Olympic basketball team, Bill Bradley of Princeton, looks things over from a high perch during the Olympic trials.

With two additional gold medals in shooting, the United States finished with a total of thirty-six, leading the world, for the first time since 1952, in gold medals. The Soviet Union, which had gathered forty-three gold medals in 1960 and thirty-seven in 1956, slumped to thirty, fully half of them in boxing, weightlifting, wrestling, and gymnastics, fields where the United States salvaged only a single championship. The Russians produced brilliant stars, of course: Vyacheslav Ivanov became the first man to win the single sculls three Olympics in a row; Grigori Kriss won the epée fencing, an area dominated by Italians for thirty-two years; and a lovely gymnast named Larisa Latynina picked up two gold medals, two silver medals, and two bronze medals, lifting her career total, spread over three Olympics, to nine gold, five silver, and three bronze medals.

Judo was introduced to the Olympic program, and the host Japanese, the masters of the sport, won the lightweight, middleweight, and heavyweight championships, fattening their haul of gold medals to sixteen, only nine less than they had won in all previous Olympic competition. Yet the Japanese

Lidija Skoblikova of the Soviet Union shows her championship form in the 1,000-meter speed skating race.

suffered a startling upset in the open class of judo competition. A 265-pound Dutchman, Anton Geesink, pinned the favored Japanese champion, Akio Kaminaga, in nine minutes, prompting one Tokyo columnist to offer Geesink "humble thanks" for lending an international flavor to the sport of judo.

There was, happily, good humor in Japan throughout the Games and, unhappily, tension throughout the world. The Olympics had been going less than a week when Nikita

Khrushchev lost his post as leader of the Soviet Union. "I knew we were doing pretty well against the Russians," said Kenneth Wilson, the president of the American Olympic Committee, "but I didn't know it would cause Khrushchev to resign."

The Russians had cosmonauts circling the globe at the start of the Olympic Games, the Chinese celebrated by exploding a nuclear device, a few Hungarians defected to the West (practically an Olympic ritual by 1964), and a Nationalist Chinese pistol shooter defected to the East. Yet with all the turmoil, despite the political bitterness that caused four nations to withdraw at the scene of the Olympics, leaving a record ninety-four countries represented, the Japanese staged a magnificent show.

Japan spent $3 billion brightening the face of Tokyo for visitors; Olympic themes dominated all the stores and hotels, and everywhere athletes and foreign visitors went, they could hear the Nikons clicking away at them. A new high-speed rail system hurtled spectators to the National Stadium, and along

Terry McDermott of the United States shows his championship form in the 500-meter speed skating race.

the Ginza the signs advertising naked beauties grew bolder and brighter. The Japanese wanted to make visitors feel comfortable, and when a pair of Australian weightlifters were overcharged in a Ginza bar, police officials ordered the bar to return half of the Australians' money. "It isn't necessary," said one of the Australians. "We had a fine time."

The ceremonies were spectacular as always, and some 100,000 different Japanese helped relay the Olympic flame to the National Stadium. The New Zealanders brightened the closing celebration. Carried away perhaps by Peter Snell's brilliance or simply by the mood of Tokyo, the New Zealanders broke into a dance as they circled the stadium, and one of them, the distance runner Bill Baillie, who had earlier performed a partial strip in a Ginza night club, got so enthusiastic he threw a kiss to Emperor Hirohito of Japan.

Most of the showing off at the Winter Olympic Games, held in Innsbruck, Austria, early in 1964, was done by Russians. The Soviets thoroughly dominated the winter sports, winning eleven gold medals in thirty-four events. No other nation captured more than four championships.

For the Soviet Union, two women, each twenty-four years old, each a schoolteacher in Siberia—sent there not for punishment, but for conditioning—contributed seven of the eleven gold medals. Lidija Skoblikova, who won two titles at Squaw Valley in 1960, became the first athlete, male or female, ever to win four individual gold medals in a Winter Olympics. Miss Skoblikova won all four women's speed skating competitions, a dazzling blend of sprinting speed and endurance, finishing first at 500 meters, 1,000 meters, 1,500 meters, and 3,000 meters.

Her fellow Siberian demonstrated even greater staying power. Claudia Boyarski specialized in long-distance skiing, and she won the 5,000-meter and 10,000-meter cross-country runs. Then she led her country to victory in the 15,000-meter cross-country relay.

The United States, unable to win a gold medal in figure skating for the first time since 1936, managed its only championship in men's speed skating, its first in the sport since World War II. Terry McDermott won the 500-meter race for the United States in 40.1 seconds, an Olympic record, upsetting Russia's Evgeni Grishin, the 1960 and 1956 champion.

But the most stirring performance, from the American point of view, came in the Alpine skiing competition, men's division. Never in the history of the Olympics had any American male threatened the superiority of the Scandinavian and Alpine nations. Not one American had won as much as a bronze medal in downhill or slalom skiing. But in Innsbruck in 1964, the United States suddenly emerged as a world threat in the sport.

By less than two tenths of a second, Pepi Stiegler of Austria won the men's slalom championship. Billy Kidd of the United States, wearing cap and goggles, captured second place, swirling down the slopes faster than any American had ever skied before, and Jimmy Heuga of the United States, racing bareheaded, captured the bronze medal.

"They're the touchdown twins," cheered the American coach, Bob Beattie.

Two athletes died in the 1964 Olympics themselves. An Englishman suffered fatal injuries when his toboggan crashed off the course, and an Australian died when, skiing downhill at more than sixty miles an hour, he slammed into a tree.

When the 1964 Winter Olympics drew to a close, the dominant nation was, clearly, the Soviet Union. But a startling development had passed almost unnoticed in all the excitement over competition. In the 1964 Winter Olympic Games—setting a pattern that would be followed in the Summer Games—nobody, no newspaper, no magazine, no wire service, maintained a point-scoring system by nations, official or unofficial.

Certainly, everyone knew how many gold and how many silver and how many bronze medals each nation had won, but for the first time since the Soviet Union and the United States began their athletic cold war, the number of points each nation scored was not publicly compiled.

Al Oerter wins his third of four consecutive gold medals in the discus throw.

Olympic teams fill the infield of the Mexico City Stadium in preparation
for the opening of the XIX Games.

# Gloved Fists, Clenched Fists

## CHAPTER NINETEEN : 1968—MEXICO CITY AND GRENOBLE

*"George is nimble,*
*And George is quick.*
*Watch me, folks,*
*'Cause I can really stick."*
—GEORGE FOREMAN
In Mexico City

The most valuable property in sports is the heavyweight boxing championship of the world. The man who holds it not only can say, with justification, "I can lick any man in the world in a fair fight"; he can also say, "I can make more money in one night than any man in the world."

That last boast is quite likely overstatement—if one of the Rockefellers ever decided of an evening to auction off his family's art collection, he could probably clear a profit greater than any fighter ever conceived—but it is close to the truth, close enough for men to tremble at the opportunity to become associated, especially financially, with a future heavyweight champion. There are grown men who have spent most of their lives hunting for a fighter who could someday win the heavyweight championship of the world.

Since 1952, there has been only one good place to look for a future heavyweight champion: in the ring at the Olympic Games. The future champion, however, hasn't always been easy to recognize. The 1952 Olympics produced two future heavyweight champions of the world, but one of them, Floyd Patterson, was disguised as a middleweight, and the other, Ingemar Johansson, was disguised as a loser, disqualified for his unwillingness to mix with his opponent. The 1956 Olympics did not produce a future professional heavyweight champion, merely a future challenger for the title; the 1956 Olympic heavyweight champion had the distinction of fighting his first professional fight for the heavyweight championship

America's women athletes wave to the crowd during the first day's ceremonies.

of the world. His name was Pete Rademacher, and he fell easy victim to Floyd Patterson, but not before being guaranteed the largest purse any boxer ever received for his professional debut. The 1960 Games sent forth the future champion Cassius Clay, who was only a light-heavyweight champion in the Olympics, and the 1964 Games offered Joe Frazier, the first man to win both the Olympic and the professional heavyweight championships of the world.

George Foreman was the second.

Two years before the 1968 Olympic Games were held in Mexico City, George Foreman had never been in a ring. He had been in fights, sure, but most of them took place in the streets of the Fifth Ward, a black slum in Houston, Texas. Foreman was the fifth of seven children of a construction worker, and as a youngster, he had one ambition: to be *bad*. He dropped out of junior high school, he once said, not because of bad marks, but "because of bad everything."

Away from school, Foreman found out he couldn't be as bad as he wanted to be. "I had these ambitions," he said, after he became the world's heavyweight champion, "to be a great thief, a great burglar, a great hijack man, an all-around hustler. But I was a complete failure." As a thief, Foreman's weakness was that whenever a victim yelled at him to drop whatever he'd stolen he would drop it. As a mugger—or, as he called it, a "hijacker"—his weakness was that he feared the victim might get hurt. He even flopped as a purse-snatcher; too many of his potential victims reminded him of his mother.

In 1965, at the age of sixteen, Foreman joined the Job Corps, a government project designed to train dropouts for useful employment. He went to a conservation center in Oregon, then to a school in California, studied bricklaying, carpentry, and electronics and earned the equivalent of a high school diploma. He also earned a reputation as a pretty tough young man. One night, with a group of fellow Corpsmen, he listened to the Clay-Patterson fight on the radio. "Why don't you go pick on them," one of his buddies suggested, "instead of always picking on us?" Not long after that, Foreman stepped into a ring for the first time; a much smaller man, a clever middleweight, bloodied his nose. Stung, Foreman began working at the sport, but he didn't take it very seriously; it certainly wasn't going to be a career.

The Job Corps graduated Foreman back to Houston, but when he couldn't find employment and was in danger of slipping back into his old *bad* habits, he reupped. He wound up on the Job Corps recreation staff in Pleasanton, California, coaching boxing and fighting an occasional amateur bout. A former lightweight fighter named Doc Broadus was in charge of the boxing program. "I sat him down," Broadus recalled years later, "and I said, 'George, I'm gonna tell you somethin', and I want an answer now, not tomorrow, or next week, or next year. George, you can't get no amateur bouts. They all know you can whip their butts. We can turn pro right now—or we can go for the gold medal!' "

*The gold medal!* Foreman was thrilled. He had only one question: What's the gold medal?

Broadus explained that a gold medal went to the heavyweight champion of the Olympic Games, the best amateur fighter in the whole world.

"Okay, Doc," said Foreman, suitably impressed, "let's go for the gold medal."

With his sights on the Olympics, Foreman immediately went into training. He trained hard. He ran five miles each morning, spent the day coaching and sparring and shadowboxing, then ran five miles more each evening. By the time the 1968 Games began, he had fought only twenty-one amateur bouts (and, in the early stages, had lost three of them), yet his skill and reputation were such that Cus D'Amato, the man who had managed Floyd Patterson to the heavyweight

George Foreman lands a right on Russia's Ionas Chepulis.

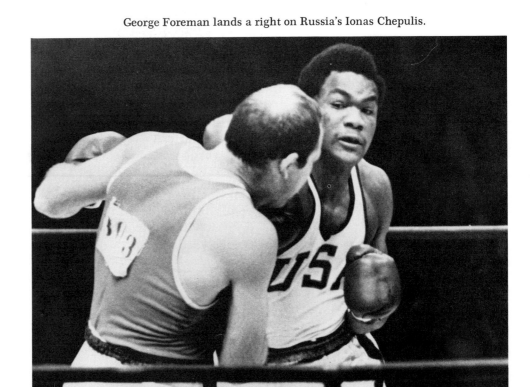

championship of the world, came to Mexico City specifically to watch Foreman. "He's got promise," said D'Amato, with his usual caution, "but he's not ready for the pros. He needs seasoning."

Yet in one respect, Foreman had already surpassed Cassius Clay: he wrote bad poetry that was worse than Clay's bad poetry. Clay had penned a lengthy ode to Floyd Patterson after the two men met during the 1960 Olympics; in 1968, Foreman's rhymes were shorter and more personal. He composed a tribute to his own left jab:

> "I can move to your right,
> Stick all night.
> Move to your left,
> Cause your death."

Foreman needed all of his weapons in his first Olympic match. He came up against a five-foot-seven Polish fireplug named Lucjan Trela; even after he destroyed Joe Frazier to win the world heavyweight championship (but before he lost the title to Muhammad Ali a/k/a Cassius Clay), Foreman said the fight against Trela was the toughest of his career. The great difference in heights—at 218 pounds, Foreman was six-foot-three and a fraction—threw off Foreman's timing, and his aim. He was happy to settle for a close decision.

In the quarter-finals, Foreman beat a Rumanian named Ion Alexe; the fight was stopped in the third round when the American opened a big cut over Alexe's eye. In the semi-finals, in the second round, Foreman jolted Giorgi Bambini of Italy with a left, then knocked him out with a right. In the final bout for the gold medal, Foreman came up against a Russian, Iones Chepulis, who had won his first three Olympic fights by knockouts. Foreman wasn't overconfident; before the bout, he told himself he wouldn't be unhappy if he lost—a silver medal would be just fine.

But the Russian never had a chance. In the first round, Foreman's jab bloodied Chepulis's nose. In the second, Foreman concentrated on the body, pounding his experienced opponent with such fury that, in the final minute of the round, the referee stopped the fight and declared Foreman the winner by a technical knockout.

As the bout ended, Foreman's American teammates presented him with a bouquet of roses, and Foreman, in turn, gave the roses to his defeated opponent. The crowd roared its approval of the gesture, and the roar grew even louder when Foreman made a second gesture that would link him forever with the 1968 Olympics, and win him millions of friends and millions of enemies. It was a gesture that would have caused barely a ripple in different times, in different circumstances.

*George Foreman walked around the ring and waved a small American flag.*

For that gesture, some people called him a patriot. And some called him an Uncle Tom.

"I'm just proud to be an American," Foreman explained. "That wasn't intended as any kind of a demonstration."

Foreman waves a small American flag after winning the Olympic heavyweight title.

Foreman may have had no intention that his flag-waving be interpreted as a demonstration, but such an interpretation was inevitable in light of what had happened only ten days earlier. After the finals of the 200-meter dash, the two black Americans who had placed first and third strode to the victory stand and, as "The Star-Spangled Banner" rang out in the Olympic Stadium, both lowered their heads and each lifted high over his head one black-gloved fist. It was a demonstration of black solidarity, of black militancy, a protest against bigotry in the United States and racism in the Olympic Games, a quiet, dignified, yet fierce display of a new mood that had struck black American athletes a year earlier.

The man who had inspired the new mood was an instructor in sociology and anthropology at San Jose State College in California. His name was Harry Edwards and, like George Foreman, he was the survivor of a tough black slum, in East St. Louis, Illinois. An imposing man, six-foot-eight and 240 pounds, a former junior college discus-throwing champion, Edwards had earned his master's degree in sociology at Cornell University and was at work on a doctoral thesis on black militancy when he came up with the idea of a black American boycott of the Olympic Games.

Edwards had felt for a while that success in sports gave the black American an arena in which he could make his protests heard—and make them effective. In the fall of 1967, he had presented to the president of San Jose State a list of grievances on behalf of fifty-nine of the school's two hundred black students. A few of the complaints were aimed squarely at the San Jose athletic program. Edwards had compiled a list of indignities suffered by black athletes, and unless these indignities were halted, Edwards warned, he and his group would "physically interfere" with the playing of San Jose's opening football game. The college called off the game, then moved to alleviate many of the problems cited by Edwards. The football season resumed, and so did Edwards.

On November 23, 1967, in a Sunday school classroom at the Second Baptist Church in Los Angeles, Edwards announced plans for a black boycott of the Olympic Games, a boycott that, if successful, would strip the American team of almost twenty percent of its medal-winners and a far greater percentage in track and field. Edwards' goal, he said, was black dignity. "I will use whatever tool is necessary, political or otherwise," he said, "to bring about unity within the black race. If it means an Olympic boycott, I'll do it. If it means taking to the streets, I'll do it."

A charismatic figure, a man who could be violently militant one minute—threatening to blow up a stadium to dramatize his protest—and utterly charming the next, Edwards attracted a dedicated following. One of his earliest, and staunchest, disciples was a San Jose State sprinter named Tommie Smith.

Tommie Smith ranked among the world's top sprinters; he was a strong bet for a gold medal in Mexico City, yet he committed himself completely to the boycott. "Winning gold medals for a country where I don't have my freedom is irrelevant," he said. Another time, Smith said, "People here [at San Jose] recognize me as a fast nigger—but that still means a nigger. Nobody sees that I'm a serious student. That's not my role to the white folks." And Smith added he would give up his life if "it will open a door by which the oppression and injustice suffered by my people can be alleviated."

For a few months, Edwards' proposed boycott existed, but did not flourish. Then, in February, 1968, the boycott got a big boost—from, of all people, the International Olympic Committee. The IOC decided—on the basis of a three-man study led by Lord Killanin of Ireland, the man who would eventually succeed Avery Brundage as president of the IOC—that South Africa, barred from the Tokyo Olympics because of its apartheid policies in sports, had changed those policies and should be readmitted to the Olympics.

Reaction to the IOC ruling was swift and harsh. Thirty-two African nations said they would not compete if South Africa did, Harry Edwards said that his boycott would expand and intensify, and the Soviet Union fanned the controversy by threatening to pull its large, gifted, and all-white team out of the Olympics.

Under pressure from all those directions—and, most strenuously, from the Mexican Organizing Committee, which feared that four years of planning and building might be wasted on an emasculated Olympics—the IOC quickly agreed to reconsider the reinstatement of South Africa. In April, 1968, six months before the Games were to begin, the IOC reversed its decision. South Africa was again out of the Olympics. Avery Brundage, clearly, was not pleased by the development, a contradiction of his contention that the Games were above politics, but he explained that the IOC had faced "a profound cleavage in world public opinion which threatened to split the Olympic family and threatened the success of the Olympics." Brundage took even deeper refuge in semantics; the IOC, he said, had not bowed to political pressure, but had acted to avoid "ugly violence."

The reversal embittered South African officials and athletes (including some black athletes), guaranteed black Africa's and Russia's participation in the 1968 Olympics, and defused Harry Edwards' boycott movement. "This is one of the things we were after," said Tommie Smith, hinting that he would now run in Mexico City.

The strength of the movement was ebbing, and on August 31, Harry Edwards formally called off the boycott. "The majority of athletes will participate in the Olympics," he said, "but will not participate in victory-stand ceremonies or victory marches. Some athletes have decided to boycott the Games and lesser forms of protest shall be carried out by others."

Edwards' credibility suffered from the death of the boycott, and as the Games grew close, his threats of milder forms of protest tended to be forgotten, especially as a more grievous, more immediate problem arose. Civil war erupted in Mexico—

332

a limited civil war between the Mexican government and university students in Mexico City.

The war began in small, sporadic battles in the summer of 1968 with students rioting to protest the actions of President Gustavo Díaz Ordaz and his government, rioting to protest against Mexico's low rate of literacy and high rate of homicide, against the squalor of Mexico's slums and the severity of Mexico's police, against an economic system that seemed designed to make the rich steadily richer and the poor poorer. Only two weeks before the Olympics were to begin, the Mexican government made what appeared to be a conciliatory move; the troops that had been occupying Mexico City's two main university campuses were withdrawn. On October 2, students organized a victory rally in a public square called the Plaza of the Three Cultures. At first, the rally was impassioned, but peaceful.

Then, in the early evening, Mexican army helicopters dropped green flares on the Plaza of the Three Cultures, and within minutes, a thousand soldiers and riot police had charged into the square. The crowd of 5,000 panicked, and in the panic, soldiers and police clubbed and clawed at the students. Almost inevitably, gunfire broke out. The government said snipers fired first; other witnesses said the government forces fired first. In the end, it made no difference; the battle raged for almost an hour, and when the shooting and the screaming finally stopped, more than thirty students were dead, more than one hundred injured, and more than three hundred jailed. The toll was so terrible that, temporarily at least, the war between the Mexican students and their government was over. Avery Brundage consulted with Mexican officials, then announced, "We have been assured that nothing will interfere with the peaceful entrance of the Olympic flame into the stadium on October 12."

The ceremonies began on schedule, in peace, with 6,300 pigeons and five interlocking helium-filled Olympic rings drifting above the stadium, and in the opening days of competition, the South African question and the American boycott and even Mexico City's "Night of Sadness" faded before a dazzling display of athletic genius.

Then, on October 16, two weeks after the massacre at the Plaza of the Three Cultures, four days after a twenty-year-old Mexican named Norma Enriqueta Basilio had become the first woman to ignite the Olympic flame, eight men lined up for the final of the 200-meter dash. Three of them were Americans, and two came from the same college, San Jose State in California.

Tommie Smith and John Carlos, two of Harry Edwards' protégés, were ready to make their bids for a gold medal.

The twenty-four-year-old Smith, six-foot-three and 185 pounds, held the recognized world record for the 200-meter dash, 20 seconds flat. The twenty-three-year-old Carlos, six-foot-four and 200 pounds, held the pending world record of 19.7

seconds, set in the U.S. Olympic trials. Carlos, born and raised in New York City's Harlem, once explained why he and Smith could run so fast: "Everything is hustle and bustle for a young black. Run to the bus, run with other kids, run from the cops. Maybe that's how we got so good at sprinting."

Both men had once planned to boycott Mexico City, and neither had forgotten Harry Edwards' promise that there would be milder forms of protest. In their preliminary heats for the 200-meter dash, both had worn long black socks, the kind known as "pimp socks" in the black ghettos. The socks were definitely symbolic; when Stan Wright, a black assistant U.S. track coach, had urged all his runners to take pride in their American uniforms, Carlos had snapped, "Coach, I think I'll run barefoot just to show my poverty."

In the semi-finals of the 200, held only a few hours before the final, the two San Jose sprinters wore their black socks shortened. Jesse Owens, the star of the 1936 Olympics, on hand in Mexico City as a radio commentator, claimed credit for the slight change in the militants' outfits; an outspoken foe of the boycott, himself often a target for Harry Edwards' barbs, Owens said he had warned the young runners that the long socks might cut down their blood circulation and harm their chances for victory. Smith and Carlos qualified easily for the final, but both came out of the semi-finals hurting.

Carlos had a minor injury, a sore back, but Smith had a pulled groin muscle, a pull so painful he was placed on a stretcher right after the semi-finals. "Lying on that stretcher," he said later, "I saw a lot of plans collapsing."

For almost two hours, Smith lay with his leg packed in ice. Then he was taped from his waist almost to the bottom edge of his running shorts. Then he went out to run.

In the final, Carlos took the lead early and held it until about fifty meters from the finish. Then he half turned to look for Smith, and as he yelled, "Come on up here, Tommie," his San Jose teammate flew past him on his way to a new Olympic record of 19.8 seconds. At the finish line, an Australian named Peter Norman nipped Carlos for second place.

Smith, of course, was in agony after the race, pain shooting up his leg, but he did not think of a stretcher or of an ice pack. He walked over to his wife and borrowed a black scarf and tied the scarf around his neck. Carlos borrowed a black shirt from a friend on the Jamaican Olympic team.

Then the two Americans walked toward the victory stand, to receive their medals, each barefooted, each carrying a track shoe in one hand, each with his free hand tucked inside his USA windbreaker. Stan Wright, the assistant coach, heard that the two men were going to make some form of protest on the victory stand, and he rushed to tell the American head track coach, Payton Jordan. "They'll regret this for the rest of their lives," warned Jordan.

As they stood on the victory stand, accepting their medals from the president of the International Amateur Athletic Foundation, the Marquis of Exeter—who himself had stood

334

Tommie Smith, center, and John Carlos, right, both of the USA, extend their black-gloved fists skyward and stare downward during the playing of the "Star-Spangled Banner," after they had received gold and bronze medals for their performances in the 200-meter dash. At left, silver medalist Peter Norman of Australia.

atop the victory stand forty years earlier, as Lord David Burghley, the 1928 400-meter hurdles champion—Smith and Carlos both had their sweatpants legs rolled up, exposing their black socks. And as "The Star-Spangled Banner" was played, Smith, on the top rung of the stand, pulled his right hand out of his windbreaker and raised it high. Carlos, on the bottom rung, pulled out his left hand and raised it high. Each fist wore a black glove, and each was clenched in protest. Both men's heads were bowed, ignoring the flag.

The gesture Harry Edwards had promised had been made, starkly and defiantly, but surprisingly only a small percentage of the 80,000 people within the Olympic Stadium noticed the protest. But the word spread quickly, among the press, among American Olympic officials, and among the members of the IOC.

"This was a victory for black people everywhere," Tommie Smith told a press gathering after he left the victory stand.

"White people seem to think we're animals," added John Carlos, the more volatile, and more talkative, of the two medalists. "I want people to know we're not animals, not inferior animals like cats and rats and roaches. They think we're some kind of a show horse. They think we can perform and they can throw us some peanuts and say, 'Good boy, good boy.' "

Carlos' statement, for all its underlying bitterness, was comical on the surface; he had managed to span almost the entire animal kingdom, from roaches to elephants, in three sentences. But the United States Olympic Committee wasn't smiling. The members met for hours after the incident, then decided to issue a statement strongly reprimanding Smith and Carlos, and apologizing for their actions to the IOC, the Mexican Organizing Committee, and the Mexican people. That should have been enough to close the incident, but the IOC did it again: just as its readmittance of South Africa had brought the Olympic boycott back to life, the IOC now seemed determined to turn Carlos and Smith into martyrs. The international group exerted tremendous pressure on the U.S. Olympic Committee, reportedly to the point of threatening the expulsion of the entire American Olympic team unless strong disciplinary action was taken against Smith and Carlos.

Shortly after midnight on October 18, thirty hours after the clenched-fist ceremony, Douglas F. Roby, the president of the USOC, announced that Smith and Carlos had been suspended from the team and expelled from the Olympic Village. Since the athletes had already moved into downtown hotels with their wives, and since the USOC could not deprive them of their medals, the punishment was mainly verbal: "The untypical exhibitionism of these athletes violates the basic standards of good manners and sportsmanship. . . . Such immature behavior is an isolated incident . . . a repetition of such incidents by other members of the United States team can only be considered a willful disregard of Olympic principles that would warrant the imposition of the severest penalties. . . ."

335

The expulsion triggered a wide range of reactions, from the outraged ("It is unfair, it is ridiculous," said Art Walker, a black American hop-step-and-jumper) to the outrageous ("It wouldn't happen to us," said Gabriel Korobkov, the Soviet track coach, "because we don't mix sports and politics").

Within the American team, reaction was split, and not only by color. The white members of the water polo team sided with the USOC ("In my opinion," said Barry Weisenberg, "an act like that in the medal ceremony defiles the American flag"), but the white members of the Harvard eight-oared crew, openly sympathetic to the black movement from its start, sided with Smith and Carlos (to which Carlos, no diplomat, retorted, "We don't need Whitey"). Most of the black track and field athletes supported Smith and Carlos, but most of the black boxers did not. "That stuff's for college kids," said George Foreman, before he waved his flag. "They live in a different world."

The day Smith and Carlos were suspended was the worst and the best day of Lee Evans' life. It was the day of the 400-meter final. Evans was favored to win the race; he was also a San Jose State student who had planned his own protest in Mexico City. All day, he agonized over whether he should run. John Carlos made the decision for him; Carlos told him to go for the gold. Still, Evans wondered what he should or should not do on the victory stand. The pressure on him was enormous. Douglas Roby read the USOC statement on Smith and Carlos to Evans and his fellow black American 400-meter finalists, Larry James and Ron Freeman. One of his coaches warned Evans that his future might depend on whether he demonstrated. "If I don't do anything," Evans told his wife, Linda, "it will be for you."

"If you want to do something for me," said Linda, "then stand up to those devils."

Before the race began, Evans, James, and Freeman decided upon a mutual course of action on the victory stand. Then they set out to make that course possible.

Larry James held the lead going into the last twenty or thirty meters, but then, somehow, Evans found extra strength in reserve. "The last yards are very painful," Evans had once said. "Maybe I can take more pain than some others." Straining, stretching, Evans drew up to James on the outside, then, in the closing strides, overtook him and won the gold medal. Freeman placed third, the first American one-two-three sweep in a track and field event since the 1960 Olympics in Rome. "A lot of things were on my mind," said Evans, "but I just had to push them out of my mind and concentrate on winning the gold medal—just like a friend of mine did."

Evans' winning time of 43.8 was more than a second under the recognized world record, held, ironically, by his friend— Tommie Smith.

On their way to the victory stand, Evans, James, and Freeman all donned black berets and all waved their fists to the crowd, but the fists were not gloved, and the looks on their faces were not looks of defiance, but of happiness. They mounted the stand and, when "The Star-Spangled Banner" was played, each removed his beret and stood at attention. At the end of the ceremony—and this time everyone was watching—the three waved their berets and marched away, smiling proudly.

"Tommie Smith and I have grown a lot in the past year," Evans told the press after his victory. "I learned a lot about people by being in the boycott movement. If I had to do it all over again, I'd support the movement. I never knew people until I supported something people were against.

"I feel I won this gold medal for black people in the United States and black people all over the world."

Someone asked Evans the significance of the black berets, and the twenty-one-year-old college student smiled. "It was rainin'," he said. "We didn't want to get wet."

There was no hint of disciplinary action against the 400-meter runners for their mild display. The crisis was past. The emphasis turned to competition again, the focus once more on performance.

And no one could have asked for more brilliant performances than those that came out of the 1968 Olympic Games. There had been some fear that Mexico, the first Latin American country to host the Olympics, might not have the experience or the resources or the dedication to provide a first-class show, and a corollary fear that the high altitude of Mexico City (7,350 feet above sea level) might depress the level of performances. Both fears proved, for the most part, unfounded.

Wealthy industrial Japan had spent close to $2 billion on the 1964 Olympics, but Mexico kept its expenses down to $150 million and, under the direction of Pedro Ramirez Vasquez, a renowned architect and a gifted planner, still did a magnificent job. The Olympic complex was a blend of striking architecture and bold sculpture. The Olympic Village, twenty-nine buildings, some six stories tall and some ten, provided living and dining facilities for 10,000 athletes, coaches, trainers, and journalists, all at a cost of $12.4 million. The Olympic Stadium, originally constructed in 1952, was enlarged from 65,000 seats to 80,000 at a cost of $3.6 million. Another $8 million went into the Sports Palace, a geodesic maze of steel beams meeting under a copper-sheathed dome, and a little more than $10 million went into the improvement of highways leading to the Olympic complex. One of the smallest investments, and one of the most significant, was the purchase of four Tartan tracks, three for training and one within the Olympic Stadium; the synthetic running surface may have contributed greatly to the record-breaking performances in all running events up to a distance of 1,500 meters.

The thin air at the high altitude may have helped, too, at the shorter distances. But at greater distances, it had a punishing effect, particularly upon runners unaccustomed to paying what became known as "the oxygen debt." Dr. Roger Bannister, the first human to run a four-minute mile, warned that competitors in distance events might do themselves serious harm. Asked how long it would take for a sea-level runner to adjust to Mexico City, Dr. Bannister replied, "Twenty-five years."

The altitude problem surfaced in the very first race of the Olympics, the 10,000-meter run. Australia's Ron Clarke, thirty-one years old, a man who had set seventeen world records in his career, was trying one last time for an Olympic gold medal. He was running well until, with three laps to go, he tried to step up his pace. His legs deadened, then his arms, and his vision blurred. He said later he felt as if his heart was rapping through the wall of his chest. "The straightaway looked two miles long," he said. At the finish, for the first time in his long career, he collapsed. Clarke had always been amused by runners who collapsed at the finish. "I apologize to them all," he said.

Clarke was in miserable shape, but within two days, after a series of electrocardiograms showed he had suffered no lasting damage, he was running again, qualifying for the finals of the 5,000-meter run.

The 10,000-meter run signaled much more than the start of the foot-racing phase of the 1968 Olympics; it marked the most sudden emergence of an athletic nation in the modern history of the Games. The nation was Kenya, which had never won a gold or a silver medal in its three previous Olympic appearances, and its specialty was long-distance running.

With only half a lap to go in the 10,000-meter run, with Ron Clarke fading to sixth place, three men were bunched in the lead, three Africans, Mamo Wolde of Ethiopia, then Mohamed Gammoudi of Tunisia, then Naftali Temu of Kenya. "That's when I decided to sprint," said Temu later.

Temu's sprint overtook Gammoudi as they came around the final turn and overtook Wolde in the homestretch. The Kenyan won the race by six-tenths of a second in 29:27.4, more than a minute slower than the Olympic record, almost two minutes slower than Ron Clarke's world record.

Two days later, Kenya earned its first silver medal in its brief Olympic history. Wilson Kiprugut—who had earned Kenya's only pre-1968 Olympic medal, a bronze, for running third to Peter Snell at 800 meters in Tokyo—placed second this time at the same distance, behind Australia's Ralph Doubell. Both Doubell and Kiprugut broke Snell's Olympic record, but for a Kenyan, it developed, 800 meters just isn't a long enough distance to work up full speed.

One day later, Kenya doubled its total of gold and silver medals. In the 3,000-meter steeplechase, Amos Biwott broke away from his fellow Kenyan, Benjamin Kogo, in the last few hundred meters. Biwott, who had just turned twenty-one, was a rare steeplechaser who cleared the water jump almost every time without splashing into it.

The following day, Kenya added to its honors. Kipchoge Keino was the favorite to win the 5,000-meter run even though, a few days earlier, he had collapsed three laps from the finish

Kipchoge Keino of Kenya nears the tape in the 1500-meter run, which he won in Olympic record time of 3:34.9 over Jim Ryun.

of the 10,000 meters. With one lap left in the 5,000, Gammoudi, the Tunisian, was leading, but a pair of Kenyans, Temu and Keino, were right behind him. In the home stretch, Keino made his move. He passed Temu and pulled up even with Gammoudi. Keino seemed certain to overtake the Tunisian, but Gammoudi, twice deprived of a gold medal, at 10,000 meters in Mexico City and in Tokyo, was not going to be deprived this time. He fought off Keino's surge and won by a couple of yards, leaving Kenya with a silver and a bronze medal. (In both the 5,000- and 10,000-meter runs, the fourth-place finisher, behind three Africans, was a Mexican, Juan Martinez, to the delight of the home crowd.)

Kenya still had one great fling left—exactly seven days after Temu gave the African nation its first Olympic gold medal. The race was the 1,500-meter run, still a glamor event, and the spotlight, from the American point of view, was on Jim Ryun, the world record-holder from Kansas. Four years earlier, in Tokyo, at the age of seventeen, Ryun had finished last in a semi-final heat of the 1,500 meters. But since then, he had established himself as the greatest middle-distance runner in the world. Yet 1968 had not been an easy year for him. He had suffered from mononucleosis, a pulled hamstring muscle, a kidney infection, and a surprising failure to qualify at 800 meters in the U.S. Olympic trials. Still, Ryun was the favorite to win the Olympic 1,500 meters.

At the start, Ben Jipcho of Kenya took the lead, setting a stunningly fast pace, and Ryun, in his usual style, lay back, all the way back in next-to-last place. Jipcho's pace was so swift that, by the halfway mark, when he faded far back, his countryman, Kip Keino, found himself holding a huge lead. There was simply no human way to catch Keino. Ryun made a magnificent effort and overtook the rest of the field, but he didn't come within twenty yards of Keino. If the high altitude had caused sub-record performances at 3,000 5,000, and 10,000 meters, it didn't seem to slow down Keino; his winning time was 3:34.9, an Olympic record and the second-fastest 1,500 meters ever run, second only to Ryun's 3:33.1.

Kenya had its third gold medal of the 1968 Games, all three earned at distances of 1,500 meters or more, a feat no nation had performed since 1936, when three Finns won the 5,000, the 10,000, and the steeplechase. But the Finns had a rich tradition of long-distance excellence, a tradition that had reached its peak in 1924 when Finland won all five distance races, from the 1,500 meters to the Marathon.

Kenya had come up from nowhere, an incredible achievement diminished only slightly by the fact that the Kenyans were accustomed to living and running at high altitudes. ("This feels just like Africa," said Temu when he arrived in Mexico City.) Not coincidentally, Gammoudi, the veteran Tunisian who won at 5,000 meters, had trained for Mexico City at a site high in the Pyrenees, and Wolde, the Ethiopian who succeeded his countryman Abebe Bikila as the Marathon champion (Bikila, at the age of thirty-seven, dropped out before the finish), lived and trained, like the Kenyans, far above sea level.

If the Kenyans had every reason to be proud of their emergence as a track and field power, the United States had reason to be proud, too. The U.S. reaffirmed its position as the world's dominant track and field nation. The American men surrendered the 5,000- and 10,000-meter titles they had taken by surprise in Tokyo, but still managed to win twelve gold medals, one more than their Tokyo total. The United States retained championships in six running events, setting Olympic records in all six—at 100 meters (Jim Hines, an outspoken black opponent of the black boycott), at 200 (Smith) and at 400 (Evans), in the 110-meter hurdles (Willie Davenport) and in both the 400- and 1,600-meter relays. The U.S. added gold medals in six field events, if the decathlon can be considered a field event.

"In the decathlon," Bill Toomey once said of his specialty, "you have ten mistresses instead of one, all keeping you busy. It's more work—but more fun, too."

Toomey's affair with the decathlon had begun in 1963, when he was already twenty-four years old. He quickly fell in love with the event. Helped by a wealthy father, a wine company executive, Toomey spent four years preparing for Mexico City, including five months in Germany, training under Friedel Schirmer, considered the best of decathlon instructors.

All the work paid off in Mexico City. After an early scare, when he twice missed the opening height in the pole vault ("Can you imagine? Eleven feet! My name would have been mud!"), Toomey went on to win the decathlon and set an Olympic record. "I couldn't miss," he said afterward. "Ten's my favorite number. Ten letters in my name, born on January 10th, always wore No. 10 as a ballplayer. It had to be the decathlon."

Randy Matson, the world record-holder, set an Olympic record in winning the shot-put without great difficulty, without much drama. The other four American gold medals were the results of memorable performances.

The most spectacular performance came in the long jump; it may have been the most spectacular single track and field performance since Jesse Owens leaped twenty-six feet five and three eighths inches in the 1936 Games, setting an Olympic mark that endured for almost a quarter of a century. The record set in Mexico City may last just as long.

On his first jump in the finals, Bob Beamon, a tall, slender, twenty-two-year-old New Yorker out of the University of Texas at El Paso, sprinted down the runway, propelled himself off the board with his right foot, pulled his arms back, then flung them forward down between his legs. Legs spread-eagled, body folded like a jackknife, Beamon landed in the pit twenty-nine feet two and one half inches from the takeoff. He had broken the world record by almost two feet, the Olympic record by almost three. Beamon leaned his forehead against the ground and cried and prayed. "I was thanking that good man up there,"

Bob Beamon of the USA sails to a world record of 29 feet, 2½ inches in the finals of the long jump at Mexico City.

he said, "for letting me hit the ground right there." He took only one more jump of his allotted six—a much shorter one, of course—and then relaxed and waited for his gold medal. On the victory stand, Beamon had his sweatpants rolled up, revealing black socks, a quiet tribute to Smith and Carlos. The bronze medalist, Ralph Boston, who had won a gold medal in Rome and a silver in Tokyo, accepted his award barefooted.

The Olympic pole-vault record took almost as severe a beating as the long-jump mark. Before Mexico City, no man had vaulted seventeen feet in the Olympics. But in Mexico City, a Spaniard, a Frenchman, a Russian, and a Greek all cleared seventeen feet—and not one of them managed to win even a bronze medal. A total of nine men went above seventeen feet, including two Americans and two West Germans, and the championship came down to a three-way battle among Bob Seagren of the U.S., Claus Schiprowski of West Germany, and Wolfgang Nordwig of East Germany.

Seagren, who did not even begin to vault till the bar reached seventeen feet, saved his shrewdest move for later. After six men cleared seventeen feet four and three quarters inches, Seagren passed up his turn at seventeen feet six and three

341

quarters inches; four of his five rivals cleared that height, and the bar was raised to seventeen feet eight and one half inches, higher than the world record. If Seagren had failed at seventeen feet eight and a half, he would have dropped to fifth place. But he cleared the world-record height on his second try; so did the West German, Schiprowski. The East German, Nordwig, made it on his third attempt. They were the only three survivors, and all three then failed at seventeen feet ten and a half inches. On the basis of fewest misses—Schiprowski had missed once at seventeen feet six and three quarters inches, the height Seagren passed—Seagren won the gold medal.

The high jump introduced another American gold medalist —and a revolutionary technique. Dick Fosbury, a twenty-one-year-old Oregonian, brought the "Fosbury Flop" to the Olympics. Instead of running up to the bar, leaping off his inside foot, throwing his outside foot over the bar and then rolling the rest of his body over—the conventional method—Fosbury ran up to the bar, leaped off his outside foot, turned his back to the bar, went over backward, head first and feet last, and landed, hopefully, on his shoulder blades. At first glance, the Flop looked impossible—even to Fosbury. "Sometimes I see movies," he said, "and I wonder how I do it."

Scientifically, the method was sound. The Flop lowered his center of gravity, which—as Fosbury, a civil engineering student, knew—made it easier for him to get high off the ground. As a high school jumper who had never gone above five feet four inches, Fosbury cleared five feet ten inches as soon as he invented the Flop. By the time he graduated from

The "Fosbury Flop" that carried Dick Fosbury to the Olympic high jump victory.

Al Oerter wins his fourth consecutive gold medal in the discus, with an Olympic record throw of 212 feet, 1½ inches.

high school, Fosbury was up to six feet seven inches, and in Mexico City, he soared seven feet four and a quarter inches, setting an Olympic record. "I think quite a few kids will begin trying it my way now," said Fosbury, after his victory. He proved as reliable a prophet as a jumper; within six years, most of the best jumpers in the world were Floppers.

Fosbury, Seagren, and Beamon all produced stunning performances in Mexico City, but discus thrower Al Oerter produced the most stunning *victory*. Oerter was thirty-two years old in 1968, and was not expected to challenge seriously for the gold medal he had won in Melbourne, in Rome, and in Tokyo. But Oerter took the Games very seriously. "I get fired up for the Olympics," he said. "Something happens to me. The people, the pressure, everything about the Olympics is special to me."

Oerter followed a thirteen-month training program designed to bring him to a peak in Mexico City, and the plan worked perfectly. The favorites were Ludvik Danek of Czechoslovakia, holder of the recognized world record, and Jay Silvester of the United States, who had shattered Danek's record in the American Olympic trials. But neither Silvester nor Danek could approach his best previous effort in Mexico City, and Oerter did exactly what he had done in Melbourne, in Rome, and in Tokyo: he threw the discus farther than he had ever thrown it before in his life. Despite a torn thigh muscle, despite a chronically painful cervical disc, with his wife and his two daughters sitting and watching in the rain, Oerter spun the discus two hundred twelve feet six and a half inches, five feet beyond his own previous best. A supervisor of computer communications for an aircraft company, Oerter immediately began thinking about the 1972 Olympics. "I think I can continue to improve until I'm forty or so," he said.

Oerter knew that he would certainly not be favored in Munich in 1972, but that was all right. He hadn't been favored in Melbourne or in Rome or in Tokyo or in Mexico City. And yet he was only the second man in Olympic history to win four gold medals in the same event in four separate Olympics; the only other, Ray Ewry, won four gold medals in the standing high jump and four in the standing broad jump, but all in an *eight-year* span, 1900 through 1908, including the semi-official Olympics of 1906.

In addition to Oerter, the U.S. track and field team boasted another former gold medalist whose Olympic experience dated back to 1956. Harold Connolly, the hammer-throwing champion in Melbourne, did not reach the finals in Mexico City. During the qualifying round, on the one throw he made that would have put him into the finals, Connolly forgot the Olympic rule that says a thrower must enter the circle from the back and exit through the back. Connolly exited to the side. His wife, the former Olga Fikotova of Czechoslovakia, was in the stands when Connolly was disqualified. "I was crushed," she said. Mrs. Connolly managed to finish sixth in the women's discus—at the age of thirty-six.

No other nation came close to matching the American total of twelve gold medals in men's track and field; Kenya and the Soviet Union came closest, with three apiece. For the Russians, the total was disappointing, but not nearly so disappointing as the performance of the Soviet women. For the first time since the Russians entered the Olympic fold in 1952, they were completely shut out of gold medals in women's track and field. And at the same time, for the first time since 1932, the American women won more gold medals in track and field than any other nation. Wyomia Tyus had a hand (or, more accurately, a pair of legs) in two of the three U.S. victories. She anchored the world record-breaking 400-meter relay team, and she won the 100-meter dash, repeating her triumph in Tokyo. She was the first Olympic sprinter, male or female, to retain an individual championship four years later. (More than half a century earlier, Archie Hahn had repeated in the men's 100-meter dash, but his victories came only two years apart, in 1904 and 1906.)

After the relay race, Wyomia Tyus told a news conference, "I would like to say that we dedicate our win to John Carlos and Tommie Smith."

Wyomia Tyus (105) of the USA wins the 100-meter dash. Raelene Boyle (33) of Australia and Chi Cheng (223) of Taiwan look close, but they actually finished fourth and seventh, respectively.

Once again, as in Tokyo, no one cared about the comparative point scores of the U.S. and the U.S.S.R.—that touch of nationalism seemed to have faded from the Games—and once again, as in Tokyo, the Americans led all nations in gold medals, with a total of forty-five. The U.S. still couldn't legitimately claim to be the best all-around sports country in the world; it was, instead, the best two-sports country in the world. Of the forty-five gold medals, fifteen came in track and field, and twenty-three in swimming.

America's Debbie Meyer en route to her third gold medal in the 800-meter free style, winning by 20 yards and setting a new Olympic record.

No nation had ever before won twenty-three gold medals in swimming, for a very good reason: no previous Olympics had offered twenty-three swimming events. But in 1968, the Olympic swimming program grew to thirty-three events, and the swimmer expected to dominate the expanded show was an eighteen-year-old Californian named Mark Spitz. He was considered capable of winning an incredible six gold medals in Mexico City—three in individual events and three in relay races.

The swimming star of Mexico City did turn out to be a teenaged Californian, but it wasn't Mark Spitz. It was sixteen-year-old Debbie Meyer who, only a couple of days before her first race, was suffering from a sore throat and a stomach disorder so severe she was not expected to compete. Penicillin put her back in the pool.

Debbie Meyer won the 200-meter free style, the 400-meter free style, and the 800-meter free style, the first time any swimmer, male or female, had ever won three individual events. Four of her female teammates—Jan Henne, Kay Hall, Claudia Kolb, and Sue Pedersen—each won two gold medals, but only Claudia Kolb's both came in individual events. Sue Pedersen, who also collected a silver medal and a bronze, turned fifteen during the Games. Ironically, four years later, at Munich, not one of the 1968 multiple gold-medal winners— not even Sue Pedersen, who was then eighteen—was a member of the American Olympic team; presumably, they were all past their peaks. (Perhaps they had fallen victim to *thought*; George Haines, who coached many of the women, once said: "Thinking complicates the road to physical perfection. Don't think, don't talk, swim!")

Spitz wasn't past his peak in Mexico City; he was between peaks. Holder of the world record for both the 100-meter and the 200-meter butterfly, Spitz finished second in the shorter event, a dismal eighth in the longer. He could do no better than third in the 100-meter free style. Spitz did pick up gold medals in both free style relay races, but he did not swim in the medley relay.

345

Two Americans each won a pair of individual gold medals, Mike Burton in the longer free style races, and Charles Hickcox in the individual medleys. So did an Australian, Mike Wenden, in the shorter free style races, and an East German, Roland Matthes, in the backstroke events. And the old man of the American team, Don Schollander, an ancient twenty-two, swam the anchor leg of the victorious 800-meter free style relay team to add a fifth gold medal to the four he had collected in Tokyo.

The rest of the American gold medals were picked up here and there, a pair in boxing and a pair in yachting, the opposite extremes of sporting violence, and one, of course, in basketball. The American team was missing many of the top collegiate stars—the top collegiate star, Lew Alcindor of UCLA, who later changed his name to Kareem Abdul-Jabbar, had been an early supporter of the Harry Edwards boycott; even after the boycott was dropped, Alcindor elected to pass up the Olympics—yet it maintained its nation's unbeaten record in Olympic competition. Led by Jo Jo White and then-unknown Spencer Haywood, two future professional stars, the U.S. team won its opening game by five points, over Puerto Rico, and all its other games by wider margins. In the final, against Yugoslavia, the Americans turned a one-point halftime lead into a fifteen-point rout at the finish.

While all the U.S. gold medals were earned in seven sports, the Russians demonstrated considerably more versatility, spreading their twenty-nine gold medals among twelve different sports (of the nineteen contested in Mexico City). Weight-lifting was one of the Soviets' strongest areas—three gold medals—and the strongest of the Soviets was their heavyweight, the world record-holder and the defending Olympic champion, Leonid Zhabotinsky.

Zhabo, as his friends called him—and a heavyweight weightlifter has no enemies—began psyching his opponents right in the opening parade. He was the Soviet flag-bearer, and every other flag-bearer in the parade, representing 7,886 athletes from 112 nations, carried the shaft of the flag tucked in a leather cup strapped to his waist, or to hers. (The American flag-bearer, for the first time, was a woman, Janice Lee York Romary, a forty-year-old fencer appearing in her sixth Olympics.) Not Zhabo. He held the Russian flag straight out in front of him, in a firm left hand, with no support.

But Zhabo almost ruined his Olympic chances when, a few days before his event, he got sick from eating an entire cantaloupe, skin and all. It was probably the most logical case of *turista*, the intestinal disorder that tends to strike many visitors to Mexico, during the whole Olympic festival. And it may have been the one spactacular event that the forty-five ABC television cameras, beaming forty-five hours of color coverage to 400 million viewers around the world, failed to pick up.

Zhabo recovered in time to pick up 1,259.5 pounds—and his gold medal.

The 1968 Winter Games were scattered throughout the French Alps, fanning out in a forty-mile radius from Grenoble, the headquarters for a competition that was plagued by wind and fog and snow and rain. A dedicated mailman would have done his job in Grenoble; so did a dedicated Frenchman named Jean Claude Killy.

Killy was the most gifted Alpine skier since Austria's Toni Sailer—and the most charming. A darkly handsome twenty-four-year-old, who had been skiing the French Alps since he was three, Killy made his first assault upon Olympic gold in the downhill race.

"Why do you think more highly of the downhill race than any other Alpine event?" an Austrian journalist asked a group of Olympic skiers.

"Because the downhill tests character and courage," said Killy.

"Because the downhill does not leave room for a compromise," said Guy Perillat, another Frenchman. "You're either in front or you perish."

"The downhill demands everything a skier is able to give," said Austria's Karl Schranz. "No coward will ever win."

France's Jean Claude Killy in the Giant Slalom, his second gold medal in 1968.

Perillat was the first man down the course, almost two miles long, with a vertical drop of almost half a mile. The Frenchman raced down the hill in 1:59.93, and none of the next dozen entrants could break two minutes. Then came Killy. With a magnificent run, he covered the course in 1.59.85, winning his first gold medal by eight-hundredths of a second.

Three days later, Killy collected his second gold medal, in the giant slalom, his time more than two seconds faster than the second-place finisher's, an enormous margin in an Alpine event.

Five days later, Killy was ready to match the Alpine triple achieved by Tony Sailer in 1956 at Cortina. Killy made it—but not quite so convincingly as Sailer. The Frenchman's chief threat was the Austrian, Schranz. Each man made two runs, the first through sixty-two gates, the second through sixty-nine, and on his second run, with the course shrouded in fog, Schranz knew he had a good chance to spoil Killy's dreams of a triple. But when he reached the twenty-second

Peggy Fleming of the USA doing a compulsory figure on her way to the figure skating title in the Winter Olympics at Grenoble.

348

gate on his second run, Schranz skidded to a halt. He told Olympic officials that a spectator had wandered onto the course, forcing him to stop. The officials sent Schranz back to the top of the hill to start his run again. This time, he flashed through all sixty-nine gates in a time fast enough to defeat Killy. But then, and only then, Olympic authorities announced that Schranz had missed two gates on his original second run —two gates *before* the spectator interfered with him—and because of that, he was ineligible for a rerun. No one will ever be able to explain—to the satisfaction of Austrians—why this verdict was not handed down *before* Schranz made his rerun.

Killy got his third gold medal and, like Sailer before him, headed off toward a rich professional career of endorsements and public appearances.

Next to Killy, the two most glamorous champions at Grenoble were a teenaged American and a forty-year-old Italian, the American for her youth and grace, the Italian for his age and perseverance. Peggy Fleming gave the United States its only gold medal of the Winter Games in figure skating and she gave the audience a free-skating display they would never forget. For her free-skating performance, she earned a score of 5.9 (6.0 is perfection), the highest ever recorded in the Olympics.

Eugenio Monti, the Italian veteran, had won nine world championships, two Olympic silver medals, and two Olympic bronze medals—but no gold before Grenoble. In 1968, he earned two gold medals, in the two-man bobsled and the four-man bobsled. "I'm done now," Monti said. "I'm satisfied. I'll retire peacefully."

Norway wound up with the most gold medals at Grenoble, six, the Soviet Union captured five, and France and Italy four apiece.

General Charles de Gaulle presided over the opening of the Games, in a handsome stadium built for 60,000 spectators. The stadium was constructed solely for the opening ceremonies; the following day, workmen began to demolish it.

A few days later, the International Olympic Committee voted to readmit South Africa to the Games and, with that vote, came perilously close to the most massive demolition job in Olympic history.

Mark Spitz winning a heat in the 200-meter butterfly at Munich.

# *Mark and the Massacre*

## CHAPTER TWENTY : 1972—MUNICH AND SAPPORO

*"It could have happened to a nicer guy."*

—DOUG RUSSELL
Former Olympic champion,
On Mark Spitz at Munich

One night during the 1972 Olympic Games, several days before the massacre that was to tarnish every medal and haunt every memory, Mark Andrew Spitz was sitting in a Munich restaurant, dining with his coach, Sherman Chavoor, and complaining endlessly about a mild cold. "You know something about those antibiotics I took?" said Spitz. "They made me dizzy."

Chavoor didn't even look up from his meal. "Dizzier," he said.

Chavoor's affectionate put-down was one of the nicest things anyone had ever said about Mark Spitz. He had been called arrogant, stupid, immature, and even crazy. But Mark Spitz wasn't *mad* in Munich. He was, at worst, eccentric—an eccentric genius.

Spitz's genius was of a limited variety, extending only the length and width of a swimming pool, but within those confines, he was Einstein, he was da Vinci, he was Aristotle, all in one. He put on a display of individual excellence unprecedented in Olympic history, a display doubly impressive because it followed, by four years, dismal failure in Mexico City.

If an election had been held to determine the most disappointing performer in the 1968 Olympics, Spitz would have won in a landslide. He was expected by many people—including himself—to win six gold medals in Mexico City. Instead, he was forced to settle for two gold medals, both in relay races, and a silver and a bronze medal. For anyone else, the four-medal haul would have been a stunning achievement, but for

Spitz, a swimming god at the age of eighteen, four medals meant a flop. "He was a small boy," said Sherman Chavoor in Munich, "and the big studs on the team browbeat him. Now he can't be psyched. He's the stud this time around."

If another election had been held to determine the least popular performer in the 1968 Olympics, Spitz would have been a strong contender. His teammates did everything short of publicly applauding each of his defeats. If he had a friend on the team, the friend was harder to find than a safe glass of Mexican tap water. Most of the abuse aimed at Spitz focused on his attitude, his cockiness, but some was fouler. "Hey, Jew-boy," a teammate had yelled to him in Mexico City, "you aren't going to win *any* gold medals."

Between the shame of Mexico City and his revenge in Munich, Spitz grew up—at least a little. He went to the University of Indiana, led the school to three straight national collegiate swimming championships, learned enough tact and diplomacy to be elected co-captain of the team and, along the way, managed to break twenty-eight world records in free style and butterfly events. He was, by far, the best swimmer in the world, and in Munich, where he was entered in four individual and three relay events, experts said he would win *seven* gold medals. Spitz agreed, but not quite so forcefully as he had shared the six-medal predictions in Mexico.

At the outset of the 1972 Games, the memories of Mexico City lingered. People wondered if the six-foot, 170-pound body of the twenty-two-year-old Indiana graduate was merely a shell to hide the eighteen-year-old Californian who had cracked once before under Olympic pressure. Spitz wasn't talking too much—since Mexico City he had grown wary of the press—but on August 28, the first day of swimming competitions, he began to answer his critics.

His first race was the 200-meter butterfly, in which he was an overwhelming favorite. He had been an overwhelming favorite to win the 200-meter butterfly in 1968, too, and then he had finished dead last in the final. But in Munich, Spitz splashed through the water with such controlled fury, with such grace, that he finished two full seconds in front of the runner-up. His time—only seven tenths of a second more than two minutes—set a new world record. It was an accurate harbinger—and a psychological turning point. "If Mark had lost his first race," said Peter Daland, head coach of the American men's swimming team, "he could have been discouraged. But the Mark Spitz of '72 is a tough person."

The same day, Spitz anchored the American 400-meter free style relay team to a smashing victory, establishing another world record. "I like Mark," said Dave Edgar, one of Spitz's relay teammates, in a confession more startling than the world record. "He talks a lot about himself, but how can you blame him? That's all people ever ask him about." Ironically, Edgar had earlier been a target of Spitz's arrogance; even though Edgar had defeated him in collegiate meets, held in short pools emphasizing turning ability, Spitz had dismissed

Spitz's seventh gold medal hangs around his neck, after the American victory in the 400-meter medley relay. He had previously won gold medals in the 100- and 200-meter free style, the 100- and 200-meter butterfly, and the 400- and 800-meter free style relays.

his rival's chances in the Olympic trials by saying, "This is swimming, not turns."

On the second day of Olympic swimming competition, Spitz faced one of his sternest tests—the 200-meter free style. His stiffest competition was supposed to come from Mike Wenden, Australia's defending champion; the best of his American rivals, Steve Genter, was not in perfect condition. Only a few days earlier, Genter had undergone minor surgery, a fifteen-minute operation, for a collapsed lung. The day before the final, Spitz told Genter he didn't think it was such a good idea for Genter to be swimming, that he might be risking permanent physical harm. Spitz said later he was only trying to show his concern, but Genter interpreted the remarks as pure psych, an attempt to shatter his concentration and weaken his performance. If it was an attempt to psych, it worked only in reverse. Genter's concentration intensified, his dedication increased. At the start of the final, shaking, twitching, jabbering, his standard pre-race ritual, Genter was determined to kill Spitz's bid for seven gold medals.

Halfway through the race, Genter held the lead. He was still in front at one hundred fifty meters. But then, either the aftereffects of his operation or Spitz's sheer swimming genius caught up to Genter. Spitz passed him and won by less than a second. Once again, Spitz's time—1:52.78—set a world record. "Nothing would have pleased me more than to beat him," said Genter, unhappily.

With three gold medals in his grasp, Spitz still could not relax. "This isn't fun, not yet at least," he said, in a candid moment. "It's tremendous—the pressure of not losing. I'd rather win six out of six, or even four out of four, than six out of seven. It's reached a point where my self-esteem comes into it. I just don't want to lose." Obviously, the specter of Mexico City lingered.

The handsome specter of Spitz himself was already dominating the 1972 Olympics. With his neat mustache and his dark good looks, Spitz reminded people of Omar Sharif, the movie actor. And with his ability, Spitz reminded people of Johnny Weissmuller, the dominant swimmer in Olympic history, except that Weissmuller never swam nearly so fast. "Mark's so loose and long-muscled," said Sherman Chavoor. "The way he slips through the water is simply mystifying." Arnold Spitz, Mark's father, an engineer, offered his own non-technical explanation. "Mark's whole body is so flexible the water just seems to slip by him." Mark's father had moved his family to Honolulu when Mark was two, had watched Mark start swimming then and had pushed him toward greatness ever since. "Swimming isn't everything," Arnold Spitz once said, in a moment Vince Lombardi would have been proud of. "Winning is."

Spitz followed his father's advice perfectly in Munich; swimming *wasn't* everything. He was seen often in the company of Jo Ann Harshbarger, a fifteen-year-old American swimmer; before the Games, he had been dating Ann Simmons, who, like Harshbarger, was a free style distance swimmer. "The least he could have done," said one member of the American women's team, a bit cattily, "was put the make on someone from a different event."

But if swimming wasn't everything, winning was. Two days after his dramatic victory over Genter, Spitz was in the pool, bidding for two more gold medals. He got them—in the 100-meter butterfly and in the 800-meter free style relay. For both events, of course, world records were set. In the butterfly, Spitz's margin was incredible—almost a second and half in a race that lasted less than a minute. The relay was a joke. Steve Genter, ironically, swam the third leg and handed Spitz a big lead that he increased to six full seconds over the second-place team.

Then, on September 3, in the 100-meter free style—the race in which he was considered most beatable—Spitz took the lead right at the start and churned to his sixth gold medal and his sixth world record. Suddenly, he stood alone, the first man in the history of the modern Olympics to win six gold medals in one year. (There had been four winners of five gold medals: Anton Heida, an American gymnast, in 1904; Nedo Nadi, an Italian fencer, in 1920; Willis Lee, an American shooter, in 1920; and Paavo Nurmi, the Finnish distance runner, in 1924. Heida's feat included four individual golds and one team gold; Nadi won two as an individual and three as a team member; Lee won all his medals in team events; and Nurmi, although he took three individual titles and shared in two team titles, ran only four races, one of them counting toward both an individual and a team championship.)

Jerry Heidenreich, an American who finished third in the 100-meter free style, said afterward that Spitz's secret is "in the way he's built. His legs are so long. He's so hyperextended that he can kick six inches deeper than anyone else. His legs are like a bow. When he puts on a pair of pants, the stripes on the seams go in different directions."

Spitz's seventh gold medal was almost anticlimactic. He was a member of the American 400-meter medley relay team. The U.S. did brilliantly. With Spitz swimming the third leg, the butterfly leg, the Americans won by four seconds. Spitz pulled himself out of the water for the final time as an amateur competitor, the winner of seven Olympic gold medals, the holder of seven new world records. He had come as close to perfection as any athlete in any sport at any time.

From the glory of Munich, Spitz was supposed to move to the drudgery of dental school, but Sherman Chavoor predicted, "He'll never go to dental school."

Chavoor was right. There were too many temptations awaiting the winner of seven gold medals. There were millions of dollars waiting in endorsements and in appearances, opportunities to hawk razors for the Schick Company, to plug milk for the California Milk Advisory Board, to clown with Bob Hope on a television special, to do everything in the world to turn Olympic gold into hard cash.

Spitz couldn't resist. No human could have. But before he could leave Munich and go home to a hero's welcome, Spitz—along with most of the world—was shaken by a barbaric act of terrorism that made all the past problems of the modern Olympics, all the feuds and arguments that had torn for three-quarters of a century at Baron de Coubertin's lofty ideals, seem like petty squabbles.

The morning after Spitz won his seventh gold medal, an hour before dawn, eight men slipped into the Olympic Village. Some of them wore disguises, one a face mask. They carried machine guns and hand grenades concealed in athletic equipment bags. They scaled a six-foot, six-inch fence, easily avoided the minimal security guards and made their way to Building 31 on Connollystrasse, a street named after Harold and Olga Connolly, symbols, ironically, of international harmony.

The eight men represented the Black September movement, the most violent of Arab terrorist groups, dedicated to the destruction of Israel. Building 31, which housed the Israeli Olympic team, was neither locked nor guarded. The Arabs climbed to the second floor and began knocking on doors. "I heard the knocking and then a terrible cry," said Tuvia Sokolsky, a weightlifting coach and one of the Israelis who managed to escape from Building 31. "I knew instinctively that it was an Arab attack. Then I heard my friends yelling, 'Get out! Escape!' I couldn't open the window, so I broke it and ran out."

One of the Arab terrorists who seized the Israeli team quarters appears on a balcony in the Olympic Village.

Yosef Gutfreund, a wrestling referee; Joseph Romano, a weightlifter; and Moshe Weinberg, the wrestling coach, were the first Israelis to confront the Arabs. They were strong men, and briefly they held back the terrorists at their door. But then machine-gun bullets ripped through the door. Weinberg, thirty-three years old, collapsed and died. Romano, also thirty-three, was mortally wounded. Gutfreund was captured.

Half a dozen Israelis fled from the building. One, a boxer, ran under fire, zigzagging between pillars. "I think I broke the world record for the dash," he said later. "I heard the bullets whistling by my ears."

The terrorists rounded up eight more Israelis, including the country's track and field coach, Amitzur Schapira; an eighteen-year-old wrestler named Mark Slavin, a recent Israeli immigrant who spoke no language but his native Russian; and a twenty-six-year-old weightlifter named David Berger, born in Ohio, an American lawyer who had moved to Israel specifically to become an Olympic athlete.

The hostages were crowded into one room on the second floor of Building 31, their hands tied behind their backs, their bodies linked together by ropes circling their waists.

The escapees spread word of the invasion, and soon West German government and police officials converged on the scene and made contact with the terrorists. The guerrillas put forward a list of demands that were to be met before they would release the nine surviving Israeli hostages. Most significantly, they wanted the Israeli government to release two hundred imprisoned Palestinian terrorists and they wanted their own safe passage guaranteed to an Arab nation.

Premier Golda Meir's Israeli government immediately turned down the demand for the release of the two hundred Palestinians and advised the West Germans to stall for time. The terrorists' initial deadline—nine A.M.—kept getting pushed back, and the world waited and watched.

The American Broadcasting Company's television crews, primed to cover this spectacular athletic show, suddenly found themselves reporting a nightmare. For hours, ABC beamed live broadcasts of the terrifying wait in the Olympic Village around the world, and Jim McKay, a capable sportscaster, distinguished himself with a calm, reasoned account of an event far more tense than any he had ever covered on "Wide World of Sports."

West German authorities sealed off the Olympic Village, not so securely that athletes eager to train and a few imaginative newsmen couldn't find their way in and out, and desperate negotiations continued. Hans Dietrich Genscher, West Germany's minister of the interior, made several trips to Building 31 to attempt to bargain with the terrorists, whose leader wore a conspicuous floppy white hat. Chancellor Willy Brandt hurried to Munich to offer his diplomatic aid. The terrorists rejected the offer of a huge ransom and dismissed an offer by German officials to put themselves in Black September hands in exchange for the Israelis.

356

Irony screamed out of the situation. The setting was Germany, the country where Hitler had elevated anti-Semitism to a murderous art, and the backdrop was an Olympics dominated by a gifted Jewish athlete, and the theme of the whole gathering was supposed to have something to do with international peace and understanding.

But in the horrifying hours of September 5, irony took second place to reality. Nine innocent lives were at stake, and all over the world, viewers could see the stakeout at Building 31, could catch an occasional glimpse of a terrorist, could hear the fear and concern and outrage in the voices of authorities and commentators.

Olympic officials from Arab nations tried to reason with the terrorists but failed; all they emerged with was a threat that, if the demands were not soon met, the hostages would be killed publicly, two at a time, in front of Building 31. Willy Brandt sought to contact Egyptian President Anwar Sadat, to solicit his help, but could not. Brandt did reach the Egyptian Premier, Aziz Sidky, who replied: "I cannot pre-empt a decision of the guerrillas. We do not want to get involved in this."

Brandt's government decided early that under no circumstances would the terrorists be allowed to escape from West Germany. As troops massed in the Olympic Village, rumors spread that the Germans would storm Building 31. But an assault would have meant instant death for the hostages. As the hours dragged slowly on, and the hostages still survived, some observers began to think that further bloodshed might be avoided. "It is difficult to be optimistic," argued one Israeli woman, "when your friends have machine guns pointed at them."

Meanwhile, insanely, the Olympics went on, small scale. Few events had been scheduled for September 5, yet almost twelve hours after the terrorists launched their attack, Russian and Polish volleyball teams were competing in a building not far from Connollystrasse.

By early evening, the Games had been suspended, and the West German officials had decided upon a course of action. They would pretend to accede to the Black September demands of safe passage out of Germany. They would send a bus to Building 31, pick up the guerrillas and their hostages and transport them through an underground ramp to a nearby helicopter pad. Then two helicopters would carry them to a military air base at Fürstenfeldbruck, fifteen miles away, to a waiting Lufthansa 727.

The 727 was never intended to take off. Five of the best marksmen in the Munich police force were waiting at the airport, positioned to pick off the Arab terrorists as they walked from the helicopters to the 727.

Sometime around 11 P.M., shooting broke out at the airport, and in the confusion that followed, a report went out that the terrorists had been killed and the hostages saved.

But the good news was false. The West German plan, approved by Israeli authorities, had backfired. The snipers had been told not to fire until all the Arabs were visible, but they started shooting when only four of the Arabs were between the helicopters and the airplane. The Arabs swiftly retaliated; they immediately shot their Israeli hostages. Eight of the Israelis died of bullet wounds; the ninth died when a terrorist tossed a hand grenade into one of the helicopters. The West Germans poured bullets on the Arabs, and an hour later, the death toll was known: besides the Israelis, five of the terrorists and one West German policeman were dead. Three of the terrorists were taken prisoner.

Willy Brandt was shattered—"a catastrophe," was all he could say. Pope Paul VI called the massacre an act that "truly dishonors our times." Kurt Waldheim, the secretary-general of the United Nations, spoke of "a dastardly act," and at a news conference, before he was whisked away from Munich amid fears for his safety, Mark Spitz said, "As a human being and as a Jew, I am profoundly shocked." Red Smith, the veteran sports columnist, expressed eloquent outrage:

> MUNICH, West Germany, Sept. 5—Olympic Village was under siege. Two men lay murdered and nine others were held at gunpoint in imminent peril of their lives. Still, the Games went on. Canoeists paddled through their races. Fencers thrust and parried in make-believe duels. Boxers scuffled. Basketball players scampered across the floor like happy children. Walled off in their dream world, appallingly unaware of the realities of life and death, the aging playground directors who conduct this quadrennial muscle dance ruled that a little blood must not be allowed to interrupt play.
>
> It was 4:30 A.M. when Palestinian terrorists invaded. . . . More than four hours later, word came down from Avery Brundage, retiring president of the International Olympic Committee, that sport would proceed as scheduled. . . . Not until 4 P.M. did some belated sense of decency dictate suspension of the obscene activity, and even then exception was made for games already in progress. . . . The men who run the Olympics are not evil men. Their shocking lack of awareness can't be due to callousness. It has to be stupidity.

Sentiment mounted for the rest of the Games to be canceled, out of shock and out of respect for the dead. The Israeli government favored such a move. "How could anyone even think about competing in the face of death?" asked Kenny Moore, an American Marathon runner. "It would be very difficult for me to suggest that the Games go on," conceded Willi Daume, the chairman of the West German Organizing Committee.

But the International Olympic Committee took the opposite view, that an end to the Games would mean a victory for terrorism, a concession to horror, an admission that the Olympic ideal was a sham. Instead of canceling the Games, the IOC scheduled a memorial ceremony at the Olympic Stadium less than ten hours after the shootout at the airport.

The ceremony was a strange one. The Arab nations were absent; so were the Russians. Not even half the American team

Eddie Hart receives the baton from Gerald Tinker on the final leg of the 400-meter relay. The French and Russian teams are in contention.

turned out. The flags of one hundred twenty-two competing nations and the Olympic banner hung at half-mast, and West Germany's President Gustav Heinemann said, "We stand helpless before a truly despicable act"; yet the ceremony did not so much honor the dead as stain their memory. Again, Red Smith was a clear eyewitness, his column in *The New York Times* a moving blend of sadness and fury:

MUNICH, West Germany, Sept. 7—This time surely, some thought, they would cover the sandbox and put the blocks aside. But no. "The Games must go on," said Avery Brundage, high priest of the playground, and 80,000 listeners burst into applause. The occasion was yesterday's memorial service for eleven members of Israel's Olympic delegation murdered by Palestinian terrorists. It was more like a pep rally.

"Sadly in this imperfect world," Brundage told survivors in the Israeli party and the thousands come to join them in their grief, "the greater and the more important the Olympic Games become, the more they are open to commercial, political and now criminal attack. The Games of the Twentieth Olympiad have been subjected to two savage attacks. We lost the Rhodesian battle against naked political pressure. . . ."

On some faces in Olympic Stadium there was incredulity. That first "savage attack" had been a threat by African nations to boycott the carnival if white-dominated Rhodesia were allowed to participate. Now the retiring president of the International Olympic Committee was equating this with a cold-blooded guerrilla operation that had wiped out seventeen lives.

Here in this solemn assemblage, Brundage was beating the tired old horse of commercialism, deploring again the practice of bribing amateur footracers to wear a certain brand of spiked shoe. How insensitive can the closed mind get?

The voice was reedy and thin, the 84-year-old voice that for twenty years has enunciated the last word in Olympic policy.

"We have only the strength of a great ideal. I am sure the public will agree that we cannot allow a handful of terrorists to destroy this nucleus of international cooperation and goodwill we have in the Olympic movement. The Games must go on and we must continue our efforts to keep them clean, pure and honest, and try to extend the sportsmanship of the athletic field into other areas."

Applause was loud. Obviously, not everyone has been repelled by the spectacle of children returning to their play almost as soon as the killing ended.

The play went on, almost a mockery within the magnificent setting the West Germans had constructed for the Olympic festival that was going to wipe out the bad taste of the last German Games in 1936. Physically, the $650-million Olympic complex was dominated by an incredible $60-million acrylic glass roof, curving and dipping over acre after acre, covering part of the Olympic Stadium, the Sports Hall and the swimming pool.

But the theme of the 1972 Olympics could not be traced to its physical setting. The theme was not nearly so grand: the Games of the XX Olympiad were riddled with stupidity, with insensitivity, and with poor judgment—the traits that were displayed, on a far more significant scale, when the massacre occurred. The first blunder was the admission, then the banning of Rhodesia, a process that required the ultimate in doubletalk and doublethink. The Rhodesians were allowed to come into the Games under the condition that they pretend that they were still part of the British Commonwealth, a status the country had unilaterally surrendered in 1965. To maintain the pretense, the Rhodesians agreed to march under the nation's colonial flag, hum "God Save the Queen," and carry identification stating they were loyal British subjects. The IOC figured this subterfuge would keep everybody happy. But when the black-dominated African nations threatened to boycott the Games, which meant that the gifted runners from Kenya and Ethiopia would not compete, the IOC, after a bitter internal struggle, banned the Rhodesians, again using a transparently manufactured excuse: the Rhodesians had no passports proving they were British subjects.

Once the Games began, idiocy still reigned, and not only in the councils of the IOC. Two American sprinters, Eddie Hart and Rey Robinson, suffered in one classic case of stupidity. The two of them, and a third sprinter, Rob Taylor, were sitting in the Olympic Village one afternoon, calmly watching the day's events on television. Suddenly, Hart and Robinson couldn't believe the picture they were seeing: athletes lining up for the quarter-final heat of the 100-meter dash, the heat they were entered in. It was 4:15 in the afternoon, and they had been told by their coach, Stan Wright, the man who feuded with John Carlos in Mexico City, that their heat would be run at 6:15 P.M. But now they saw themselves being called to the starting line. Hart, Robinson, and Taylor rushed out of the room, into a car and sped to the Olympic Stadium. Hart and Robinson were too late. When they arrived, their heat had been run, and they had been disqualified. Rob Taylor still had time to run in his quarter-final heat (which he did, qualifying for the semi-finals), but Hart's Olympic hopes, and Robinson's, were dead. "How do you explain it?" said Hart, with tears in his eyes. "How do you tell your father that you aimed for something for two years and blew it like this?"

"I can't believe it," echoed Robinson. "I don't believe it. What about three years? What about torn ligaments? What about pulled muscles, a broken leg? Stan Wright can go on being a coach, but what can I go on being?"

"There's nothing I can say that can describe how bad I feel about Eddie and Rey," said Stan Wright. "I just can't put it in words." Wright had read 1615 hours on the schedule as 6:15—instead of 4:15.

Hart and Robinson were among the holders of the world record of 9.9 seconds for 100 meters. With them sidelined, a Russian won the Olympic 100-meter dash for the first time, Valery Borzov, in 10.1 seconds. Rob Taylor was the runner-up, a tenth of a second behind Borzov. The Russian, a muscular five-foot-eleven and 182 pounds, then went on to win the 200-meter dash, establishing himself as the world's fastest human, the first double sprint winner among Olympic men since Bobby Morrow sixteen years earlier.

Some people said that Hart and Robinson had no one to blame but themselves, that they should not have depended on a coach to get them to the line on time, but Chuck Smith, a 200-meter sprinter, defended his fellow athletes. "Wright told us when to get up, when to eat, when to work out," said Smith. "He insisted on running the whole show. Fine. He made us depend on him. Whatever he said, we did. Man, that's the way he wanted it. And look what happened."

Hart and Robinson were not the only victims of official blunders. Rick DeMont, a sixteen-year-old American swimmer, won the 400-meter free style in a dramatic race, coming from last place to beat Bradford Cooper of Australia by one-hundredth of a second. But after the race, DeMont underwent a standard drug test, and the medical committee of the IOC discovered traces of ephedrine, a stimulant prohibited in the Olympics.

DeMont suffered from asthma, and as part of his normal treatment, he took a prescription drug called Malax, which contained ephedrine. He had been taking the drug since early childhood, and when he had filled out his Olympic forms, he had carefully listed the special medication. But U.S. medical officials never bothered to clear the drug with the IOC medical authorities, and because of their ignorance or laziness, DeMont had broken the Olympic rules. The IOC had little choice but to disqualify him.

While Julius Sang of Kenya, bronze medalist in the 400-meter run, stands at attention during the playing of the United States National Anthem, America's Vince Matthews, gold medal winner, and Wayne Collett, silver medalist in the race, stand at ease.

American officials suggested that they be reprimanded instead, punished in some way—perhaps spanked—and that the teenager should be allowed to keep his gold medal. The IOC said no. Bradford Cooper was elevated to first place and DeMont disqualified, "robbed," said American swimming coach Peter Daland, with scorn, "because of the mistakes of adults."

Stupidity had to share the stage in Munich with insensitivity. On the second day of competition, a North Korean named Ho Jun Li broke the world and Olympic record in small-bore rifle shooting from a prone position. Ho Jun Li scored 599 points out of a possible 600, then capped his near-perfect performance with a statement of perfect callousness. "Our prime minister," said Ho Jun Li, "told us to shoot as if we were fighting against our enemies, and that's what I did."

But Ho Jun Li's statement, at least, came before the terrorists invaded Munich; two American runners, Vince Matthews and Wayne Collett, who finished first and second in the 400-meter run, had no such excuse. Their race came only two days after the massacre of the Israeli sportsmen, and after they mounted the victory stand, they slouched and giggled and ignored the playing of "The Star-Spangled Banner." When the national anthem ended, Matthews walked off twirling his gold medal.

Matthews insisted that he and Collett had staged no protest, that they were not trying to emulate Tommie Smith and John Carlos, that they were simply relaxed and happy and acting natural. Matthews was not guilty of protest, an understandable act; he was guilty of thoughtlessness, injecting an air of uncaring carelessness into an atmosphere still charged with the sadness and shock of the massacre.

The IOC then proceeded, in its usual fashion, to make a poor situation terrible. Matthews and Collett were banned from all future Olympic competition, including the 1,600-meter relay they were expected to run three days later. The felony compounded, Matthews and Collett were transformed, like Smith and Carlos, into martyrs.

On top of stupidity and insensitivity came poor judgment, or downright cheating, depending on the harshness of each observer. If "*Heil Hitler*" had been the recurring cry in 1936, the most popular slogan in 1972 was "*Räuber*," the German word for "robber." It was hurled at officials in dozens of contests, but never with the fury that followed a light-middleweight boxing bout between Reginald Jones of the United States and Valery Tregubov of the Soviet Union. Jones completely dominated the match, opening a big gash over Tregubov's right eye in the second round, almost flooring Tregubov in the third, avoiding all damage himself. At the end, as they flanked the referee and awaited his decision, Jones was smiling, the Russian glum. Then the referee lifted Tregubov's hand; he was the winner, the choice of three judges out of five. "I just stood there and closed my eyes for a second," said Jones. "There was a big blur. I knew it was no dream. I knew I was not gonna get a medal."

America's Kevin Joyce (14) grabs a loose ball in the final game against Russia. Looking on are Zurab Sakandelidze (6), Dwight Jones (9) and Alshan Sharmukhamedov (7).

Soviet player Ivan Edeshko (9) raises his arms in victory, after the last-second Russian triumph, 51–50, the first American defeat in 36 years of Olympic basketball.

Many of the 6,000 spectators hurled debris into the ring and almost all capped cries of *"Räuber"* with shouts of *"Schieber"* and *"Schande"*—"crook" and "shame." For fifteen minutes, the fans whistled and hooted their displeasure, while Jones, a twenty-one-year-old fighter out of the ghettos of Newark, New Jersey, came to a bitter decision, later rescinded, that "I'll never fight again."

But only one American was *Räubed* in that boxing match; a whole team of Americans got ripped off in basketball. The United States had never lost an Olympic basketball game before 1972; no one knew that better than Willi Daume, the head of the Organizing Committee, who had played on the German basketball team that lost to the United States in 1936, the year basketball became part of the Olympic program, by a score of 130 to 8.

The United States team in Munich was certainly not the strongest ever put together, but it did include several excellent professional prospects, and as a unit, under the coaching of Hank Iba, the veteran from Oklahoma A. & M., it won its first seven games in the 1972 Olympics, extending the American Olympic winning streak to sixty-three games. Then came the final contest, against the Soviet Union, which had also won seven straight, and the Russians got off to an early lead, built it to ten points with ten minutes to play, and led by eight with six minutes to go. But in the closing minutes, the Americans went to a full-court press, and the Soviet lead shrank under the pressure. In the final half-minute, Russia still led by a point. Then Doug Collins of the U.S. picked up a loose ball at midcourt and drove for the basket. He went up to shoot and, with three seconds to play, was fouled. Under the most intense pressure—and the distraction of an official horn that blared just before his second shot—Collins converted both foul shots. The U.S. led for the first time in the whole game, 50–49.

The Russians took the ball out of bounds and passed it to midcourt. An American player deflected the pass, and immediately the crowd poured onto the court, thinking the U.S. had won. But the clock still showed one second to play; officials cleared the court, and instructed the Russians to bring the ball inbounds again. This time, the inbounds pass fell short of its mark, and the final second ticked off, and the American players once again began jumping up and down and laughing and celebrating their victory. Not yet. A British official of the International Amateur Basketball Federation ruled that the clock had been incorrectly set at one second, that it should have been reset at three. The Russians were given a third chance to inbounds the ball from under the American basket.

Tom McMillen, a six-foot-ten American, was guarding the inbounds passer, waving his long arms high in the air to block a pass or, at least, distract the passer. A referee ordered McMillen to back up. As he did, the Russian inbounding the ball uncorked a baseball throw the length of the court, aimed at Alexander Belov, a six-foot-eight Soviet forward. Belov leaped for the pass; so did Kevin Joyce and Robert Forbes of the U.S.

Valery Borzov of the Soviet Union wins the 100-meter dash from Robert Taylor of the USA.

The three collided; Joyce and Forbes fell to the floor. Belov caught the ball at the full extension of his jump, came down, then went up again and dropped the ball into the basket. Russia won, 51–50.

The U.S. team was furious. Even though international rules state that the clock does not start until a player on the court touches an inbound pass, coach Iba insisted there was no way Belov could have scored within three seconds. Iba rushed to file a protest—which turned out to be as successful as his trip to lodge the protest. On his way through the confused, chaotic crowd, Iba had his pocket picked of $370.

In track and field, as always, there were many Olympic heroes, and the Soviet Union could boast two of the most able, Borzov, the sprinting specialist, and Nikolai Avilov, a decathlon generalist. Avilov, a twenty-four-year-old Ukrainian, slender, sinewy, six-foot-three, broke Bill Toomey's Olympic and world decathlon-records. And then Avilov refused to call himself the world's greatest athlete, a title often accorded the Olympic decathlon champion. "Every sport has its star," he said.

The star of the gymnastics competition was another Russian, a seventeen-year-old girl named Olga Korbut who captured the imagination of the world. Her appeal was not only in her talent—she and an East German named Karin Janz each won two individual gold medals—but also in her petite charm, beauty, and grace. Olga Korbut stood only four-foot-eleven and weighed a mere 84 pounds.

Another luminary of the women's sports was even younger than Olga Korbut, but not nearly so small. Shane Gould, a fifteen-year-old Australian, five-foot-seven and 132 pounds, was the Games' female Mark Spitz. Her reputation had preceded her to Munich, and in an attempt to psych themselves up, several of Shane's American rivals donned T-shirts proclaiming, "All that glitters is not Gould." Two Americans had the satisfaction of proving that point; Sandra Neilson won the 100-meter freestyle, in which Shane finished third, and Keena Rothhammer won the 800-meter free style, in which Shane finished second. But to go with her silver and bronze medals, Shane Gould picked up three gold medals—in the 200-meter free style, the 400-meter free style, and the 200-meter individual medley. She set world records in all her victories, and she earned a tribute from the chief fifteen-year-old girl-watcher at the 1972 Olympics: "She looks pretty good with her braces off," said Mark Spitz.

Cuba sprang a surprising hero, a man as big as Olga Korbut and Shane Gould combined, a heavyweight fighter named

LEFT: Olga Korbut wins the gold medal for the balance beam in Olympic gymnastics.   RIGHT: The Soviet sweep of the women's free standing gymnastic event: from left, Ludmila Tourischeva, silver medal; Olga Korbut, gold medal; Tamara Lazakovitch, bronze medal.

Australia's Shane Gould winning a heat of the 400-meter free style.

Shane Gould wearing her third gold medal after breaking the world record in the 200-meter free style.

Teofilo Stevenson. The favorite to win the heavyweight division, to succeed George Foreman and Joe Frazier to the most prestigious boxing title, was an American named Duane Bobick. Bobick had defeated Stevenson in the Pan American Games in 1971, but in their quarter-final match in the Olympics, the American was no match for the West Indian-born Cuban. The fight ended in the third round when Stevenson twice knocked Bobick down. Then Stevenson went on to win the gold medal, and, immediately, boxing promoters around the world began to anticipate the ultimate heavyweight championship grudge match, an American against a Cuban, an ideological superfight, democracy versus socialism, each in trunks, a sure multimillion-dollar gate. But Stevenson destroyed those dreams; he fought for the glory of the state, he said—socialism put the power in his punches—and he was not going to turn professional.

Cuba earned three gold medals in boxing, a proud total for a country that had won only six gold medals in all sports in all previous Olympics, but Cuba's pride was nothing compared to Uganda's. The little African nation won its first gold medal ever from a remarkable 400-meter hurdler, John Akii-Bua, who broke the world record in his race. Afterward, Akii-Bua revealed a statistic even more stunning than his winning time: he was one of forty-three children in his family. He quickly explained that his father had eight wives, not consecutively, but concurrently.

If Uganda emerged as a track and field nation in 1972, Finland re-emerged. Once the dominant force in distance running, but shut out since 1936, Finland made up for its long drought in Munich. The Finns took the 1,500 meters, the 5,000, and the 10,000, and victory in both longer events went to a twenty-three-year-old policeman named Lasse Viren. Viren fell down halfway through the 10,000-meter run, yet recovered swiftly enough to set a world record.

Kenya's Kip Keino, who ran second to Finland's Pekka Vasala at 1,500 meters, captured the steeplechase, and, wonder of all, an American won the Marathon. No American had won the Marathon since Johnny Hayes's dramatic victory over Dorando Pietri in 1908, but Frank Shorter, a Yale graduate and a law student, shattered the myth that to go farther than 1,500 meters, an American needed a car. Shorter knew the turf; he was born in Munich twenty-four years before the 1972 Olympics, the son of an American serviceman.

Shorter's triumph provided a measure of consolation for a United States track and field team that was for the most part disappointing. The Americans won only six gold medals in men's track and field—Dave Wottle took the 800-meter run, Rod Milburn the 110-meter hurdles, and Randy Williams the long jump—six fewer than they had won in Mexico City. The 1,600-meter relay (won by the U.S. four straight times) went to Kenya; the pole vault (won by the U.S. in every Olympics since 1896) went to East Germany's Wolfgang Nordwig; the shot-put (won by the U.S. in every Olympics since World War

Down goes Duane Bobick, TKO'd in the heavyweight final by Teofilo Stevenson of Cuba.

II) went to Poland's Wladyslaw Komar; and the discus throw (won four straight times by Al Oerter) went to Czechoslovakia's Ludvik Danek. Those defeats hurt, statistically, but emotionally the worst defeat was Jim Ryun's. The Kansan had put himself through a tortuous psychological and physical obstacle course to enter his third Olympics, and while he was not favored, he was certainly a threat. But in his heat, Billy Fordjour of Ghana accidentally bumped into Ryun and knocked him off his feet. By the time he struggled to his feet, spiked in both ankles, Ryun had no chance to qualify for the finals. He gamely finished the race, on the brink of tears. Kip Keino tried to console him, but Ryun pulled away from Keino's grasp and, fist clenched, face agonized, walked away from his last chance for an Olympic gold medal.

In women's track and field, the United States didn't win a single gold medal; of fourteen gold medals, ten remained in Germany, four won by West Germans and six by East Germans. An East German girl named Renate Stecher won both sprints, the first women to achieve that double since Wilma Rudolph in 1960.

For both German teams, the 1972 Olympics were, in competition, a satisfying experience. East Germany captured twenty gold medals, West Germany thirteen, and combined, the two Germanys won more total medals—gold, silver, and bronze—than any other nation, including the United States and the Soviet Union. For the first time since 1960, the Russians had the largest collection of gold medals, a total of fifty. The U.S. won thirty-three (the same as Germany's combined),

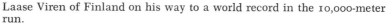

Laase Viren of Finland on his way to a world record in the 10,000-meter run.

more than half of them in swimming, two in archery, and one
—earned by an impressive athlete named Dan Gable—in
wrestling.

As the Games finally, mercifully, came to an end, a new
president assumed command of the International Olympic
Committee, a fifty-eight-year-old Irishman, Michael Morris,
Baron Killanin, of Dublin. Lord Killanin had already proved
that he possessed at least one trait his predecessor certainly
seemed to lack, a sense of humor. Once, when an IOC member
showed up late for a meeting and blamed his tardiness on a
commercial airline—by name—Lord Killanin looked at him
sternly and said, "No advertising, please. This is the Olympic
movement."

At the closing ceremonies, the scoreboard in Munich flashed
a farewell to the IOC's outgoing president. The sign read:
"Thank you, Avery *Brandage*."

The name of the octogenarian Brundage had been mis-
spelled. It was a fitting final error in an Olympics of mistakes
—and madness.

The Winter Olympics of 1972 marked the first time the Winter
Games came to Asia, and the Japanese put on a splendid show
in Sapporo, a show even more impressive because the competition—as was becoming habit—was almost ruined before it
began.

The villain was Avery Brundage's favorite—commercialism
—specifically commercialism among Alpine skiers, pure
amateurs who always seemed to have plenty of money, presumably as a reward for strapping on the right boots and the
right skis at the right time. There was no such thing as a pure
amateur European skier—not one who was any good, anyway
—and when the IOC threatened to bar the most flagrant pro/
amateurs from Sapporo, the Alpine skiing federation threatened to boycott the event.

Shortly before the Games opened, Brundage announced that
the IOC was disqualifying one skier from the Olympics—Karl
Schranz, of Austria, an Olympic veteran who, at thirty-three,
was considered the most likely candidate to match Jean Claude
Killy's 1968 Alpine triple. Schranz was certainly not the only
Alpine skier whose personal commercial ethic violated the
Olympic spirit, but he was among the most blatant.

Since the rest of the Alpine skiers had already traveled to
Japan, and since every nation except Austria figured to gain
from the absence of Schranz, the threat of a boycott disappeared. The Austrian team did talk of withdrawing, but
Schranz urged them to carry on without him. His teammates
took his advice, and Schranz flew home to Vienna, to the most
spectacular hero's welcome in the city's history. One hundred
thousand Austrians greeted him, as proud of his martyrdom
as they would have been of a triple victory.

Without Schranz, Austria went without an Alpine first place;
the three gold medals were divided among a Spaniard, an
Italian, and a Swiss. And in Schranz's absence, a Dutchman,

Ard Schenk of the Netherlands swings toward his
third gold medal in the 10,000-meter speed skating
event at Sapporo, Japan.

368

a speed skater named Ard Schenk, emerged as the glamour figure of the 1972 Winter Games. A tall, muscular, blue-eyed blond, Schenk won the 1,500-, 5,000-, and 10,000-meter races, and might have won the 500 meter if he hadn't fallen during his turn.

In the women's half of speed skating, a pair of American girls, Anne Henning and Dianne Holum, both from Northbrook, Illinois, won gold medals. Henning won at 500 meters, Holum at 1,500, and Northbrook promptly declared itself the speed-skating capital of the world, or at least of the Western Hemisphere.

The victories of Henning and Holum, the first ever for American women in speed skating, were surprising. Even more surprising was Barbara Cochran's gold medal in the slalom, the first Alpine victory for the U.S. since Andrea Mead Lawrence's double twenty years earlier. The other two Alpine events for women went to Marie Therese Nadig of Switzerland.

The United States settled for three gold medals in Sapporo—Russia led all nations with eight—and earned none in figure skating. But an American figure skater, clearly, was the popular favorite, blonde Janet Lynn, the most gifted of the free skaters.

Janet Lynn left Japan with only a bronze medal, but with the cheers of the crowd ringing in her ears and offers of a lucrative professional career, a chance to follow in the skate-steps of Sonja Henie and Peggy Fleming, stretching in front of her.

The 1972 Olympic Games left bad memories, bad vibrations, a nightmare of bloodshed, a carnival of blunders, a frustrating feeling that the Olympic ideal was no longer reachable. Olga Fikotova Connolly, the former Czech discus-throwing champion who carried the American flag in the opening parade at Munich, captured the frustration in wistful words. "The flag was feeling beautiful and cuddly," Olga Connolly said, "and I was in love with it. I wanted it to be a flag of peace . . . not of war."

Ironically, sadly, within two years after the end of the Munich Olympics, Olga and Harold Connolly—living symbols of the possibilities of international understanding—were divorced. The perfect union of East and West had lasted less than twenty years.

# Distribution of Gold Medals 1896-1972

## COUNTRIES WITH TWENTY-FIVE OR MORE

| Nation | Summer | Winter | Total |
|---|---|---|---|
| United States | 583 | 27 | 610 |
| U.S.S.R. | 211 | 36 | 247 |
| Great Britain | 143 | 3 | 146 |
| Sweden | 123 | 22 | 145 |
| France | 121 | 12 | 133 |
| Italy | 116 | 9 | 125 |
| Germany* | 108 | 14 | 122 |
| Finland | 83 | 21 | 104 |
| Hungary | 102 | 0 | 102 |
| Norway | 39 | 46 | 85 |
| Japan | 65 | 1 | 66 |
| Australia | 63 | 0 | 63 |
| Switzerland | 37 | 14 | 51 |
| Netherlands | 41 | 8 | 49 |
| Czechoslovakia | 38 | 2 | 40 |
| Austria | 15 | 20 | 35 |
| East Germany** | 29 | 5 | 34 |
| Canada | 23 | 10 | 33 |
| Poland | 30 | 1 | 31 |
| Denmark | 28 | 0 | 28 |

\* Germany credited with only one national entry through 1964 Games.
\*\* Statistics through the 1968 and 1972 Games where East Germany competed as separate nation.

# Participation in the Modern Olympics

| Year | Site | Men | Women | Total | Nations |
|---|---|---|---|---|---|
| | | **SUMMER GAMES** | | | |
| 1896 | Athens | 285 | 0 | 285 | 13 |
| 1900 | Paris | 1060 | 6 | 1066 | 20 |
| 1904 | St. Louis | 496 | 0 | 496 | 11 |
| 1906 | Athens | 900 | 0 | 900 | 21 |
| 1908 | London | 2023 | 36 | 2059 | 22 |
| 1912 | Stockholm | 2484 | 57 | 2541 | 28 |
| 1920 | Antwerp | 2543 | 63 | 2606 | 29 |
| 1924 | Paris | 2956 | 136 | 3092 | 44 |
| 1928 | Amsterdam | 2725 | 290 | 3015 | 46 |
| 1932 | Los Angeles | 1281 | 127 | 1408 | 37 |
| 1936 | Berlin | 3741 | 328 | 4069 | 49 |
| 1948 | London | 4030 | 438 | 4468 | 59 |
| 1952 | Helsinki | 4407 | 518 | 4925 | 69 |
| 1956 | Melbourne | 3186 | 353 | 3539 | 67 |
| 1960 | Rome | 4859 | 537 | 5396 | 84 |
| 1964 | Tokyo | 4833 | 732 | 5565 | 94 |
| 1968 | Mexico City | 5238 | 844 | 6082 | 109 |
| 1972 | Munich | 6547 | 1636 | 8183 | 123 |
| | | **WINTER GAMES** | | | |
| 1924 | Chamonix | 280 | 13 | 293 | 16 |
| 1928 | St. Moritz | 464 | 27 | 491 | 25 |
| 1932 | Lake Placid | 277 | 30 | 307 | 17 |
| 1936 | Garmisch-Partenkirchen | 680 | 76 | 756 | 28 |
| 1948 | St. Moritz | 688 | 90 | 778 | 28 |
| 1952 | Oslo | 624 | 108 | 732 | 30 |
| 1956 | Cortina | 777 | 146 | 923 | 32 |
| 1960 | Squaw Valley | 534 | 159 | 693 | 30 |
| 1964 | Innsbruck | 1107 | 225 | 1332 | 36 |
| 1968 | Grenoble | 1129 | 230 | 1359 | 37 |
| 1972 | Sapporo | 904 | 226 | 1130 | 35 |

# Olympic Champions

## COMPLETE ROSTER OF WINNERS 1896–1972

Note: Results of competition in Athens in 1906 were unofficial and were not recognized by the International Olympic Committee

* denotes Olympic Record

### TRACK AND FIELD—MEN

#### 100-METER DASH                                    Sec.
1896—Thomas E. Burke, United States . . 12.0
1900—Francis W. Jarvis, United States . . 10.8
1904—Archie Hahn, United States . . . . . . 11.0
1906—Archie Hahn, United States . . . . . . 11.2
1908—Reginald E. Walker, South Africa . 10.8
1912—Ralph C. Craig, United States . . . . 10.8
1920—Charles W. Paddock, United States 10.8
1924—Harold M. Abrahams, Great Britain 10.6
1928—Percy Williams, Canada . . . . . . . . 10.8
1932—Eddie Tolan, United States . . . . . . 10.3
1936—Jesse Owens, United States . . . . . . 10.3
1948—Harrison Dillard, United States . . . 10.3
1952—Lindy J. Remigino, United States . . 10.4
1956—Bobby J. Morrow, United States . . 10.5
1960—Armin Hary, Germany . . . . . . . . . . 10.2
1964—Bob Hayes, United States . . . . . . . 10.0 *
1968—Jim Hines, United States . . . . . . 9.9*
1972—Valery Borzov, U.S.S.R. . . . . . . . . 10.14

#### 200-METER DASH
1900—J. Walter Tewksbury,
        United States . . . . . . . . . . . . . 22.2
1904—Archie Hahn, United States . . . . . . 21.6
1908—Robert Kerr, Canada . . . . . . . . . . 22.6
1912—Ralph C. Craig, United States . . . . 21.7
1920—Allan Woodring, United States . . . 22.0
1924—Jackson V. Scholz, United States . . 21.6
1928—Percy Williams, Canada . . . . . . . . 21.8
1932—Eddie Tolan, United States . . . . . . 21.2
1936—Jesse Owens, United States . . . . . . 20.7
1948—Mel Patton, United States . . . . . . 21.1
1952—Andrew W. Stanfield, United States 20.7
1956—Bobby J. Morrow, United States . . 20.6
1960—Livio Berruti, Italy . . . . . . . . . . . 20.5
1964—Henry Carr, United States . . . . . . 20.3 *
1968—Tommie Smith, United States . . . . 19.8*
1972—Valery Borzov, U.S.S.R. . . . . . . . . 20.0

#### 400-METER DASH
1896—Thomas E. Burke. United States . . 54.2
1900—Maxey W. Long, United States . . . 49.4
1904—Harry I. Hillman, United States . . . 49.2
1906—Paul Pilgrim, United States . . . . . . 53.2
1908—Wyndham Halswelle,
        Great Britain (walkover) . . . . . . 50.0
1912—Charles D. Reidpath, United States 48.2
1920—Bevil G. D. Rudd, South Africa . . . 49.6
1924—Eric H. Liddell, Great Britain . . . . 47.6
1928—Ray Barbuti, United States . . . . . . 47.8
1932—William Carr, United States . . . . . 46.2
1936—Archie Williams, United States . . . 46.5
1948—Arthur Wint, Jamaica . . . . . . . . . 46.2
1952—George Rhoden, Jamaica . . . . . . . 45.9
1956—Charles L. Jenkins, United States . . 46.7
1960—Otis Davis, United States . . . . . . . 44.9*
1964—Mike Larrabee, United States . . . . 45.1
1968—Lee Evans, United States . . . . . . . 43.8*
1972—Vince Matthews, United States . . . 44.66

#### 800-METER RUN                                 Min.-Sec.
1896—Edwin H. Flack, Great Britain . . . . 2:11.0
1900—Alfred E. Tysoe, Great Britain . . . 2:01.4
1904—James D. Lightbody, United States 1:56.0
1906—Paul Pilgrim, United States . . . . . . 2:01.2
1908—Melvin W. Sheppard, United States 1:52.8
1912—James T. Meredith, United States . 1:51.9
1920—Albert G. Hill, Great Britain . . . . . 1:53.4
1924—Douglas G. A. Lowe, Great Britain 1:52.4
1928—Douglas G. A. Lowe, Great Britain 1:51.8
1932—Thos. Hampson, Great Britain . . . . 1:49.8
1936—John Woodruff, United States . . . . 1:52.9
1948—Mal Whitfield, United States . . . . 1:49.2
1952—Mal Whitfield, United States . . . . 1:49.2

#### 1956—Thomas W. Courtney,
        United States . . . . . . . . . . . . . 1:47.7
1960—Peter Snell, New Zealand . . . . . . . 1:46.3
1964—Peter Snell, New Zealand . . . . . . . 1:45.1 *
1968—Ralph Doubell, Australia . . . . . . 1:44.3*
1972—Dave Wottle, United States . . . . 1:45.9

#### 1,500-METER RUN
1896—Edwin H. Flack, Great Britain . . 4:33.2
1900—Charles Bennett, Great Britain . . 4:06.2
1904—James D. Lightbody, United States 4:05.4
1906—James D. Lightbody, United States 4:12.0
1908—Melvin W. Sheppard, United States 4:03.4
1912—Arnold N. S. Jackson,
        Great Britain . . . . . . . . . . . . 3:56.8
1920—Albert G. Hill, Great Britain . . . . . 4:01.8
1924—Paavo Nurmi, Finland . . . . . . . . . 3:53.6
1928—Harry E. Larva, Finland . . . . . . . 3:53.2
1932—Luigi Beccali, Italy . . . . . . . . . . . 3:51.2
1936—Jack E. Lovelock, New Zealand . . . 3:47.8
1948—Henry Eriksson, Sweden . . . . . . . . 3:49.8
1952—Joseph Barthel, Luxembourg . . . . . 3:45.2
1956—Ron Delany, Ireland . . . . . . . . . . . 3:41.2
1960—Herbert Elliott, Australia . . . . . . . 3:35.6*
1964—Peter Snell, New Zealand . . . . . . . 3:38.1
1968—Kipchoge Keino, Kenya . . . . . . . . 3:34.9*
1972—Pekka Vasala, Finland . . . . . . . . . 3:36.3

#### 5,000-METER RUN
1912—Hannes Kolehmainen, Finland . . .14:36.6
1920—Joseph Guillemot, France . . . . . .14:55.6
1924—Paavo Nurmi, Finland . . . . . . . . .14:31.2
1928—Willie Ritola, Finland . . . . . . . . . .14:38.0
1932—Lauri Lehtinen, Finland . . . . . . . .14:30.0
1936—Gunnar Hockert, Finland . . . . . . .14:22.2
1948—Gaston Reiff, Belgium . . . . . . . . .14:17.6
1952—Emil Zatopek, Czechoslovakia . .14:06.6
1956—Vladimir Kuts, U.S.S.R. . . . . . . .13:39.6*
1960—Murray Halberg, New Zealand . . .13:43.4
1964—Bob Schul, United States . . . . . . .13:48.8
1968—Mohamed Gammoudi, Tunisia . . .14:05.0
1972—Lasse Viren, Finland . . . . . . . . . .13:26.4*

#### 10,000-METER RUN
1912—Hannes Kolehmainen, Finland . . .31:20.8
1920—Paavo Nurmi, Finland . . . . . . . . .31:45.8
1924—Willie Ritola, Finland . . . . . . . . .30:23.2
1928—Paavo Nurmi, Finland . . . . . . . . .30:18.8
1932—Janusz Kusocinski, Poland . . . . . .30:11.4
1936—Ilmari Salminen, Finland . . . . . . .30:15.4
1948—Emil Zatopek, Czechoslovakia . . .29:59.6
1952—Emil Zatopek, Czechoslovakia . . .29:17.0
1956—Vladimir Kuts, U.S.S.R. . . . . . . .28:45.6
1960—Petr Bolotnikov, U.S.S.R. . . . . . .28:32.2
1964—Billy Mills, United States . . . . . . .28:24.4 *
1968—Naftali Temu, Kenya . . . . . . . . . .29:27.4
1972—Lasse Viren, Finland . . . . . . . . . .27:38.4*

#### MARATHON                                      Hr.-Min.-Sec.
1896—Spiridon Loues, Greece . . . . . . 2:58:50.0
1900—Michel Teato, France . . . . . . . . 2:59:45.0
1904—Thomas J. Hicks,
        United States . . . . . . . . . . . . 3:28:53.0
1906—William Sherring, Canada . . . . . 2:51:23.6
1908—John J. Hayes, United States . . . 2:55:18.4
1912—Kenneth McArthur,
        South Africa . . . . . . . . . . . . 2:36:54.8
1920—Hannes Kolehmainen, Finland 2:32:35.8
1924—Albin Stenroos, Finland . . . . . . 2:41:22.6
1928—El Ouafi, France . . . . . . . . . . . 2:32:57.0
1932—Juan Zabala, Argentina . . . . . . . 2:31:36.0
1936—Kitei Son, Japan . . . . . . . . . . . 2:29:19.2
1948—Delfo Cabrera, Argentina . . . . . 2:34:51.6
1952—Emil Zatopek, Czechoslovakia . 2:23:03.2
1956—Alain Mimoun, France . . . . . . . 2:25:00.0
1960—Abebe Bikila, Ethiopia . . . . . . . 2:15:16.2
1964—Abebe Bikila, Ethiopia . . . . . . . .2:12:11.2 *

#### 1968—Mamo Wolde, Ethiopia . . . 2:20:26.4
1972—Frank Shorter, United States . .2:12:19.8

#### 110-METER HURDLES                             Sec.
1896—Thomas P. Curtis, United States . . 17.6
1900—Alvin E. Kraenzlein, United States 15.4
1904—Frederick W. Schule, United States 16.0
1906—R. G. Leavitt, United States . . . . . 16.2
1908—Forrest Smithson, United States . . 15.0
1912—Frederick W. Kelley, United States 15.1
1920—Earl J. Thomson, Canada . . . . . . . 14.8
1924—Daniel C. Kinsey, United States . . . 15.0
1928—Sydney Atkinson, South Africa . . . 14.8
1932—George Saling, United States . . . . 14.6
1936—Forrest Towns, United States . . . . 14.2
1948—William Porter, United States . . . . 13.9
1952—Harrison Dillard, United States . . . 13.7
1956—Lee Q. Calhoun, United States . . . 13.5*
1960—Lee Q. Calhoun, United States . . . 13.8
1964—Hayes Jones, United States . . . . . . 13.6
1968—Willie Davenport, United States . . 13.3
1972—Rod Milburn, United States . . . . . 13.24*

#### 400-METER HURDLES
1900—J. Walter Tewksbury,
        United States . . . . . . . . . . . . . 57.6
1904—Harry L. Hillman, United States . . . 53.0
1908—Charles J. Bacon, United States . . 55.0
1920—Frank F. Loomis, United States . . . 54.0
1924—F. Morgan Taylor, United States . . 52.6
1928—Lord David Burghley, Great Britain 53.4
1932—Robert Tisdall, Ireland . . . . . . . . . 51.8
1936—Glenn Hardin, United States . . . . . 52.4
1948—Roy Cochran, United States . . . . . 51.1
1952—Charles Moore, United States . . . . 50.8
1956—Glenn A. Davis, United States . . . 50.1
1960—Glenn A. Davis, United States . . . 49.3*
1964—Rex Cawley, United States . . . . . . 49.6
1968—Dave Hemery, Great Britain . . . . . 48.1
1972—John Akii-Bua, Uganda . . . . . . . 47.82*

#### 3,000-METER STEEPLECHASE                  Min.-Sec.
1920—Percy Hodge, Great Britain . . . . .10:00.4
1924—Willie Ritola, Finland . . . . . . . . . . 9:33.6
1928—Toiva A. Loukola, Finland . . . . . . 9:21.8
1932—Volmari Iso-Hollo, Finland . . . . . .10:33.4
        (3,460 meters—extra lap by error)
1936—Volmari Iso-Hollo, Finland . . . . . . 9:03.8
1948—Thore Sjostrand, Sweden . . . . . . . 9:04.6
1952—Horace Ashenfelter, United States 8:45.4
1956—Chris Brasher, Great Britain . . . . . 8:41.2
1960—Zdzislaw Krzyszkowiak, Poland . . . 8:34.2
1964—Gaston Roelants, Belgium . . . . . . 8:30.8 *
1968—Amos Biwott, Kenya . . . . . . . . . . 8:51.0
1972—Kipchoge Keino, Kenya . . . . . . . 8:23.6*

#### 20,000-METER WALK                          Hr.-Min.-Sec.
1956—Leonid Spirine, U.S.S.R. . . . . . . 1:31.27
1960—Vladimir Golubnichy,
        U.S.S.R. . . . . . . . . . . . . . . 1:34.07.2
1964—Kenneth Mathews, Great Britain 1:29:34.0 *
1968—Vladimir Golubnichiy, U.S.S.R. 1:33:58.4
1972—Peter Frenkel, East Germany 1:26:42.4*

#### 50,000-METER WALK
1932—Thomas W. Green,
        Great Britain . . . . . . . . . . . 4:50:10.0
1936—Harold Whitlock, Great Britain 4:30:41.4
1948—John A. Ljunggren, Sweden . . . . 4:41:52.0
1952—Guiseppe Dordoni, Italy . . . . . 4:28:07.8
1956—Norm. Read, New Zealand . . . . 4:30:42.8
1960—Donald Thompson,
        Great Britain . . . . . . . . . . . 4:25:30.0
1964—Abdon Pamich, Italy . . . . . . . . 4:11:12.4 *
1968—Christoph Hohne,
        East Germany . . . . . . . . . . 4:20:13.6
1972—Bernd Kannenberg,
        West Germany . . . . . . . . . . 3:56:11.6*

**400-METER RELAY** — Sec.

1912—Great Britain (D. H. Jacobs, H. M. Macintosh, Victor d'Arcy, William Applegarth) . . . 42.4
1920—United States (Charles Paddock, Jackson Scholz, Morris Kirksey, Loren Murchison) . . . 42.2
1924—United States (Louis Clarke, Francis Hussey, Loren Murchison, Alfred Leconey) . . . 41.0
1928—United States (Frank Wykoff, James Quinn, Charles Borah, Henry Russell) . . . 41.0
1932—United States (Robert Kiesel, Emmett Toppino, Hector Dyer, Frank Wykoff) . . . 40.0
1936—United States (Jesse Owens, Ralph Metcalfe, Foy Draper, Frank Wykoff) . . . 40.0
1948—United States (Norwood Ewell, Lorenzo Wright, Harrison Dillard, Mel Patton) . . . 40.3
1952—United States (Dean Smith, Harrison Dillard, Lindy Remigino, Andrew Stanfield) . . . 40.1
1956—United States (Ira Murchison, Leamon King, Thane Baker, Bobby J. Morrow) . . . 39.5
1960—Germany (Bernd Cullman, Armin Hary, Walter Mahlendorf, Martin Lauer) . . . 39.5
1964—United States (Paul Drayton, Gerry Ashworth, Dick Stebbins, Bob Hayes) . . . 39.0*
1968—United States (Charlie Greene, Mel Pender, Ronald Ray Smith, Jim Hines) . . . 38.2
1972—United States (Larry Black, Robert Taylor, Gerald Tinker, Eddie Hart) . . . 38.2*

**1,600-METER RELAY** — Min.-Sec.

1908—United States (William F. Hamilton, Nathan J. Cartmell, John Taylor, Melvin W. Sheppard) (200-200-400-800 m) . . . 3:29.4
1912—United States (Melvin W. Sheppard, Edward F. Lindberg, James T. Meredith, Charles D. Reidpath) . . . 3:16.6
1920—Great Britain (Robert Lindsay, Guy Butler, John Ainsworth, Cecil Griffiths) . . . 3:22.2
1924—United States (C. S. Cochran, William E. Stevenson, J. O. McDonald, Allen Helffrich) . . . 3:16.0
1928—United States (George Baird, Fred Alderman, Emerson Spencer, Ray Barbuti) . . . 3:14.2
1932—United States (Ivan Fuqua, Edgar Ablowich, Karl Warner, William Carr) . . . 3:08.2
1936—Great Britain (Frederick Wolff, Godfrey Rampling, William Roberts, Arthur Brown) . . . 3:09.0
1948—United States (Cliff Bourland, Art Harnden, Roy Cochran, Mal Whitfield) . . . 3:10.4
1952—Jamaica (Herbert McKenley, Leslie Laing, Arthur Wint, George Rhoden) . . . 3:03.9
1956—United States (Charles Jenkins, Lou Jones, Jesse Mashburn, Tom Courtney) . . . 3:04.8
1960—United States (Jack Yerman, Earl Young, Glenn Davis, Otis Davis) 3:02.2
1964—United States (Ollan Cassell, Mike Larrabee, Ulis Williams, Henry Carr) . . . 3:00.7*
1968—United States (Vincent Matthews, Ron Freeman, Larry James, Lee Evans) . . . 2:56.1*
1972—Kenya (Charles Asati, Hezahiah Nyamau, Robert Ouko, Julius Sang) . . . 2:59.8

**POLE VAULT** — Ft.-In.

1896—Welles Hoyt, United States . . . 10′ 9¾″
1900—Irving K. Baxter, United States . . . 10′ 9.9″
1904—Charles E. Dvorak, United States . . . 11′ 6″
1906—Fernand Gouder, France . . . 11′ 6″
1908—Albert C. Gilbert, United States; Edward T. Cook, Jr., United States . . . 12′ 2″
1912—Harry S. Babcock, United States . . . 12′ 11½″
1920—Frank K. Foss, United States 12′ 5 9/16″
1924—Lee S. Barnes, United States 12′ 11½″
1928—Sabin W. Carr, United States 13′ 9⅜″
1932—William Miller, United States 14′ 1⅞″
1936—Earle Meadows, United States 14′ 3¼″
1948—O. Guinn Smith, United States 14′ 1¼″
1952—Robert Richards, United States . . . 14′ 11¼″
1956—Robert Richards, United States . . . 14′ 11½″
1960—Donald Bragg, United States 15′ 5⅛″
1964—Fred Hansen, United States . . 16′ 8¾″*
1968—Robert Seagren, United States 17′ 8½″
1972—Wolfgang Nordwig, East Germany 18′ 0½″*

**HIGH JUMP**

1896—Ellery Clark, United States . . . 5′ 11¼″
1900—Irving Baxter, United States . . 6′ 2 4/5″
1904—Samuel Jones, United States . . 5′ 11″
1906—Con Leahy, Ireland . . . 5′ 9⅞″
1908—Harry Porter, United States . . . 6′ 3″
1912—Alma Richards, United States 6′ 4″
1920—Richard Landon, United States 6′ 4¼″
1924—Harold Osborn, United States . . 6′ 5 15/16″
1928—Robert W. King, United States 6′ 4⅜″
1932—Duncan McNaughton, Canada 6′ 5⅝″
1936—Cornelius Johnson, United States . . . 6′ 7 15/16″
1948—John Winter, Australia . . . 6′ 6″
1952—Walter Davis, United States . . . 6′ 8¼″
1956—Charles E. Dumas, United States . . . 6′ 11¼″
1960—Robert Shavlakadze, U.S.S.R. . . 7′ 1″
1964—Valery Brumel, U.S.S.R. . . . 7′ 1¾″*
1968—Richard Fosbury, United States 7′ 4½″*
1972—Yuri Tarmak, U.S.S.R. . . . 7′ 3¾″

**LONG JUMP (originally called "Broad" Jump)**

1896—Ellery Clark, United States . . . 20′ 10″
1900—Alvin Kraenzlein, United States 23′ 6⅞″
1904—Myer Prinstein, United States 24′ 1″
1906—Myer Prinstein, United States 23′ 7½″
1908—Frank Irons, United States . . . 24′ 6½″
1912—Albert Gutterson, United States . . . 24′ 11¼″
1920—William Pettersson, Sweden . . 23′ 5½″
1924—DeHart Hubbard, United States . . . 24′ 5⅛″
1928—Edward Hamm, United States 25′ 4¾″
1932—Edward Gordon, United States 25′ ¾″
1936—Jesse Owens, United States . . 26′ 5⅜″
1948—Willie Steele, United States . . 25′ 8″
1952—Jerome Biffle, United States . . 24′ 10″
1956—Gregory C. Bell, United States 25′ 8¼″
1960—Ralph Boston, United States . . 26′ 7¾″*
1964—Lynn Davies, Great Britain . . . 26′ 5½″
1968—Robert Beamon, United States 29′ 2½″*
1972—Randy Williams, United States 27′ 0½″

**TRIPLE JUMP (originally called Hop, Step, and Jump)**

1896—James Connolly, United States 45′
1900—Myer Prinstein, United States 47′ 4¼″
1904—Myer Prinstein, United States 47′
1906—P. O'Connor, Ireland . . . 46′ 2″
1908—Timothy Ahearne, Great Britain . . . 48′ 11¼″
1912—Gustaf Lindblom, Sweden . . . 48′ 5⅛″
1920—Vilho Tuulos, Finland . . . 47′ 6⅞″
1924—Archibald Winter, Australia . . . 50′ 11⅛″
1928—Mikio Oda, Japan . . . 49′ 10 13/16″
1932—Chuhei Nambus, Japan . . . 51′ 7″
1936—Naoto Tajima, Japan . . . 52′ 5⅞″
1948—Arne Ahman, Sweden . . . 50′ 6¼″
1952—Adhemar Ferreira da Silva, Brazil . . . 53′ 2½″
1956—Adhemar Ferreira da Silva, Brazil . . . 53′ 7½″
1960—Jozef Schmidt, Poland . . . 55′ 1¾″
1964—Jozef Schmidt, Poland . . . 55′ 3½″*
1968—Viktor Saneev, U.S.S.R. . . . 57′ 0¾″*
1972—Viktor Saneev, U.S.S.R. . . . 56′ 11″

**16-LB. SHOT-PUT**

1896—Robert Garrett, United States 36′ 9¾″
1900—Richard Sheldon, United States . . . 46′ 3⅛″
1904—Ralph Rose, United States . . . 48′ 7″
1906—M. J. Sheridan, United States 40′ 4 4/5″
1908—Ralph Rose, United States . . . 46′ 7½″
1912—Patrick McDonald, United States . . . 50′ 4″
1920—Ville Porhola, Finland . . . 48′ 7⅛″
1924—Clarence Houser, United States . . . 49′ 2½″
1928—John Kuck, United States . . . 52′ 11/16″
1932—Leo Sexton, United States . . . 52′ 6 3/16″
1936—Hans Woellke, Germany . . . 53′ 1¾″
1948—Wilbur Thompson, United States . . . 56′ 2″
1952—Parry O'Brien, Jr., United States . . . 57′ 1½″
1956—Parry O'Brien, Jr., United States . . . 60′ 11″
1960—William Nieder, United States 64′ 6¾″
1964—Dallas Long, United States . . . 66′ 8½″*
1968—J. Randel Matson, United States . . . 67′ 4¾″
1972—Wladyslaw Komar, Poland . . 69′ 6″*

**DISCUS THROW**

1896—Robert Garrett, United States 95′ 7½″
1900—Rudolf Bauer, Hungary . . . 118′ 2.9″
1904—Martin Sheridan, United States . . . 128′ 10½″
1906—Martin Sheridan, United States . . . 136′ ⅓″
1908—Martin Sheridan, United States . . . 134′ 2″
1912—Armas Taipale, Finland . . . 145′ 9/16″
1920—Elmer Niklander, Finland . . . 146′ 7″
1924—Clarence Houser, United States . . . 151′ 5¼″
1928—Clarence Houser, United States . . . 155′ 2 4/5″
1932—John Anderson, United States . . . 162′ 4⅞″
1936—Kenneth Carpenter, United States . . . 165′ 7½″
1948—Adolfo Consolini, Italy . . . 173′ 2″
1952—Sim Iness, United States . . 180′ 6½″
1956—Alfred A. Oerter, United States . . . 184′ 10½″
1960—Alfred A. Oerter, United States . . . 194′ 2″
1964—Alfred A. Oerter, United States 200′ 1½″*
1968—Alfred A. Oerter, United States . . . 212′ 6½″*
1972—Ludvik Danek, Czechoslovakia . . . 211′ 3″

**16-LB. HAMMER THROW**

1900—John Flanagan, United States . . . 167′ 4″
1904—John Flanagan, United States . . . 168′ 1″
1908—John Flanagan, United States . . . 170′ 4¼″
1912—Matthew McGrath, United States . . . 179′ 7⅛″
1920—Patrick Ryan, United States . . . 173′ 5⅝″
1924—Frederick Tootell, United States . . . 174′ 10¼″
1928—Patrick O'Callaghan, Ireland . . . 168′ 7½″

1932—Patrick O'Callaghan, Ireland . . . 176′ 11⅛″
1936—Karl Hein, Germany . . . 185′ 4¼″
1948—Imre Nemeth, Hungary . . . 183′ 11½″
1952—Jozsef Csermak, Hungary . . 197′ 11¾″
1956—Harold Connolly, United States . . . 207′ 3½″
1960—Vasily Rudenkov, U.S.S.R. . . 220′ 1⅝″
1964—Romuald Klim, U.S.S.R. . . . 228′ 10½″*
1968—Gyula Zsivotzky, Hungary . 240′ 8″
1972—Anatoli Bondarchuk, U.S.S.R. . . . 248′ 8″*

### JAVELIN THROW

1906—Erik Lemming, Sweden . . . 175′ 6″
1908—Erik Lemming, Sweden . . . 179′ 10½″
1912—Erik Lemming, Sweden . . . 198′ 11¼″
1920—Jonni Myyra, Finland . . . 215′ 9¾″
1924—Jonni Myyra, Finland . . . 206′ 6¾″
1928—Erik Lundquist, Sweden . . . 218′ 6⅛″
1932—Matti Jarvinen, Finland . . . 238′ 7″
1936—Gerhard Stoeck, Germany . . . 235′ 8⁵⁄₁₆″
1948—Tapio Rautavaara, Finland . . 228′ 10½″
1952—Cy C. Young, United States . . . 242′ ¾″
1956—E. Danielson, Norway . . . 281′ 2¼″*
1960—Viktor Cybulenko, U.S.S.R. . . 277′ 8⅜″
1964—Pauli Nevala, Finland . . . 271′ 2¼″
1968—Janis Lusis, U.S.S.R. . . . 295′ 7″
1972—Klaus Wolfermann, West Germany . . . 296′ 10″*

### DECATHLON — Points

1912—Hugo Wieslander, Sweden . . . 7724.49
1920—Helge Lovland, Norway . . . 6804.35
1924—Harold Osborn, United States . . 7710.77
1928—Paavo Yrjola, Finland . . . 8053.29
1932—James Bausch, United States . . 8462.23
(Old points system used 1912 to 1932)
1936—Glenn Morris, United States . . 7900.00
1948—Robert Mathias, United States 7139.00
1952—Robert Mathias, United States 7887.00
1956—Milton G. Campbell, United States . . . 7937.00
1960—Rafer Johnson, United States . . 8392.00*
1964—Willi Holdorf, Germany . . . 7877.00
1968—William A. Toomey, United States . . . 8,193.00
1972—Nikolai Avilov, U.S.S.R. . . . 8,454.00*

## TRACK AND FIELD—WOMEN

### 100-METER DASH — Sec.

1928—Elizabeth Robinson, United States 12.2
1932—Stanislawa Walasiewicz, Poland . . . 11.9
1936—Helen Stephens, United States . . . 11.5
1948—Fanny Blankers-Koen, Netherlands 11.9
1952—Marjorie Jackson, Australia . . . 11.5
1956—Betty Cuthbert, Australia . . . 11.5
1960—Wilma Rudolph, United States . . . 11.0*
1964—Wyomia Tyus, United States . . . 11.4
1968—Wyomia Tyus, United States . . . 11.0*
1972—Renate Stecher, East Germany . . 11.07

### 200-METER DASH

1948—Fanny Blankers-Koen, Netherlands 24.4
1952—Marjorie Jackson, Australia . . . 23.7
1956—Betty Cuthbert, Australia . . . 23.4
1960—Wilma Rudolph, United States . . . 24.0
1964—Edith McGuire, United States . . . 23.0*
1968—Irena Kirszenstein, Poland . . . 22.5
1972—Renate Stecher, East Germany . . 22.4*

### 800-METER RUN — Min.-Sec.

1928—Linda Radke, Germany . . . 2:16.8
1960—Ljudmila Shevcova, U.S.S.R. . . . 2:04.3
1964—Ann Packer, Great Britain . . . 2:01.1*
1968—Madeline Manning, United States 2:00.9
1972—Hildegard Falck, West Germany 1:58.6*

### 400-METER RELAY — Sec.

1928—Canada . . . 48.4
1932—United States . . . 47.0
1936—United States . . . 46.9
1948—Netherlands . . . 47.5
1952—United States . . . 45.9
1956—Australia . . . 44.5
1960—United States . . . 44.5
1964—Poland . . . 43.6*
1968—United States (Barbara Ferrell, Margaret Bailes, Mildrette Netter, Wyomia Tyus) . . . 42.8
1972—West Germany (Christiane Krause, Ingred Mickler, Annegret Richter, Heidemarie Rosendahl) . . 42.8

### 400-METER RUN — Sec.

1964—Betty Cuthbert, Australia . . . 52.0
1968—Colette Besson, France . . . 52.0
1972—Monika Zehrt, East Germany . . . 51.08*

### 1500-METER RUN — Min.-Sec.

1972—Ludmila Bragina, U.S.S.R. . . . 4:01.4*

### 80-METER HURDLES

1932—Mildred Didrikson, United States . . 11.7
1936—Trebisonda Villa, Italy . . . 11.7
1948—Fanny Blankers-Koen, Netherlands 11.2
1952—Shirley Strickland de la Hunty, Australia . . . 10.9
1956—Shirley Strickland de la Hunty, Australia . . . 10.7
1960—Irina Press, U.S.S.R. . . . 10.8
1964—Karin Balzer, Germany . . . 10.5*
1968—Maureen Caird, Australia . . . 10.3*
**NOTE:** Discontinued after 1968 Games.

### 100-METER HURDLES — Sec.

1972—Annelie Ehrhardt, East Germany 12.59*

### HIGH JUMP — Ft.-In.

1928—Ethel Catherwood, Canada . . . 5′ 3″
1932—Jean Shiley, United States . . . 5′ 5¼″
1936—Ibolya Csak, Hungary . . . 5′ 3″
1948—Alice Coachman, United States . . . 5′ 6⅛″
1952—Esther Brand, South Africa . . . 5′ 5¾″
1956—Mildred L. McDaniel, United States . . . 5′ 9¼″
1960—Iolanda Balas, Rumania . . . 6′ ¼″
1964—Iolanda Balas, Rumania . . . 6′ 2⅔″*
1968—Miloslava Rezkova, Czechoslovakia . . . 5′ 11¾″
1972—Ulrike Meyfarth, West Germany . . . 6′ 3¾″*

### DISCUS THROW

1928—Helena Konopacka, Poland . . 129′ 11⅞″
1932—Lillian Copeland, United States . . . 133′ 2″
1936—Gisela Mauermayer, Germany . . . 156′ 3³⁄₁₆″
1948—Micheline Ostermeyer, France . . . 137′ 6½″
1952—Nina Romaschkova, U.S.S.R. . . . 168′ 8½″
1956—Olga Fikotova, Czechoslovakia . . . 176′ 1½″
1960—Nina Ponomareva, U.S.S.R. . . . 180′ 8¼″
1964—Tamara Press, U.S.S.R. . . . 187′ 10¾″*
1968—Lia Manoliu, Rumania . . . 191′ 2½″
1972—Faina Melnik, U.S.S.R. . . . 218′ 7″*

### JAVELIN THROW

1932—Mildred Didrikson, United States . . . 143′ 4″
1936—Tilly Fleischer, Germany . . . 148′ 2¾″
1948—Herma Bauma, Austria . . . 149′ 6″
1952—Dana Zatopekova, Czechoslovakia . . . 165′ 7″
1956—Inessa Janzeme, U.S.S.R. . . 176′ 8″
1960—Elvira Ozolina, U.S.S.R. . . . 183′ 8″
1964—Mihaela Penes, Rumania . . . 198′ 7½″*
1968—Angela Nemeth, Hungary . . 198′ 0½″
1972—Ruth Fuchs, East Germany 209′ 7″*

### 8-LB.-13⅘-OZ. SHOT-PUT

1948—Micheline Ostermeyer, France 45′ 1½″
1952—Galina Zybina, U.S.S.R. . . . 50′ 1½″
1956—Tamara Tishkyevich, U.S.S.R. 54′ 5″
1960—Tamara Press, U.S.S.R. . . . 56′ 9⅞″
1964—Tamara Press, U.S.S.R. . . . 59′ 6¼″*
1968—Margitta Gummel, East Germany . . . 64′ 4″
1972—Nadezhda Chizhova, U.S.S.R. 69′ 0″*

### LONG JUMP (originally called "Broad" Jump)

1948—Olga Gyarmati, Hungary . . . 18′ 8¼″
1952—Yvette Williams, New Zealand 20′ 5¾″
1956—Elzbieta Krzeskinska, Poland 20′ 9¾″
1960—Vera Krepkina, U.S.S.R. . . . 20′ 10¾″
1964—Mary Rand, Great Britain . . . 22′ 2½″*
1968—Viorica Viscopoleanu, Rumania . . . 22′ 4½″*
1972—Heidemarie Rosendahl, West Germany . . . 22′ 3″

### PENTATHLON — Points

1964—Irina Press, U.S.S.R. . . . 5,246
1968—Ingrid Becker, West Germany . . 5,098
1972—Mary Peters, Great Britain . . . 4,801*

## BASKETBALL

| | | | |
|---|---|---|---|
| 1904 | *United States | 1956 | United States |
| 1936 | United States | 1960 | United States |
| 1948 | United States | 1964 | United States |
| 1952 | United States | 1968 | United States |
| | | 1972 | U.S.S.R. |

*Demonstration

## BOXING

### LIGHT FLYWEIGHT

1968—Francisco Rodriguez, Venezuela
1972—Gyoergy Gedeo, Hungary

### FLYWEIGHT

1904—George V. Finnegan, United States
1920—Frank De Genaro, United States
1924—Fidel LaBarba, United States
1928—Anton Kocsis, Hungary
1932—Stephen Enekes, Hungary
1936—Willi Kaiser, Germany
1948—Pascual Perez, Argentina
1952—Nathan Brooks, United States
1956—Terence Spinks, Great Britain
1960—Gyula Torok, Hungary
1964—Fernando Atzori, Italy
1968—Ricardo Delgado, Mexico
1972—Gheorghi Kostadinov, Bulgaria

### BANTAMWEIGHT

1904—O. L. Kirk, United States
1908—H. Thomas, Great Britain
1920—Clarence Walker, South Africa
1924—William Smith, South Africa
1928—Vittorio Tamagnini, Italy
1932—Horace Gwynne, Canada
1936—Ulderico Sergo, Italy
1948—Tibor Csik, Hungary
1952—Pentti Hamalainen, Finland
1956—Wolfgang Behrendt, Germany
1960—Oleg Grigoryev, U.S.S.R.
1964—Takao Sakurai, Japan
1968—Valery Sokolov, U.S.S.R.
1972—Orlando Martinez, Cuba

### FEATHERWEIGHT

1904—O. L. Kirk, United States
1908—R. K. Gunn, Great Britain
1920—Paul Fritsch, France
1924—John Fields, United States
1928—L. Van Klaveren, Holland
1932—Carmelo Robledo, Argentina
1936—Oscar Casanovas, Argentina

1948—Ernesto Formenti, Italy
1952—Jan Zachara, Czechoslovakia
1956—Vladimir Safronov, U.S.S.R.
1960—Francesco Musso, Italy
1964—Stanislav Stepashkin, U.S.S.R.
1968—Antonio Roldan, Mexico
1972—Boris Kousnetsov, U.S.S.R

## LIGHTWEIGHT

1904—H. J. Spanger, United States
1908—F. Grace, Great Britain
1920—Samuel Mosberg, United States
1924—Harold Nielson, Denmark
1928—Carlo Orlandi, Italy
1932—Lawrence Stevens, South Africa
1936—Imre Harangi, Hungary
1948—Gerald Dreyer, South Africa
1952—Aureliano Bolognesi, Italy
1956—Richard McTaggart, Great Britain
1960—Kazimierz Pazdzior, Poland
1964—Josef Grudzein, Poland
1968—Ronald Harris, United States
1972—Jan Szczepanski, Poland

## LIGHT-WELTERWEIGHT

1952—Charles Adkins, United States
1956—Vladimir Enguibarian, U.S.S.R.
1960—Bonumil Nemecek, Czechoslovakia
1964—Jerzy Kulei, Poland
1968—Jerzy Kulei, Poland
1972—Ray Seales, United States

## WELTERWEIGHT

1904—Albert Young, United States
1920—T. Schneider, Canada
1924—Jean Delarge, Belgium
1928—Edward Morgan, New Zealand
1932—Edward Flynn, United States
1936—Sten Suvio, Finland
1948—Julius Torma, Czechoslovakia
1952—Zigmunt Chycha, Poland
1956—Necalae Linca, Rumania
1960—Giovanni Benvenuti, Italy
1964—Marian Kasprzyk, Poland
1968—Manfred Wolke, East Germany
1972—Emilio Correa, Cuba

## LIGHT-MIDDLEWEIGHT

1952—Laszlo Papp, Hungary
1956—Laszlo Papp, Hungary
1960—Wilbert McClure, United States
1964—Boris Lagutin, U.S.S.R.
1968—Boris Lagutin, U.S.S.R.
1972—Dieter Kottysch, West Germany

## MIDDLEWEIGHT

1904—Charles Mayer, United States
1908—John Douglas, Great Britain
1920—Harry Mallin, Great Britain
1924—Harry Mallin, Great Britain
1928—Piero Toscani, Italy
1932—Carmen Barth, United States
1936—Jean Despeaux, France
1948—Laszlo Papp, Hungary
1952—Floyd Patterson, United States
1956—Guennadii Chatkov, U.S.S.R.
1960—Edward Crook, United States
1964—Valery Popenchenko, U.S.S.R.
1968—Christopher Finnegan, Great Britain
1972—Viatchesiav Lemechev, U.S.S.R.

## LIGHT-HEAVYWEIGHT

1920—Edward Eagan, United States
1924—Harry Mitchell, Great Britain
1928—Victorio Avendano, Argentina
1932—David E. Carstens, South Africa
1936—Roger Michlot, France
1948—George Hunter, South Africa
1952—Norvel Lee, United States
1956—James F. Boyd, United States
1960—Cassius Clay, United States
1964—Cosimo Pinto, Italy
1968—Dan Pozdniak, U.S.S.R.
1972—Mate Parlov, Yugoslavia

## HEAVYWEIGHT

1904—Samuel Berger, United States
1908—A. L. Oldham, Great Britain
1920—R. Rawson, Great Britain
1924—Otto von Porath, Norway
1928—Rodriguez Jurado, Argentina
1932—Santiago A. Lovell, Argentina
1936—Herbert Runge, Germany
1948—Rafael Iglesias, Argentina
1952—Edward Sanders, United States
1956—Peter Rademacher, United States
1960—Francesco De Piccoli, Italy
1964—Joseph Frazier, United States
1968—George Foreman, United States
1972—Teofilo Stevenson, Cuba

# CANOEING

## KAYAK SINGLES—1,000 METERS

| | Min.-Sec. |
|---|---|
| 1936—Gregor Hradetzky, Austria | 4:22.9 |
| 1948—Gert Fredriksson, Sweden | 4:33.2 |
| 1952—Gert Fredriksson, Sweden | 4:07.9 |
| 1956—Gert Fredriksson, Sweden | 4:12.8 |
| 1960—Erik Hansen, Denmark | 3:53.0 |
| 1964—Rolf Peterson, Sweden | 3:57.13 |
| 1968—Mihaly Hesz, Hungary | 4:02.63 |
| 1972—Aleksandr Shaperenko, U.S.S.R. | 3:48.06 |

## KAYAK PAIRS—1,000 METERS

| | |
|---|---|
| 1936—Austria (Adolf Kainz, Alfons Dorfner) | 4:03.8 |
| 1948—Sweden (Hans Berglund, Lenart Klingstroem) | 4:07.3 |
| 1952—Finland (Kurt Wires, Yrjo Hietanen) | 3:51.1 |
| 1956—Germany (Michel Scheuer, Minrad Miltenberger) | 3:49.6 |
| 1960—Sweden (Gert Fredriksson, Sven Sjodelius) | 3:34.73 |
| 1964—Sweden (Sven Sjodelius, Gunnar Utterberg) | 3:38.54 |
| 1968—U.S.S.R. (Alexander Shaparenko, Vladimir Morozov) | 3:37.54 |
| 1972—U.S.S.R. (Nikolai Gorbachev, Viktor Kratassyuk) | 3:31.23 |

## 4 x 500-METER KAYAK RELAY

| | |
|---|---|
| 1960—Germany (Dieter Krause, Gunther Perleberg, Paul Lange, Friedhelm Wentzke) | 7:39.43 |
| 1964—U.S.S.R. (1,000 m.) | 3:14. 67 |

## CANADIAN SINGLES—1,000 METERS

| | |
|---|---|
| 1936—Francis Amyot, Canada | 5:32.1 |
| 1948—Joseph Holocek, Czechoslovakia | 5:42.0 |
| 1952—Joseph Holocek, Czechoslovakia | 4:56.3 |
| 1956—Leon Rottman, Rumania | 5:05.3 |
| 1960—Janos Parti, Hungary | 4:33.9 |
| 1964—Jurgen Eschert, Germany | 4:35.14 |
| 1968—Tibor Tatai, Hungary | 4:36.14 |
| 1972—Ivan Patzaichin, Rumania | 4:08.94 |

## CANADIAN PAIRS—1,000 METERS

| | |
|---|---|
| 1936—Czechoslovakia (Vladimir Syrovatka, F. Jan Brzak) | 4:50.1 |
| 1948—Czechoslovakia (Jan Brzak, Bohumil Kudrna) | 5:07.1 |
| 1952—Denmark (Bent Rasch, Finn Haunstoft) | 4:38.3 |
| 1956—Rumania (Alex Dumitru, Simon Jsmailciuc) | 4:47.4 |
| 1960—U.S.S.R. (Leonid Geyshter, Sergey Makarenko) | 4:17.9 |
| 1964—Russia (Andrey Khimich, Stepan Oschepkov) | 4:04.65 |
| 1968—Rumania (Ivan Patzaichin, Serghei V. Covaliov) | 4:07.18 |
| 1972—U.S.S.R. (Vladas Chessyunas, Yuri Lobanov) | 3:52.60 |

## KAYAK SINGLES—WOMEN—500 METERS

| | |
|---|---|
| 1948—K. Hoff, Denmark | 2:31.9 |
| 1952—Sylvi Saimo, Finland | 2:18.4 |
| 1956—Elisaveta Dementieva, U.S.S.R. | 2:18.9 |
| 1960—Antonina Seredina, U.S.S.R. | 2:08.08 |
| 1964—Ludmila Khoedosiuk, U.S.S.R. | 2:12.87 |
| 1968—Ludmila Pinaeva, U.S.S.R. | 2:11.09 |
| 1972—Yulia Ryabchinskaya, U.S.S.R. | 2:03.17 |

## KAYAK PAIRS—WOMEN—500 METERS

| | |
|---|---|
| 1960—U.S.S.R.—(Maria Shubina, Antonina Seredina) | 1:54.76 |
| 1964—Germany (Roswitha Esser, Annemie Zimmermann) | 1:56.95 |
| 1968—West Germany (Annemarie Zimmermann, Roswitha Esser) | 1:56.44 |
| 1972—U.S.S.R. (Ludmila Pinaeva, Ekaterina Kuryshko) | 1:53.50 |

# CYCLING

## ROAD RACE, INDIVIDUAL

| | Hr.-Min.-Sec. |
|---|---|
| 1896—A. Konstantinidis, Greece (87 km.) | 3:22:31.0 |
| 1906—Vast and Bardonneau, France tied (84 km.) | 2:41:28.0 |
| 1912—Rudolph Lewis, South Africa (320 km.) | 10:42:39.0 |
| 1920—Harry Stenquist, Sweden (175 km.) | 4:40:01.8 |
| 1924—Armand Blanchonnet, France (188 km.) | 6:20:48.0 |
| 1928—Henry Hansen, Denmark (168 km.) | 4:47:18.0 |
| 1932—Attilo Pavesi, Italy (100 km.) | 2:28:53.6 |
| 1936—Robert Charpentier, France (100 km.) | 2:33:05.0 |
| 1948—Jose Bayaert, France (194.633 km.) | 5:18:12.6 |
| 1952—Andre Noyelle, Belgium (190.4 km.) | 5:06:03.4 |
| 1956—E. Baldini, Italy (188.1 km.) | 5:21:17.0 |
| 1960—Viktor Kapitonov, U.S.S.R. | 4:20:37.0 |
| 1964—Marko Zanin, Italy | 4:39:51.63 |
| 1968—Pier-franco Vianelli, Italy (196 km.) | 4:41:25.24 |
| 1972—Hennie Kuiper, Netherlands (200 km.) | 4:14:37.0 |

## ROAD RACE, TEAM

| | |
|---|---|
| 1912—Sweden (Friborg, Malm. Persson, Lonn) | 44:35:33.6 |
| 1920—France (Canteloube, Detreille, Souchard, Gobillot) | 19:16:43.4 |
| 1924—France (Blanchonnet, Hamel, Wambst) | 19:30:14.0 |
| 1928—Denmark (H. Hansen, Nielsen, Jorgensen) | 15:09:14.0 |
| 1932—Italy (Olmo, Segato, Pavesi) | 7:27:15.2 |
| 1936—France (Charpentier, Lapebie, Dorgebray) | 7:39:16.2 |
| 1948—Belgium (Wouters, Delathower, Van Roosbroeck) | 15:58:17.4 |
| 1952—Belgium (A. Noyelle, R. Grondelaers, Lucien Victor) | 15:20:46.6 |
| 1956—France (A. Geyre, M. Moucherard, M. Vermeulin) | 5:21:17.0 |
| 1960—Italy (A. Bailetti, O. Cogliati, G. Fornoni, L. Trape) | 2:14:33.53 |
| 1964—Netherlands (Evert Gerardus Dolman, Johannes A. M. Pieterse; Gerben Karstens, Hubertus Balthazar Zoet) | 2:26:31.19 |
| 1968—Netherlands (Marinus Pijnen, Fedor den Hertog, Jan Krekels Gerardes Zoetemelk) | 2:07:49.06 |
| 1972—U.S.S.R. (Boris Chouhov, Valery Lardy, Gennadi Komnatov, Valery Likhachev) (100 km.) | 2:11:17.8 |

## 1,000 METERS SCRATCH

| | Min.-Sec. |
|---|---|

1896—Paul Masson, France (2,000 m.) 4:56.0
1900—G. Taillendier, France
1906—Francesco Verri, Italy
1908—Void, time limit exceeded
1920—Maurice Peeters, Holland
1924—Lucien Michard, France
1928—R. Beaufrand, France
1932—Jacobus van Edmond, Holland
1936—Toni Merkens, Germany
1948—Mario Ghella, Italy (920 m.)
1952—Enzo Sacchi, Italy
1956—M. Rousseau, France ......... 0:11.4
1960—Sante Gaiardoni, Italy
1964—Giovanni Pettenella, Italy
1968—Daniel Morelon, France
1972—Daniel Morelon, France

## 4,000-METER INDIVIDUAL PURSUIT

1964—Jiri Daller, Czechoslovakia .... 5:04.75
1968—Daniel Rebillard, France      4:41.71
1972—Knut Kundsen, Norway ...... 4:45.74

## 2,000 METERS TANDEM

1906—Great Britain—Matthews, Rushen
1908—France—Schilles, Auffray
1920—Great Britain—Ryan, Lance
1924—France—Choury, Cugnot
1928—Holland—Leene, van Dijk
1932—France—Perrin, Chaillot
1936—Germany—Ihbe, Lorenz
1948—Italy—Teruzzi, Perona
1952—Australia—Mockridge, Cox
1956—Australia—Browne, Marchant
1960—Italy—S. Bianchetto, G. Beghetto
1964—Italy—Angelo Damiano, Sergio Bianchetto
1968—France—Daniel Morelon, Pierre Trentin
1972—U.S.S.R.—Vladimir Sements, Igor Tselovalnikov

## 4,000 METERS TEAM PURSUIT

| | Min.-Sec. |
|---|---|

1908—Great Britain (Meredith, Jones, Payne, Kingsbury)—1810.5 m. 2:18.6
1920—Italy (Giorgetti, Ferrario, Carli, Magnani) ............. 5:20.0
1924—Italy (di Martino, Dinale, Menegazzi, Zuchetti) ...... 5:15.0
1928—Italy (Tasselli, Cattaneo, Facciani, Luisiani) ........... 5:01.8
1932—Italy (Cimatti, Pedretti, Ghilardi, Borsari) ............ 4:53.0
1936—France (Charpentier, Goujon, Lapebie, Le Niherzy) ...... 4:45.0
1948—France (Coste, Blusson, Decanali, Adam) ............. 4:57.8
1952—Italy (Morettini, Messina, DeRossi, Campana) ......... 4:46.1
1956—Italy (L. Faggin, V. Gasparella, A. Domenicali, F. Gandino) .. 4:37.4
1960—Italy (L. Arienti, F. Testa, M. Vallotto, M. Vigna) ...... 4:30.9
1964—Germany (Lothar Glaesges, Karl Link, Karl-Heinz Henrichs, Ernst Streng) ............. 4:35.67
1968—Denmark (Gunnar Asmussen, Per Lyngemark, Reno Olsen, Mogens Jensen) ............. 4:22.44
1972—West Germany (Juergen Colombo, Guenter Haritz, Udo Hempel, Guenther Schumacher) ..... 4:22.14

## 1,000 METERS TIME TRIAL

1928—Willy Falck-Hansen, Denmark... 1:14.4
1932—Edgar Gray, Australia ........ 1.13.0
1936—Arie Gerrit van Vliet, Holland .. 1:12.0
1948—Jacques Dupont, France ...... 1:13.5
1952—Russell Mockridge, Australia ... 1:11.1
1956—L. Faggin, Italy ............. 1:09.8
1960—Sante Gaiardoni, Italy ....... 1:07.27
1964—Patrick Sercu, Belgium ...... 1:09.52
1968—Pierre Trentin, France ...... 1:03.91
1972—Niels Fredborg, Denmark ..... 1:06.44

## EQUESTRIAN

### THREE-DAY EVENT, TEAM

1912—Sweden (Nordlander, Aldercreutz, Casparsson) ........... 139.06 pts.
1920—Sweden (H. Morner, Lundstrom, von Braun) ...........5058.00 pts.
1924—Holland (van Zijp, de Mortanges, G. de Kruiff Sr.) ....... 5294.50 pts.
1928—Holland (van Zijp, de Mortanges, G. de Kruiff Jr.) ....... 5865.68 pts.
1932—United States (Lt. E. F. Thomson, Maj. H. D. Chamberlain, Capt. E. Y. Argo) .......5038.08 pts.
1936—Germany (Stubbendorff, Lippert, von Wangenheim) ....... 676.65 pts.
1948—United States (Col. F. S. Henry, Lt. Col. C. H. Anderson, Col. E. F. Thomson) ....161.50 marks
1952—Sweden (von Blixen-Finecke, Stahre, Frolen) ........ 221.94 marks
1956—Great Britain (A. E. Hill, F. W. C. Welden, A. L. Rock) .... 355.48 marks
1960—Australia (L. Morgan, N. Lavis, W. Roycroft) ............128.18 marks
1964—Italy (Mauro Checcoli, Paolo Angioni, Giuseppe Ravano) .. 85.80 pts.
1968—Great Britain (Derek S. Allhusen, Richard Meade, Reuben S. Jones) ........... minus 175.93
1972—Great Britain (Mary Gordon-Watson, Bridget Parker, Richard Meade) ........ 95.53 pts.

### THREE-DAY EVENT, INDIVIDUAL

1912—Lt. Axel Norlander, Sweden .. 46.59 pts.
1920—Lt. Helmer Morner, Sweden ..1775.00 pts.
1924—A. D. C. Van Der Voort, van Zijp, Holland ........1976.00 pts.
1928—Lt. Ferdinand Pahud de Mortanges, Holland .........1969.82 pts.
1932—Lt. Ferdinand Pahud de Mortanges, Holland .........1813.82 pts.
1936—Ludwig Stubbendorff, Germany .......... 362.30 pts.
1948—Capt. Bernard Chevallier, France ........... 4 plus marks
1952—Hans von Blixen-Finecke, Sweden ........ 28.33 fault points
1956—P. Kastenman, Sweden .... 66.53 marks
1960—Lawrence Morgan, Australia ........ 7.15 plus marks
1964—Mauro Checcoli, Italy ....... 64.40 pts.
1968—Jean J. Guyon (riding Pitou), France ........ minus 38.86
1972—Richard Meade (riding Laurieston), Great Britain ...... 57.73 pts.

### DRESSAGE, TEAM

1928—Germany (v. Langen, Lindenbach, v. Lotzbeck) ........ 669.7 pts.
1932—France (Lesage, Marion, Jousseaume) ......... 939.6 pts.
1936—Germany (Pollay, Gerhard, v. Oppeln-Bronikowski) ....1014.8 pts
1948—France (Jousseaume, Paillard, Buret) ............ 1269 pts.
1952—Sweden (St. Cyr, Boltenstern, Persson) ........1592.5 marks
1956—Sweden (Maj. H. St. Cyr. G. Persson, G. Boltenstern) ...... 860 marks
1960—Event Not Held
1964—Germany (Harry Boldt, Reiner Klimke, Josef Neckermann) ......... 2,558.0 marks
1968—West Germany (Josef Neckermann, Liselott Linsenhoff, Rainer Klimke) ......... 2,699 pts.
1972—U.S.S.R. (Elena Petushkova, Ivan Kizimov, Ivan Kalita) 5,095 pts.

### DRESSAGE, INDIVIDUAL

1912—Capt. Carl Bonde, Sweden .. 15.000 pts.

1920—Capt. Janne Lundblad, Sweden ..........27.937 pts.
1924—Ernst v. Linder, Sweden .... 276.004 pts.
1928—Carl von Langen, Germany . 237.042 pts.
1932—Francois Lesage, France .... 343.075 pts.
1936—Heinz Pollay, Germany .... 352.000 pts.
1948—Capt. Hans Moser, Switzerland .......... 492.005 pts.
1952—Henri St. Cyr, Sweden .... 556.005 pts.
1956—Henri St. Cyr, Sweden .... 860.000 pts.
1960—Sergey Filatov, U.S.S.R. .. 2144.000 pts.
1964—Henri Chammartin, Switzerland 1,504 pts.
1968—Ivan Kozomov (riding Ijor), U.S.S.R. .......... 1,572 pts.
1972—Liselott Lisenhoff (riding Piaff), West Germany .......... 1,229 pts.

### PRIX DES NATIONS, INDIVIDUAL

1912—Capt. J. Cariou, France...... 186 pts.
1920—Lt. Tommaso Lequio, Italy.... 2 faults
1924—Lt. Alphons Gemuseus, Switzerland .......... 6 faults
1928—F. Ventura, Czechoslovakia.... no faults
1932—Takeichi Nishi, Japan ..... 8 faults
1936—Kurt Hasse, Germany ..... 4 faults
1948—Mariles Cortes, Mexico ....6¼ faults
1952—Pierre Jonqueres d'Oriola, France .......... 0 faults
1956—H. G. Winkler, Germany...... 4 faults
1960—Raimondo D'Inzeo, Italy ..... 12 faults
1964—Jonquieres d'Orlola, France .. 9 faults
1968—William Steinkraus, United States 4 pts.
1972—Graziano Mancinelli, Italy .... 8 faults

### PRIX DES NATIONS, TEAM

1912—Sweden (Lewenhaupt, Kilman, von Rosen) ...........545 pts.
1920—Sweden (von Rosen, Koenig, Norling) .......... 14 faults
1924—Sweden (Thelning, Stahle, Lundstrom) .............42.25 pts.
1928—Spain (de los Truxillos, Morenes, Fernandez) .......... 4 faults
1932—All teams participating disqualified.
1936—Germany (v. Barnekow, Hasse, Brandt) .......... 44 faults
1948—Mexico (Cortes, Uriza, Valdes) 34¼ faults
1952—Great Britain (White, Stewart, Llewellyn) ...........40.75 faults
1956—Germany (H. G. Winkler, F. Thiedemann, A. L. Westhues) ..... 40 faults
1960—Germany ...........46½ pen-points
1964—Germany (Hermann Schridde, Kurt Jarasinski, Hans G. Winkler).. 68.50
1968—Canada (Thomas Gayford, James Day, James Elder) ....... 102.75
1972—West Germany (Fritz Ligges, Gerhard Wiltfang, Hartwig Steenken, Hans-Guenter Winkler) .......... 32 faults

## FENCING—MEN

### FOILS, INDIVIDUAL

1900—C. Coste, France
1904—Ramon Fonst, Cuba
1906—M. Dillon-Cavanaugh, France
1908—Demonstration
1912—Nedo Nadi, Italy
1920—Nedo Nadi, Italy
1924—Roger Ducret, France
1928—Lucien Gaudin, France
1932—Gustavo Marzi, Italy
1936—Giulio Gaudini, Italy
1948—Jean Buhan, France
1952—Christian D'Oriola, France
1956—Christian D'Oriola, France
1960—Viktor Zhdanovich, U.S.S.R.
1964—Egon Franke, Poland
1968—Ian Drimbu, Rumania
1972—Witold Woyda, Poland

## FOIL, TEAM

1904—Cuba
1920—Italy
1924—France
1928—Italy
1932—France
1936—Italy
1948—France
1952—France
1956—Italy
1960—U.S.S.R.
1964—U.S.S.R.
1968—France
1972—Poland

## EPEE, INDIVIDUAL

1896—E. Gravelotte, France
1900—Ramon Fonst, Cuba
1904—Ramon Fonst, Cuba
1906—Count de la Falaise, France
1908—Gaston Alibert, France
1912—Paul Anspach, Belgium
1920—Armand Massard, France
1924—Charles Delporte, Belgium
1928—Lucien Gaudin, France
1932—Giancarlo Cornaggia-Medici, Italy
1936—Franco Riccardi, Italy
1948—Luigi Cantone, Italy
1952—Edoardo Mangiarotti, Italy
1956—Carlo Pavesi, Italy
1960—Giuseppe Delfino, Italy
1964—Grigori Kriss, U.S.S.R.
1968—Gyozo Kulcsar, Hungary
1972—Dr. Csaba Fenyvesi, Hungary

## EPEE, TEAM

1906—France
1908—France
1912—Belgium
1920—Italy
1924—France
1928—Italy
1932—France
1936—Italy
1948—France
1952—Italy
1956—Italy
1960—Italy
1964—Hungary
1968—Hungary
1972—Hungary

## SABER, INDIVIDUAL

1896—Jean Georgiadis, Greece
1900—Count de la Falaise, France
1904—Manuel Diaz, Cuba
1906—Jean Georgiadis, Greece
1908—Dr. Jeno Fuchs, Hungary
1912—Dr. Jeno Fuchs, Hungary
1920—Nedo Nadi, Italy
1924—Alexandre Posta, Hungary
1928—Odon Tersztyanszky, Hungary
1932—George Piller, Hungary
1936—Endre Kabos, Hungary
1948—Aladar Gerevich, Hungary
1952—Pal Kovacs, Hungary
1956—Rudolf Karpati, Hungary
1960—Rudolf Karpati, Hungary
1964—Tibor Pezsa, Hungary
1968—Jerzy Pawlowski, Poland
1972—Viktor Sidiak, U.S.S.R.

## SABER, TEAM

1904—Cuba
1906—Germany
1908—Hungary
1912—Hungary
1920—Italy
1924—Italy
1928—Hungary
1932—Hungary
1936—Hungary
1948—Hungary
1952—Hungary

1956—Hungary
1960—Hungary
1964—U.S.S.R.
1968—U.S.S.R.
1972—Italy

## FENCING—WOMEN

### FOILS, INDIVIDUAL

1924—Mrs. Ellen Osiier, Denmark
1928—Helene Mayer, Germany
1932—Ellen Preis, Austria
1936—Ilona Schacherer-Elek, Hungary
1948—Ilona Elek, Hungary
1952—Irene Camber, Italy
1956—Gillian Sheen, Great Britain
1960—Adelheid Schmid, Germany
1964—Ujalki Rejto, Hungary
1968—Elene Novikova, U.S.S.R.
1972—Antonella Ragno Lonzi, Italy

### FOILS, TEAM

1960—U.S.S.R.
1964—Hungary
1968—U.S.S.R.
1972—U.S.S.R.

## FIELD HOCKEY

| | |
|---|---|
| 1908—Great Britain | 1960—Pakistan |
| 1920—Great Britain | 1964—India |
| 1928—British India | 1968—Pakistan |
| 1936—British India | 1972—West Germany |
| 1948—India | |
| 1952—India | |
| 1956—India | |

## GYMNASTICS—MEN

### LONG HORSE (VAULTS)    Points

1896—Karl Schumann, Germany
1904—Anton Heida, George Eyser,
    United States ............ 36.00
1924—Frank Kriz, United States ...... 9.98
1928—Eugen Mack, Switzerland ...... 28.75
1932—Savino Guglielmetti, Italy ...... 54.10
1936—Karl Schwarzmann, Germany ... 19.20
1948—Paavo Aaltonen, Finland ...... 39.10
1952—Viktor Tchoukarine, U.S.S.R. ... 19.20
1956—H. Bantz, Germany and
    V. Mouratov, U.S.S.R. Tied at .. 18.85
1960—Boris Shakhlin, U.S.S.R., tied with
    Takashi Ono, Japan ........ 19.350
1964—Haruhiro Yamashita, Japan .... 19.600
1968—Mikhail Voronin, U.S.S.R. ...... 19.000
1972—Klaus Koeste, East Germany ... 18.850

### SIDE (POMMELED) HORSE

1896—Louis Zutter, Switzerland
1904—Anton Heida, United States .... 42.00
1924—Joseph Wilhelm, Switzerland ... 21.23
1928—Hermann Hanggi, Switzerland ... 59.25
1932—Stephen Pelle, Hungary ....... 57.20
1936—Konrad Frey, Germany ........ 19.33
1948—Paavo Aaltonen, Finland ...... 38.70
1952—Viktor Tchoukarine, U.S.S.R. ... 19.50
1956—Boris Shakhlin, U.S.S.R. ...... 19.25
1960—Eugen Ekman, Finland, tied with
    Boris Shakhlin, U.S.S.R. ..... 19.375
1964—Miroslav Cerar, Yugoslavia ..... 19.525
1968—Miroslav Cerar, Yugoslavia ..... 19.325
1972—Viktor Klimenko, U.S.S.R. ..... 19.125

### HORIZONTAL BAR

1896—Herman Weingaertner, Germany
1904—Anton Heida and E. A. Hennig,
    United States ............ 40.00

1924—Leon Stukelj, Yugoslavia ....... 19.73
1928—George Miez, Switzerland ...... 57.50
1932—Dallas Bixler, United States .... 55.00
1936—Aleksanteri Saarvala, Finland ... 19.367
1948—Joseph Stalder, Switzerland .... 39.70
1952—Jack Gunthard, Switzerland .... 19.55
1956—Takashi Ono, Japan .......... 19.60
1960—Takashi Ono, Japan .......... 19.600
1964—Boris Shakhlin, U.S.S.R. ...... 19.625
1968—Michael Voronin, U.S.S.R. and
    Akinori Nakayama, Japan ... 19.550
1972—Mitsuo Tsukahara, Japan ...... 19.725

### PARALLEL BARS

1896—Alfred Flatow, Germany
1904—George Eyser, United States ... 44.00
1924—August Guttinger, Switzerland . 21.63
1928—Ladislav Vacha, Czechoslovakia . 56.50
1932—Romeo Neri, Italy ........... 56.90
1936—Konrad Frey, Germany ....... 19.07
1948—Michael Reusch, Switzerland.... 39.50
1952—Hans Eugster, Switzerland ..... 19.65
1956—Viktor Tchoukarine, U.S.S.R. ... 19.20
1960—Boris Shakhlin, U.S.S.R. ...... 19.400
1964—Yukio Endo, Japan .......... 19.675
1968—Akinori Nakayama, Japan ..... 19.475
1972—Sawao Kato, Japan .......... 19.475

### RINGS

1896—Jean Mitropoulos, Greece
1904—Herman T. Glass, United States .. 45.00
1924—Franco Martino, Italy ........ 21.55
1928—Leon Stukelj, Yugoslavia ...... 57.75
1932—George Gulack, United States ... 56.90
1936—Alois Hudec, Czechoslovakia ... 19.43
1948—Karl Frei, Switzerland ........ 39.60
1952—Grant Chaguinian, U.S.S.R. .... 19.75
1956—Albert Azaryen, U.S.S.R. ...... 19.35
1960—Albert Azaryen, U.S.S.R. ...... 19.725
1964—Takuji Hayata, Japan ........ 19.475
1968—Akinori Nakayama, Japan ..... 19.450
1972—Akinori Nakayama, Japan ..... 19.350

### ALL-AROUND INDIVIDUAL

1900—S. Sandras, France .......... 320.00
1904—Anton Heida, United States.... 161.00
1906—Lavielle, France, 5 events
    Weber, Germany, 6 events
1908—Alberto Braglia, Italy ........ 317.00
1912—Alberto Braglia, Italy ........ 135.00
1920—Giorgio Zampori, Italy ....... 88.35
1924—Leon Stukelj, Yugoslavia ...... 110.34
1928—George Miez, Switzerland...... 247.50
1932—Romeo Neri, Italy ........... 140.625
1936—Alfred Schwarzmann, Germany . 113.10
1948—Veikko Huhtanen, Finland .... 229.70
1952—Viktor Tchoukarine, U.S.S.R. ... 115.70
1956—Viktor Tchoukarine, U.S.S.R. ... 114.25
1960—Boris Shakhlin, U.S.S.R. ...... 115.95
1964—Yukio Endo, Japan .......... 115.95
1968—Sawao Kato, Japan .......... 115.90
1972—Sawao Kato, Japan .......... 114.650

### TEAM GYMNASTICS

1896—Germany
1904—United States
1906—Denmark and Norway (tie)
1908—Sweden ............... 438.000
1912—Italy ................. 265.750
1920—Italy ................. 359.855
1924—Italy ................. 839.058
1928—Switzerland .......... 1718.625
1932—Italy ................. 541.850
1936—Germany ............. 657.430
1948—Finland .............. 1358.300
1952—U.S.S.R. ............. 574.400
1956—U.S.S.R. ............. 568.250
1960—Japan ............... 575.20
1964—Japan ............... 577.95
1968—Japan ............... 575.90
1972—Japan ............... 571.25

### FREE EXERCISE

1956—Valentine Mouratov, U.S.S.R. ... 19.20

1960—Nobuyuki Aihara, Japan . . . . . . 19.450
1964—Franco Menichelli, Italy . . . . . . . 19.450
1968—Sawao Kato, Japan . . . . . . . . . . 19.475
1972—Nikolai Andrianov, U.S.S.R. . . . . 19.175

## GYMNASTICS—WOMEN

### BALANCE BEAM, INDIVIDUAL

1952—Nina Botcharova, U.S.S.R. . . . . . 19.22
1956—Agnes Keleti, Hungary . . . . . . . . 18.800
1960—Eva Bosakova, Czechoslovakia . . 19.283
1964—Vera Caslauska, Czechoslovakia . . 19.499
1968—Natalia Kutchinskaya, U.S.S.R. . . 19.650
1972—Olga Korbut, U.S.S.R. . . . . . . . 19.400

### PARALLEL BARS, INDIVIDUAL

1952—Margit Korondi, Hungary . . . . . . 19.40
1956—Agnes Keleti, Hungary . . . . . . . . 18.966
1960—Polina Astakhova, U.S.S.R. . . . . 19.616
1964—Polina Astakhova, U.S.S.R. . . . . 19.332
1968—Vera Caslavska, Czechoslovakia . . 19.650
1972—Karin Janz, East Germany . . . . . 19.675

### LONG-HORSE VAULT (side horse)

1952—Yekaterina Kalinchouk, U.S.S.R. . . 19.20
1956—Larisa Latynina, U.S.S.R. . . . . . 18.833
1960—Margarita Nikolaeva, U.S.S.R. . . 19.316
1964—Vera Caslauska, Czechoslovakia . . 19.483
1968—Vera Caslavska, Czechoslovakia . . 19.775
1972—Karin Janz, East Germany . . . . . 19.525

### FREE STANDING (floor exercises)

1952—Agnes Keleti, Hungary . . . . . . . 19.36
1956—Larisa Latynina, U.S.S.R. . . . . . 18.732
1960—Larisa Latynina, U.S.S.R. . . . . . 19.583
1964—Larisa Latynina, U.S.S.R. . . . . . 19.599
1968—Vera Caslavska, Czechoslovakia
    and Larissa Petrik, U.S.S.R. . . 19.675
1972—Olga Korbut, U.S.S.R. . . . . . . . 19.575

### ALL-AROUND, INDIVIDUAL

1952—Maria Gorokhovskaja, U.S.S.R. . . 76.78
1956—Larisa Latynina, U.S.S.R. . . . . . 74.931
1960—Larisa Latynina, U.S.S.R. . . . . . 77.031
1964—Vera Caslauska, Czechoslovakia . . 77.56
1968—Vera Caslavska, Czechoslovakia . . 78.25
1972—Ludmila Turischeva, U.S.S.R. . . 77.025

### TEAM

1928—Holland . . . . . . . . . . . . . . . . . 316.75
1936—Germany . . . . . . . . . . . . . . . . 506.50
1948—Czechoslovakia . . . . . . . . . . . . 445.45
1952—U.S.S.R. . . . . . . . . . . . . . . . . 527.03
1956—U.S.S.R. . . . . . . . . . . . . . . . . 444.80
1960—U.S.S.R. . . . . . . . . . . . . . . . . 382.320
1964—U.S.S.R. . . . . . . . . . . . . . . . . 380.890
1968—U.S.S.R. . . . . . . . . . . . . . . . . 382.85
1972—U.S.S.R. . . . . . . . . . . . . . . . . 380.50

## JUDO Event First Held in 1964
## Final Ranking

### LIGHTWEIGHT CLASS (149.6 lbs. or 68 kgs.)

Takehide Nakatani, Japan . . . . . . . . . . . 5    0
1972—Takao Kawaguchi, Japan

### WELTERWEIGHT

1972—Toyokazu Nomura, Japan

### MIDDLEWEIGHT CLASS (176.4 lbs. or 80 kgs.)

Isao Okano, Japan . . . . . . . . . . . . . 5    0
1972—Shinobu Sekine, Japan

### LIGHT HEAVYWEIGHT

1972—Shota Chochoshvili, U.S.S.R.

### HEAVYWEIGHT CLASS (over 176.4 lbs. or 80 kgs.)

Isao Inokuma, Japan . . . . . . . . . . . . . 5    0
1972—Wim Ruska, Netherlands

### OPEN CLASS (No weight limitations)

Anton Geesink, Netherlands . . . . . . . . . 4    0
1972—Wim Ruska, Netherlands

## MODERN PENTATHLON

### INDIVIDUAL                                       Points

1912—Gustaf Lilliehook, Sweden . . . . . . . . 27.0
1920—Gustaf Dyrssen, Sweden . . . . . . . . . 18.0
1924—Bo Lindman, Sweden . . . . . . . . . . . 18.0
1928—Sevn Thofelt, Sweden . . . . . . . . . . 47.0
1932—Johan Oxenstierna, Sweden . . . . . . . 32.0
1936—Gotthard Handrick, Germany . . . . . . 31.5
1948—Capt. William Grut, Sweden . . . . . . . 16.0
1952—Lars Hall, Sweden . . . . . . . . . . . . 32.0
1956—Lars Hall, Sweden . . . . . . . . . . . 4,833.0
1960—Ferenc Nemeth, Hungary . . . . . . . . 5,024.0
1964—Ferenc Torok, Hungary . . . . . . . . . 5,116.0
1968—Bjoern Ferm, Sweden . . . . . . . . . . 4,964.0
1972—Andras Balczo, Hungary . . . . . . . . 5,412.0

### TEAM (Official since 1952)

1952—Hungary . . . . . . . . . . . . . . . . . . 166.0
1956—U.S.S.R. . . . . . . . . . . . . . . . . 13,690.5
1960—Hungary . . . . . . . . . . . . . . . . 14,863.0
1964—U.S.S.R. . . . . . . . . . . . . . . . . 14,961.0
1968—Hungary . . . . . . . . . . . . . . . . 14,325.0
1972—U.S.S.R. . . . . . . . . . . . . . . . . 15,968.0

## ROWING

### SINGLE SCULLS                                    Min.-Sec.

1900—H. Barrelet, France . . . . . . . . . . . 7:35.6
1904—Frank Greer, United States (dem-
    onstration) (3,218 m.) . . . . . . . . 10:08.5
1908—Harry Blackstaffe, Great Britain . . 9:26.0
1912—William Kinnear, Great Britain . . . 7:47.6
1920—John Kelly, United States . . . . . . 7:35.0
1924—Jack Beresford, Great Britain . . . 7:49.2
1928—Henry Pearce, Australia . . . . . . . 7:11.0
1932—Henry Pearce, Australia . . . . . . . 7:44.4
1936—Gustav Schafer, Germany . . . . . . 8:21.5
1948—Mervyn Wood, Australia . . . . . . . 7:24.4
1952—Yuri Tjukalov, U.S.S.R. . . . . . . . 8:12.8
1956—Vyacheslav Ivanov, U.S.S.R. . . . . 8:02.5
1960—Vyacheslav Ivanov, U.S.S.R. . . . . 7:13.96
1964—Vyacheslav Ivanov, U.S.S.R. . . . . 8:22.51
1968—Jan Henri Wienese, Netherlands 7:47.80
1972—Yuri Malishev, U.S.S.R. . . . . . . . 7:10.12

### DOUBLE SCULLS

1904—United States (demonstration)
    (3,218 m.) . . . . . . . . . . . . . . 10:03.3
1920—United States, John Kelly,
    Paul V. Costello . . . . . . . . . . 7:09.0
1924—United States, John Kelly,
    Paul V. Costello . . . . . . . . . . 6:34.0
1928—United States, Paul V. Costello,
    Charles McIlvaine . . . . . . . . . 6:41.4
1932—United States, Kenneth Myers,
    Garrett Wm. Gilmore . . . . . . . 7:17.4
1936—Great Britain, Jack Beresford,
    Leslie Southwood . . . . . . . . . 7:20.8
1948—Great Britain, R. D. Burnell,
    B. H. Bushnell . . . . . . . . . . . 6:51.3
1952—Argentina, T. Cappozzo,
    E. Guerrero . . . . . . . . . . . . . 7:32.2
1956—U.S.S.R., A. Berkoutov,
    Turi Tiukalov . . . . . . . . . . . . 7:24.0
1960—Czechoslovakia, Vaclav Kozak,
    Pavel Schmidt . . . . . . . . . . . 6:47.50
1964—U.S.S.R., Oleg Tiurin, Boris
    Dubrovsky . . . . . . . . . . . . . 7:10.66
1968—U.S.S.R. (Anatoly Sass, Aleksandr
    Timoshinin) . . . . . . . . . . . . 6:51.82
1972—U.S.S.R. (Aleksandr Timoshinin,
    Gennadi Korshikov) . . . . . . . 7:01.77

### COXSWAINLESS PAIRS

1908—Great Britain, J. Fenning,
    G. Thompson . . . . . . . . . . . 9:41.0

1920—Italy, M. Olgeni, G. Scatturini . . . 7:56.0
1924—Holland, W. H. Rosingh,
    A. C. Beynen . . . . . . . . . . . . 8:19.4
1928—Germany, K. Moeschter,
    B. Muller . . . . . . . . . . . . . . 7:06.4
1932—Great Britain, L. Clive,
    H. R. A. Edwards . . . . . . . . . 8:00.0
1936—Germany, W. Eichhorn,
    Hugo Strauss . . . . . . . . . . . 8:16.1
1948—Great Britain, J. Wilson, W. Laurie 7:21.1
1952—United States, C. P. Logg,
    T. S. Price . . . . . . . . . . . . . 8:20.7
1956—United States, James Fifer,
    Duvall Hecht . . . . . . . . . . . 7:55.4
1960—U.S.S.R., Valentin Boreiko,
    Oleg Golovanou . . . . . . . . . . 7:02.01
1964—Canada, George W. Hungerford,
    Roger C. Jackson . . . . . . . . . 7:32.94
1968—East Germany (Jorge Lucke,
    Heinz Bothe) . . . . . . . . . . . 7:26.56
1972—East Germany (Siegfried
    Brietzke, Wolfgang Mager) . . . 6:53.16

### PAIRS WITH COXSWAIN

1900—Holland . . . . . . . . . . . . . . . . . 7:34.2
1906—Italy, Brunna, Fontanella,
    G. Cesana . . . . . . . . . . . . . 7:32.4
1924—Switzerland, M. Candeveau,
    A. Felber, E. Lachapelle . . . . 8:39.0
1928—Switzerland, H. Schochlin,
    C. Schochlin-Bourquin . . . . . . 7:42.6
1932—United States, J. A. Schauers,
    C. M. Kieffer, E. F. Jennings . . 8:25.8
1936—Germany, G. Gustmann,
    H. Adamski, Dieter Arend . . . . 8:36.9
1948—Denmark, F. Pedersen,
    T. Henriksen, C. E. Andersen . . 8:00.5
1952—France, Salles, Mercier, Malivoire 8:28.6
1956—United States, Art Ayrault,
    Conn Findlay, Kurt Seiffert . . 8:26.1
1960—Germany, Bernhard Knubel,
    Heinz Renneberg, Klaus Zerta 7:29.14
1964—United States, Edward P. Ferry,
    Conn F. Findlay, Kent Mitchell . 8:21.33
1968—Italy (Primo Baran, Renzo
    Sambo, Bruno Cipolla, cox) . . 8:04.81
1972—East Germany (Wolfgang Gunkel,
    Jorge Lucke, Klaus-Dieter
    Neubert, cox) . . . . . . . . . . 7:17.25

### COXSWAINLESS FOURS

1908—Great Britain . . . . . . . . . . . . . 8:34.0
1924—Great Britain . . . . . . . . . . . . . 7:08.6
1928—Great Britain . . . . . . . . . . . . . 6:36.0
1932—Great Britain . . . . . . . . . . . . . 6:58.2
1936—Germany . . . . . . . . . . . . . . . . 7:01.8
1948—Italy . . . . . . . . . . . . . . . . . . 6:39.0
1952—Yugoslavia . . . . . . . . . . . . . . . 7:16.0
1956—Canada . . . . . . . . . . . . . . . . . 7:08.8
1960—United States . . . . . . . . . . . . . 6:26.26
1964—Denmark . . . . . . . . . . . . . . . . 6:59.30
1968—East Germany . . . . . . . . . . . . . 6:39.18
1972—East Germany . . . . . . . . . . . . . 6:24.27

### FOURS WITH COXSWAINS

1906—Italy . . . . . . . . . . . . . . . . . . 8:13.0
1912—Germany . . . . . . . . . . . . . . . . 6:59.4
1920—Switzerland . . . . . . . . . . . . . . 6:54.0
1924—Switzerland . . . . . . . . . . . . . . 7:18.4
1928—Italy . . . . . . . . . . . . . . . . . . 6:47.8
1932—Germany . . . . . . . . . . . . . . . . 7:19.0
1936—Germany . . . . . . . . . . . . . . . . 7:16.2
1948—United States . . . . . . . . . . . . . 6:50.3
1952—Czechoslovakia . . . . . . . . . . . . 7:33.4
1956—Italy . . . . . . . . . . . . . . . . . . 7:19.4
1960—Germany . . . . . . . . . . . . . . . . 6:39.12
1964—Germany . . . . . . . . . . . . . . . . 7:00.44
1968—New Zealand . . . . . . . . . . . . . . 6:45.62
1972—West Germany . . . . . . . . . . . . . 6:31.85

### EIGHT-OARED SHELL

1900—United States (Vesper B.C.) . . . . 6:09.8
1904—United States (demonstration)

| | |
|---|---|
| 1908—Great Britain | 7:52.0 |
| 1912—Great Britain | 6:15.0 |
| 1920—United States (Navy) | 6:02.6 |
| 1924—United States (Yale) | 6:33.4 |
| 1928—United States (California) | 6:03.2 |
| 1932—United States (California) | 6:37.6 |
| 1936—United States (Washington) | 6:25.4 |
| 1948—United States (California) | 5:56.7 |
| 1952—United States (Navy) | 6:25.9 |
| 1956—United States (Yale) | 6:35.2 |
| 1960—Germany | 5:57.18 |
| 1964—United States (Vesper B. C.) | 6:18.23 |
| 1968—West Germany | 6:07.00 |
| 1972—New Zealand | 6:08.94 |

## SHOOTING

### CLAY PIGEON (TRAP) INDIVIDUAL    Points

| | |
|---|---|
| 1908—W. H. Ewing, Canada | 72 |
| 1912—James Graham, United States | 96 |
| 1920—Mark Arie, United States | 95 |
| 1924—Gyula Halasy, Hungary | 98 |
| 1952—George Genereux, Canada | 192 |
| 1956—Galliano Rossini, Italy | 195 |
| 1960—Ion Dumitrescu, Rumania | 192 |
| 1964—Ennio Mattarelli, Italy | 198 |
| 1968—John Braithwaite, Great Britain | 198 |
| 1972—Angelo Scalzone, Italy | 199* |

### CLAY PIGEON, TEAM

| | |
|---|---|
| 1908—Great Britain | 407 |
| 1912—United States (Charles Billings, Ralph Spotts, John Hendrickson, James Graham, Edward Gleason, Frank Hall) | 532 |
| 1920—United States (Mark Arie, Frank Troeh, Frank Wright, Fred Plum, Horace Bonser, Martin McNeir) | 547 |
| 1924—United States (Frank Hughes, Fred R. Etchen, John H. Noel, S. H. Sharman, William S. Silkworth) | 363 |

### RAPID-FIRE PISTOL, 25 Meters

| | |
|---|---|
| 1936—Cornelius van Oyen, Germany | 36 |
| 1948—Karoly Takacs, Hungary | 580 |
| 1952—Karoly Takacs, Hungary | 579 |
| 1956—Stefan Petrescu, Rumania | 587 |
| 1960—William McMillan, United States | 587 |
| 1964—Pentti Linnosvuo, Finland | 592 |
| 1968—Josef Zapedzki, Poland | 593 |
| 1972—Josef Zapedzki, Poland | 595* |

### SPORT (FREE) PISTOL, 50 Meters

| | |
|---|---|
| 1936—Thorsten Ullman, Sweden | 539 |
| 1948—Cam E. Vasquez, Peru | 545 |
| 1952—Huelet Benner, United States | 553 |
| 1956—Pentii Linnosvuo, Finland | 556 |
| 1960—Alexey Gustchin, U.S.S.R. | 560 |
| 1964—V. Markhanen, Finland | 560 |
| 1968—Grigory Kosykh, U.S.S.R. | 562 |

**NOTE:** Heinz Mertel, West Germany, also 562

| | |
|---|---|
| 1972—Ragnar Skanaker, Sweden | 567* |

### FULL-BORE RIFLE (FREE RIFLE)
### 300 Meters, 3 Positions

| | |
|---|---|
| 1900—Emil Kellenberger, Switzerland | 930 |
| 1948—Emil Grunig, Switzerland | 1120 |
| 1952—Anatoli Bogdanov, U.S.S.R. | 1123 |
| 1956—Vassili Borissov, U.S.S.R. | 1138 |
| 1960—Hubert Hammerer, Australia | 1129 |
| 1964—Gary L. Anderson, United States | 1153 |
| 1968—Gary L. Anderson, United States | 1,157* |
| 1972—Lones Wigger, United States | 1,155 |

### SMALL-BORE RIFLE—PRONE—50 Meters

| | |
|---|---|
| 1948—Arthur Cook, United States | 599 |
| 1952—Josif Sarbu, Rumania | 400 |
| 1956—Gerald Ouellette, Canada | 600 |
| 1960—Peter Kohnke, Germany | 590 |
| 1964—Laszlo Hammerl, Hungary | 597 |

| | |
|---|---|
| 1968—Jan Kurka, Czechoslovakia | 598 |
| 1972—Ho Jun Li, North Korea | 599* |

### SMALL-BORE RIFLE—Combined, 3 Positions

| | |
|---|---|
| 1952—Erling Kongshang, Norway | 1164 |
| 1956—Anatole Bogdanov, U.S.S.R. | 1172 |
| 1960—Viktor Shamburkim, U.S.S.R. | 1149 |
| 1964—Lones Wigger, United States | 1164 |
| 1968—Bernd Klinger, West Germany | 1,157 |
| 1972—John Writer, United States | 1,166* |

## SOCCER FOOTBALL

| | |
|---|---|
| 1900—Great Britain | 1936—Italy |
| 1904—Canada | 1948—Sweden |
| 1906—Denmark | 1952—Hungary |
| 1908—Great Britain | 1956—U.S.S.R. |
| 1912—Great Britain | 1960—Yugoslavia |
| 1920—Belgium | 1964—Hungary |
| 1924—Uruguay | 1968—Hungary |
| 1928—Uruguay | 1972—Poland |

## SWIMMING—MEN

### 100-METER FREE STYLE    Min.-Sec.

| | |
|---|---|
| 1896—Alfred Hajos, Hungary | 1:22.2 |
| 1904—Zoltan de Halmay, Hungary (yds.) | 1:02.8 |
| 1906—Charles Daniels, United States | 1:13.4 |
| 1908—Charles Daniels, United States | 1:05.6 |
| 1912—Duke Kahanamoku, United States | 1:03.4 |
| 1920—Duke Kahanamoku, United States | 1:01.4 |
| 1924—John Weissmuller, United States | 59.0 |
| 1928—John Weissmuller, United States | 58.6 |
| 1932—Yasuji Miyazaki, Japan | 58.2 |
| 1936—Ferenec Csik, Hungary | 57.6 |
| 1948—Walter Ris, United States | 57.3 |
| 1952—Clarke Scholes, United States | 57.4 |
| 1956—Jon Hendricks, Australia | 55.4 |
| 1960—John Devitt, Australia | 55.2 |

NOTE: Lance Larson, United States, also credited with same record time although placed second.

| | |
|---|---|
| 1964—Don Schollander, United States | 53.4 * |
| 1968—Mike Wenden, Australia | 52.2 |
| 1972—Mark Spitz, United States | 51.22* |

### 200-METER FREE STYLE

| | |
|---|---|
| 1900—Frederick C. V. Lane, Australia | 2:25.2 |
| 1968—Mike Wenden, Australia | 1:55.2 |
| 1972—Mark Spitz, United States | 1:52.78* |

### 400-METER FREE STYLE

| | |
|---|---|
| 1896—Paul Neumann, Austria (500 m.) | 8:12.6 |
| 1904—Charles Daniels, United States (440 yds.) | 6:16.2 |
| 1906—Otto Scheff, Austria | 6:23.8 |
| 1908—Henry Taylor, Great Britain | 5:36.8 |
| 1912—George Hodgson, Canada | 5:24.4 |
| 1920—Norman Ross, United States | 5:26.8 |
| 1924—John Weissmuller, United States | 5:04.2 |
| 1928—Albert Zorilla, Argentina | 5:01.6 |
| 1932—Clarence Crabbe, United States | 4:48.4 |
| 1936—Jack Medica, United States | 4:44.5 |
| 1948—William Smith, United States | 4:41.0 |
| 1952—Jean Boiteux, France | 4:30.7 |
| 1956—Murray Rose, Australia | 4:27.3 |
| 1960—Murray Rose, Australia | 4:18.3 |
| 1964—Don Schollander, United States | 4:12.2 * |
| 1968—Michael J. Burton, United States | 4:09.0 |
| 1972—Bradford Cooper, Australia | 4:00.27* |

### 1,500-METER FREE STYLE

| | |
|---|---|
| 1896—Alfred Hajos, Hungary (1200 m.) | 18:22.2 |
| 1900—John Jarvis, Great Britain (1000 m.) | 13:40.2 |
| 1904—Emil Rausch, Germany (1609 m.) | 27:18.2 |

| | |
|---|---|
| 1906—Henry Taylor, Great Britain (1609 m.) | 28:28.0 |
| 1908—Henry Taylor, Great Britain | 22:48.4 |
| 1912—George Hodgson, Canada | 22:00.0 |
| 1920—Norman Ross, United States | 22:23.2 |
| 1924—Andrew Charlton, Australia | 20:06.6 |
| 1928—Arne Borg, Sweden | 19:51.8 |
| 1932—Kusuo Kitamura, Japan | 19:12.4 |
| 1936—Noburo Terada, Japan | 19:13.7 |
| 1948—James P. McLane, United States | 19:18.5 |
| 1952—Ford Konno, United States | 18:30.0 |
| 1956—Murray Rose, Australia | 17:58.9 |
| 1960—John Konrads, Australia | 17:19.6 |
| 1964—Robert Windle, Australia | 17:01.7 * |
| 1968—Michael J. Burton, United States | 16:38.9 |
| 1972—Michael J. Burton, United States | 15:52.58* |

### 100-METER BACKSTROKE

| | |
|---|---|
| 1900—Ernst Hoppenberg, Germany (200 m.) | 2:47.0 |
| 1904—Walter Brack, Germany (100 yds.) | 1:16.8 |
| 1908—Arno Bieberstein, Germany | 1:24.6 |
| 1912—Harry Hebner, United States | 1:21.2 |
| 1920—Warren Kealoha, United States | 1:15.2 |
| 1924—Warren Kealoha, United States | 1:13.2 |
| 1928—George Kojac, United States | 1:08.2 |
| 1932—Masaji Kiyokawa, Japan | 1:08.6 |
| 1936—Adolph Kiefer, United States | 1:05.9 |
| 1948—Allen Stack, United States | 1:06.4 |
| 1952—Yoshinobu Oyakawa, United States | 1:05.4 |
| 1956—David Thiele, Australia | 1:02.2 |
| 1960—David Thiele, Australia | 1:01.9 |
| 1964—Jed Graef, United States (200 m.) | 2:10.3 |
| 1968—Roland Matthes, East Germany | 0:58.7 |
| 1972—Roland Matthes, East Germany | 0:56.58* |

### 200-METER BACKSTROKE

| | |
|---|---|
| 1900—Ernst Hoppenberg, Germany | 2:47.0 |
| 1964—Jed R. Graef, United States | 2:10.3 |
| 1968—Roland Matthes, East Germany | 2:09.6 |
| 1972—Roland Matthes, East Germany | 2:02.82* |

### 100-METER BREASTSTROKE

| | |
|---|---|
| 1968—Donald McKenzie, United States | 1:07.7 |
| 1972—Nobutaka Taguchi, Japan | 1:04.94* |

### 200-METER BREAST STROKE

| | |
|---|---|
| 1908—Frederick Holman, Great Britain | 3:09.2 |
| 1912—Walter Bathe, Germany | 3:01.8 |
| 1920—Haken Malmroth, Sweden | 3:04.4 |
| 1924—Robert Skelton, United States | 2.56.6 |
| 1928—Yoshiyuki Tsuruta, Japan | 2:48.8 |
| 1932—Yoshiyuki Tsuruta, Japan | 2:45.4 |
| 1936—Tetsuo Hamuro, Japan | 2:41.5 |
| 1948—Joseph Verdeur, United States | 2:39.3 |
| 1952—John Davies, Australia | 2:34.4 |
| 1956—Masura Furukawa, Japan | 2:34.7 |
| 1960—William Mulliken, United States | 2:37.4 |
| 1964—Ian O'Brien, Australia | 2:27.8 * |
| 1968—Felipe Muñoz, Mexico | 2:28.7 |
| 1972—John Hencken, United States | 2:21.55* |

### 100-METER BUTTERFLY STROKE

| | |
|---|---|
| 1956—William Yorzyk, United States | 2:19.3 |
| 1960—Michael Troy, United States | 2:12.8 |
| 1964—Kevin Berry, United States | 2:06.6 * |
| 1968—Douglas Russell, United States | 55.9 |
| 1972—Mark Spitz, United States | 54.27* |

### 200-METER BUTTERFLY STROKE

| | |
|---|---|
| 1968—Carl Robie, United States | 2:08.7 |
| 1972—Mark Spitz, United States | 2:00.70* |

### 200-METER INDIVIDUAL MEDLEY

| | |
|---|---|
| 1968—Charles Hickcox | 2:12.0 |
| 1972—Gunnar Larsson, Sweden | 2:07.17* |

## 400-METER INDIVIDUAL MEDLEY
1964—Richard W. Roth, United States 4:45.4
1968—Charles Hickcox, United States 4:48.4
1972—Gunnar Larsson, Sweden .... 4:31.98*

| SPRINGBOARD DIVING | Points |
| --- | --- |
| 1908—Albert Zurner, Germany | 85.50 |
| 1912—Paul Guenther, Germany | 79.23 |
| 1920—Louis Kuehn, United States | 675.00 |
| 1924—Albert C. White, United States | 696.40 |
| 1928—Pete Desjardins, United States | 185.04 |
| 1932—Michael Galitzen, United States | 161.38 |
| 1936—Richard Degener, United States | 163.57 |
| 1948—Bruce Harlan, United States | 163.64 |
| 1952—David Browning, United States | 205.29 |
| 1956—Robert L. Clotworthy, United States | 159.56 |
| 1960—Gary Tobian, United States | 170.00 |
| 1964—Ken Sitzberger, United States | 159.90 |
| 1968—Bernard Wrightson, United States | 170.15 |
| 1972—Vladmir Vasin, U.S.S.R. | 594.09 |

| HIGH DIVING | |
| --- | --- |
| 1904—Dr. G. E. Sheldon, United States | 12.75 |
| 1906—Gottlob Walz, Germany | 156.00 |
| 1908—Hjalmar Johansson, Sweden | 83.75 |
| 1912—Erik Adlerz, Sweden | 73.94 |
| 1920—Clarence Pinkston, United States | 100.67 |
| 1924—Albert White, United States | 97.46 |
| 1928—Pete Desjardins, United States | 98.74 |
| 1932—Harold Smith, United States | 124.80 |
| 1936—Marshall Wayne, United States | 113.58 |
| 1948—Dr. Samuel Lee, United States | 130.05 |
| 1952—Dr. Samuel Lee, United States | 156.28 |
| 1956—Joaquin Capilla, Mexico | 152.44 |
| 1960—Robert Webster, United States | 165.56 |
| 1964—Robert Webster, United States | 148.58 |
| 1968—Klaus Dibiasi, Italy | 164.18 |
| 1972—Klaus Dibiasi, Italy | 504.12 |

| 400-METER MEDLEY RELAY | Min.-Sec. |
| --- | --- |
| 1960—United States | 4:05.4 |
| 1964—United States | 3.58.4 * |
| 1968—United States | 3:54.9 |
| 1972—United States | 3:48.16* |

## 400-METER FREE STYLE RELAY
1964—United States ................ 3:33.2
1968—United States ................ 3:31.7
1972—United States ................ 3:26.42*

## 800-METER FREE STYLE RELAY
1908—Great Britain ..............10:55.6
1912—Australia ..................10:11.6
1920—United States .............10:04.4
1924—United States ............. 9:53.4
1928—United States ............. 9:36.2
1932—Japan ..................... 8:58.2
1936—Japan ..................... 8:51.5
1948—United States ............. 8:31.1
1952—United States ............. 8:31.1
1956—Australia ................. 8:23.6
1960—United States ............. 8:10.2
1964—United States ............. 7:52.1 *
1968—United States ............. 7:52.3
1972—United States ............. 7:35.78*

## SWIMMING—WOMEN

| 100-METER FREE STYLE | Min.-Sec. |
| --- | --- |
| 1912—Fanny Durack, Australia | 1:22.2 |
| 1920—Ethelda Bleibtrey, United States | 1:13.6 |
| 1924—Ethel Lackie, United States | 1:12.4 |
| 1928—Albina Osipowich, United States | 1:11.0 |
| 1932—Helene Madison, United States | 1:06.8 |
| 1936—Hendrika Mastenbroek, Holland | 1:05.9 |
| 1948—Greta Andersen, Denmark | 1:06.3 |
| 1952—Katalin Szoke, Hungary | 1:06.8 |
| 1956—Dawn Fraser, Australia | 1:02.0 |
| 1960—Dawn Fraser, Australia | 1:01.2 |
| 1964—Dawn Fraser, Australia | 0:59.5 * |

1968—Margo Jan Henne, United States 1:00.0
1972—Sandra Neilson, United States 0:58.59*

## 200-METER FREE STYLE
1968—Deborah Meyer, United States 2:10.5
1972—Shane Gould, Australia ..... 2:03.56*

## 100-METER BUTTERFLY STROKE
1956—Shelley Mann, United States . 1:11.0
1960—Carolyn Schuler, United States . 1:09.5
1964—Sharon Stouder, United States . 1:04.7 *
1968—Lynn McClements, Australia .. 1:05.5
1972—Mayumi Aoki, Japan ........ 1:03.34*

## 400-METER FREE STYLE
1920—Ethelda Bleibtrey, United States (300 m.) .............. 4:34.0
1924—Martha Norelius, United States . 6:02.2
1928—Martha Norelius, United States . 5:26.4
1932—Helene Madison, United States . 5:28.5
1936—Hendrika Mastenbroek, Holland . 5:26.4
1948—Ann Curtis, United States ... 5:17.8
1952—Valeria Gyenge, Hungary ..... 5:12.1
1956—Lorraine Crapp, Australia .... 4:54.6
1960—Chris Von Saltza, United States 4:50.6
1964—Virginia Duenkel, United States 4:43.3 *
1968—Deborah Meyer, United States . 4:31.8
1972—Shane Gould, Australia ...... 4:19.04*

## 800-METER FREE STYLE
1968—Deborah Meyer, United States 9:24.0
1972—Keena Rothammer, United States ..................... 8:53.68*

## 400-METER FREE STYLE RELAY
1912—Great Britain ............... 5:52.8
1920—United States .............. 5:11.6
1924—United States .............. 4:58.8
1928—United States .............. 4:47.6
1932—United States .............. 4:38.0
1936—Holland .................... 4:36.0
1948—United States .............. 4:29.2
1952—Hungary .................... 4:24.4
1956—Australia .................. 4:17.1
1960—United States .............. 4:08.9
1964—United States .............. 4:03.8 *
1968—United States .............. 4:02.5
1972—United States .............. 3:55.19*

## 100-METER BACKSTROKE
1924—Sybil Bauer, United States .... 1:23.2
1928—Marie Braun, Holland ........ 1:22.0
1932—Eleanor Holm, United States ... 1:19.4
1936—Dina Senff, Holland ......... 1:18.9
1948—Karen Harup, Denmark ...... 1:14.4
1952—Joan Harrison, South Africa .... 1:14.3
1956—J. Grinham, Great Britain ..... 1:12.9
1960—Lynn Burke, United States .... 1:09.3
1964—Cathy Ferguson, United States . 1:07.7 *
1968—Kaye Hall, United States ..... 1:06.2
1972—Melissa Belote, United States 1:05.78*

## 200-METER BACKSTROKE
1968—Lillian (Pokey) Watson, United States ........... 2:24.8
1972—Melissa Belote, United States 2:19.19*

## 100-METER BREASTSTROKE
1968—Djurdjica Bjedov, Yugoslavia .. 1:15.8
1972—Catherine Carr, United States 1:13.58*

## 200-METER BREAST STROKE
1924—Lucy Morton, Great Britain ..... 3:33.2
1928—Hilde Schrader, Germany ...... 3:12.6
1932—Clare Dennis, Australia ...... 3:06.3
1936—Hideko Maehata, Japan ...... 3:03.6
1948—Nel Van Vliet, Netherlands .... 2:57.2
1952—Eva Szekely, Hungary ........ 2:51.7
1956—U. Happe, Germany ......... 2:53.1
1960—Anita Lonsbrough, Great Britain 2:49.5
1964—Galina Prozumenschikova, U.S.S.R. .................. 2:46.4 *
1968—Sharon Wichman, United States 2:44.4
1972—Beverly Whitfield, Australia .. 2:41.71*

## 200-METER BUTTERFLY
1968—Ada Kok, Netherlands ...... 2:24.7
1972—Karen Moe, United States ... 2:15.57*

## 200-METER INDIVIDUAL MEDLEY
1968—Claudia Kolb, United States . 2:24.7
1972—Shane Gould, Australia ..... 2:23.07*

## 400-METER INDIVIDUAL MEDLEY
1964—Donna de Varona, United States 5:18.7
1968—Claudia Kolb, United States . 5:08.5
1972—Gail Neall, Australia ........ 5:02.97*

## 400-METER MEDLEY RELAY
1960—United States ............. 4:41.1
1964—United States ............. 4:33.9 *
1968—United States ............. 4:28.3
1972—United States ............. 4:20.75*

| SPRINGBOARD DIVING | Points |
| --- | --- |
| 1920—Aileen Riggin, United States | 539.90 |
| 1924—Elizabeth Becker, United States | 474.50 |
| 1928—Helen Meany, United States | 78.62 |
| 1932—Georgia Coleman, United States | 87.52 |
| 1936—Marjorie Gestring, United States | 89.27 |
| 1948—Victoria Draves, United States | 108.74 |
| 1952—Patricia McCormick, United States | 147.30 |
| 1956—Patricia McCormick, United States | 142.36 |
| 1960—Ingrid Kramer, Germany | 155.81 |
| 1964—Ingrid Engel-Kramer, Germany | 145.00 |
| 1968—Sue Gossick, United States | 150.77 |
| 1972—Capt. Micki King, USAF | 450.03 |

| HIGH DIVING | |
| --- | --- |
| 1912—Greta Johansson, Sweden | 39.90 |
| 1920—Stefani Fryland-Clausen, Denmark | 34.60 |
| 1924—Caroline Smith, United States | 33.20 |
| 1928—Elizabeth Pinkston, United States | 31.60 |
| 1932—Dorothy Poynton, United States | 40.26 |
| 1936—Dorothy Poynton Hill, United States | 33.93 |
| 1948—Victoria Draves, United States | 68.87 |
| 1952—Patricia McCormick, United States | 79.37 |
| 1956—Patricia McCormick, United States | 84.85 |
| 1960—Ingrid Kramer, Germany | 91.28 |
| 1964—Lesley Bush, United States | 99.80 |
| 1968—Milena Duchkova, Czechoslovakia | 109.59 |
| 1972—Ulrike Knape, Sweden | 390.00 |

## VOLLEYBALL

| | Men | Women |
| --- | --- | --- |
| 1964 | U.S.S.R. | Japan |
| 1968 | U.S.S.R. | U.S.S.R. |
| 1972 | Japan | U.S.S.R. |

## WATER POLO

| | |
| --- | --- |
| 1900—Great Britain | 1936—Hungary |
| 1904—United States | 1948—Italy |
| 1908—Great Britain | 1952—Hungary |
| 1912—Great Britain | 1956—Hungary |
| 1920—Great Britain | 1960—Italy |
| 1924—France | 1964—Hungary |
| 1928—Germany | 1968—Yugoslavia |
| 1932—Hungary | 1972—U.S.S.R. |

## WEIGHT-LIFTING

### FLYWEIGHT
1972—Zygmunt Smalcerz, Poland .. 745.000*

| BANTAMWEIGHT | Pounds |
| --- | --- |
| 1948—Joe N. DePietro, United States | 677.915 |
| 1952—Ivan Udovov, U.S.S.R. | 694 |

1956—Charles Vinci, United States ... 754½
1960—Charles Vinci, United States .. 760
1964—Aleksei Vakhonin, U.S.S.R. ... 788.15
1968—Mohammed Nassiri Seresht,
    Iran ................. 808.500
1972—Imre Foldi, Hungary ....... 833.000*

**FEATHERWEIGHT**         **Pounds**
1920—L. de Haes, Belgium........ 485
1924—Paolo Gabetti, Italy......... 887.35
1928—Franz Andrysek, Austria...... 633.822
1932—Raymond Suvigny, France.... 633.822
1936—Anthony Terlazzo, United States 688.937
1948—Mahmoud Fayad, Egypt...... 733.02
1952—Rafael Chimishyan, U.S.S.R.... 743½
1956—Isaac Berger, United States.... 776¾
1960—Evgeni Minaev, U.S.S.R...... 821
1964—Yoshinobu Miyake, Japan..... 875.5
1968—Yoshinobu Miyake, Japan ... 863.500
1972—Norair Nourikian, Bulgaria ... 888.000*

**LIGHTWEIGHT**
1920—Alfred Neyland, Estonia....... 567.68
1924—Edmond Decottignies, France... 970.02
1928—Kurt Helbig, Germany, and
    Hans Hass, Austria ....... 710.98
1932—Rene Duverger, France....... 716.495
1936—Mohammed Mesbah, Egypt.... 755.085
1948—Ibrahim Shams, Egypt....... 793.656
1952—Tommy Kono, United States ... 798¾
1956—Igors Rybak, U.S.S.R....... 837
1960—Viktor Bushuev, U.S.S.R....... 876
1964—Waldemar Baszanowski, Poland 951.5
1968—Waldemar Baszanowski, Poland 962.500
1972—Mukharbi Kirzhinov, U.S.S.R. 1,014.000*

**MIDDLEWEIGHT**
1920—B. Gance, France ......... 540.012
1924—Carlo Galimberti, Italy....... 1085.725
1928—Francois Roger, France...... 738.54
1932—Rudolf Ismayr, Germany..... 760.507
1936—Khadr El Touni, Egypt...... 854.28
1948—Frank Spellman, United States.. 859.794
1952—Peter George, United States ... 881½
1956—F. Bogdanovskii, U.S.S.R..... 925½
1960—Alexander Kurynov, U.S.S.R.... 964¼
1964—Hans Zdrazila, Czechoslovakia.. 979
1968—Viktor Kurentsov, U.S.S.R. .. 1,045.000
1972—Yordan Bikov, Bulgaria .... 1,069.000*

**LIGHT-HEAVYWEIGHT**
1920—E. Cadine, France........... 639.334
1924—Charles Rigoulot, France...... 1107.811
1928—Saied Nosseir, Egypt........ 782.63
1932—Louis Hostin, France........ 804.679
1936—Louis Hostin, France........ 821.213
1948—Stanley Stanczyk, United States 920.42
1952—Trofim Lomakin, U.S.S.R..... 920¼
1956—Tommy Kono, United States ... 986¼
1960—Ireneusz Palinski, Poland..... 975¼
1964—Rudolf Plyukfeider, U.S.S.R..... 1045
1968—Boris Selitsky, U.S.S.R. .... 1,067.000
1972—Leif Jenssen, Norway ...... 1,118.000*

**MIDDLE-HEAVYWEIGHT**
1952—Norbert Schemansky,
    United States ........... 980¾
1956—A. Vorobiev, U.S.S.R........ 1019¼
1960—Arkady Vorobiev, U.S.S.R...... 1041¼
1964—Vladimir Golovanov, U.S.S.R.... 1072.5
1968—Kaarlo Kangasniemi, Finland 1,138.500*
1972—Andon Nikolov, Bulgaria ... 1,157.000*

**HEAVYWEIGHT**
1920—Filippo Bottini, Italy ........ 595.24
1924—Giuseppe Tonani, Italy........ 1140.879
1928—Joseph Strassberger, Germany 821.213
1932—Jaroslaw Skobla, Czechoslovakia 837.748
1936—Joseph Manger, Germany..... 903.886
1948—John Davis, United States .... 997.581
1952—John Davis, United States .... 1013¾
1956—Paul E. Anderson, United States 1102
1960—Yuriy Vlasov, U.S.S.R......... 1184¼

1964—Leonid Zhabotinsky, U.S.S.R. ...1259.5
1968—Leonid Zhabotinsky, U.S.S.R. 1,259.500
1972—Yan Talts, U.S.S.R. ....... 1,278.000*

**SUPER HEAVYWEIGHT**
1972—Vassili Alexeev, U.S.S.R. ... 1,411.000*


# WRESTLING
## FREE STYLE

**PAPERWEIGHT**
1972—Roman Dimtriev, U.S.S.R.

**FLYWEIGHT**
1948—Lennart Viitala, Finland
1952—Hasan Gemici, Turkey
1956—Marian Tzalkalmanidze, U.S.S.R.
1960—Ahmet Bilek, Turkey
1964—Yoshoikatsu Yoshida, Japan
1968—Shigeo Nakata, Japan
1972—Kiyomi Kato, Japan

**BANTAMWEIGHT**
1908—George N. Mehnert, United States
1924—Kustaa Pihlajamaki, Finland
1928—Kaarie Makinen, Finland
1932—Robert E. Pearce, United States
1936—Odon Zombori, Hungary
1948—Nasuch Akar, Turkey
1952—Shohachi Ishii, Japan
1956—Mustafa Dagistanli, Turkey
1960—Terrence McCann, United States
1964—Yojiro Uetake, Japan
1968—Yojiro Uetake, Japan
1972—Hideaki Yanagida, Japan

**FEATHERWEIGHT**
1908—George S. Dole, United States
1920—Charles E. Acklerly, United States
1924—Robin Reed, United States
1928—Allie Morrison, United States
1932—Herman Pihlajamaki, Finland
1936—Kustaa Pihlajamaki, Finland
1948—Ganzanfer Bilge, Turkey
1952—Bayram Sit, Turkey
1956—Shozo Sasahara, Japan
1960—Mustafa Daginstanii, Turkey
1964—Osamu Watanabe, Japan
1968—Masaaki Kaneko, Japan
1972—Zegalav Abdulbekov, U.S.S.R.

**LIGHTWEIGHT**
1908—G. de Relwyskow, Great Britain
1920—Kalle Antilla, Finland
1924—Russell Vis, United States
1928—Osvald Kapp, Estonia
1932—Charles Pacome, France
1936—Karoly Karpati, Hungary
1948—Celal Atik, Turkey
1952—Olle Anderberg, Sweden
1956—Emmali Habibi, Iran
1960—Shelby Wilson, United States
1964—Enio Dimov, Bulgaria
1968—Abdollah Movahed, Iran
1972—Dan Gable, United States

**WELTERWEIGHT**
1924—Hermann Gehri, Switzerland
1928—Arve Haavisto, Finland
1932—Jack F. Van Bebber, United States
1936—Frank Lewis, United States
1948—Yasar Dogu, Turkey
1952—William Smith, United States
1956—Mitsuo Ikeda, Japan
1960—Douglas Blubaugh, United States
1964—Ismail Ogan, Turkey
1968—Mahmud Atalay, Turkey
1972—Wayne Wells, United States

**MIDDLEWEIGHT**
1908—Stanley Bacon, Great Britain

1920—Eino Leino, Finland
1924—Fritz Haggmann, Switzerland
1928—Ernst Kyburz, Switzerland
1932—Ivar Johansson, Sweden
1936—Emile Poilve, France
1948—Glen Brand, United States
1952—David Cimakuridze, U.S.S.R.
1956—Nikola Nikolov, Bulgaria
1960—Hasan Gungor, Turkey
1964—Prodan Goardjev, Bulgaria
1968—Boris Gurevitch, U.S.S.R.
1972—Levan Tediashvili, U.S.S.R.

**LIGHT-HEAVYWEIGHT**
1920—Anders Larsson, Sweden
1924—John Spellman, United States
1928—Thure Sjostedt, Sweden
1932—Peter J. Mehringer, United States
1936—Knut Fridell, Sweden
1948—Henry Wittenberg, United States
1952—Wiking Palm, Sweden
1956—Gholam Takhti, Iran
1960—Ismet Atli, Turkey
1964—Alexandr Medved, U.S.S.R.
1968—Ahmet Ayuk, Turkey
1972—Ben Peterson, United States

**HEAVYWEIGHT**
1908—G. C. O'Kelly, Great Britain
1920—Robert Roth, Switzerland
1924—Harry Steele, United States
1928—John C. Richthoff, Sweden
1932—John C. Richthoff, Sweden
1936—Kristjan Palusalu, Estonia
1948—Gyula Bobis, Hungary
1952—Arsen Mekokishvili, U.S.S.R.
1956—Hamid Kaplan, Turkey
1960—Wilfried Dietrich, Germany
1964—Alexandr Ivanitsky, U.S.S.R.
1968—Aleksandr Medved, U.S.S.R.
1972—Ivan Yarygin, U.S.S.R.

**SUPER-HEAVYWEIGHT**
1972—Aleksandr Medved, U.S.S.R.


# WRESTLING
## GRECO-ROMAN STYLE

**PAPERWEIGHT**
1972—Gheorghe Berceanu, Rumania

**FLYWEIGHT**
1948—Pietro Lombardi, Italy
1952—Boris Gourevitch, U.S.S.R.
1956—Nikolai Soloviev, U.S.S.R.
1960—Dumitru Pirvulescu, Rumania
1964—Tsutomu Hanahara, Japan
1968—Petar Kirov, Bulgaria
1972—Peter Kirov, Bulgaria

**BANTAMWEIGHT**
1924—Edward Puttsepp, Esthonia
1928—Karl Leucht, Germany
1932—Jakob Brendel, Germany
1936—Marton Lorincz, Hungary
1948—Kurt Petersen, Sweden
1952—Imre Hodos, Hungary
1956—Konstantin Vyropaev, U.S.S.R.
1960—Oleg Karavaev, U.S.S.R.
1964—Masamitsu Ichiguchi, Japan
1968—Janos Varga, Hungary
1972—Rustem Kazakov, U.S.S.R.

**FEATHERWEIGHT**
1912—Kalle Koskelo, Finland
1920—Oskari Friman, Finland
1924—Kalle Anttila, Finlánd
1928—Voldemar Wali, Esthonia
1932—Giovanni Gozzi, Italy
1936—Yasar Erkan, Turkey
1948—Mohammed Oktav, Turkey
1952—Yakov Punkin, U.S.S.R.

1956—Rauno Makinen, Finland
1960—Muzahir Sille, Turkey
1964—Imre Polyak, Hungary
1968—Roman Rurua, U.S.S.R.
1972—Gheorghi Markov, Bulgaria

## LIGHTWEIGHT

1906—Watzl, Austria
1908—E. Porro, Italy
1912—Emil Ware, Finland
1920—Emil Ware, Finland
1924—Oskari Friman, Finland
1928—Lajos Keresztes, Hungary
1932—Eric Malmberg, Sweden
1936—Lauri Koskela, Finland
1948—Karl Freij, Sweden
1952—Chasame Safine, U.S.S.R.
1956—Kyosti Lehtonen, Finland
1960—Avtandil Kordidze, U.S.S.R.
1964—Kazim Ayvaz, Turkey
1968—Muneji Mumemura, Japan
1972—Shamil Khisamutdinov, U.S.S.R.

## WELTERWEIGHT

1932—Ivar Johansson, Sweden
1936—Rudolf Svedberg, Sweden
1948—Gosta Andersson, Sweden
1952—Miklos Szilvasi, Hungary
1956—Mithat Bayrak, Turkey
1960—Mithat Bayrak, Turkey
1964—Anatoly Kolesov, U.S.S.R.
1968—Rudolph Vesper, East Germany
1972—Vitezslav Macha, Czechoslovakia

## MIDDLEWEIGHT

1906—Weckmann, Finland
1908—Fritjof Martenson, Sweden
1912—Claes Johansson, Sweden
1920—Carl Westergren, Sweden
1924—Edward Westerlund, Finland
1928—Vaino A. Kokkinen, Finland
1932—Vaino A. Kokkinen, Finland
1936—Ivar Johansson, Sweden
1948—Axel Gronberg, Sweden
1952—Axel Gronberg, Sweden
1956—Guivi Kartozia, U.S.S.R.
1960—Dimitro Dobrev, Bulgaria
1964—Branislav Simic, Yugoslavia
1968—Lothar Metz, East Germany

1972—Csaba Hegedus, Hungary

## LIGHT-HEAVYWEIGHT

1908—Verner Weckmann, Finland
1912—Anders Ahlgren, Sweden, and
　　　Ivar Boling, Finland
1920—Claes Johansson, Sweden
1924—Carl Westergren, Sweden
1928—Ibrahim Moustafa, Egypt
1932—Rudolf Svensson, Sweden
1936—Axel Cadier, Sweden
1948—Karl Nilsson, Sweden
1952—Kaelpo Grondahl, Finland
1956—V. Nikolaev, U.S.S.R.
1960—Tevfik Kis, Turkey
1964—Boyan Alexanirov, Bulgaria
1968—Boyan Radev, Bulgaria
1972—Valeri Rezantsev, U.S.S.R.

## HEAVYWEIGHT

1896—Karl Schumann, Germany
1906—S. Jensen, Denmark
1908—Richard Weisz, Hungary
1912—Yrjo Saarela, Finland
1920—Adolf Lindfors, Finland
1924—Henri Deglane, France
1928—Rudolph Svensson, Sweden
1932—Carl Westergren, Sweden
1936—Kristjan Palusalu, Esthonia
1948—Ahmed Kirecci, Turkey
1952—Johannes Kotkas, U.S.S.R.
1956—Anatolii Parfenov, U.S.S.R.
1960—Ivan Bogdan, U.S.S.R.
1964—Istvan Kozma, Hungary
1968—Istvan Kozma, Hungary
1972—Nicolae Martinescu, Rumania

## SUPER-HEAVYWEIGHT

1972—Anatoly Roshin, U.S.S.R.


# YACHTING
### SKIPPER (YACHT NAME) NATION

## 5.5-METER CLASS

1952—Dr. Britton Chance (COMPLEX II)
　　　United States
1956—Skipper not listed (RUSH V) Sweden
1960—George O'Day (MINOTAUR) United States

1964—James Sargeant (BARRANJOEY) Australia
1968—Ulf Sundelin (WASA IV) Sweden

## STAR CLASS

1932—Gilbert Gray (JUPITER) United States
1936—Dr. Peter Bischoff (WANNESEE) Germany
1948—Hilary Smart (HILARIUS) United States
1952—Agosto Straulino (MEROPE) Italy
1956—Herbert Williams (KATHLEEN)
　　　United States
1960—Timir Pinegin (TORNADO) U.S.S.R.
1964—Durward Knowles (GEM) Bahamas
1968—Lowell North (NORTH STAR)
　　　United States
1972—David Forbes (SIMBA V) Australia

## FINN MONOTYPE CLASS

1952—Paul Elvstrom, Denmark
1956—Paul Elvstrom, Denmark
1960—Paul Elvstrom, Denmark
1964—Wilhelm Kuhweide, Germany
1968—Valentin Alentin, U.S.S.R.
1972—Serge Maury, France

## DRAGON CLASS

1948—Thor Thorvaldsen (PAN) Norway
1952—Thor Thorvaldsen (PAN) Norway
1956—Skipper not listed (SLAGHOKEN II)
　　　Sweden
1960—Constantino di Grecia (NIREFS) Greece
1964—O. V. H. Berntsen (WHITE LADY) Denmark
1968—George Frederichs (WILLIWAW)
　　　United States
1972—John Bruce (WYUANA) Australia

## SOLING CLASS

1972—Harry Melges (TEAL) United States

## FLYING-DUTCHMAN CLASS

1960—Peder Lunde (SIRENE) Norway
1964—Earle Wells (PANDORA) New Zealand
1968—Rodney Pattisson (SUPER-
　　　CALIFRAGISTICEXPIALIDOCIOUS)
　　　Great Britain
1972—Rodney Pattisson, Christopher Davies,
　　　Great Britain

## TEMPEST CLASS

1972—Valentin Mankin (ESKIMO II) U.S.S.R.

# WINTER GAMES

## BIATHLON
### (Skiing and Shooting)

**INDIVIDUAL** — Hr.-Min.-Sec.
1960—Klas Lestander, Sweden . . . . . 1:33:21.6
1964—Vladimir Melanin, U.S.S.R. . . . 1:20:26.8
1968—Magnar Solberg, Norway . . . 1:13:45.9
1972—Magnar Solberg, Norway . . . 1:15:55.50

**40 KILOMETER RELAY**
1968—U.S.S.R. . . . . . . . . . . . . . 2:13:02.4
1972—U.S.S.R. . . . . . . . . . . . . . 1:51:44.92

## BOBSLED

**4-MAN BOB** — Min.-Sec.
1924—Switzerland (Edward Scherrer) . . 5:45.54
1928—United States (William Fiske) . . 3:20.5
1932—United States (William Fiske) . . 7:53.68
1936—Switzerland (Pierre Musy) . . . . 5:19.85
1948—United States (Edward Rimkus) . . 5:20.1
1952—Germany (Andreas Ostler) . . . . 5:07.84
1956—Switzerland (Franz Kapus) . . . . 5:10.44
1964—Canada (Victor Emery) . . . . . . . . 4:14.46
1968—Italy (Monti, De Paolis,
Zandonella, Armano) . . . . . . 2:17.39
(only 2 races instead of usual 4)
1972—Switzerland (Jean Wicki, Hans
Leutenegger, Werner Camichel,
Edy Hubacher) . . . . . . . . . . . 4:43.07

**2-MAN BOB**
1932—United States (Hubert Stevens) . . 8:14.74
1936—United States (Ivan Brown) . . . . 5:29.29
1948—Switzerland (Endrich) . . . . . . . . 5:29.2
1952—Germany (Andreas Ostler) . . . . . 5:24.54
1956—Italy (Dalla Costa) . . . . . . . . . 5:30.14
1964—Great Britain (Antony Nash) . . . . 4:21.90
1968—Italy (Monti, De Paolis) . . . . . . 4:41.54
1972—West Germany (Wolfgang
Zimmerer, Peter
Utzschneider) . . . . . . . . . . . 4:57.07

**SKELETON**
1928—James Heaton, United States . . . 3:01.8
1948—Nino Bibbia, Italy . . . . . . . . 5:23.2

## TOBOGGANING (LUGE)

**SINGLE SEATER—MEN** — Min.-Sec.
1964—Thomas Koehler, Germany . . . . 3:26.77
1968—Manfred Schmid, Austria . . . . . 2:52.48
1972—Wolfgang Scheidel, East Germany 3:27.58

**SINGLE SEATER—WOMEN**
1964—Otrum Enderlein, Germany . . . . 3:24.67
1968—Erica Lechner, Italy . . . . . . . . 2:28.66
1972—Anna Maria Muller, East Germany 2:59.18

**TWO SEATER—MEN**
1964—Austria . . . . . . . . . . . . . . 1:41.62
1968—East Germany . . . . . . . . . . . 1:35.85
1972—Italy and East Germany . . . . . 1:28.35

## FIGURE SKATING
(Note—Scoring systems have varied with the Games.)

**MEN'S SINGLES** — Points
1908—Ulrich, Sweden . . . . . . . . . . 2,641.00
1920—Gillis Grafstrom, Sweden . . . . 2,838.50
1924—Gillis Grafstrom, Sweden . . . . 2,575.25
1928—Gillis Grafstrom, Sweden . . . . 2,698.25
1932—Karl Schaefer, Austria . . . . . . 2,602.00
1936—Karl Schaefer, Austria . . . . . . 2,959.00
1948—Richard T. Button, United States 191.177
1952—Richard T. Button, United States 192.256
1956—Hayes Alan Jenkins,
United States . . . . . . . . . . . 166.430
1960—David W. Jenkins, United States 1,440.2
1964—Manfred Schnelldorfer,
Germany . . . . . . . . . . . . . . 1,916.9
1968—Wolfgang Schwarz, Austria . . . 1,904.10
1972—Ondrej Nepela, Czechoslovakia 2,739.10

**WOMEN'S SINGLES**
1908—Madge Syers, Great Britain . . . 1,767.50
1920—Madam Julin, Sweden . . . . . . . 1,278.90
1924—Mrs. Herma von Szabo-Planck,
Austria . . . . . . . . . . . . . . . 2,094.25
1928—Sonja Henie, Norway . . . . . . . 2,452.25
1932—Sonja Henie, Norway . . . . . . . 2,302.50
1936—Sonja Henie, Norway . . . . . . . 2,971.40
1948—Barbara Ann Scott, Canada . . . 163.077
1952—Jeannette Altwegg,
Great Britain . . . . . . . . . . . 161.756
1956—Tenley E. Albright,
United States . . . . . . . . . . . 169.670
1960—Carol Heiss, United States . . . . 1,490.1
1964—Sjoukje Dijkstra, Netherlands . . 2,018.5
1968—Peggy Gale Fleming,
United States . . . . . . . . . . . 1,970.50
1972—Beatrix Schuba, Austria . . . . . 2,751.50

**PAIRS**
1908—Miss Hubler and H. Burger,
Germany . . . . . . . . . . . . . . 78.40
1920—Mr. & Mrs. Jacobsson, Finland . . 80.70
1924—Helen Engelman and A. Berger,
Austria . . . . . . . . . . . . . . . 74.50
1928—Andree Joly and Pierre Brunet,
France . . . . . . . . . . . . . . . 78.20
1932—Andree and Pierre Brunet, France 76.70
1936—Maxie Herber and Ernst Baier,
Germany . . . . . . . . . . . . . . 103.30
1948—Micheline Lannoy and Pierre
Baugniet, Belgium . . . . . . . . 11.227
1952—Ria and Paul Falk, Germany . . . 11.400
1956—Elizabeth Schwarz and Kurt
Oppelt, Austria . . . . . . . . . . 11.310
1960—Barbara A. Wagner and Robert
Paul, Canada . . . . . . . . . . . 80.4
1964—Ludmilla Belousova and Oleg
Protopopov, U.S.S.R. . . . . . . 104.4
1968—Ludmilla Belousova and
Oleg Protopopov, U.S.S.R. . . . 315.20
1972—Irina Rodnina and Alexei
Ulanov, U.S.S.R. . . . . . . . . 420.40

## ICE HOCKEY

1920—CANADA . . . . . . . . . . . . . . . (W-3 L-0)*
1924—CANADA . . . . . . . . . . . . . . . (W-2 L-0)*
1928—CANADA . . . . . . . . . . . . . . . (W-3 L-0)*
1932—CANADA . . . . . . . . . . . . . . . (W-5 L-0 T-1)*
1936—GREAT BRITAIN . . . . . . . (W-2 L-0 T-1)*
1948—CANADA . . . . . . . . . . . . . . . (W-7 L-0 T-1)*
1952—CANADA . . . . . . . . . . . . . . . (W-7 L-0 T-1)*
1956—U.S.S.R. . . . . . . . . . . . . . . (W-5 L-0)*
1960—UNITED STATES . . . . . . . . . (W-5 L-0)*
1964—U.S.S.R. . . . . . . . . . . . . . . (W-7 L-0)*
1968—U.S.S.R.
1972—U.S.S.R.
* Championship final round standings.

## SKIING—ALPINE

**MEN'S DOWNHILL** — Min.-Sec.
1948—Henry Oreiller, France . . . . . . 2:55.0
1952—Zeno Colo, Italy . . . . . . . . . . 2:30.8
1956—Anton Sailer, Austria . . . . . . 2:52.2
1960—Jean Vuarnet, France . . . . . . . 2:06.0
1964—Egon Zimmerman, Austria . . . . 2:18.16
1968—Jean Claude Killy, France . . . . 1:59.85
1972—Bernhard Russi, Switzerland . . . 1:51.43

**MEN'S GIANT SLALOM**
1952—Stein Eriksen, Norway . . . . . . 2:25.0
1956—Anton Sailer, Austria . . . . . . 3:00.1
1960—Roger Staub, Switzerland . . . . 1:48.3
1964—François Bonlieu, France . . . . . 1:46.71
1968—Jean Claude Killy, France . . . . 3:29.28
1972—Gustavo Thoeni, Italy . . . . . . 3:09.62

**MEN'S SLALOM** — Min.-Sec.
1948—Edi Reinalter, Switzerland . . . . 2:10.3
1952—Othmar Schneider, Austria . . . . 2:00.0
1956—Anton Sailer, Austria . . . . . . *194.7 pts.
1960—Ernst Hinterseer, Austria . . . . 2:08.9
1964—Pepi Steigler, Austria . . . . . . 131.13
1968—Jean Claude Killy, France . . . . 1:39.73
1972—Francesco Fernandez Ochoa,
Spain . . . . . . . . . . . . . . . 1:49.27
* Scoring system changed in 1956 and 1964.

**ALPINE COMBINATION—DOWNHILL
AND SLALOM** — Points
1936—Franz Pfnur, Germany . . . . . . 99.25
1948—Henri Oreiller, France . . . . . . 3.27

**WOMEN'S DOWNHILL** — Min.-Sec.
1948—Hedi Schlunegger, Switzerland . . 2:28.3
1952—Trude Jochum-Beiser, Austria . . 1:47.1
1956—Madeleine Berthod, Switzerland . 1:40.7
1960—Heidi Biebl, Germany . . . . . . 1:37.6
1964—Christi Haas, Austria . . . . . . 1:55.39
1968—Olga Pall, Austria . . . . . . . . 1:40.87
1972—Marie-Therese Nadig,
Switzerland . . . . . . . . . . . . 1:36.68

**WOMEN'S GIANT SLALOM**
1952—Andrea Mead Lawrence,
United States . . . . . . . . . . . 2:06.8
1956—Ossi Reichert, Germany . . . . . 1:56.5
1960—Yvonne Ruegg, Switzerland . . . 1:39.9
1964—Marielle Goitschel, France . . . . 1:52.24
1968—Nancy Greene, Canada . . . . . 1:51.97
1972—Marie-Therese Nadig,
Switzerland . . . . . . . . . . . . 1:29.90

**WOMEN'S SLALOM**
1948—Gretchen Fraser, United States . . 1:57.2
1952—Andrea Mead Lawrence,
United States . . . . . . . . . . . 2:10.6
1956—Renee Colliard, Switzerland . . *112.3 pts.
1960—Anne Heggtveigt, Canada . . . . 1:49.6
1964—Marielle Goitschel, France . . . . 89.86
1968—Marielle Goitschel, France . . . . 1:25.86
1972—Barbara Cochran, United States . 1:31.24
* Scoring system changed in 1956 and 1964.

**ALPINE COMBINATION—DOWNHILL
AND SLALOM** — Points
1936—Christel Cranz, Germany . . . . . 97.06
1948—Trude Beiser, Austria . . . . . . 6.58

## SKIING—NORDIC

**MEN'S 18-KILOMETER CROSS-COUNTRY**
1924—Thorlief Haug, Norway . . . . . . 1:14:31.0
1928—Johan Grottumsbraaten,
Norway . . . . . . . . . . . . . . *1:37:01.0
1932—Sven Utterstrom, Sweden . . **1:23:07.0
1936—Erik-August Larsson, Sweden . . 1:14:38.0
1948—Martin Lundstroem, Sweden . . 1:13:50.0
1952—Hallgeir Brenden, Norway . . . . 1:01:34.0
* 19,700-meter course.
** 18,214-meter course.

**MEN'S 15-KILOMETER CROSS-COUNTRY** — Hr.-Min.-Sec.
1956—Hallgeir Brenden, Norway . . . . 0:49:39.0
1960—Hakon Brusveen, Norway . . . . 0:51:55.5

1964—Eero Mantyranta, Finland . . . . . .0:50.54.1
1968—Harold Groenningen, Norway . . 47:54.2
1972—Sven-Ake Lundback, Sweden . . 45:28.24

## MEN'S 30-KILOMETER CROSS-COUNTRY
1956—Veikko Hakulinen, Finland . . . . 1:44:06.0
1960—Sixten Jernberg, Sweden . . . . . 1:51:03.9
1964—Eero Mantyranta, Finland . . . . .1:30:50.7
1968—Franco Nones, Italy . . . . . . 1:35:39.2
1972—Vatscheslav Vedenin, U.S.S.R. 1:36:31.15

## MEN'S 50-KILOMETER CROSS-COUNTRY
1924—Thorlief Haug, Norway . . . . . 3:44:32.0
1928—Per E. Hedlund, Sweden . . . . . 4:52:03.0
1932—Veli Saarinen, Finland . . . . . . *4:28:00.0
1936—Elis Viklund, Sweden . . . . . . . . 3:30:11.0
1948—Nils Karlsson, Sweden . . . . . 3:47:48.0
1952—Veikko Haukulinen, Finland . . 3:33:33.0
1956—Sixten Jernberg, Sweden . . . . 2:50:27.0
1960—Kalevi Hamalainen, Finland . . 2:59:06.3
1964—Sixten Jernberg, Sweden . . . . 2:43:52.6
1968—Ole Ellefsaeter, Norway . . . . 2:28:45.8
1972—Paal Tyldum, Norway . . . . . . 2:43:14.75
* 48,238-meter course.

## MEN'S 40-KILOMETER CROSS-COUNTRY RELAY
1936—Finland . . . . . . . . . . . . . . . 2:41:33.0
1948—Sweden . . . . . . . . . . . . . . . 2:32:08.0
1952—Finland . . . . . . . . . . . . . . . 2:20:16.0
1956—U.S.S.R. . . . . . . . . . . . . . . . 2:15:30.0
1960—Finland . . . . . . . . . . . . . . . 2:18:45.6
1964—Sweden . . . . . . . . . . . . . . . 2:18:34.6
1968—Norway . . . . . . . . . . . . . . . 2:08:33.5
1972—U.S.S.R. . . . . . . . . . . . . . . . 2:04:47.94

## MEN'S NORDIC COMBINED (15 KM. CROSS-COUNTRY & JUMPING)    Points
1924—Thorlief Haug, Norway . . . . . . . 453.800
1928—Johan Grottumsbraaten, Norway 427.800
1932—Johan Grottumsbraaten, Norway 446.200
1936—Oddbjorn Hagen, Norway . . . . . 430.300
1948—Heikki Hasu, Finland . . . . . . . . 448.800
1952—Simon Slattvik, Norway . . . . . . 451.621
1956—Sverre Stenersen, Norway . . . . 455.000
1960—Georg Thoma, Germany . . . . . . 457.952
1964—Tormod Knutsen, Norway . . . . . 469.28
1968—Franz Keller, West Germany . . 449.040
1972—Ulrich Wehling, East Germany . . 413.340

## WOMEN'S NORDIC SKIING (5 KILOMETER CROSS COUNTRY    Min.-Sec.
1964—Klaudia Boyarskikh, U.S.S.R. . . 16:45.2
1968—Toini Gustafsson, Sweden . . . . 16:45.2
1972—Galina Kulakova, U.S.S.R. . . . . 17:00.50

## WOMEN'S 10-KILOMETER CROSS-COUNTRY
Min.-Sec.
1952—Lydia Wideman, Finland . . . . . . .41:40.0
1956—Ljubovj Kozyreva, U.S.S.R. . . . . . .38:11.0

1960—Marija Gusakova, U.S.S.R. . . . . .39:46.6
1964—Claudia Boyarski, U.S.S.R. . . . . . .40:24.3
1968—Toini Gustafsson, Sweden . . . . . 36:46.5
1972—Galina Kulakova, U.S.S.R. . . . . 34:17.82

## WOMEN'S 15-KILOMETER CROSS-COUNTRY RELAY    Hr.-Min.-Sec.
1956—Finland . . . . . . . . . . . . . . . 1:09:01.0
1960—Sweden . . . . . . . . . . . . . . . 1:04:21.4
1964—U.S.S.R. . . . . . . . . . . . . . . . 0:59:20.2
1968—Norway . . . . . . . . . . . . . . . 57:30.0
1972—U.S.S.R. . . . . . . . . . . . . . . . 48.46.15

## SKI JUMPING    Points
1924—Jacob T. Thams, Norway . . . . . . . 227.5
1928—Alfred Andersen, Norway . . . . . . 230.5
1932—Birger Ruud, Norway . . . . . . . . . 228.0
1936—Birger Ruud, Norway . . . . . . . . . 232.0
1948—Petter Hugsted, Norway . . . . . . . 228.1
1952—A. Bergmann, Norway . . . . . . . . 226.0
1956—Antti Hyvarinen, Finland . . . . . . 227.0
1960—Helmut Recknagel, Germany . . . . 227.2
1964—Toralf Engan, Norway
            (90 Meter Special Jumping) . . . 230.70
1964—Veikko Kankkonen, Finland
            (70 Meter Special Jumping) . . . 229.90

## MEN'S SKI JUMPING (70 METERS)
1964—Veikko Kankkonen, Finland . . . .229.900
1968—Jiri Raska, Czechoslovakia . . . . .216.500
1972—Yukio Kasaya, Japan . . . . . . .244.200

## MEN'S SKI JUMPING (90 METERS)
1968—Vladimir Beloussov, U.S.S.R. . .231.300
1972—Wojciech Fortuna, Poland . . . . .219.900

# SPEED SKATING

## MEN'S 500 METERS    Min.-Sec.
1924—Charles Jewtraw, United States . . 0:44.0
1928—Clas Thunberg, Finland and
            Bernt Evensen, Norway (tied) . . 0:43.4
1932—John A. Shea, United States . . . . 0:43.4
1936—Ivar Ballangrud, Norway . . . . . . . 0:43.4
1948—Finn Helgesen, Norway . . . . . . . . 0:43.1
1952—Kenneth Henry, United States . . 0:43.2
1956—Evgeni Grishin, U.S.S.R. . . . . . . 0:40.2
1960—Evgeni Grishin, U.S.S.R. . . . . . . 0:40.2
1964—Richard McDermott, United States 0:40.1
1968—Erhard Keller, West Germany . . 0:40.3
1972—Erhard Keller, West Germany . . 0:39.44

## MEN'S 1,500 METERS
1924—Clas Thunberg, Finland . . . . . . . 2:20.8
1928—Clas Thunberg, Finland . . . . . . . 2:21.1
1932—John A. Shea, United States . . . . . 2:57.5
1936—Charles Mathisen, Norway . . . . . . 2:19.2
1948—Sverre Farstad, Norway . . . . . . . . 2:17.6
1952—Hjalmar Anderson, Norway . . . . . 2:20.4
1956—Evgeni Grishin, U.S.S.R. . . . . . . 2:08.6

1960—Edgar Roadaas, Norway . . . . . . . 2:10.4
1964—Ants Antson, U.S.S.R. . . . . . . . . 2:10.3
1968—Kees Verkerk, Netherlands . . . . 2.03.4
1972—Ard Schenk, Netheralnds . . . . . 2:02.96

## MEN'S 5,000 METERS
1924—Clas Thunberg, Finland . . . . . . . 8:39.0
1928—Ivar Ballangrud, Norway . . . . . . . 8:50.5
1932—Irving Jaffee, United States . . . . 9:40.8
1936—Ivar Ballangrud, Norway . . . . . . . 8:19.6
1948—Reidar Liaklev, Norway . . . . . . . . 8:29.4
1952—Hjalmar Anderson, Norway . . . . . 8:10.6
1956—Boris Shilkov, U.S.S.R. . . . . . . . . 7:48.7
1960—Viktor Kosichkin, U.S.S.R. . . . . . 7:51.3
1964—Knut Johannesen, Norway . . . . . 7:38.4
1968—F. Anton Maier, Norway . . . . . . . 7:22.4
1972—Ard Schenk, Netherlands . . . . . 7:23.61

## MEN'S 10,000 METERS
1924—Julien Skutnabb, Finland . . . . . . 18:04.8
1928—No decision, thawing of ice
(Note—Irving Jaffee, United States, had best time
    of 18:36.5)
1932—Irving Jaffee, United States . . . . . 19:13.6
1936—Ivar Ballangrud, Norway . . . . . . . 17:24.3
1948—Ake Seyffarth, Norway . . . . . . . . 17:26.3
1952—Hjalmar Anderson, Norway . . . . . 16:45.8
1956—Sigvard Ericsson, Sweden . . . . . 16:35.9
1960—Knut Johannesen, Norway . . . . . 15:46.6
1964—Jonny Nilsson, Sweden . . . . . . . 15:50.1
1968—Jonny Hoeglin, Sweden . . . . . . 15:23.6
1972—Ard Schenk, Netherlands . . . . 15:01.35

## WOMEN'S 500 METERS    Min.-Sec.
1932—Jean Wilson, Canada . . . . . . . . . . 0:58.0
1960—Helga Haase, Germany . . . . . . . . . 0:45.9
1964—Lidija Skoblikova, U.S.S.R. . . . . . 0:45.0
1968—Ludmila Titova, U.S.S.R. . . . . . . 0:46.1
1972—Anne Henning, United States . . 0:43.33

## WOMEN'S 1,000 METERS
1932—Elizabeth DuBois, United States . . 2:04.0
1960—Klara Guseva, U.S.S.R. . . . . . . . 1:34.1
1964—Lidija Skoblikova, U.S.S.R. . . . . . 1:33.2
1968—Carolina Geijssen, Netherlands . . 1:32.6
1972—Monika Pflug, West Germany . . 1:31.40

## WOMEN'S 1,500 METERS
1932—Kit Klein, United States . . . . . . . . 3:06.0
1960—Lidija Skoblikova, U.S.S.R. . . . . . . 2:52.2
1964—Lidija Skoblikova, U.S.S.R. . . . . . . 2:25.2
1968—Kaija Mustonen, Finland . . . . . . . 2:22.4
1972—Dianne Holum, United States . . 2:20.85

## WOMEN'S 3,000 METERS
1960—Lidija Skoblikova, U.S.S.R. . . . . . . 5:14.3
1964—Lidija Skoblikova, U.S.S.R. . . . . . . 5:14.9
1968—Johanna Schut, Netherlands . . 4:56.2
1972—Stien Baas-Kaiser, Netherlands . 4:52.14
Note—Women's events in 1932 were not considered official.

# DISCONTINUED EVENTS

## TRACK AND FIELD—MEN

**60-METER DASH** Sec.
1900—Alvin E. Kraenzlein, United States ... 7
1904—Archie Hahn, United States ........ 7

**5-MILE RUN** Min.-Sec.
1906—H. Hawtrey, Great Britain ..... 26:11.8
1908—Emil R. Voigt, Great Britain ... 25:11.2

**200-METER HURDLES** Sec.
1900—Alvin E. Kraenzlein, United States.. 25.4
1904—Harry L. Hillman, United States .. 24.6

**STEEPLECHASE** Min.-Sec.
1900—George W. Orton, United States 7:34.4
    (2,500 meters)
1900—John Rimmer, Great Britain ... 12:58.4
    (4,000 meters)
1904—James D. Lightbody,
    United States ............ 7:36.9
    (2,590 meters)
1908—A. Russell, Great Britain ...... 10:47.8
    (3,200 meters)

**3,000-METER TEAM RACE** Points
1908—Great Britain (4,828 meters) ...... 6
1912—United States ................. 9
1920—United States ................. 10
1924—Finland ..................... 8

**CROSS-COUNTRY, INDIVIDUAL** Min.-Sec.
1912—Hannes Kohlemainen, Finland.. 45:11.6
    (8,000 meters)
1920—Paavo Nurmi, Finland ....... 27:15
    (10,000 meters)
1924—Paavo Nurmi, Finland ....... 32:54.8
    (10,650 meters)

**CROSS-COUNTRY, TEAM** Points
1900—Great Britain (5,000 meters) ...... 26
1904—United States (6,437 meters) ..... 27
1912—Sweden (8,000 meters) ........ 10
1920—Finland (10,000 meters) ....... 10
1924—Finland (10,650 meters) ....... 11

**1,500-METER WALK** Min.-Sec.
1906—George V. Bonhag, United States 7:12.6

**3,000-METER WALK**
1920—Ugo Frigerio, Italy ......... 13:14.2

**3,500-METER WALK**
1908—George E. Larner, Great Britain .. 14:55

**10-MILE WALK** Hr.-Min.-Sec.
1908—George E. Larner, Great Britain 1:15:57.4

**10,000-METER WALK** Min.-Sec.
1912—G. H. Goulding, Canada ..... 46:28.4
1920—Ugo Frigerio, Italy .......... 48:06.2
1924—Ugo Frigerio, Italy .......... 47:49.0
1948—J. F. Mikaelsson, Sweden ..... 45:13.2
1952—J. F. Mikaelsson, Sweden ..... 45:02.8

**STANDING HIGH JUMP**
1900—Ray C. Ewry, United States.. 5' 5"
1904—Ray C. Ewry, United States.. 4' 11"
1906—Ray C. Ewry, United States.. 5' 1⅝"
1908—Ray C. Ewry, United States.. 5' 2"
1912—Platt Adams, United States.. 5' 4⅛"

**STANDING BROAD JUMP**
1900—Ray C. Ewry, United States.. 10' 6⅖"
1904—Ray C. Ewry, United States.. 11' 4⅞"
1906—Ray C. Ewry, United States.. 10' 10"
1908—Ray C. Ewry, United States.. 10' 11¼"
1912—Konstantin Tsicilitiras, Greece 11' ¼"

**STANDING HOP, STEP, AND JUMP**
1900—Ray C. Ewry, United States.. 34' 8½"
1904—Ray C. Ewry, United States.. 34' 7¼"

**16-LB. SHOT-PUT (BOTH HANDS)**
1912—Ralph Rose, United States ... 90' 10⁹⁄₁₆"

**56-LB. WEIGHT THROW**
1904—Etienne Desmarteau, Canada.. 34' 4"
1920—Pat J. McDonald,
    United States .......... 36' 11⅝"

**DISCUS THROW, GREEK STYLE**
1906—Werner Jarvinen, Finland ... 115' 4"
1908—Marty J. Sheridan,
    United States ........ 124' 8"

**DISCUS THROW (BOTH HANDS)**
1912—Armas Taipale, Finland.... 271' 1⅛"

**JAVELIN THROW, FREE STYLE**
1908—Erik Lemming, Sweden.... 178' 7½"

**JAVELIN THROW (BOTH HANDS)**
1912—Julius J. Saaristo, Finland.. 358' 11½"

**PENTATHLON** Points
1906—H. Mellander, Sweden ........... 24
1912—Ferdinand R. Bie, Norway ....... 16
1920—Eero R. Lehtonen, Finland........ 18
1924—Eero R. Lehtonen, Finland........ 14

**TUG OF WAR**
1900—United States
1904—United States
1906—Germany
1908—Great Britain
1912—Sweden
1920—Great Britain

## ARCHERY

**DOUBLE YORK ROUND—MEN** Points
1904—Phillips Bryant, United States.... 820
1908—W. Dodd, Great Britain.......... 815

**CONTINENTAL ROUND—MEN**
1908—E. G. Grisot, France............ 263

**NATIONAL ROUND—WOMEN**
1908—Miss Q. Newall, Great Britain.... 688

**FIXED BIRD TARGET—MEN, INDIVIDUAL**
1920—(Small Bird)—E. Van Meer, Belgium 11
1920—(Large Bird)—E. Clostens, Belgium 13

**TEAM**
1908—Small Bird—Belgium
1920—Large Bird—Belgium

**MOVING BIRD TARGET—MEN**
1920—(28 meters)—H. Van Innis, Belgium 144
1920—(33 meters)—H. Van Innis, Belgium 139
1920—(50 meters)—Louis Brule, France.. 134

**TEAM**
1920—(28 meters)—Netherlands....... 3087
1920—(33 meters)—Belgium.......... 2958
1920—(50 meters)—Belgium.......... 2698

**60- & 50-YARD INDIVIDUAL—WOMEN**
1920—Miss Q. Newall, Great Britain.... 132

**SHORT DISTANCE, AMERICAN ROUND—MEN**
1904—H. Taylor, United States........ 811

**LONG DISTANCE, DOUBLE YORK ROUND—MEN**
1904—Phillips Bryant, United States.... 820

**TEAM COMPETITION—MEN—60 YARDS**
1904—Robert Williams, William Thompson,
    L. W. Maxon, and Spencer (Wash-
    ington, D.C.), United States ... 1344

**SHORT DISTANCE, DOUBLE COLUMBIA ROUND—WOMEN**
1904—M. C. Howell, United States..... 867

**LONG DISTANCE, DOUBLE NATIONAL ROUND—WOMEN**
1904—M. C. Howell, United States..... 620

**TEAM COMPETITION—WOMEN—60-48-50 YARDS**
1904—M. C. Howell, H. C. Pollock, L.
    Woodruff, A. Taylor (Cincinnati
    A. C.), United States ......... 506

## CANOEING

**FOLDING KAYAK SINGLES—10,000 METERS** Min.-Sec.
1936—G. Hradetzky, Austria......... 50:01.2

**FOLDING KAYAK PAIRS—10,000 METERS**
1936—Sweden (Sven Johansson, Eric
    Bladstroem) ............ 45:48.9

**KAYAK SINGLES—10,000 METERS**
1936—Ernst Krebs, Germany ........ 46:01.6
1948—Gert Fredriksson, Sweden ..... 50:47.7
1952—Thorvald Stromberg, Finland ..47:22.8
1956—Gert Fredriksson, Sweden ..... 47:43.4

**KAYAK PAIRS—10,000 METERS**
1936—Germany (Paul Wevers, Ludwig
    Landen) ................ 41:45.0
1948—Sweden (Gunnar Akerlund, Hans
    Wetterstroem) ............ 46:09.4
1952—Finland (Kurt Wires, Yrjo
    Hietanen) ............... 44:21.3
1956—Hungary (Janos Uranyl, Laszle
    Fabian) ................ 43:37.0

**CANADIAN SINGLES—10,000 METERS**
1948—F. Capek, Czechoslovakia ..... 62:05.2
1952—Frank Havens, United States... 57:41.1
1956—Leon Rottman, Rumania ...... 56:41.0

**CANADIAN PAIRS—10,000 METERS**
1936—Czechoslovakia (Vaclav Mottle,
    Zdenek Skrdlant) ......... 50:33.5
1948—United States (Stephen Lysak,
    Stephen Macknowski) ...... 55:55.4
1952—France (Georges Turlier,
    Jean Laudet) ............ 54:08.3
1956—U.S.S.R. (Pavel Kharine,
    Gratsian Botev) .......... 54:02.4

## CYCLING

**333.3 METERS TIME TRIAL** Sec.
1896—Emile Masson, France........... 24
1906—Francesco Verri, Italy......... 22.8

**440-YARD SPRINT**
1904—Marcus Hurley, United States ..... 31.8

**ONE-THIRD MILE**
1904—Marcus Hurley, United States ..... 43.8

**660-YARD SPRINT**
1906—V. L. Johnson, Great Britain...... 51.2

**880 YARDS**                                    Min.-Sec.
1904—Marcus Hurley, United States .... 1:09.0

**ONE MILE**
1904—Marcus Hurley, United States .... 2:41.4

**5 KILOMETERS**
1906—Francesco Verri, Italy ......... 8:35
1908—Ben Jones, Great Britain ...... 8:36.2

**10 KILOMETERS**                                Min.-Sec.
1906—P. Mason, France .......... 17:54.2

**20 KILOMETERS**
1906—W. J. Pett, Great Britain .....29
1908—C. Kingsbury, Great Britain.... 34:13.6

**50 KILOMETERS**                           Hr.-Min.-Sec.
1920—H. George, Belgium....... 1:16:43.5
1924—J. Willems, Holland....... 1:18:25

**100 KILOMETERS**
1896—C. Flameng, France ....... 3:08:19.2
1908—C. Bartlett, Great Britain.... 2:41.48.6

**12-HOUR RACE**
1896—A. Schmall, Austria....... 314.997 km.

## FENCING

**Individual Swords**
1904—Ramon Fonst, Cuba

**Single Sticks**
1904—A. V. Z. Post, Cuba

**Three-Cornered Saber**
1906—Gustav Casmir, Germany

## FIELD HANDBALL

1936—Germany

## GOLF—MEN

1900—Charles Sands, United States
1904—George S. Lyon, Canada

## GOLF—WOMEN

1900—Margaret Abbot, United States

## GYMNASTICS

**CALISTHENICS**                                  Points
1948—F. Pataki, Hungary............. 38.7
1952—Karl Thoresson, Sweden ........ 19.25

**TEAM—SWEDISH SYSTEM**
1912—Sweden ................... 937.46
1920—Sweden ................... 1364

**TEAM—FREE SYSTEM (Exercises, Apparatus)**
1912—Norway ................... 114.25
1920—Denmark

**TEAM—HORIZONTAL BARS**
1896—Germany

**TEAM—PARALLEL BARS**
1896—Germany

**ROPE CLIMB**                                      Sec.
1896—Andriakopoulos, Greece ......... 23.4

1904—George Eyser, United States (25 ft.)  7
1906—G. Aliprantis, Greece (10 m) ...... 11.4
1924—B. Supcik, Czechoslovakia ....... 7.2
1932—Raymond Bass, United States (8 m)  6.7

**SIDE HORSE, VAULTS**                           Points
1924—A. Seguin, France .............. 10

**TUMBLING**
1932—Rowland Wolfe, United States ..... 56.7

**INDIAN CLUB**
1904—E. A. Hennig, United States....... 13
1932—George Roth, United States....... 26.9

## LACROSSE

1904—Canada
1908—Canada

## LAWN TENNIS

**MEN'S SINGLES**
1896—J. P. Boland, Great Britain
1900—Lawrence H. Doherty, Great Britain
1904—Beals C. Wright, United States
1906—Max Decugis, France
1908—M. J. G. Ritchie, Great Britain
1912—C. L. Winslow, South Africa
1920—Louis Raymond, South Africa
1924—Vincent Richards, United States

**LADIES' SINGLES**
1900—Miss C. Cooper, Great Britain
1906—Miss Simiriotou, Greece
1908—Mrs. Dorothea Chambers, Great Britain
1912—Miss Marguerite Broquedis, France
1920—Miss Suzanne Lenglen, France
1924—Miss Helen Wills, United States

**MIXED DOUBLES**
1900—Miss C. Cooper and Reginald Doherty, Great Britain
1906—Mr. and Mrs. Max Decugis, France
1912—Miss Dora Koring and Heinrich Schomburgk, Germany
1920—Miss Suzanne Lenglen and Max Decugis, France
1924—Mrs. Hazel Wightman and R. N. Williams, United States

**MEN'S DOUBLES**
1896—J. P. Boland, Great Britain, and Fritz Traun, Germany
1900—Reginald Doherty and Lawrence Doherty, Great Britain
1904—E. W. Leonard and Beals C. Wright, United States
1906—Max Decugis and M. Germot, France
1908—George Hillyard and Reginald Doherty, Great Britain
1912—H. A. Kitson and C. Winslow, South Africa
1920—O. Turnbull and Max Woosnam, Great Britain
1924—Vincent Richards and Frank T. Hunter, United States

**LADIES' DOUBLES**
1920—Mrs. J. McNair and Miss Kitty MacKane, Great Britain
1924—Miss Helen Wills and Mrs. Hazel Wightman, United States

## COVERED COURTS TENNIS

**MEN'S SINGLES**
1908—Arthur W. Gore, Great Britain
1912—Andre H. Gobert, France

**LADIES' SINGLES**
1908—Miss G. Eastlake-Smith, Great Britain
1912—Mrs. E. M. Hannam, Great Britain

**MEN'S DOUBLES**
1908—Arthur W. Gore and Herbert Roper-Barrett, Great Britain
1912—Andre H. Gobert and Maurice Germot, France

**MIXED DOUBLES**
1912—Mrs. E. M. Hannam and C. P. Dixon, Great Britain

## PAUME

**MEN'S SINGLES**
1908—Jay Gould, United States

## RACQUETS

**MEN'S SINGLES**
1908—E. B. Noel, Great Britain

**MEN'S DOUBLES**
1908—V. H. Pennell and J. J. Astor, Great Britain

## POLO

1908—Great Britain
1920—Great Britain
1924—Argentina
1936—Argentina

## ROWING

**MAN-OF-WAR BOATS**                              Min.-Sec.
1906—Italy, 2,000-m. course ........ 10:45
      Greece, 3,000-m. course ........ 16:35

**FOURS, INRIGGERS WITH COXSWAIN**
1912—Denmark ................... 7:47

## RUGBY FOOTBALL

1908—Australia
1920—United States
1924—United States

## PISTOL SHOOTING

**PISTOL, 30 Meters**                             Points
1896—Sumner Paine, United States...... 442

**SERVICE REVOLVER, 25 Meters**
**PISTOL, 25 Meters**
1896—John Paine, United States........ 442
1896—Jean Phrangudis, Greece .......... 344

**REVOLVER AND PISTOL, 50 Meters**
1908—Paul Van Asbroeck, Belgium ....... 490
1912—Alfred Lane, United States ....... 499
1920—Carl Frederick, United States .... 496
1932—Renzo Morigi, Italy.............. 42

**DUELING PISTOL, 30 Meters—Team**
1912—Sweden ................... 1145

**DUELING PISTOL, 30 Meters**
1912—Alfred Lane, United States........ 287

**REVOLVER AND PISTOL, 50 Meters—Team**

1912—United States (Alfred Lane, Harry Sears, P. F. Dolfen, John Dietz) . . 1916
1920—United States (Carl Frederick, Alfredo Lane, Raymond Bracken, James Snook, Michael Kelly) . . . . . . . . 2374

**PISTOL AND REVOLVER, 30 Meters**

1920—Guilherme Paraense, Brazil . . . . . . . 274

**PISTOL AND REVOLVER, 30 Meters—Team**

1920—United States (Louis Harant, Alfred Lane, Carl Frederick, James Snook, Michael Kelly) . . . . . . . . . . . . . 1310

**AUTOMATIC PISTOL, 25 Meters—Team**

1924—United States (Sgt. H. M. Bailey, Sgt. B. G. Betke, Maj. H. D. Frazer, Lt. W. J. Whaling) . . . . . . . . . . . . . 10

**AUTOMATIC PISTOL, 25 Meters**

1924—H. N. Bailey, United States . . . . . . . 18

**ARMY GUN, 200 Meters—Individual**

1896—Pantelis Karasevdas, Greece . . . . . . .2320

**ARMY GUN, 300 Meters—Individual**

1896—Georges Orphanidis, Greece . . . . . . .1583
1900—Albert Helgerard, United States . . . . 909
1912—Sandor Prokopp, Hungary . . . . . . . . 97

**ARMY GUN, 600 Meters—Individual**

1912—P. Colas, France . . . . . . . . . . . . . . . 94

**ARMY GUN—TEAM INTERNATIONAL 200-500-800-900-1000 Yards**

1900—United States (no score or personnel given)

1908—United States (William Leushner, Maj. W. B. Martin, Maj. C. B. Winder, Capt. K. K. V. Casey, Cpl. Al Eastman, Capt. C. S. Benedict) . . . . . .2531

**ARMY GUN—INDIVIDUAL INTERNATIONAL 200-500-800-900-1000 Yards**

1900—J. K. Millner, Great Britain (see note)
1908—J. K. Millner, Great Britain (see note) 98
NOTE—1900 records sometimes credit Millner with being an American.

**ARMY GUN, 300 Meters—Team**

1900—Norway (no score given)

**ARMY GUN—TEAM INTERNATIONAL 200-400-500-600 Yards**

1912—United States (Capt. C. L. Burdette, Allan Briggs, Harry Adams, John Jackson, Carl Osburn, Warren Sprout) . . . . . . . . . . . . . . . . . . .1687

**FULL-BORE RIFLE, 300 Meters—Team, 3 Positions**

1900—Switzerland . . . . . . . . . . . . . . . .4399

**FULL-BORE RIFLE, 300 Meters—Standing**

1900—Lars Jorgen Madsen, Denmark, no score given.

**FULL-BORE RIFLE, 300 Meters—Kneeling**

1900—Konrad Staeheli, Switzerland, no score given.

**FULL-BORE RIFLE, 300 Meters—Prone**

1900—A. Paroche, France, no score given.

**RUNNING DEER—Team Single—100 Meters**

1908—Sweden . . 86      1920—Norway . .178
1912—Sweden . .151      1924—Norway . .160

**RUNNING DEER—Individual Singles—100 M.**

1908—Oscar Swahn, Sweden . . . . . . . . . 25
1912—Alfred Swahn, Sweden . . . . . . . . . 41

1920—Otto Olsen, Norway . . . . . . . . . . . . 43
1924—John Boles, United States . . . . . . . . 40
1952—John Larsen, Norway . . . . . . . . . .413*
1956—Vitalli Romaneko, U.S.S.R. . . . . . . .441*
*New scoring on 50 single shots, 25 double shots.

**RUNNING DEER—Individual Doubles—100 M.**

1908—Walter Winans, United States . . . . . 46
1912—Ake Lundeberg, Sweden . . . . . . . . 79
1920—Ole Lilloe-Olsen, Norway . . . . . . . . 82
1924—Ole Lilloe-Olsen, Norway . . . . . . . . 76

**RUNNING DEER—Team Doubles—100 M.**

1920—Norway . . . . . . . . . . . . . . . . . 343
1924—Great Britain . . . . . . . . . . . . . . 263

**SMALL-BORE RIFLE, 50 & 100 Yards—Team**

1908—Great Britain . . . . . . . . . . . . . . . 77

**SMALL-BORE RIFLE, 50 & 100 Yards—Individual**

1908—A. A. Carnell, Great Britain . . . . . . . 387

**SMALL-BORE RIFLE—25 Yards Vanishing Target**

1908—W. K. Styles, Great Britain . . . . . . . 45
1912—Wilhelm Carlberg, Sweden . . . . . . . 242

**SMALL-BORE RIFLE—25 Yards Moving Target**

1908—A. F. Gleming, Great Britain . . . . . . . 24

**SMALL-BORE (Miniature) RIFLE, 50 Meters**

1912—Frederick Hird, United States . . . . . . 194
1920—Lawrence Nuesslein, United States . . 391
1924—Charles Coquelin de Lisle, France . . . 398
1928—Bartil Ronmark, Sweden . . . . . . . . 294
1936—Willy Rogeberg, Norway . . . . . . . . 300

**SMALL-BORE (Miniature) RIFLE, 50 Meters—Team**

1912—Great Britain . . . . . . . . . . . . . . . 762
1920—United States (Lawrence Nuesslein, Art Rothrock, Willis Lee, Dennis Fenton, Gunnery Schriver) . . . . . .1899
1924—France . . . . . . . . . . . . . . . . . . .' 10

**SMALL-BORE RIFLE, 25 Yards—Team, Vanishing Target**

1912—Sweden . . . . . . . . . . . . . . . . . . 925

**FREE RIFLE, 300 Meters—Team**

1908—Norway . . . . . . . . . . . . . . . . . .5055

**FREE RIFLE, 300 Meters—Individual**

1908—Albert Helgerud, Norway . . . . . . . . 909

**OPTIONAL RIFLE, 300 Meters—3 Positions**

1912—P. Colas, France . . . . . . . . . . . . . 987

**OPTIONAL RIFLE, 300 Meters—Team, 3 Positions**

1912—Sweden . . . . . . . . . . . . . . . . . .5655

**OPTIONAL RIFLE, 400 & 600 Meters**

1924—Sgt. Morris Fisher, United States . . . 95

**OPTIONAL RIFLE, 400 & 600 Meters—Team**

1924—United States (Morris Fisher, Walter Stokes, J. Crockett, Chan Coulter, Sidney Hinds) . . . . . . . . . . . . . 676

**MILITARY RIFLE, 300 Meters—2 Positions**

1920—Sgt. Morris Fisher, United States . . . 997

**MILITARY RIFLE, 300 Meters—Team, 2 Positions**

1920—United States (Morris Fisher, Carl Osburn, Dennis Fenton, Lloyd Spooner, Willis Lee) . . . . . . . . . .4876

**MILITARY RIFLE, 300 Meters—Team, Standing**

1920—Denmark . . . . . . . . . . . . . . . . . 266

**MILITARY RIFLE, 300 Meters—Standing**

1920—Carl Osburn, United States . . . . . . . 56

**MILITARY RIFLE, 300 Meters—Prone**

1920—Otto Olsen, Norway . . . . . . . . . . . . 60

**MILITARY RIFLE, 300 Meters—Team, Prone***

1920—United States (Carl Osburn, Lloyd Spooner, Morris Fisher, Willis Lee, Joseph Jackson) . . . . . . . . . . . 289

**MILITARY RIFLE, 300 & 600 Meters—Team, Prone**

1920—United States (Joe Jackson, Willis Lee, Gunnery Schriver, Carl Osburn, Lloyd Spooner) . . . . . . . . . 573

**MILITARY RIFLE, 600 Meters—Team, Prone**

1920—United States (Dennis Fenton, Gunnery Schriver, Willis Lee, Lloyd Spooner, Joe Jackson) . . . . . . . . 287

**MILITARY RIFLE, 600 Meters—Prone**

1920—Hugo Johansson, Sweden . . . . . . . . 58


# SWIMMING

| **RELAY RACES** | **Min.-Sec.** |
| --- | --- |
| 1900—Germany—5 x 40 m. | |
| 1904—United States—4 x 50 yds . . . . . | 2:04.6 |
| 1906—Hungary—4 x 250 m. . . . . . . . . | 16:52.4 |

**200-METER FREE STYLE**

1900—F. C. V. Lane, Australia . . . . . . . 2:25.5

**200-YARD FREE STYLE**

1904—Charles Daniels, United States . . . 2:44.2

**400-METER BREAST STROKE**

1904—Georg Zacharias, Germany (440 yds.) . . . . . . . . . . . . . . . 7:27
1912—Walter Bathe, Germany . . . . . . . 6:29.6
1920—H. Malmroth, Sweden . . . . . . . . 6:31.8

| **50-YARD FREE STYLE** | **Min.-Sec.** |
| --- | --- |
| 1904—Zoltan de Halmy, Hungary . . . . . | 0:28 |

**880-YARD FREE STYLE**

1904—Emil Rausch, Germany . . . . . . . .13:11.6

**4,000-METER FREE STYLE**

1900—John Jarvis, Great Britain . . . . . .58:24

**200 METERS (Hindernisschwimmen)**

1900—F. C. V. Lane, Australia . . . . . . . 2:31.4

**PLUNGE**

1900—de Vaudeville, France
1904—W. E. Dickey, United States

| **PLAIN HIGH DIVING** | **Points** |
| --- | --- |
| 1912—Eric Adlerz, Sweden . . . . . . . . . | 40 |
| 1920—Arvid Wallman, Sweden . . . . . . | 183.5 |
| 1924—Richard Eve, Australia . . . . . . . | 160 |


# WEIGHT-LIFTING

| **ONE HAND** | **Pounds** |
| --- | --- |
| 1896—L. Elliot, Great Britain . . . . . . . . | 156.52 |
| 1904—O. C. Osthoff, United States . . . . | 48 pts. |
| 1906—Josef Steinbach, Austria . . . . . . | 168.872 |

| **TWO HANDS** | |
| --- | --- |
| 1896—V. Jensen, Denmark . . . . . . . . . | 245.812 |
| 1904—P. Kakousis, Greece . . . . . . . . . | 245.799 |
| 1906—D. Tofolas, Greece . . . . . . . . . | 313.925 |

## YACHTING

**6-METER CLASS**

1900—H. de Pourtales (LERINA) Switzerland
1908—G. U. Laws (DORMY) Great Britain
1912—O. Thube (MAC MICHE) France
1920—Andreas Bracke (JO) Norway (new)
1920—E. Corneille (EDELWEISS II) Belgium (old)
1924—Eugen Lunde (ELISABETH V) Norway
1928—Prince Olav (NORMA) Norway
1932—Thore Holm (BISSBI) Sweden
1936—M. A. Belville (LALAGE) Great Britain
1948—Herman Whiton (LLANORIA) United States
1952—Herman Whiton (LLANORIA) United States

**6.5-METER CLASS**

1920—J. R. Carp (ORANJE) Holland

**7-METER CLASS**

1908—C. J. Rivett-Carnac (HEROINE)
    Great Britain
1920—Dorothy Winifred (ANCORA) Great Britain

**8-METER CLASS**

1900—Exshaw (OLLE) Great Britain
1908—Blair Cochrane (COBWEB) Great Britain
1912—Thoralf Glad (TAIFUN) Norway
1920—Magnus Konow (SILDRA) Norway (new)
1920—August Ringvold (IRENE) Norway (old)
1924—August Ringvold (BERA) Norway
1928—Mme V. Heriot (L'AIGLE) France
1932—Owen Churchill (ANGELITA) United States
1936—M. Reggio (ITALIA) Italy

**10-METER CLASS**

1900—M. Wiesner (ASHENBRODEL) Germany
1912—Nils Asp (KITTY) Sweden
1920—Willy Gilbert (MOSK II) Norway (new)
1920—Erik Herseth (ELEDA) Norway (old)

**12-METER CLASS**

1908—T. C. Glen-Coats (HERA) Great Britain
1912—Alfred Larson (MAGDA IV) Norway
1920—Johan Friele (HERA) Norway (new)
1920—Henrik Ostervold (ATLANTA) Norway (old)
1956—Skipper not listed (JEST) New Zealand

**FIREFLY CLASS**

1948—Paul Elvstrom, Denmark

**SWALLOW CLASS**

1948—S. Morris (SWIFT) Great Britain

**MONOTYPE CLASS (Old)**

1920—A. E. Van der Biesen (BEATRISS) Holland
    (2-man dinghy)
1924—Leon Huybrechts, Belgium
1928—Sven Thorell, Sweden
1932—Jacques Lebrun, France
1936—Daniel Kagchelland, Holland

**30-METER CLASS**

1920—Gosta Lundquist (KULLAN) Sweden

**40-METER CLASS**

1920—Tore Holm (SIF) Sweden

**18-FOOT CENTERBOARD BOAT**

1920—Skipper not listed (BRAT) Holland

## DEMONSTRATIONS

In some Olympiads, host countries conducted demonstration sports on a competitive basis, some as exhibition contests.

| MILITARY SKI PATROL | Hr.-Min.-Sec. |
|---|---|
| 1924—Switzerland (30,000 m.) | 3:56:06 |
| 1928—Norway (28,050 m.) | 3:50:47 |
| 1936—Italy (25,000 m.) | 2:28:35 |
| 1948—Switzerland (27,000 m.) | 2:34:25 |

**SLED-DOG RACING**

1932—St. Goddard, Canada . . . . . . . . 4:23:12.5

| SPEED SKATING—MEN—FOUR EVENTS | Points |
|---|---|
| 1924—Clas Thunberg, Finland | 5.5 |

| CURLING | |
|---|---|
| 1924—Great Britain | 4 |
| 1932—Canada (Manitoba) | |
| 1936—Austria (Tirol) | |
| 1948—Gustav Lindh, Sweden | 14 |

| WINTER PENTATHLON | Points |
|---|---|
| 1948—Gustav Lindh, Sweden | 14 |

## BANDY
### (FOOTBALL ON ICE)

1952—Sweden defeated Norway and Finland, in round-robin series.

## BASEBALL

1912—United States
1936—United States
1952—Exhibition of Basque Pelota
    (Finnish Baseball)
1956—Exhibition of American baseball
    (U.S. Army Teams)

## FIELD HANDBALL

1952—Sweden defeated Denmark 19-11 in exhibition.

## FOOTBALL

1932—American collegiate exhibition
    (East vs. West All Stars)
1956—Australian rules exhibition
    (selected Australian teams)

## ICE SHOOTING

**INTERNATIONAL TEAM EVENT**

1936—Austria

**INDIVIDUAL DISTANCE SHOOTING**

1936—Georg Edenhauser, Austria

**INDIVIDUAL TARGET SHOOTING**

1936—Ignaz Reiterer, Austria

## GLIDING

1936—Herman Schreiber, Germany

## ROQUE

1904—Charles Jacobus, United States

## LA CROSSE

1928—United States defeated Canada 6-3 and
    Great Britain 7-6 in round-robin exhibition series.
1932—United States defeated Canada in two out
    of three exhibition games.
1948—United States and Great Britain tied 5-5 in
    exhibition game.

## MOTOR BOATING

| CLASS A (40 SEA MILES) | Hr.-Min.-Sec. |
|---|---|
| 1908—E. B. Thubrow, France | 2:26:53.0 |

| CLASS B (40 SEA MILES) | |
|---|---|
| 1908—Thomas Thorneycroft, Great Britain | 2:28:58.8 |

| CLASS C (40 SEA MILES) | |
|---|---|
| 1908—Thomas Thorneycroft, Great Britain | 2:28:26.0 |

# Index

# Index

ii

# Picture Credits

## A NOTE ON THE TYPE

THE TEXT of this book was set on the Linotype in a new face called PRIMER, designed by *Rudolph Ruzicka*, earlier responsible for the design of Fairfield and Fairfield Medium, Linotype faces whose virtues have for some time now been accorded wide recognition.

The complete range of sizes of Primer was first made available in 1954, although the pilot size of 12 point was ready as early as 1951. The design of the face makes general reference to Linotype Century (long a serviceable type, totally lacking in manner or frills of any kind) but brilliantly corrects the characterless quality of that face.